COURTROOM
MODIFICATIONS
FOR CHILD WITNESSES

The LAW AND PUBLIC POLICY: PSYCHOLOGY AND THE SOCIAL SCIENCES series includes books in three domains:

Legal Studies—writings by legal scholars about issues of relevance to psychology and the other social sciences, or that employ social science information to advance the legal analysis;

Social Science Studies—writings by scientists from psychology and the other social sciences about issues of relevance to law and public policy; and

Forensic Studies—writings by psychologists and other mental health scientists and professionals about issues relevant to forensic mental health science and practice.

The series is guided by its editor, Bruce D. Sales, PhD, JD, University of Arizona; and coeditors, Bruce J. Winick, JD, University of Miami; Norman J. Finkel, PhD, Georgetown University; and Valerie P. Hans, PhD, University of Delaware.

* * *

Preventing Sexual Violence: How Society Should Cope With Sex Offenders
        John Q. La Fond
Homophobia and the Law
        Amy D. Ronner
Experts in Court: Reconciling Law, Science, and Professional Knowledge
        Bruce D. Sales and Daniel W. Shuman
More Than the Law: Behavioral and Social Facts in Legal Decision Making
        Peter W. English and Bruce D. Sales
Laws Affecting Clinical Practice
        Bruce D. Sales, Michael Owen Miller, and Susan R. Hall
Constructive Divorce: Procedural Justice and Sociolegal Reform
        Penelope Eileen Bryan
Violent Offenders: Appraising and Managing Risk, Second Edition
        Vernon L. Quinsey, Grant T. Harris, Marnie E. Rice, and
        Catherine A. Cormier
Reforming Punishment: Psychological Limits to the Pains of Imprisonment
        Craig Haney
Criminal Profiling: Developing an Effective Science and Practice
        Scotia J. Hicks and Bruce D. Sales
Emotions and Culpability: How the Law is at Odds With Psychology, Jurors, and Itself
        Norman J. Finkel and W. Gerrod Parrott
Scientific Jury Selection
        Joel D. Lieberman and Bruce D. Sales
Sex Offending: Causal Theories to Inform Research, Prevention, and Treatment
        Jill D. Stinson, Bruce D. Sales, and Judith V. Becker
Courtroom Modifications for Child Witnesses: Law and Science in Forensic Evaluations
        Susan R. Hall and Bruce D. Sales

COURTROOM MODIFICATIONS

FOR CHILD WITNESSES

LAW AND SCIENCE IN FORENSIC EVALUATIONS

SUSAN R. HALL AND BRUCE D. SALES

AMERICAN PSYCHOLOGICAL ASSOCIATION • WASHINGTON, DC

Published by
American Psychological Association
750 First Street, NE
Washington, DC 20002
www.apa.org

To order
APA Order Department
P.O. Box 92984
Washington, DC 20090-2984
Tel: (800) 374-2721; Direct: (202) 336-5510
Fax: (202) 336-5502; TDD/TTY: (202) 336-6123
Online: www.apa.org/books/
E-mail: order@apa.org

In the U.K., Europe, Africa, and the Middle East, copies may be ordered from
American Psychological Association
3 Henrietta Street
Covent Garden, London
WC2E 8LU England

Typeset in Goudy by Page Grafx, Inc., St. Simon's Island, GA

Printer: Maple-Vail Book Manufacturing, Binghamton, NY
Cover Designer: Mercury Publishing Services, Rockville, MD
Technical/Production Editor: Tiffany L. Klaff

The opinions and statements published are the responsibility of the authors, and such opinions and statements do not necessarily represent the policies of the American Psychological Association.

Library of Congress Cataloging-in-Publication Data

Hall, Susan R.
   Courtroom modifications for child witnesses : law and science in forensic evaluations / Susan R. Hall and Bruce D. Sales.
      p. cm. — (The law and public policy: psychology and the social sciences series)
   Includes bibliographical references and index.
   ISBN-13: 978-1-4338-0354-3
   ISBN-10: 1-4338-0354-2
   1. Child witnesses—United States.   2. Examination of witnesses—United States. 3. Conduct of court proceedings—United States—Psychological aspects.   4. Forensic psychology—United States.   5. Forensic sciences—United States.   I. Sales, Bruce Dennis.
KF9673.H35 2008
347.73′66083—dc22

2007050835

British Library Cataloguing-in-Publication Data
A CIP record is available from the British Library.

Printed in the United States of America
First Edition

For Robert Scholz
    —*SRH*

For Mary Elizabeth
    —*BDS*

CONTENTS

ACKNOWLEDGMENTS

The authors extend their appreciation for the able research assistance of Tanisha R. Douglas, Daniel Hackman, Kelly Leon, Meghan Owenz, Brian J. Swanson, Leslie Vaccarello, Reena Vogt, and Kaycie L. Zielinski.

COURTROOM MODIFICATIONS

for Child Witnesses

1

INTRODUCTION: NEED FOR COURTROOM MODIFICATIONS

Most civil and criminal courtrooms are designed as if all witnesses were adults. Yet common sense and science teach that although courtrooms can be anxiety-provoking settings for people of all ages, for a child witness "the courtroom is at best a place of confusion, at worst a terrifying world" (McGough, 1994, p. 10). Child witnesses must overcome a number of "daunting hurdles in order for their voices to be heard" (Task Force on Child Witnesses of the American Bar Association Criminal Justice Section [Task Force], 2002, p. 3). From a child's point of view, the physical surroundings of the courtroom can be formal, austere, and intentionally intimidating (McGough, 1994). Compared with other familiar people in their lives, parties in the courtroom play strange roles and may wear more formal attire (Warren-Leubecker, Tate, Hinton, & Ozbeck, 1989). In one case, a 5-year-old child was reported to be "so intimidated by the judge in his long black robe that she refused to raise her head and look at him during her testimony" (Tebo, 2003, p. 53).

Child witnesses may have little or no understanding of the trial process—its goals, rules, setting, actors, and procedures. Understanding can provide a frame of reference in which an individual (adult or child) can make sense of the experience and be ready to respond to the expectations of others within the system. Children, especially those under 10 years of age, can be at a developmental disadvantage because their knowledge about commonly used legal terms may be limited (Saywitz, 2002; Warren-Leubecker et al., 1989; Whitcomb, 1992b). Children do not obtain a full understanding of the legal system and the various roles within a courtroom until their teenage years (Saywitz, 1989), although studies have demonstrated that adolescents still misunderstand some important legal terms (e.g., jury, cross-examination; Crawford & Bull, 2006b). The resulting misconceptions can often lead to false expectations, mistakes, and/or unrealistic fears (Flin, Stevenson, & Davies, 1989; Sas, 1991; Saywitz, 1989; Saywitz, Jaenicke, & Camparo, 1990; Spencer & Flin, 1990; Warren-Leubecker et al., 1989). Some misconceptions occur when children and adolescents familiar with court settings and procedures through television programs erroneously believe that judges will be mean, sarcastic, and/or yell at them; that the courtroom will be packed with noisy spectators; and that they will be on television (Finnegan, 2000). Across the cognitive psychology and developmental research traditions, there is consensus that prior knowledge and expectations about events being experienced can affect cognitive processing (e.g., perception and interpretation, encoding and later retrieval of information; Ornstein et al., 1998). Accordingly, some researchers have suggested that individual factors, including lack of knowledge and fear of the unknown, can interfere with memory (Baker-Ward & Ornstein, 2002; Saywitz, Goodman, & Lyon, 2002), which in turn can affect children's participation in the process. Readers interested in additional information on children's memory and other developmental differences in children's cognitive skills that can affect child testimony should see Baker-Ward and Ornstein (2002); Bruck, Ceci, and Principe (2006); Fivush (2002); Lindsay (2002); J. E. B. Myers, Saywitz, and Goodman (1996); Pezdek and Hinz (2002); Powell and Thomson (2002); and Schaaf et al. (2002).

Normal developmental differences in speech and language abilities (not to mention the presence of communication disorders and/or challenges faced by children whose primary language is not English) also affect children's abilities to comprehend and communicate in courtroom proceedings. For example, young children can be very literal in their understanding of attorneys' questions. In one case, a young child who was asked whether she was wearing clothes at the time an alleged incident of sexual abuse occurred answered "no" because she was wearing pajamas (Tebo, 2003). Receptive language issues become more problematic when adults in the courtroom speak to children in more complex, grammatically confusing, and even incomprehensible terms (Saywitz & Snyder, 1993; Zajac, Gross, & Hayne, 2003) and ask adversarial questions (Flin, 1993). Use of linguistically complex lawyer jargon is confusing even to adolescents and college students (Perry et al., 1995). Young children may not be aware of comprehension problems, and confused school-age children may not ask for clarification and may try to answer attorneys' questions anyway (Saywitz, 2002). In addition, children may lack the vocabulary with which to express their experiences in words.

To improve receptive and expressive skills in the courtroom, age-appropriate questioning techniques and education programs have been recommended for use with child witnesses (e.g., American Prosecutors Research Institute [APRI] National Center for Prosecution of Child Abuse, 2004; Plotnikoff & Woolfson, 1995; A. G. Walker, 2000; N. E. Walker & Hunt, 1998; Walters, 2000).

Developmental differences interact with other individual and contextual differences and can affect a child's ability to testify competently in a courtroom setting. Children who raise special concerns and needs in this regard are those who reportedly experienced maltreatment and are later asked to testify in court against the defendant who allegedly caused or contributed to the abuse. Such differences may result in varying degrees of the severity and length of emotional effects and variances in children's memory of the event, their willingness to report, and their ability to participate fully in legal processes.

CHILD WITNESSES IN ABUSE CASES

The legal system's need to receive accurate testimony from allegedly abused child witnesses is critical given the increased awareness of child abuse in this country. Starting in the 1980s, an upsurge in public awareness and media attention contributed to a significant increase in child abuse and neglect incidents being reported to law enforcement and child protection agencies, as well as in child abuse cases being prosecuted or pursued through civil litigation. Reported cases climbed from 850,000 in 1981 to nearly 2.7 million in 1991. The issue of child abuse appeared so severe in the United States that the federal government declared the situation a national emergency in 1990 (R. G. Marks, 1995).

Children continue to be victims with "alarming frequency" (Task Force, 2002, p. 6). The number of child maltreatment cases reported to child protective services in 1995 was 3,111,000, a 49% increase from 1986 (Kelley, Thornberry, & Smith, 1997). About one third of such reports were substantiated, and of these, 54% involved neglect, 25% physical abuse, 11% sexual abuse, and 3% emotional maltreatment. Although some researchers believe that the numbers of sexual abuse cases in particular are on the decline (L. Jones & Finkelhor, 2001), more recent statistics reveal similar numbers of reported and substantiated cases of sexual abuse and other forms of maltreatment in 2005 (U.S. Department of Health and Human Services, 2007). Other forms of maltreatment include exposure to domestic and community violence (Berman, Silverman, & Kurtines, 2002; Kerig & Fedorowitz, 1999). Some commentators believe that these incidents will increase given more recent laws that create a new offense or category of an existing offense or enhanced penalties for domestic violence committed in the presence of children (Whitcomb, 2003). Such laws have been enacted in a number of states (e.g., Or. Rev. Stat. § 163.160, 2005 [Oregon]; Ga. Code Ann. § 16-5-70, 2007 [Georgia]; see also http://www.mincava.umn.edu/link/documents/statutes/statutes.shtml for a 50-state review of relevant state statutes).

Official numbers, however, do not tell the whole story. Despite increased awareness of child maltreatment, a substantial but unknown number of cases are probably not reported. Some commentators fear that this may be partly due to a backlash against reporting abuse because of negative publicity about false allegations and lawsuits seeking damages against mandated reporters in sexual abuse cases (e.g., Faller, 2003). Also, even though a case may be reported, it may not be investigated in an efficient and coordinated manner, or it may not even be pursued. Investigation errors can have serious ramifications and fatal costs. Inaccurate investigations may result in innocent people being labeled child molesters or abusers, but they may also mean that perpetrators are set free to continue abusing children, at times with fatal results (Pence & Wilson, 1994). The U.S. Advisory Board on Child Abuse and Neglect estimated that every day in the United States, five children die from child abuse and neglect (Kelley et al., 1997). Approximately 1,300 children died of abuse or neglect in 2001, a rate of 1.81 per 100,000 children in the population, 84.5% of whom were younger than 6 years of age (U.S. Department of Health and Human Services, n.d.).

Assuming that a child was abused but not mortally injured and assuming that an investigation of the alleged abuse ensues, some of these children will be adversely affected through their involvement with the criminal justice system (Goodman, Pyle-Taub, et al., 1992; Hall, 1995; Lipovsky, 1994; Lipovsky & Stern, 1997; Quas, Goodman, & Ghetti, 2005; Runyan, Everson, Edelsohn, Hunter, & Coulter, 1988). Ceci and Bruck (1993a, 1998) conservatively estimated that more than 100,000 children testify in criminal and civil cases each year in the United States, including more than 13,000 in sexual abuse cases. Whether the case is brought to a juvenile, family, domestic relations, civil, or criminal court, the child may eventually be asked to testify and/or other child and adult witnesses will be called to testify as to what the child told them. For example, consider a child suspected of being physically or sexually assaulted by his or her day-care provider. If the provider had a questionable work history that the current employer ignored, it is likely that there would be criminal (e.g., statutory rape, abuse of a child) and civil charges (e.g., assault and battery, intentional infliction of emotional distress) filed against the individual, as well as civil charges against the employer for negligent hiring and supervision.

For "at least three decades . . . professionals have expressed concern about the 'revictimization' of child victims who are involved in the justice system, and particularly those who testify in criminal court" (Whitcomb, 2003, p. 150). Criminal abuse cases "demand the most" of the child witness (Whitcomb, p. 149). Their involvement in the criminal justice system may begin with investigative interviews by child protection, forensic, and/or law enforcement professionals. Children often are asked to provide a formal statement. In some jurisdictions, they may be required to provide sworn testimony for depositions or preliminary hearings at which the defendant may be present. Even though the majority of cases are resolved before trial, prosecutors approach each case as if it will go to trial. Thus, child witnesses will also be involved in evaluations and trial preparations. In some cases, children may be asked to testify and to prepare statements for sentencing hearings if there is a conviction (Whitcomb, 2003).

Serving as a child witness is not categorically harmful or beneficial (Task Force, 2002). Individual, family, and other contextual factors appear to contribute to the impact of courtroom testimony on children. Some child witnesses required to confront the person who allegedly harmed them in the past find the experience devastating. For example, some may lose their ability to testify accurately or otherwise be afraid to testify when confronted by the alleged perpetrator. Not all child witnesses will react this way, however. Some children may find the experience empowering. Clinicians have noted that testifying can be beneficial, "especially if a child's testimony is believed and a perpetrator is found guilty" (Schroeder & Gordon, 2002, p. 255).

It is also important to remember that not all children who are asked to testify in abuse cases have been abused. Small but vocal groups of people and professionals believe that the number of false reports is substantial. For example, Wakefield and Underwager (1981) claimed that a significant proportion of allegations of sexual abuse are false and reported that three fourths of the cases they had seen had involved false allegations. In an online manuscript, they noted, "There is disagreement over how many of these accusation [sic] are false, although most estimates range between 20% and 80%" (Wakefield & Underwager, 1991, updated 2007, ¶ 9).

Empirical research indicates that false allegations are rare, however, occurring in approximately 2% to 8% of cases (APRI, 2004; Everson & Boat, 1989; D. Jones & McGraw, 1987). Statistics may be similar or only slightly higher in divorce cases (Faller, 2003). For example, sexual abuse allegations in one representative study occurred in only 2% of child custody disputes, and of these 8% to 16.5% were estimated to be false (Penfold, 1995). According to the American Psychological Association's Ad Hoc Committee on Legal and Ethical Issues in the Treatment of Interpersonal Violence (2008), "[t]he incidents of intentionally false reports appear to be approximately 5–8% of all cases" (n.p.). The law penalizes false reporting of child maltreatment, however rare, in approximately 31 states (Child Welfare Information Gateway, 2003).

Regardless of whether the abuse actually occurred, developmental issues and confrontational stress can have an impact on a child's memory and performance as a witness (Saywitz, 1995). Premised on the thesis that the physical, social, and psychological setting in which remembering takes place influences the ability to recall information, the term *confrontational stress* was adopted on the basis of studies in which (a) young children's autobiographical memory was better in a supportive social atmosphere than in a neutral one, (b) children were less able to identify an unfamiliar adult when the adult was present during testimony, and (c) children had fears of recrimination and worries about angering the adult. Facing the defendant has been shown to be one of the most frequently expressed or worst fears of children who testify (Flin, 1990; Goodman, Pyle-Taub, et al., 1992; Murray, 1995; Sas, Hurley, Hatch, Malla, & Dick, 1993; Wade, 2002).

Because of the developmental and psychological issues related to the alleged incident, the legal process, or both, and because of the additional negative psychological sequelae that some children may experience if courtroom confrontation with the alleged abuser were required, child advocates and prosecutors in the 1980s raised concerns about the lack of accommodations or modifications for the growing numbers of children in criminal courtrooms. Legislatures and courts responded by fashioning specific rules and procedures to protect child witnesses, typically only in child abuse cases. In some countries (e.g., England), special measures are extended to vulnerable and intimidated witnesses of any age. Depending on a jurisdiction's laws and practices, some procedural modifications have become standard practice, others are underused or have fallen into disuse, and others, although introduced in the 1980s, are still considered innovative (for detailed reviews, see Task Force [2002], APRI [2004], and J. E. B. Myers [1996a, 1996b]). The following sections review these laws and practices.

Standard Practices

- Educating child witnesses regarding courtroom appearances through individually tailored instruction by counselors, prosecutors, or other court personnel, or through formalized court schools (in larger jurisdictions);
- Asking children developmentally appropriate questions;
- Allowing support persons (e.g., parent, guardian, adult friend), interpreters, or intermediaries for child witnesses;
- Appointing counsel, a guardian *ad litem*, or a court-appointed special advocate;
- Using support items (e.g., teddy bear);
- Using physical courtroom changes (e.g., altered seating arrangements);
- Instructing child witnesses on options when giving in-court testimony (e.g., avoiding eye contact with the defendant, having the child witness testify with his or her back to the defendant but facing the judge and attorneys, having the child testify with his or her profile to the defendant);

- Clearing or closing the courtroom;
- Conducting testimony outside the courtroom (e.g., in the judge's chambers, at the child's school); and
- Using schedule adaptations (e.g., limiting length of child's testimony, allowing testimony during appropriate hours).

Rarely Used or Underused Practices

- Using screens or partitions to shield the child witness from seeing the defendant;
- Allowing the use of demonstrative aids during in-court witness questioning; and
- Using vertical prosecution (i.e., keeping the same prosecutor throughout proceedings).

Practices Considered Innovative in Some Jurisdictions

- Using remote testimony (e.g., closed-circuit television [CCTV], videoconferencing) to remove the child witness from physical face-to-face interaction with the defendant;
- Using videotaped testimony and depositions; and
- Having a private waiting area for child witnesses.

Practices Considered Standard, Rarely Used, or Innovative Depending on the Jurisdiction

- Using child hearsay statements (i.e., a statement made by a child outside of court, e.g., videotaped investigative interviews);
- Giving precedence in the criminal docket to cases involving child witnesses;
- Allowing leading questions to be asked of child witnesses during direct testimony; and
- Allowing greater judicial control over proceedings and questioning.

Many of these modifications do not raise legal concerns. However, those that attempt to block or prevent face-to-face confrontation have state and federal constitutional implications. Specifically, the uses of screens; videotaped, remote (typically CCTV), or child hearsay testimony; and excluding the defendant from hearings have been argued to violate the defendant's Sixth Amendment right to confront witnesses against him or her, and the Fourteenth Amendment right to due process. The Confrontation Clause of the Sixth Amendment, made applicable to the states through the Fourteenth Amendment, specifically provides that "In all criminal prosecutions, the accused shall enjoy the right . . . to be confronted with the witnesses against him."

THE U.S. SUPREME COURT ADDRESSES
CHILD WITNESS MODIFICATIONS

Given the ongoing importance of the constitutional status of modifications for child witnesses, it is important to consider how the U.S. Supreme Court has responded to this issue. The Court has ruled in two cases involving the use of courtroom modifications that prevent face-to-face confrontation (*Coy v. Iowa*, 1988; *Maryland v. Craig*, 1990b). The more recent case involved Sandra Ann Craig, the owner and operator of a kindergarten and prekindergarten center who was charged with committing child abuse, first- and second-degree sexual offenses, perverted sexual practice, assault, and battery against a 6-year-old girl who attended her center from August 1984 to June 1986. The child and other children from the center were to be called as witnesses against Craig at the trial. Before the trial began, however, the State of Maryland requested that the court allow the children to testify by one-way CCTV. Maryland had a statute that permitted witness questioning through CCTV if there was a finding that the child's courtroom testimony would result in that child suffering serious emotional distress such that he or she could not reasonably communicate. The procedure involves the child, prosecutor, and defense counsel going to another room where the child is examined and cross-examined while the judge, jury, and defendant remain in the courtroom where the testimony is displayed. One-way CCTV allows the defendant to see the child, but the child cannot see the defendant. The defendant remains in electronic communication with counsel, and objections may be made and ruled on as if the witness were in the courtroom.

In support of its request, the state presented expert testimony suggesting the following:

> that each child would have some or considerable difficulty in testifying in Craig's presence. For example, as to one child, the expert said that what "would cause him the most anxiety would be to testify in front of Mrs. Craig . . ." The child "wouldn't be able to communicate effectively." As to another, an expert said she "would probably stop talking and she would withdraw and curl up." With respect to two others, the testimony was that one would "become highly agitated, that he may refuse to talk or if he did talk, that he would choose his subject regardless of the questions" while the other would "become extremely timid and unwilling to talk." (*Maryland v. Craig*, 1989, pp. 568–569, 1128–1129)

Craig objected to allowing the child witnesses to be interviewed in another room and not being able to face her accusers, basing her argument on the U.S. Constitution's Confrontation Clause noted earlier. The trial judge ruled in favor of the state, holding that although CCTV would take away the defendant's ability to be face to face with her accuser, the procedure preserved the essence of confrontation: The defendant's attorney would be present with the child witnesses and able to observe and cross-examine them, and the jury would be able to view the child witnesses' demeanor during testimony.

Craig was convicted on all counts, with the conviction being affirmed by Maryland's appellate court (*Craig v. State*, 1988). Maryland's supreme court reversed the decision in 1989. Although it agreed with the trial court that the Confrontation Clause does not require a face-to-face courtroom encounter between the accused and accusers, it disagreed with the emotional distress standard used by the trial court to justify permitting the special questioning procedure for child witnesses. The Maryland high court held that in addition to requiring a finding that the child's courtroom testimony would result in that child suffering serious emotional distress such that he or she could not reasonably communicate, two additional requirements had to be met: (a) the child must initially be questioned in the defendant's presence (inside or outside the courtroom) to demonstrate the validity of the two conclusions (i.e., the child would suffer serious emotional distress from facing the defendant and because of that would not be able to communicate effectively) and (b) it had to be shown that the child would suffer severe emotional distress if he or she were to testify by two-way CCTV (i.e., in which both the accused and the accuser could see each other during the questioning), which is a less restrictive alternative (in terms of the confrontation concerns) to the one-way CCTV procedure.

Craig appealed the case from the Maryland high court to the U.S. Supreme Court, which held that face-to-face confrontation is not an absolute constitutional requirement. However, it "may not be easily dispensed with" (*Maryland v. Craig*, 1990b, p. 850). The right to confront one's accusers may be satisfied without face-to-face confrontation only when (a) the procedure is necessary to further an important public policy interest and (b) the reliability of the testimony is otherwise assured. The testimony's reliability was shown by its satisfaction of the elements of confrontation (E. J. O'Brien, 2000), notably the opportunity to cross-examine the child witnesses, have them testify under oath, and be observed by the judge, jury, and defendant as they testified. Maryland's interest in protecting the physical and psychological well-being of child abuse victims, including protecting them from the possible trauma of testifying in court in front of the defendant, qualified as one such public policy interest. Regarding the showing of necessity, the Court established a three-part test. There must be a case-specific finding that (a) the procedure is necessary to protect the welfare of the child witness; (b) the child witness would be traumatized by the presence of the defendant, not by the courtroom generally; and (c) the emotional distress suffered by the child witness in the defendant's presence is more than *de minimis* (i.e., more than mere nervousness, excitement, or reluctance to testify).

Although the U.S. Supreme Court left it up to the states to determine their specific procedures for satisfying these requirements, the Court rejected the two additional requirements imposed by the Maryland supreme court. It did not find that the observation of the allegedly abused child victims' behavior in the defendant's presence or the consideration of less restrictive alternatives to the one-way CCTV procedure were prerequisites to use of televised testimony as a matter of federal constitutional law. "Although we think such evidentiary requirements could strengthen the grounds for use of protective measures, we decline to establish, as a matter of federal constitutional law, any such categorical evidentiary prerequisites for the use of the one-way television procedure" (*Maryland v. Craig*, 1990b, p. 860).

When *Craig* was remanded to the Court of Appeals of Maryland, it clarified the steps to be taken by a trial judge when considering the use of CCTV in light of the U.S. Supreme Court's ruling and other state law. It accepted the need for a case-specific finding of necessity as outlined by the U.S. Supreme Court and reevaluated the two additional prerequisite requirements. The Maryland supreme court determined that it was within the judge's discretion to allow the defendant to be present when the judge observed and interviewed the child witness to determine whether he or she was available to testify. In addition, it also found that the means of carrying out CCTV was at the discretion of the judge. Instead of mandating the consideration of less restrictive alternatives, it noted that "the prudent judge will consider the reasonable availability of measures which would be the least restrictive of confrontation, yet serve the purpose of § 9-102, and seek to utilize such measures, if that can be accomplished without undue delay or inconvenience" (*Craig v. State*, 1991, p. 433). The Maryland Court of Appeals then sent the case back to the Court of Special Appeals with directions to reverse the judgment of the circuit court and remand the case for a new trial.[1]

The U.S. Supreme Court's decision in *Craig* puts a lower limit, not a ceiling, on state law. At a minimum, courts must find that a child's testimony with a modification meets the requirements of reliability and necessity as set out in the U.S. Supreme Court's three-part test in *Craig*. State legislatures

---

[1]The history of this case began with a hearing before the Circuit Court in Howard County, Maryland. The defendant was found guilty and appealed to the Court of Special Appeals. This court affirmed the decision of the trial court (*Craig v. State*, 1988). The defendant petitioned for a writ of certiorari to the state's supreme court, the Court of Appeals of Maryland. It reversed the judgment of the Court of Special Appeals and remanded the case to that court with directions to reverse the judgment of the circuit court for Howard County and remand to the latter court for a new trial in accordance with its opinion (*Craig v. State*, 1989). The U.S. Supreme Court granted certiorari to resolve the Confrontation Clause issues raised in this case (*Maryland v. Craig*, 1990a). The U.S. Supreme Court vacated the judgment of the Court of Appeals of Maryland and remanded the case for further proceedings not inconsistent with their opinion (*Maryland v. Craig*, 1990b). The Court of Appeals of Maryland remanded the case to the Court of Special Appeals with directions to reverse the judgment of the Circuit Court and remand the case for a new trial (*Craig v. State*, 1991). There is no record regarding the occurrence or disposition of the new trial ordered by the Court of Special Appeals.

can and have set tougher standards than that required by the U.S. Supreme Court (e.g., Uniform Child Witness Testimony by Alternative Methods Act, 2007 [Idaho]), and other state courts have interpreted their state constitutions as requiring higher standards than those set out in statutes and rules of evidence (e.g., *State v. Apilando*, 1995 [Hawaii]).

EXPERT TESTIMONY ON THE NEED FOR COURTROOM MODIFICATION

After the U.S. Supreme Court's decision in *Craig* (1990b) recognized that some allegedly abused children need courtroom protection, innovative testimonial and evidentiary procedures became widely available both in the United States (Kovera & Borgida, 1996; McAuliff & Kovera, 2000) and internationally (Cashmore, 2002). Public support for legislation permitting such procedures is strong (Bennett, 2003). Although research has continued to show that protections such as remote testimony and other alternative means to offering testimony can reduce children's distress and increase their ability to communicate accurately in legal proceedings, U.S. courts and other legal professionals do not frequently report using these types of courtroom modifications (Goodman, Quas, Bulkley, & Shapiro, 1999; Hafemeister, 1996; Lyon, 2004; Quas, DeCecco, Bulkley, & Goodman, 1996; B. Smith, Elstein, Trost, & Bulkley, 1993).

One reason for this is that some legal professionals (judges, lawyers, court personnel) are not aware that various forms of modifications are available or allowed in their jurisdiction. Legal professionals who are knowledgeable about courtroom modifications tend to use those procedures that they perceive as being minimally disruptive of the trial process and easy to implement (McAuliff & Kovera, 2000) rather than seeking or using the modification that fits the child witness's needs. Some prosecutors view certain techniques (e.g., CCTV) as "prohibitively expensive and administratively cumbersome" (Lyon, 2004, p. 1). These professionals need to be made aware of (a) the full range of modification practices used in other states and jurisdictions that may be desirable for their cases and courtrooms, (b) the sources of funding and technical assistance (e.g., Bureau of Justice Assistance; see http://www.ojp.usdoj.gov/BJA/; http://12.46.245.173/cfda/Programs/16_611.html; Child Welfare Information Gateway, n.d.) that can be used to help facilitate the implementation of these procedures, and (c) the latest research on the effects of courtroom modifications so that these professionals will be more likely to assess accurately whether their use might disrupt the legal process. These problems are compounded when mental health professionals (MHPs) are not aware of or informed about modifications. For example, some MHPs who provide therapy for children may not realize they could suggest to prosecutors that some of their child patients (clients) who are scheduled to testify in cases can be evaluated for use of a courtroom modification by an outside MHP forensic expert (Greenberg & Shuman, 1997; Shuman, Greenberg, Heilbrun, & Foote, 1998). Without education and external influences, legal professionals are less likely to pursue appropriate modifications and to consult with MHPs who can assist them in the process.

Once the importance of modifications is recognized, a remaining issue of concern to legal and mental health professionals is how a court determines whether an individual child meets the applicable criteria for protection and what should be the specific modification in that particular case. The specific criteria for determining whether a modification is permissible depend not only on the U.S. Supreme Court's decision in *Craig* but also on state law. Some state statutes differ in the factors that must be proved to justify a courtroom modification, which can affect the type of evaluation and testimony that the MHP will need to provide. Thus, chapters 2 and 3 (this volume) explore various state laws and legal issues that arise from state practices in this area. It is important that MHPs be familiar with the law in their jurisdiction so that the testimony they provide will be relevant (see, generally, Sales & Shuman, 2005).

Yet why is there a need for MHP evaluation and testimony in these cases? The answer is that MHP evaluators can, and in some jurisdictions are required to, describe the child's symptoms that indicate present and potential emotional distress/trauma and/or his or her inability to communicate, link that child's distress/trauma and/or communication problems to the need for protection from the defendant's presence, and describe what courtroom modifications are most likely to ameliorate the concerns. Because modification hearings are pretrial, the judge is not constrained by the rules of evidence that control the admissibility of expert testimony in a trial and can therefore listen to any expert that either side wishes to present on the topic.

Although attorneys may also offer testimony from therapists who are working with these children and courts allow such testimony, it should not supplant that which is available from independent MHP evaluators. "Compared to . . . the forensic assessor, clinicians [therapists] are usually somewhat less concerned with detailed quantitative information about experiences and symptoms"; quantitative information gathered from scientifically validated measures is necessary to obtain accurate, objective information about a client (E. B. Carlson & Dutton, 2003, p. 136). In addition, the possibility of a treating therapist to reach a biased conclusion, consciously or unconsciously, about the need for a courtroom accommodation makes her or his testimony problematic. For example, concern for the long-term emotional well-being of the child may influence the therapist to opine that an immediate courtroom accommodation is required, even though the clinical facts may not support this conclusion (see, e.g., Greenberg & Shuman, 1997; Shuman et al., 1998).

What literature can expert witnesses turn to for legal and psychological guidance on the issues they may be asked to address, and that they should address? Although many of the methods used to protect child witnesses in the courtroom have been discussed in the literature (e.g., Cashmore, 2002; Myers, 1996a, 1996b; Task Force, 2002), few have reviewed the science supporting their use (Bennett, 2003; Cashmore, 2002; Marsil, Montoya, Ross, & Graham, 2002; McAuliff & Kovera, 2002; Sandler, 2006; Whitcomb, 2003) or made recommendations regarding how to choose a particular procedural modification. In addition, no scholarship has critically considered the clinical methods MHPs use to assess child witnesses for courtroom modifications, including linking specific clinical problems to the need for courtroom modifications for allegedly abused child witnesses. Instead, the literature advises MHP expert witnesses only about general legal (e.g., only the *Craig* criteria), clinical (e.g., child's developmental age), and ethical (e.g., report the level of uncertainty in a expert opinion) issues to consider when performing these forensic evaluations (Saywitz, 1997; Small & Melton, 1994; Trowbridge, 2003; Whitcomb, Goodman, Runyan, & Hoak, 1994) and appropriately reminds experts to exercise caution in performing these predictive evaluations (Melton, Petrila, Poythress, & Slobogin, 1997; Small & Melton, 1994).

GOALS AND ORGANIZATION OF THE BOOK

This book addresses these needs of expert witnesses by comprehensively considering courtroom modifications that present confrontational concerns and providing an analytical approach that qualified MHPs can use to evaluate whether a child witness appears to need a modification. The focus is on child maltreatment cases. Although all modifications are reviewed, the book concentrates on the following:

- use of remote testimony (CCTV);
- use of videotaped testimony and depositions;
- use of videotaped investigative interviews and other hearsay statements;
- courtroom design changes—namely, the use of devices (e.g., screens) to shield child witnesses from seeing the defendant and the use of physical courtroom changes (e.g., altered seating arrangements); and
- instruction to child witnesses on how to avoid eye contact while in the presence of the defendant.

We limit our discussion to this specific category of modifications because experts are particularly susceptible to legal challenge of their work when such modifications are proposed. For example, *Craig* allows for expert testimony alone to be used to demonstrate the necessity for the courtroom modification.[2] Federal law also specifically requires MHP expert testimony to establish a "substantial likelihood of trauma" before permitting two-way CCTV and videotaped depositions (18 USCS § 3509b(1)(B)(ii); b(2)(B)(i)(II)), as do some states. To minimize the risk of successful legal challenges to MHP testimony, the goal of this book is to provide a comprehensive framework with which to approach the forensic evaluation of children and adolescents for use in these modification hearings. We do not discuss related forensic assessment issues such as how to deal with child witnesses once the court has made a modification decision.

The first step in our framework to help prepare MHPs to perform a courtroom modification assessment is to become familiar with the various alternative courtroom procedures for child witnesses and the legal standards that they will have to meet to convince the judge of the need for a courtroom modification. To accomplish this, it is necessary to determine whether the law of the jurisdiction provides for courtroom modifications and what legal requirements should be followed in a courtroom modification evaluation. Chapter 2 reviews the courtroom modifications provided for in the law that do not raise confrontation issues. Chapter 3 then concentrates on the use of courtroom modifications that raise Sixth Amendment concerns.

The second step in our framework is to assess which of the courtroom modifications that implicate the Confrontation Clause have empirical support. In other words, do social and behavioral science data demonstrate that the modification will do what it purports to do? Chapter 4 discusses the advantages and disadvantages of these modifications and makes specific recommendations for their use.

Chapter 5 then describes our analytic approach to preparing for and conducting the forensic evaluation of potential child witnesses. Note that throughout the volume, we use the terms *assessment* and *evaluation* interchangeably. Chapter 5 begins with recommendations for the requisite knowledge needed to carry out courtroom evaluations competently, followed by a discussion of the content of such evaluations and related in-court testimony.

Given *Craig's* requirement that courtroom evaluations assess for trauma/emotional distress, chapter 6 reviews these concepts as applied to modification evaluations. Chapters 7 through 9 provide the reader with more information about the common clinical conditions (e.g., posttraumatic stress disorder) that can be used to demonstrate trauma or more than *de minimis* emotional distress. Because some jurisdictions require higher degrees of trauma to be shown, we discuss idiographic (case-specific) and nomothetic (e.g., results from psychological tests comparing a child's in-

---

[2]"The trial court in this case, for example, could well have found, on the basis of the expert testimony before it, that testimony of the child witness in the courtroom by the defendant's presence 'will result in [each] child suffering serious emotional distress such that the child cannot reasonably communicate'" (*Maryland v. Craig*, 1990b, p. 860).

dividual performance with group norms) evidence for the formal diagnosis of each clinical condition that can be used to demonstrate the existence of trauma. Chapter 10 then addresses the assessment of relevant communication problems for purposes of the courtroom modification decision.

Chapter 11 concludes the book by summarizing key points discussed throughout the volume, making suggestions for improving the use of courtroom modifications and considering future directions for ensuring fair treatment of both witnesses and defendants in modification hearings. These include ideas for increasing the effectiveness of modifications, enacting legal reforms, and conducting further research to improve the value of courtroom modifications and MHP testimony in these hearings.

We hope that this book will assist MHPs in performing competently in modification hearings and educate legal professionals about the appropriate use of expert testimony in cases with child witnesses. We also hope that a careful reading of the volume will encourage further research by social scientists in this important area and that the results of this research will stimulate further policy discussion and change.

2

COURTROOM MODIFICATIONS THAT DO NOT RAISE CONFRONTATION CLAUSE CONCERNS

A child's testimony is critical in child abuse cases because often the child is the sole witness to the alleged offense (McCauley, Schwartz-Kenny, Epstein, & Tucker, 2000) and alleged child victims of sexual assault are viewed as more believable witnesses in studies with mock juries than adolescents or adults (Yozwiak, Golding, & Marsil, 2004). Children are permitted to testify in these cases because the majority of states hold every person competent to be a witness, including those as young as 2 or 3 years of age (e.g., *State v. Hunsaker*, 1984; *State v. Hussy*, 1987). Testimonial competency involves being found to (a) have the capacity to observe an event, (b) have sufficient memory to recall events, (c) be able to communicate, (d) comprehend the difference between truth and lies, and (e) understand the duty to tell the truth when testifying.

To testify, it must be determined that the child is competent at the time of trial, not at the time of the alleged abusive event (J. E. B. Myers, 1997). If a child is competent to be a witness at trial but was incompetent at the time of the crime, then the court would handle his or her offered testimony about the crime in one of two ways: the judge would either find the offered testimony so inherently unreliable that it would not be admitted or admit it and leave judgments about its credibility up to the trier of fact (i.e., the jury, or the judge when there is no jury). In some states, the law presumes that children under age 10, 12, or 14 are incompetent witnesses (Uehlein, 2007); however, this presumption can be rebutted. The trend is to allow all persons to testify regardless of age because competency issues (e.g., ability to recall events) can be addressed during examination and cross-examination of the child (Task Force on Child Witnesses of the American Bar Association Criminal Justice Section [Task Force], 2002).

Another approach to ensuring witness competency if there is doubt about a child's ability to testify is for a judge to conduct a competency hearing (Task Force, 2002). The judge or attorneys may hire a mental health professional (MHP) to conduct an evaluation to help determine whether a child is competent to testify (Trowbridge, 2003). The defendant may be excluded from the competency hearing if adequate cross-examination is afforded during trial (*Kentucky v. Stincer*, 1987). Courts allow this approach if the defendant's presence at the competency hearing would inhibit the child's ability to testify (J. E. B. Myers, 1997). A minority of states ensure that alleged child victims of abuse testify without a preliminary examination of their competence as witnesses (see, generally, National Center for Prosecution of Child Abuse, 2004).

After the determination of a child witness's competency has been made in a case, the next issue to consider is what courtroom modifications are legally available for children who may be in need of assistance. Thus, in addition to knowing about the most recent U.S. Supreme Court decision regarding modifications (see chap. 1, this volume), MHPs should also understand the law of their state or the federal jurisdiction that affects their activities on this issue.[1]

The goal of this chapter and chapter 3 is to describe the courtroom modifications for child witnesses and the laws governing their use. To achieve this goal, this chapter begins with a list of 15 statutorily authorized ways that court procedures can be altered for child witnesses. It then describes in greater detail the 10 modifications that have been found not to implicate the defendant's Sixth Amendment right to confront his or her witnesses (chap. 3 reviews those that do) because MHPs need to be aware of the full range of available modifications when assessing and planning to meet the needs of a particular child witness.

---

[1]Within the federal court system, the 94 U.S. district courts are the trial courts that hear all civil and criminal cases. There is at least one district in each state, the District of Columbia, and Puerto Rico. The district courts are organized into 12 regional circuits, each of which has a U.S. court of appeals. Each appellate court hears appeals from the district courts located within its circuit. Thus, to understand the modification rules in cases appearing in federal courts, one must understand not only the federal statutory law but also the district and appellate decision(s) governing the interpretation of that law in one's region. In addition, if a constitutional challenge, based on the U.S. Constitution, is raised to a state modification law, the appropriate federal district court can hear the case and rule on the law's constitutionality. The district court's decision can then be appealed to the appropriate federal appellate court. The state is bound by the decisions of these federal courts.

COURTROOM MODIFICATIONS AND THE LAW

All states have laws regarding at least one alternative procedure for child witnesses in criminal court. As previously discussed, there are 15 courtroom modifications in state and federal statutes: (a) providing a guardian *ad litem* (GAL), (b) providing a support person or child advocate, (c) protecting the child's identity, (d) closing the courtroom, (e) allowing the use of leading questions, (f) encouraging the use of developmentally appropriate questioning, (g) permitting the use of demonstrative aids and evidence, (h) limiting the length of child testimony, (i) limiting the number of child interviews, (j) encouraging expeditious disposition, (k) using remote testimony (CCTV), (l) using videotaped testimony, (m) using videotaped investigative interviews, (n) allowing a child hearsay exception, and (o) permitting courtroom design changes. Given the complexity of the law relating to these modifications, MHPs should consult with an attorney to determine the legal requirements of the jurisdiction in which they are working. For example, such a determination includes an examination of the state's constitution, statutes, rules of evidence, criminal and civil procedure, rules of court, and case law to learn whether a modification is already legally recognized.

In situations in which a state or federal law does not address the use of a particular modification, a court has the authority to fashion and apply a modification if it is in the best interests of the child and does not violate the defendant's constitutional rights. Trial courts are generally given wide discretion in how they conduct trials because trial judges have the inherent authority to exercise control over the child witnesses in their courtrooms (e.g., Fed. R. Evid. 611(a)).[2] Thus, judicial creativity can be applied both in deciding whether a child witness should be given a modification and what that modification should be (American Prosecutors Research Institute [APRI] National Center for Prosecution of Child Abuse, 2004). This means that courts in a state or a federal jurisdiction may use modifications not set out in existing law.

---

[2]Rule 611. "Mode and Order of Interrogation and Presentation. (a) Control by court. The court shall exercise reasonable control over the mode and order of interrogating witnesses and presenting evidence so as to (1) make the interrogation and presentation effective for the ascertainment of the truth, (2) avoid needless consumption of time, and (3) protect witnesses from harassment or undue embarrassment." This rule applies as long as the (confrontation) rights of the defendant are protected and the probative value of the evidence is weighed against the possibility that it will be used improperly or unfairly, as is required by Rule 403 (Commentary to Rule 611 by Stephen A. Saltzburg, Daniel J. Capra, and Michael M. Martin). We refer to the Federal Rules of Evidence in this chapter because it is controlling in the federal courts and the majority of states have adopted them.

COURTROOM MODIFICATIONS FOR CHILD WITNESSES THAT DO NOT IMPLICATE THE SIXTH AMENDMENT

The 10 courtroom modifications in state and federal statutes that do not raise Confrontation Clause issues include the following: (a) providing a GAL, (b) providing a support person or child advocate, (c) protecting the child's identity, (d) closing the courtroom, (e) allowing the use of leading questions, (f) encouraging the use of developmentally appropriate questioning, (g) permitting the use of demonstrative aids and evidence, (h) limiting the length of child testimony, (i) limiting the number of child interviews, and (j) encouraging expeditious disposition. Each modification is now discussed in more detail.

1. Guardian *Ad Litem* (GAL) or Child's Attorney

Because children are not the litigants (i.e., prosecution or the defendant) in a criminal child abuse case, their needs may get overlooked. To address this concern, the judge may appoint an adult representative who understands the legal system, known as a GAL, to speak on behalf of the child (J. E. B. Myers, 1997; Task Force, 2002). The GAL will identify the child's interests in the litigation and advocate for a judgment that is in the child's best interests (Whitcomb, 1988). To fulfill their responsibilities, GALs have the power to investigate and present the court with recommendations regarding the child and provide support to the child throughout the legal process.

The GAL's role is similar to that of a support person or child advocate (described later) but is often more comprehensive. Although the duties and responsibilities of GALs are not always specifically defined by statute, some state laws denote common roles and responsibilities, including the following:

- interviewing witnesses;
- making recommendations to the court;
- investigating the case to ascertain facts;
- examining and cross-examining witnesses at preliminary hearings and trial;
- attending all depositions, hearings, and trial proceedings;
- requesting additional examinations by medical doctors or MHPs;
- explaining to the court the child's ability to understand; and
- helping the child and the child's family cope with any emotional effects of the trial. (Task Force, 2002)

The GAL's responsibilities are typically different from those of an attorney. For example, an attorney advocates for the child's wishes (without making any independent judgment of the child's best interests), whereas the

GAL advocates for the best interests of the child rather than what the child wants. However, in a few states (e.g., Iowa Code § 915.37 (2006)), GALs must be attorneys. In other states, the law offers guidelines for their selection by the judge (Task Force, 2002). A few states require training for the role of a GAL (e.g., Ky. Rev. Stat. § 26A.140, 2006 [Kentucky]).

2. Support Person

Child witnesses may need support during a court appearance or testimony. These support people, also referred to as *adult attendants* or *child advocates*, may include parents, stepparents, guardians, relatives, friends, counselors, and other trusted adults not accused of a crime. Although one court has indicated a preference for use of family members rather than MHPs in this role (*State v. T.E.*, 2001 [New Jersey]), prosecutors do not recommend that parents take on this role given that they may be witnesses in the case and may become upset during the testimony (APRI, 2004).

In the role of support person, an adult is to provide appropriate support that has been shown to make the child's court experience positive while not influencing the child's testimony through prompts, coaching, or indications of approval or disapproval (Whitcomb, Goodman, Runyan, & Hoak, 1994). The extent of the emotional assistance that the support person can provide may be regulated (e.g., whether the support person is permitted physical contact with the child). A few states (e.g., 42 Pa. Cons. Stat. § 5983, 2006 [Pennsylvania]) give the support person specific duties such as explaining the legal proceedings to the child in a language understandable to him or her, advising the judge about the child's ability to understand and participate in the court proceedings, and assisting the child and his or her family in coping with the emotional effects of the alleged crime and the legal proceedings in which the child is involved. Support persons can also provide the child and family with appropriate referrals and assist the caregiver with obtaining financial assistance through victim compensation programs (Walters, 2000).

3. Protecting the Child's Identity

Given the sensitive nature of the facts involved in cases of alleged child maltreatment, there may be a need to protect the personal information of the alleged child victims of or child witnesses to these crimes. The prospect of sharing intimate details about alleged abuse can lead to feelings of fear, embarrassment, shame, and stigma in children (Ghetti, Alexander, & Goodman, 2002; Herman & Hirschman, 1981). Children are sensitive about their reputations and often do not have the power to control the dissemination of information about themselves (Finkelhor & Putnam, 2004). Some states have enacted laws to limit access to the information of child crime victims or witnesses (e.g., sealing court records and documents, amending public records laws to protect alleged child victims' identifying information, and identifying child witnesses by a pseudonym in police records, charging documents, and court filings; Armagh, 1998; Finkelhor & Putnam, 2004). In these cases, the desire to protect the privacy of alleged child victims or witnesses (e.g., name, phone number, address, picture) must be weighed against the public's common law right to access court records and documents (Task Force, 2002).

4. Courtroom Closure

During their testimony, child witnesses in child maltreatment cases may be asked to describe debasing and embarrassing acts in front of court personnel, attorneys, parties to the case, immediate family members, guardians, and others with direct interest in the case. The potential for people who are not necessary to the proceedings (i.e., members of the public, the media), to watch, listen, and possibly record and broadcast the child's testimony may cause some children to feel, or compound existing feelings of, shame or humiliation. To protect child witnesses from such an occurrence, the judge may exclude unnecessary persons from the courtroom or from the judge's chambers during a child's testimony regarding certain crimes (typically sexual offenses). This practice is allowed in a number of states and in the federal jurisdictions (e.g., S.C. Code Ann. § 16-3-1550(E), 2006 [South Carolina]). A few states, however, allow members of the media to remain and/or permit the child and her or his testimony to be broadcast by closed-circuit television out of the courtroom so that it is made public, thereby defeating the purpose of this modification (e.g., Fla. Stat. ch. 918.16, 2007 [Florida]). Several states set age restrictions (e.g., children under 16 years of age) on the child witness for this modification to apply, but many do not. Of course, even without a specific statute, the trial judge has the inherent authority to exercise discretion to close the courtroom as long as constitutional rights are protected (e.g., *Newspapers, Inc. v. Commonwealth*, 1981 [Virginia]).

Closing the courtroom implicates U.S. and state constitutional rights. The First Amendment protects the rights of free speech and freedom of the press, including a "qualified right to attend a criminal trial" (APRI, 2004, p. 460). Under the leading case in this area, *Globe Newspaper Co. v. Super. Ct.* (1982), the U.S. Supreme Court found unconstitutional a Massachusetts statute that required judges to exclude the public and press in all cases in which alleged child sex offense victims testify. Finding that the right of access to criminal trials is not absolute, the court held that closure must be justified by a "compelling government interest, and . . . narrowly tailored to serve that interest" (*Globe*, p. 607). The U.S. Supreme Court in *Waller v. Georgia* (1984) clarified the requisite findings from previous cases, which can be summarized as a four-part test:

Under *Press-Enterprise* [*Press-Enterprise Co. v. Superior Court*, 1985], the party seeking to close the hearing must advance an overriding interest that is likely to be prejudiced, the closure must be no broader than necessary to protect that interest, the trial court must consider reasonable alternatives to closing the proceeding, and it must make findings adequate to support the closure. (p. 48)

In these rulings, the U.S. Supreme Court weighed the compelling need to protect the child's physical and psychological well-being against the newspaper's First Amendment right to attend a criminal trial. It noted that a judge can close the courtroom on a case-by-case basis, after weighing factors including the alleged victim's age, psychological maturity, and understanding; the nature of the crime; the wishes of the alleged victim; and the interests of parents and relatives.

Most state statutes, however, do not address the specific factors that a judge must consider when making this decision, with case law often applying the standards set by the U.S. Supreme Court. However, California requires the court to consider all of the following:

(1) The nature and seriousness of the offense. (2) The age of the minor, or the level of cognitive development of the dependent person. (3) The extent to which the size of the community would preclude the anonymity of the victim. (4) The likelihood of public opprobrium due to the status of the victim. (5) Whether there is an overriding public interest in having an open hearing. (6) Whether the prosecution has demonstrated a substantial probability that the identity of the witness would otherwise be disclosed to the public during that proceeding, and demonstrated a substantial probability that the disclosure of his or her identity would cause serious harm to the witness. (7) Whether the witness has disclosed information concerning the case to the public through press conferences, public meetings, or other means. (8) Other factors the court may deem necessary to protect the interests of justice. (Cal. Penal Code § 859.1, 2007)

The defendant also has the right to a speedy and public trial under the Sixth Amendment. The U.S. Supreme Court clarified that this right is "no less protective of a public trial than the implicit First Amendment rights of the press and public" (*Waller v. Georgia*, 1984) discussed earlier. When closure of the courtroom is sought for a child witness, *Waller* requires a judge to apply the same four-part test to evaluate Sixth Amendment issues as when the defendant asserts his or her right to a public trial.

In a case involving a defendant charged with sexual battery of a 6-year-old child, the U.S. Court of Appeals (Eleventh Circuit) upheld the *Waller* test as the "clearly established federal law . . . on the issue of courtroom closures" (*LaPlante v. Crosby*, 2005, p. 724). Applying the four *Waller* factors, the court found that (a) the protection of the physical and psychological well-being of a minor is a compelling state interest in a child rape case; (b) the total closure of the courtroom was limited to the testimony of the alleged child victim; (c) the trial court considered other alternatives to total closure, including modifying an original order to allow the victim advocate to be present; and (d) the trial court made adequate findings to support its ruling, including considerations of the age, psychological maturity, and understanding of the child; the nature of the crime and the testimony to be given; and the interests of the alleged victim's relatives. Thus, this modification has been upheld as constitutional for child witnesses in child abuse cases.

5. Leading Questions

Leading questions are those that provide guidance as to the way that a question is expected to be answered (e.g., "You live on State Street, don't you?"). The law traditionally limits the use of such questions when an attorney is directly examining a witness, but trial courts have the inherent authority to allow this practice (Fed. R. Evid. 611(c); *Jackson v. State*, 1986 [Arkansas]). The reason they would do so for child witnesses is that leading questions can help elicit testimony when children "experience difficulty testifying due to fear, timidity, embarrassment, confusion, or reluctance" (Task Force 2002, p. 23). In addition, leading questions do not require the child to describe all of the events that allegedly occurred. Careful use of this type of questioning can make developmental sense for young children who "need more adult questions and prompts to guide their recall" (Hewitt, 1999, p. 59; Saywitz, Goodman, & Lyon, 2002). However, it also raises substantial concern because leading questions can increase the suggestibility of young children and the possibility of inaccurate responses (APRI, 2004; Saywitz et al., 2002). Although they can be problematic, leading questions with child witnesses in cases of alleged child abuse are specifically allowed in many states (e.g., N.H. Super. Ct. R. 93-A, 2007 [New Hampshire]).

6. Developmentally Appropriate Questioning

Although age-appropriate questioning of child witnesses should be standard practice in all jurisdictions (as discussed in chap. 1, this volume), attorneys, judges, and courtroom personnel may need reminding that children should be asked questions in a language that they can understand. Indeed, a few states (e.g., Fla. Stat. ch. 90.612, 2007 [Florida]) "mandate that questions be stated in a form which is appropriate for the age, understanding and developmental level of the child" and "restrict the unnecessary repetition of questions" for witnesses under age 14 (Task Force, 2002, p. 25).

7. Demonstrative Aids and Evidence

Demonstrative aids and evidence include drawings, diagrams, models, dolls, puppets, or mannequins. For example, anatomical diagrams are outline drawings of nude males and females of different ethnicities at various stages of development (young school-age children, adolescents, and adults), with age-appropriate body features (Holmes & Finnegan, 2002). Anatomically correct dolls (also called anatomical or anatomically detailed [AD] dolls) have lifelike features, including vaginal, oral, and anal openings and age-appropriate, gender-specific genitalia. They also vary in appearance (different shapes, sizes, ages, skin tones, anatomical detail).

Demonstrative aids and evidence can be used when a child does not have the words for an act, when there is a need to determine a child's words for different body parts, when the child feels too embarrassed to use words to describe what allegedly happened, or to enhance memory of an event and recall of detail (Hiltz & Bauer, 2003). The general rules of evidence allow judges to permit the use of these aids as evidence, although some states and the federal jurisdictions have added specific statutory language to clarify the limits of this use (e.g., age requirements, types of proceedings, child's need for this type of assistance when testifying).

Although widely used in many jurisdictions (J. E. B. Myers, 2000),[3] demonstrative aids and evidence are subject to criticism. For example, anatomical dolls may be overly suggestive to children, invite misuse, and be particularly problematic when used with young children who do not understand that they are to be used in a self-representative manner (Bruck, Ceci, & Principe, 2006; Hewitt, 1999). More specifically,

> when props are used in forensic interviews with young children, the risk of obtaining inaccurate memory reports (e.g. reports influenced by products of the child's imagination) is often increased, especially perhaps when distractor props or props that prompt fantasy play are included. (Goodman & Melinder, 2007, p. 8)

Such materials may also influence the interviewer's perception of the child's report (Melinder, 2002). Interpreting the meaning of a child's non-verbal testimony is a subjective process, and there is no accepted standard protocol for conducting such an analysis when using dolls and drawings in court (American Psychological Association [APA] Council of Representatives, 1991; Task Force, 2002). In addition, "there is no documentation

---

[3]Twenty guidelines for the use of anatomical dolls in investigative interviews were reviewed in 1994 (Everson & Boat), and 1 year later, the American Professional Society on the Abuse of Children (APSAC) issued guidelines on the use of anatomical dolls in child sexual abuse investigative interviews (APSAC, 1995). The APA's Council of Representatives (1991) formally adopted its *Statement on the Use of Anatomically Detailed Dolls in Forensic Evaluations*, which the APA Anatomical Doll Working Group approved subject to five caveats (Koocher et al., 1995). See, for example, *Commonwealth v. Trowbridge* (1995; permitting use of anatomically correct doll); *Phillips v. State* (1986; permitting dolls); *Pittman v. State* (1986; permitting diagrams).

of the validity of AD dolls or of suggested protocols for forensic purposes" (Koocher et al., 1995, ¶ 3). It is not surprising that consensus does not exist as to whether or when the dolls should be introduced as a demonstrative aid during interviews with children (Faller, 2003). Some courts have therefore not permitted MHP testimony when it was based on the use of anatomical dolls with children (e.g., *Gier By & Through Gier v. Educational Serv. Unit No. 16*, 1994; *In re Amber B.*, 1987). However, when anatomical dolls are used, APRI (2004) recommends that an attorney first ask the child what he or she is showing with the aid to have the record reflect what the child said he or she was demonstrating. If the child is not able to use words to describe what he or she was doing with the aid, the attorney should offer a description, followed by a request that the trial transcript reflect that the attorney's description of the child's actions with the aid is accurate.

8. Length of Child Testimony

Mindful of the developmental needs of children, a few states require courts to be sensitive to the time of day and length of time that a child witness testifies. Because young children perform best when well rested, it is recommended that their testimony be scheduled in the morning, not conflicting with nap time (Task Force, 2002). Morning testimony for young children "can make the difference between no testimony and great testimony" (APRI, 2004, p. 327). It has also been argued that school-age children do best when their testimony is scheduled during school hours, so that they do not worry all day about going to court or become too drained from the day's activities (J. E. B. Myers, 1997). California has included this recommendation in a statute: "In the court's discretion, the taking of [a minor's] . . . testimony . . . may be limited to normal school hours if there is no good cause to take the testimony of the person . . . during other hours" (Cal. Penal Code § 868.8(d), 2007).

The length of time that a child testifies should also take into account the child's developmental needs. Because children have a limited attention span, prearranged breaks (e.g., every 15 minutes for children under 5 years and at longer intervals for older children, breaks between direct and cross-examination) and a limited time for direct testimony are recommended (APRI, 2004). Recesses may be appropriate when the child shows signs of fatigue, unmanageable stress, or difficulties sustaining attention (J. E. B. Myers, 1997). The trial judge has the inherent authority and discretion (e.g., *Commonwealth v. Brusgulis*, 1986 [Massachusetts]) to provide for recesses during the proceedings at reasonable intervals during a child's testimony and can remind attorneys of this schedule (Task Force, 2002). California's statute is once again illustrative of laws regarding breaks for a child witness:

> In the court's discretion, the witness may be allowed reasonable periods of relief from examination and cross-examination during which he or

she may retire from the courtroom. The judge may also allow other witnesses in the proceeding to be examined when the . . . child witness retires from the courtroom. (Cal. Penal Code § 868.8(a), 2007)

9. Number of Child Interviews

Some states have enacted statutes that attempt to reduce repeated pretrial interviews or interviewers of child witnesses (e.g., N.D. Cent. Code § 12.1-35-04, 2007 [North Dakota]). The purpose of these laws is to eliminate unnecessary or duplicative practices and to protect children from the psychological damage of repeated interrogations (Saywitz et al., 2002). These interviews may be a part of law enforcement or child protection investigations and of attorney practices (e.g., discovery).

Evaluations by multidisciplinary teams (MDTs) or evaluations at child advocacy centers (CACs) may help reduce the number of interviews and increase their quality because of the coordination that occurs between MDT members or CAC personnel (L. M. Jones, Cross, Walsh, & Simone, 2005). The purpose of MDTs is to bring together multiple professionals (e.g., from law enforcement, child protection, medicine, victim witness, mental health, and prosecution) to guide investigations, conduct team interviews, and collaborate on decision making in child maltreatment cases (Cross, Finkelhor, & Ormrod, 2005). Similarly, CACs not only "provide coordinated investigations and MDTs, as described above, but must also meet an array of standards for quality of investigations, medical and mental health care involvement, victim support and advocacy, and culturally competent services" (Cross et al., p. 228). All states have initiatives regarding MDTs, with the majority mandating their formation (e.g., N.J. Stat. § 9:6-8.104, 2007 [New Jersey]). Many states have also enacted laws regarding the formation, coordination, and funding of CACs, which many professionals believe reduce children's stress (Task Force, 2002).

10. Expeditious Disposition

It has been shown that children whose sexual abuse cases took a longer time to resolve tended to recover more slowly than those whose cases proceeded more quickly (Runyan, Everson, Edelson, Hunter, & Coulter, 1988). For this reason, many states (e.g., Wis. Stat. § 971.105, 2006 [Wisconsin]) have enacted statutes that require speedy trials for cases involving alleged crimes against children and child witnesses and for these cases to be given precedence in the criminal docket. The court, when ruling on motions for continuance or delays in proceedings, may also be required to consider the negative effect on child witnesses (e.g., Wash. Rev. Code § 10.46.085, 2007 [Washington]). At least two courts have held that these laws do not restrict the defendant's Sixth Amendment right to prepare adequately for trial (Task

Force, 2002). Ironically, research indicates that these statutes have little practical effect because of the court's overall caseload. In addition, these statutes "are interpreted by judges to mean that the proceedings are to be expedited only *after* the trial date is set" (Task Force, 2002, p. 20, citing Oregon Task Force Report, 1993).

Another way to increase efficiency across child abuse trials is through the use of vertical prosecution, which involves one prosecutor consistently handling all parts of a case involving a child victim or witness. Although it is a growing trend to use vertical prosecution in other areas of the law (e.g., violent drug use, violent juvenile offenses), only a few states (e.g., Cal. Penal Code § 999s, 2007) mandate their use in criminal child abuse cases. In addition, municipalities within a state may include vertical prosecutions as part of their child abuse investigation protocols (e.g., Pinal County, Arizona, as described in Olson, 2005).

DISCUSSION

All of the courtroom modifications described in this chapter attempt to improve the quality of courtroom testimony, with most modifications aiming to make testifying a less stressful process for child witnesses. Because different aspects of courtroom testimony may be distressing for different children, modifications target various elements of courtroom testimony. MHPs should consider which modification to suggest on the basis of the specifics of the case and of the child under consideration. For example, young children and those with attention problems typically benefit from modifications that reduce the amount of time spent in the courtroom or that help them focus as they give testimony (Modification 7: demonstrative aids and evidence, Modification 8: limiting the length of child testimony, Modification 10: expeditious disposition). Similarly, scheduled testimony times may be altered because of the child's age; younger children, compared with adolescents, for example, may prefer the morning hours and perform better during that time period (Modification 8: limiting the length of child testimony). Young children may also lack the cognitive tools to understand or resist leading questions (Modification 5: leading questions, Modification 6: developmentally appropriate questions) and may benefit from the use of props to make up for delayed or emerging expressive language skills (Modification 7: demonstrative aids and evidence). Children afraid of unfamiliar or intimidating situations may benefit from modifications that provide support from familiar people or objects (Modification 1: GAL, Modification 2: support person), and that remove them (Modification 9: limiting the number of child interviews) or others (Modification 4: courtroom closure) from an environment that is stressful, scary, or embarrassing. Minors and their parents who are concerned about the privacy of personal information may want modifications that can protect this interest (Modification 3: protecting child's identity, Modification 4: courtroom closure).

Some modifications were designed to help with understanding and communication rather than to accommodate the child's emotional well-being. As a result, these modifications can have either positive or negative psychological effects. First, the use of developmentally appropriate questions (Modification 6) improves children's ability to communicate in court; in turn, this can indirectly reduce the child's anxiety, confusion, or frustration. Thus, this modification is recommended for all child witnesses. Second, the use of anatomical dolls or other demonstrative materials (Modification 7: demonstrative aids and evidence) were introduced as methods to help children who have difficulty using words to relate their experiences. Although these forms of nonverbal communication may help them give a report, they may be too suggestive for young children. In addition, they can be just as anxiety provoking as talking about the alleged abuse. For other children, using dolls to recount an experience may be less distressing than speaking and thus may have a protective effect. As a result, this modification is typically recommended on a case-by-case basis.

Another rationale for modifications concerns victims' rights. Current criminal trial practice involves the government and the defendant as the only parties to criminal litigation, but some commentators argue that allegedly abused child witnesses, referred to as *child victims*, should have a voice in judicial proceedings in which their interests are at stake (Beloof, 1999; Edwards & Sagatun, 1995; Haralambie, 1995). According to this position, the child victim, as a result of the harm suffered, should have standing in a criminal case and be given the right to counsel or at least a GAL (e.g., Beloof, 1999; Hobson, 1990; see also Pizzi & Perron, 1996 [regarding victims of violent crimes generally]). Children in juvenile court have this right. This position is also consistent with the United Nations Convention on the Rights of the Child (http://www.ohchr.org/english/law/crc.htm), which guarantees children the right to be heard in any judicial and administrative proceeding affecting them, either directly or through a representative or appropriate body. Some state statutes give alleged child victims the right to a GAL who can serve as the child's voice during a trial. In most other states, however, it is still in the court's discretion as to whether an alleged child victim's interests need representation by an attorney, GAL, or other adult. If the alleged child victim is not provided the opportunity to have representation at trial and the child does not serve as a witness, he or she may have the right to be present at the trial as a spectator and/or have his or her voice heard in limited ways (e.g., submit a statement to the court about the impact that the crime has had on his or her life—i.e., a victim impact statement; Alexander & Lord, 1994; Herman, 2003; U.S. Department of Justice, Office of Justice Programs, Office for Victims of Crimes, 1999, 2002, 2007).

Some states and the federal law have created other rights for alleged victims in criminal cases. When the right to a speedy trial for victims is provided, for example, courts, in deciding whether to assign priority to the adjudication, must consider any adverse impact a delay or continuance in the trial may have on the alleged child victim's well-being. As noted earlier, child witnesses may also have the right to the presence and assistance of a support person.

CONCLUSION

The majority of the courtroom modifications discussed in this chapter are fairly easy to implement legally because it is within the trial judge's discretion to adapt these procedures for child witnesses and because they do not affect the defendant's rights. These modifications can generally be used if the court finds them to be helpful (e.g., reduces witness stress), practicable (e.g., does not make the proceeding too inefficient), and in the interests of justice. In deciding whether justice is promoted, the court will weigh the child's needs against the interests of the public (e.g., to obtain information), the court (e.g., to operate efficiently), the person charged with the crime (e.g., right to a fair and speedy trial), and the alleged victim.

What remains to be considered are the courtroom modifications that raise confrontation concerns. Because the legal issues regarding these modifications are more complex than those discussed in this chapter and are more likely to involve the services of an MHP evaluator, they raise the need for special knowledge of the forensic literature. Chapter 3, as well as the rest of this book, considers these modifications and their implications for forensic assessment and testimony.

3

COURTROOM MODIFICATIONS THAT RAISE CONFRONTATION CLAUSE CONCERNS

In addition to the 10 modifications discussed in detail in chapter 2, there are 5 in use (Modifications 11–15, as listed in chap. 2, this volume) that implicate defendants' Sixth Amendment right to confront the witnesses against them: remote testimony (typically closed-circuit television [CCTV]), videotaped testimony, videotaped investigative interviews (child hearsay testimony), special child hearsay exceptions, and courtroom design changes. These modifications can involve the child not being in the physical presence of the defendant or not directly looking the defendant in the eye when giving testimony.

This chapter describes the five courtroom modifications and details the legal standards and issues relevant to their proposed use in criminal abuse cases. Mental health professionals (MHPs) need this information to prepare for the forensic assessment of the child witness regarding courtroom modifications. The chapter explains the modifications to the MHP and also provides information that can be used to shape the nature of the evaluation and the recommendations that the expert witness is likely to make in court.

DEFINITIONS AND LEGAL ISSUES

The law often dictates the factors that guide alterations to the traditional courtroom procedures and practices for child witnesses, including the following:

- where the procedure can be used (i.e., criminal, civil, and/or juvenile court cases),
- whether the procedure is available to child witnesses or alleged child victim witnesses,
- the age of children eligible for the modification,
- the type of crime that was alleged to have been committed, and
- the legal tests that govern the admissibility of the modifications.

These issues are discussed as needed throughout this chapter.

Closed-Circuit Television

What Is CCTV?

One way a child's testimony can be taken outside the traditional courtroom without the physical presence of the jury, courtroom audience, and (in most cases) the defendant is through the use of CCTV. This method allows for simultaneous transmission of the child's live testimony from a nearby location to the courtroom using audiovisual equipment. People in the courtroom observe the child's testimony on television monitors.

There are two categories of CCTV. One-way CCTV enables the defendant to view and hear the child without the child seeing or hearing the defendant. As discussed in chapter 1 (this volume), *Craig* involved the use of one-way CCTV testimony with preschool children. Two-way CCTV allows both parties to see and hear each other. The location where the child testifies is designed to be more comforting to the child, with the goals of increasing the truthfulness of the testimony and decreasing his or her inhibitions about testifying (Task Force on Child Witnesses of the American Bar Association Criminal Justice Section [Task Force], 2002).

What Is the Law Regarding CCTV?

The majority of states and the U.S. Congress have authorized CCTV as a way to present testimony from a child victim or witness in criminal trials (American Prosecutors Research Institute [APRI], 2004; e.g., *In re Stradford*, 1995 [North Carolina]; Ky. Rev. Stat. § 421.350, 2006 [Kentucky]). Most statutes define the type of case in which CCTV can be used, set age requirements for the child to be eligible for CCTV, and describe the location of the defendant during the child's testimony. All outline the legal findings that must be made regarding the child witness.

Most states allow CCTV to be used only when the proceedings pertain to the alleged physical or sexual abuse of a child (e.g., Ala. Code § 15-25-3,

2007 [Alabama]). A few states allow CCTV in other types of criminal proceedings (e.g., Ark. Code Ann. § 16-43-1001, 2007 [Arkansas]). However, states are split over whether only alleged child victims of these crimes or both alleged child victims and child witnesses are permitted to use CCTV.

A few jurisdictions permit any child under the age of 18 years to be eligible to use CCTV (e.g., 725 Ill. Comp. Stat. 5/106B-5, 2007 [Illinois]). Most states place age restrictions on its use, ranging from "16 years of age or younger" (N.J. Stat. § 2A:84A-32.4, 2007 [New Jersey]) to "under 10 years of age" (e.g., Wash. Rev. Code § 9A.44.150, 2007 [Washington]). Of these, the most frequently cited age ranges are children under 16 years of age and under 12 years of age. A few states allow CCTV for developmentally disabled people over the chronological age limit (e.g., Fla. Stat. ch. 92.54, 2007 [Florida]).

The location of courtroom participants, including the court reporter, court security personnel, defense attorney, defendant, prosecuting attorney, support person, legal guardian, interpreter, and CCTV equipment operators, varies by state. In some states, all of these participants may be in the room with the child, and only the judge, jury, and defendant are required to remain in the courtroom (e.g., Ala. Code § 15-25-3, 2007 [Alabama]). In the majority of states, the defendant is excluded from the room where the child testifies (e.g., Tenn. Code Ann. § 24-7-120, 2007 [Tennessee]). In those states that allow the defendant to remain in the room with the child, the judge may exclude the defendant if it is found that the child would be intimidated or inhibited by his or her physical presence (e.g., S.D. Codified Laws § 26-8A-30, 2007 [South Dakota]).

The court may order CCTV in a case after it is requested (usually by the prosecution) and after the court conducts an individualized finding that it is necessary to protect the child. Similar to *Craig*, most require a showing that the child required to give live testimony would suffer a certain level of trauma or emotional distress (i.e., more than *de minimis*) because of the presence of the defendant and not the courtroom generally. Note that the U.S. Supreme Court appeared to use the terms *trauma* and *emotional distress* interchangeably, whereas MHPs may or may not (see chap. 5, this volume, for further discussion of this issue). The Federal Court of Appeals for the Eighth Circuit emphasized the importance of this finding (*United States v. Bordeaux*, 2005). It held that a trial court must find that the *predominant* reason for a witness's inability to testify in the courtroom is his or her fear of the defendant and that the showing of trauma/distress had to be as high as in *Craig* (Harmon, 2005; S. McMahon, 2006). However, the legal showing does not require the child to be placed in the presence of the defendant but can be demonstrated with other evidence such as expert testimony. In addition, about half of the states that permit CCTV require a showing that testimony in the defendant's presence would result in the child "suffering serious emotional distress such that the child cannot reasonably communicate" (*Mary-*

land v. Craig, 1990b, p. 860; Lamken, n.d.; Montoya, 1992). Although states and courts are divided on this question, the U.S. Supreme Court decided in 2007 not to address the issue (i.e., whether there must be a showing that the child cannot communicate; State v. Vogelsberg, 2007). Depending on the jurisdiction, expert testimony can be used to assist the court in making the required showing of trauma/emotional distress, and/or communication impairment, either in conjunction with other evidence (E. J. O'Brien, 2000) or standing alone (e.g., Lomholt v. Iowa, 2003).

The showing must be supported by evidence that is found to meet a specific level of certainty. Most CCTV statutes require showing of necessity (defined as "the presence or pressure of circumstances that justify or compel a certain course of action"; e.g., La. Rev. Stat. § 15:283, 2007 [Louisiana]); good cause ("reasonable grounding; substantial reason put forth in good faith that is not unreasonable, arbitrary, or irrational"; e.g., Utah R. Crim. P. Rule 15.5(2), 2007); compelling ("tending to demand action or to convince") need (e.g., Ky. Rev. Stat. § 421.350, 2006 [Kentucky]); substantial likelihood (substantial can be defined as "not illusory, having merit"; e.g., Or. Rev. Stat. § 40.460; OEC 803, 2005 [Oregon]); substantial risk (e.g., Vt. R. Evid. 807, 2007 [Vermont]); or substantial evidence ("evidence greater than a scintilla of evidence that a reasonable person would find sufficient to support a conclusion"; e.g., Wash. Rev. Code § 9A.44.150, 2007 [Washington]). Necessity must be proved either by clear and convincing evidence ("evidence showing a high probability of truth of the factual matter at issue"; e.g., Conn. Gen. Stat. § 54-86g, 2003 [Connecticut]) or a preponderance of the evidence ("more probable than not"; e.g., N.H. Rev. Stat. Ann. § 517:13-a, 2007 [New Hampshire]). No jurisdictions require the most demanding standard of proof, that is, proof beyond a reasonable doubt. Being aware of the showing required in one's state will help expert witnesses prepare for the level of scrutiny that the court will use to evaluate their testimony. Standards are examined further in the Discussion section of this chapter.

The majority of CCTV statutes have withstood state and federal constitutional challenges. As noted in chapter 1 (this volume), Maryland v. Craig (1990b) upheld a one-way CCTV procedure, finding that face-to-face confrontation at trial was not required in every case. The U.S. Supreme Court found that CCTV was the "functional equivalent" of live, in-court testimony because it incorporates the following four elements of confrontation: physical presence of the witness, testifying under oath, cross-examination, and the observation of the witness's demeanor by the trier of fact. The Court pointed out that assurances provided by one-way CCTV "are far greater than those required for the admission of hearsay statements."[1] Only a handful of state courts (e.g., Commonwealth v. Bergstrom, 1988 [Massachusetts]) have found that their state CCTV statutes were facially unconstitutional (i.e., from look-

---

[1]Maryland v. Craig (1990b, p. 851); notwithstanding the majority's decision, the dissent emphasized a literal interpretation of the meaning of confrontation, requiring a face-to-face meeting.

ing at the face of the state constitution, without further inquiry, the statute appeared unconstitutional) on the basis of a literal reading of "face-to-face" confrontation in their state law; such statutes have since been modified. However, in some states that use language identical to those statutes found facially unconstitutional, the courts have upheld the use of CCTV (APRI, 2004). The federal statute regarding the use of two-way CCTV (Child Victims' and Child Witnesses' Rights Act, 18 U.S.C. § 3509, 2007, enacted in 1990) was upheld as constitutionally permissible by the Ninth Circuit Court of Appeals in 2003 (*United States v. Etimani*) but was later found unconstitutional to the extent it conflicted with *Craig* regarding the showing of distress/trauma by the Eighth Circuit Court of Appeals in 2005 (*United States v. Bordeaux*).

Videotaped Testimony

What Is Videotaped Testimony?

Videotaped testimony is the other primary way that a child's testimony can be taken outside of the courtroom, without the physical presence of the jury, courtroom observers, and, in some jurisdictions or cases, the defendant. Videotaped testimony involves a child's sworn testimony being given and videotaped during the grand jury proceeding, a preliminary hearing, or a trial. This testimony is considered a videotaped deposition when the videotape is made during a pretrial hearing (excluding the grand jury proceeding) or during the trial. For videotaped depositions, attorneys for both sides can question and cross-examine the child during the deposition. Because the child is subject to cross-examination, these depositions can be considered the functional equivalent of trial testimony (*State v. Cameron*, 1998). In some states, the child witness does not and is not permitted to testify "live" at the trial (e.g., N.M. Stat. Ann. § 30-9-17, 2007 [New Mexico]). Other states, however, require the child to give in-person testimony or to be cross-examined after the videotapes are shown, if the court deems it necessary (e.g., Wis. Stat. § 967.04, 2006 [Wisconsin]). For example, if pertinent evidence comes to light after the recorded deposition, the defendant may have the right to cross-examine the child about this new evidence in another deposition or in court (APRI, 2004).

What Is the Law Regarding Videotaped Testimony?

The majority of states and the U.S. Congress have specifically authorized the use of videotaped testimony at trials in lieu of live testimony (e.g., N.Y. Crim. Proc. Law §§ 190.25, .30, .32, 2007 [New York, grand jury only]; 18 U.S.C.S. § 3509(b)(2), 2007 [United States]) and videotaped depositions (e.g., Colo. Rev. Stat. §§ 18-3-413 & 18-6-401.3, 2006 [Colorado]). As with CCTV, state statutes specify the type of proceeding, age requirements for the alleged child victim and/or witness who may be present when the videotape is made of the testimony, and the legal showing required to bypass face-to-face confrontation. The majority of states allow videotaped testimony to be used only for prosecutions for alleged physical or sexual abuse of a child (e.g., Utah R. Crim. P. Rule 15.5(3), 2007). A few states permit it in all types of criminal prosecutions or in felony proceedings (e.g., murder; 42 Pa. Cons. Stat. § 5984.1, 2006 [Pennsylvania]).

Although states are split over whether only alleged child victims or both child victims and child witnesses are permitted to use videotaped testimony in criminal cases, the majority of states set age requirements for the child witness. As with CCTV, most states allow them only for vulnerable or developmentally disabled adults and children aged 15 or under (e.g., Ala. Code § 15-25-2, 2007 [Alabama]; Mich. Comp. Laws § 600.2163a, 2007 [Michigan]), 14 or under (e.g., Mass. Gen. Laws Ann. ch. 278 § 16 D, 2007 [Massachusetts]), 13 or under (e.g., Utah R. Crim. P. Rule 15.5(3), 2007), 12 or under (e.g., Okla. Stat. Ann. tit. 12, § 2611.4, 2007, and tit. 22, § 765, 2007 [Oklahoma]), and 11 or under (e.g., Wyo. Stat. § 7-11-408, 2007 [Wyoming]). Wisconsin (Wis. Stat. § 967.04, 2006) sets a general restriction for the use of videotaped depositions for children 11 and under at the time of the hearing but allows for those 15 and under if the court finds the "interests of justice" warrant the child's testimony be recorded. A few states (e.g., R.I. Gen. Laws § 11-37-13.2, 2007 [Rhode Island]) and federal jurisdictions (18 U.S.C.S. § 3509(b)(2), 2007) permit admission of videotaped depositions for any child under 18.

Most states require that the judge, prosecutor, defense counsel, equipment operators (who are typically required to be out of the sight and hearing of the child), and someone whose presence would contribute to the child's welfare be present with the child when his or her testimony is being videotaped (e.g., Tenn. Code Ann. § 24-7-117, 2007 [Tennessee]). An issue on which states do not agree is whether the defendant has a right to be in the same room as the child. Some states specifically allow for defendants to be excluded from the room (e.g., Ala. Code § 15-25-3, 2007 [Alabama]), whereas others require the defendant's presence (e.g., Vt. R. Evid. § 807 (2007) [Vermont]). The constitutional issues that arise when excluding the defendant from the room (not allowing the defendant to face and confront the witness) are similar to that discussed in *Craig*. Some jurisdictions require expert testimony as one source of evidence regarding the child's status before a court can allow videotaped testimony (e.g., Ind. Code Ann. § 35-37-4-8, 2007 [Indiana]). In these jurisdictions, the defendant must be able to communicate with counsel to participate in cross-examination. This is usually accomplished through the use of a two-way private telephone line. The U.S. Supreme Court underscored the importance of simultaneous, private communication during the taking of a child's testimony using this alternative procedure (*Coy v. Iowa*, 1988).

The other issue raised by videotaped testimony and depositions concerns their introduction during trial. Rule 15 of the Federal Rules of Criminal Procedure and similar state statutes permit depositions in criminal proceedings. Rule 15 allows for the testimony of a prospective witness to be taken and preserved for trial whenever a court finds that there are "exceptional circumstances" (e.g., witness unavailability) and it is "in the interests of justice" (U.S.C.S. Fed. R. Crim. P. 15(a)(1), 2006).

In addition, a deposition is traditionally admissible as trial testimony if the child witness meets the unavailability requirements of the law, which include Fed. R. Evid. 804 and applicable case law of *California v. Green* (1970)[2] and its progeny (Natali, 2007). In other words, the child's video-taped deposition can be used in court even though it was an out-of-court statement. However, use of such testimony triggers hearsay law. Stated another way, no assertion offered as testimony can be admitted into testimony unless it is or has been open to scrutiny by cross-examination or an opportunity for cross-examination. As discussed in the sections that follow on hearsay, when this occurs, the testimonial evidence of the videotaped deposition must be found to comply with the confrontation requirements of the Constitution. Under a U.S. Supreme Court case in March 2004 (*Crawford v. Washington*), this means that the judge must make a finding that the child continues to be unavailable at the time of trial and that the defense has had a prior opportunity to cross-examine the child.[3]

At least 30 state appellate courts have upheld these statutes as constitutional in their states, and some have imposed additional conditions to satisfy constitutional requirements. A few states have found videotaped testimony to violate state constitutional law because of a literal interpretation of the defendant's right to "face-to-face" confrontation (e.g., *Commonwealth v. Bergstrom*, 1988 [Massachusetts], although their current statute redressed these issues: Mass. Gen. Laws Ann. ch. 278 § 16 D, 2007). Note that this strict interpretation is a minority view because other states with identical constitutional language permit videotaped testimony with child witnesses (APRI, 2004).

Videotaped Investigative Interviews

What Are Videotaped Investigative Interviews?

When authorities receive a report of alleged child maltreatment, an investigation of the allegations is usually pursued according to local proto-

---

[2]". . . for [declarant's] statement at the preliminary hearing had already been given under circumstances closely approximating those that surround the typical trial. [The declarant] was under oath; respondent was represented by counsel—the same counsel in fact who later represented him at the trial; respondent had every opportunity to cross-examine [the declarant] as to his statement; and the proceedings were conducted before a judicial tribunal, equipped to provide a judicial record of the hearings" (*California v. Green*, 1970, p. 165).

[3]"Testimonial statements of witnesses absent from trial [are] admitted only where the declarant is unavailable and only where the defendant has had a prior opportunity to cross-examine" (*Crawford v. Washington*, 2004, p. 1369). "We leave for another day any effort to spell out a comprehensive definition of 'testimonial.' Whatever else the term covers, it applies at a minimum to prior testimony at a preliminary hearing, before a grand jury, or at a former trial; and to police interrogations" (*Crawford v. Washington*, 2004, p. 1374). See the section on hearsay for a definition of *unavailable*.

cols. As part of the investigatory process, a member or members of the local multidisciplinary or interdisciplinary team (MDT or IDT), usually trained law enforcement agents, child protective service workers, or forensic interviewers, will conduct an interview (or a series of interviews) with the alleged child victim of the abuse. The trend is to interview the children in a child advocacy center (CAC) or other facility specially designed to accommodate children and families in such cases and to videotape the interviews. Videotaping these interviews is controversial among and within states, however (for reasons for and against videotaped interviews, see APRI, 2004; Lanning, 2002; Task Force, 2002).

There are differences between investigative interviews and videotaped depositions. First, videotaped investigative interviews are less formal and less regulated than videotaped depositions because investigative interviews are not specifically made for the court or during a trial. Second, investigative interviews are not adversarial because they only involve a child and a neutral interviewer, whereas videotaped testimony involves both attorneys questioning and cross-examining the child. Third, whereas the investigative interview involves only the interviewer and the allegedly abused child, videotaped depositions may involve the defendant in some jurisdictions, as well as attorneys for the state, attorneys for the defense, support person(s), a person to operate the video equipment, and the judge.

What Is the Law Regarding Videotaped Investigative Interviews?

Although investigative interviews can be videotaped without a specific law authorizing it, about one third of states allow for the videotaping of investigative interviews through statutes and court rules. The U.S. Supreme Court ruled that videotaping can enhance the reliability of children's out-of-court statements about alleged maltreatment (*Idaho v. Wright*, 1990).

The statutes in the states that authorize videotaped investigative interviews or videotaped statements of children in court (e.g., La. Rev. Stat. § 15:440.5 (2007) [Louisiana]) generally contain a number of limiting provisions, including specifying the following:

- the type of proceeding in which the tape is allowed (e.g., Ind. Code Ann. § 35-37-4-6 (2007) [Indiana]; a few states only permit their use in grand jury proceedings, and most allow them in child sexual or physical abuse cases only (e.g., Colo. Rev. Stat. § 18-3-413 (2006) [Colorado]));
- age requirements for the alleged child victim and/or witness (most are for children 14 years and under; e.g., Mo. Rev. Stat. § 492.304, 2007 [Missouri]);
- the status of child as alleged victim and/or witness (the majority authorize for alleged victims only; e.g., Iowa Code § 915.38, 2006 [Iowa]);

- that the recording is both visual and aural and is recorded on film or videotape or through other electronic means (e.g., Kan. Stat. Ann. § 22-3433, 2006 [Kansas]);
- that the recording is accurate and has not been altered or distorted (e.g., Wis. Stat. § 908.08, 2006 [Wisconsin]);
- that every voice on the recording is identified (e.g., Ariz. Rev. Stat. § 13-4252, 2007 [Arizona]);
- that the videotaped assertion of the child is an oral and/or nonverbal statement (e.g., Okla. Stat. Ann., tit. 10, § 7003-4.2, 2007 [Oklahoma]);
- that the statement is not made in response to questioning calculated to lead the child to make a particular statement or that it is clearly shown to be the child's statement and not made solely as a result of a leading or suggestive question (e.g., R.I. Gen. Laws § 11-37-13.1, 2007 [Rhode Island]);
- that no attorney or peace officer was present when the child's statement was made (e.g., La. Rev. Stat. Ann. § 15:440.5; 2007 [Louisiana]); some states permit prosecutor members of MDTs to view but not be in the same room as a child giving a statement at a state-funded child assessment center or CAC (e.g., Mo. Rev. Stat. § 492.304, 2007 [Missouri]);
- that the interviewer is present at the proceeding and available to testify or be cross-examined by either party (e.g., Mo. Rev. Stat. § 492.304, 2007 [Missouri]); and
- that each party to the proceeding is given an opportunity to view the recording and, in some states, receive a copy of a written transcript (e.g., Kan. Stat. Ann. § 22-3433, 2006 [Kansas]).

A few statutes describe the qualifications or professional status of the interviewer or videotape custodian and the protocol to be followed during the interview (e.g., Mich. Comp. Laws § 600-2163a, 2007 [Michigan]).

Even if the statutory provisions are met, the next legal issue is whether the videotaped investigative interview can be admitted into evidence. This involves determining whether the interview can properly be admitted under a hearsay exception (explained in the next section), and, if so, whether a Confrontation Clause analysis is required to examine the admissibility of the interview as a constitutional matter.

If a child subsequently testifies in court and is cross-examined, an attorney who wants to admit his or her videotaped investigative interview (recorded prior to trial) must show that the videotape meets a hearsay exception. For example, it has been admitted under a "firmly rooted" hearsay exception (i.e., an exception that has been historically accepted under hearsay law) such as prior consistent statements (i.e., to rebut defense charges of coaching the witness or fabrication of testimony) and prior inconsistent statements (i.e., to rehabilitate a child's recantation of prior testimony; Whitcomb, 1992b). Because the child is available to be cross-examined in court, the attorney who introduces the videotaped interview does not have to address Confrontation Clause requirements. When the child witness (declarant) "appears for cross examination at trial, the *Confrontation Clause* places no constraints on the use of his prior testimonial statements" (*Crawford*, p. 1369).

To introduce the videotaped investigative interview in lieu of a child's testimony, the videotape must meet a hearsay exception, typically a residual or special child abuse hearsay exception (a discussion of this appears later in this chapter). Under previous law, only hearsay not admitted under a firmly rooted exception was also subject to Confrontation Clause analysis. The rationale was that the context of firmly rooted statements gave the statements special guarantees of credibility and trustworthiness, such that reliability was implied (*Ohio v. Roberts*, 1980; *White v. Illinois*, 1992). Statements not falling under a firmly rooted exception were treated as presumptively unreliable unless it could be shown that they were sufficiently trustworthy. Videotaped investigative interview statutes therefore often require the court to determine that the time, content, and circumstances of the statement provide sufficient indicia of reliability (i.e., a basis on which to infer that the information was reliable; e.g., Ind. Code Ann. § 35-37-4-6, 2007 [Indiana]). In addition, many of the statutes also specifically include the requirement that the child be available to testify at trial (e.g., La. Rev. Stat. Ann. § 15:440.5, 2007 [Louisiana]) or that the court needs to find the child to be unavailable before a videotaped investigative interview can be introduced at trial (e.g., Colo. Rev. Stat. § 18-3-413, 2006 [Colorado]). Courts may require medical or psychological evidence or expert testimony to make the unavailability determination (e.g., N.D. Cent. Code § 31-04-04.1, 2007 [North Dakota]).

However, the U.S. Supreme Court's decision in *Crawford v. Washington* (2004) overruled *Ohio v. Roberts* (1980)[4] and cast doubt on *Idaho v. Wright* (1990) and *White v. Illinois* (1992). As the current controlling law in this area, *Crawford* has affected the use of videotaped investigative interviews and child hearsay when the child does not testify in criminal cases. Although "most convictions have been upheld post-*Crawford*" (Hudson, 2004, citing New England School of Law Professor Wendy Murphy), and the U.S. Supreme Court decided that the case cannot be retroactively applied (*Whorton v. Bockting*, 2007), *Crawford* calls into question the constitutionality of certain provisions of many current state statutes when the child is "unavailable" to testify. This is because *Crawford* overruled the old reliability test

---

[4]Although the U.S. Supreme Court did not explicitly overrule *Ohio v. Roberts* in *Crawford*, its subsequent decisions in *Davis v. Washington* (2006) and *Whorton v. Bockting* (2007) made its holding explicit; still, some courts continue to apply *Roberts* to the admission of nontestimonial statements (e.g., *United States v. Thomas*, 2006).

and replaced it with a new test or rule of criminal procedure (*Whorton*) to be applied when a witness is unavailable at trial. The new test looks not at the firmly rooted or reliable nature of the hearsay (i.e., was the child truthful?) but whether it is testimonial. If it is testimonial, then the Sixth Amendment requires that the defendant be afforded a prior opportunity to cross-examine the witness. Because this right to confront applies to criminal and not civil cases, civil child protection proceedings are not affected by *Crawford* (Phillips, 2005b).

Whether videotaped investigative interviews in criminal cases are considered testimonial has not yet been legally established, although emerging case law suggests that they generally are (Phillips, 2006a; Raeder, 2005a, 2005b). Although some commentators believe that videotaped interviews may fall into disuse because they generally cannot be used in criminal court (Mosteller, 2005), others are more hopeful (e.g., Raeder, 2005b; Phillips, 2006a, 2006b). Given the importance of this area of emerging law, we consider it in more detail.

How do courts decide whether a child witness's investigative interview or hearsay statement is testimonial? The U.S. Supreme Court in *Crawford* "provided minimal guidance as to the definition of 'testimonial'" (Phillips, 2004b, p. 1); the same is true for *Davis v. Washington* (2006), *Hammon v. Indiana* (2006), and *Whorton v. Bockting* (2007), the cases it has heard since then. Although the U.S. Supreme Court left "for another day any effort to spell out a comprehensive definition of 'testimonial'" (*Crawford*, p. 1374), it included other relevant language (referred to as "formulations" in some case law) in its opinion.

The U.S. Supreme Court started by noting that "'Testimony,' . . . is typically '[a] solemn declaration or affirmation made for the purpose of establishing or proving some fact.' . . . an accuser who makes a formal statement to government officers bears testimony in a sense that a person who makes a casual remark does not" (*Crawford*, p. 1364). Next, it provided two factors to consider: (a) whether there is any involvement by a government officer or agent in the creation of testimony or taking of a formalized statement and (b) whether an objective person in the declarant's shoes would reasonably expect the statement, when made, to be used for prosecution purposes, such as at a trial. With regard to the first factor, the Court specifically identified statements given in the following contexts as testimonial: affidavits, depositions, prior in-court testimony at a preliminary hearing or trial, testimony before a grand jury, custodial examinations, and interrogations.[5] The Court

---

[5]Testimony includes (1) "*Ex parte* in-court testimony or its functional equivalent—that is, material such as affidavits, custodial examinations, prior testimony that the defendant was unable to cross-examine, or *similar pretrial statements that declarants would reasonably expect to be used prosecutorially* [emphasis added] . . . [(2)] extrajudicial statements . . . contained in affidavits, depositions, prior testimony, or confessions . . . [and (3)] statements that were made under circumstances which would lead an objective witness to reasonably believe that the statement would be available for use at a later trial" (*Crawford*, p. 1364).

noted that its use of the term "interrogation" was in "its colloquial, rather than any technical, legal sense. . . . Just as various definitions of 'testimonial' exist, one can imagine various definitions of 'interrogation,' and we need not select among them in this case" (p. 1365). *Crawford* involved the police arresting the petitioner for stabbing a man and then interrogating the petitioner and his wife twice in police custody (after being given *Miranda* warnings).

In the context of videotaped investigative interviews in child abuse cases, most courts have only looked at the first factor of whether the interviewer was a government agent. Most of these courts have found that the interviews were testimonial because forensic interviewers act as or with government officials or police officers (Phillips, 2005a). In fact, state statutes often require the coordination of law enforcement and child protection in reporting, investigating, and responding to allegations of child abuse. For example, the court in *State v. Mack* (2004) found that a social worker who took over a forensic interview from a police officer was a government agent and a proxy for the police. The same has held true even when the police officer was part of a joint investigation but not in the same room. In the case of *In re Rolandis G.* (2004), a child's statement to a child advocacy worker while a police officer watched through a two-way mirror was found to be testimonial, as were statements made by three alleged child abuse victims during an interview with a licensed social worker employed by child protection services (*State v. Snowden*, 2005).

It is not surprising that the testimony from child witnesses in cases involving police officers who conducted videotaped investigative interviews as part of multidisciplinary forensic teams are typically found to be testimonial (*Colorado ex rel. R.A.S.*, 2004—videotaped interview by an investigating police officer at a child abuse facility of a 4-year-old alleged sexual abuse victim; *Somervell v. Florida*, 2004—videotaped statement of an 8-year-old boy to police officer and a 10-year-old autistic boy to an officer at a CAC regarding alleged lewd and lascivious acts; Raeder, 2005a, 2005b). Some cases examine the question of whether a videotaped investigative interview is the functional equivalent of a police interrogation and therefore testimonial using *Davis/Hammon's* (2006) "primary purpose test"; a videotaped investigative interview would be considered testimonial if it is used "to establish or prove past events potentially relevant to later criminal prosecution" (pp. 2273–2274; e.g., *State v. Pitt*, 2006, 2007).

Other courts have found that being a member of a child protective team does not automatically bestow status as a governmental official. For instance, at a nongovernmental CAC, a 2-year-old girl's response to a question from the executive director of whether she had an "owie" was nontestimonial evidence because it was not made to a government employee (*People v. Geno*, 2004). *People v. Vigil* (2006) noted how there would need to be a direct and controlling police presence, such as being involved in the medical examination or present in the examination room, to find that a physician member of a child protection team was a government official. Other cases involving statements made to medical professionals have been found to be nontestimonial (e.g., *Commonwealth v. DeOliveira*, 2006; *State v. Vaught*, 2004—statements of a 4-year-old alleged sexual abuse victim to an emergency room physician were not testimonial because "there was no indication of a purpose to develop testimony for trial, nor was there an indication of government involvement in the initiation or course of the examination"; p. 326).

The second factor surrounding the circumstances of the statement involves an examination of whether the child understood that he or she was making a formal statement to a government official (i.e., "an accuser who makes a formal statement to government officers"; *Crawford*, 2004, p. 1364) and that the statements in the interview might be used in a later trial. It has been argued that the child's perspective (or that of a reasonable child witness) rather than that of an objective adult should be applied when making this determination. In the U.S. Supreme Court's words in *Crawford*, did the child "declarant . . . reasonably expect [the statements] to be used prosecutorially" (p. 1364)? Supporting this view, Vieth (2004) stated that young children are unlikely to comprehend that a videotaped investigative interview may be used at trial, and even older children may not understand that the interview may be used for testimonial purposes (given research showing that children do not understand what goes on in court). "Courts in Minnesota, Colorado, North Carolina, Ohio, Texas, and the Military Court of Appeals have also discussed what is reasonable for an objective child to understand about the investigation and court process during the phase of a forensic interview" (Phillips, 2006b, p. 1).

Although an objective child's perspective has been taken in cases involving statements made to parents, friends, counselors, and medical professionals, it is not always taken in cases involving investigative interviews. Some courts take an objective adult's view. For instance, the California Court of Appeals found a 4-year-old's statement "testimonial" (*People v. Seum Sisavath*, 2004) because it was made under circumstances that would lead an objective witness to reasonably believe that it would be used later at trial (i.e., the interview took place after the prosecution was initiated, was attended by the prosecutor and the prosecutor's investigator, and was conducted by a trained forensic interviewer). Still, the *Sisavath* court cautioned that not all statements made in forensic interviews are testimonial under *Crawford*.

Furthermore, an objective adult view will not always result in forensic interviews yielding testimonial interviews. A Minnesota supreme court case (*State v. Bobadilla*, 2006), which held that a videotaped forensic interview of a 3-year-old child with a child protection worker in the presence of a detective was nontestimonial, illustrates this point. The *Bobadilla* court reasoned that a forensic interview should be testimonial only if the child and interviewer "were acting, to a substantial degree, in order to produce a statement for trial" (p. 25), which was not found in this case. Instead, the court pointed to the statutory purposes of the interview and highlighted that the interviews are conducted for the health and welfare of the child, not just for purposes of prosecution (Phillips, 2006b). Indeed, forensic interviewers are taught to place the child's needs during the interview before those of the police or prosecution (e.g., Walters, Holmes, Bauer, & Vieth, 2003). The interviewing techniques highlighted in the *Bobadilla* case followed the following principles:

- A forensic interview is not about gaining evidence for court, but rather is done for the benefit of the child.
- A forensic interview is not about proving sexual abuse, but rather to learn whether something has happened to the child.
- A forensic interview is conducted to help the overall well-being of the child, including determining whether medical and therapeutic treatment is necessary, and determining safety issues for placement of the child. (Phillips, 2006b, p. 2)

In addition to attending to the purpose of the forensic interview, courts may also scrutinize the content of the interview and, specifically, focus on whether it involved or concentrated on testimonial issues. For example, truth-versus-lie tasks may need to be avoided (Phillips, 2005a). The court of appeals in *People v. Vigil* (2004) noted that "the interviewer's emphasis at the outset regarding the need to be truthful would indicate to an objective person in the child's position that the statements were intended for use at a later proceeding that would lead to punishment of the defendant" (p. 263).

Finally, *Crawford* may not apply to the admission of videotaped investigative interviews if a defendant can be shown to have forfeited his or her right to confront witnesses because his or her pretrial conduct (i.e., alleged abuse and threats concurrent with or subsequent to the alleged abuse) made the child witness unavailable for trial (Veith, 2004). The rule of forfeiture by wrongdoing "extinguishes confrontation claims" (*Crawford*, p. 1370; see also *Davis/Hammon*) when "the accused's own wrongful conduct is responsible for the inability of the witness to testify under the conditions ordinarily required . . . [and it] remains applicable even when the conduct that allegedly rendered the witness unavailable to testify is the same criminal conduct for which the accused is now on trial" (R. D. Friedman, 2002, p. 252). Thus, if a judge found this principle to apply, then the testimonial or nontestimonial videotaped investigative interview could be admitted without the child testifying (i.e., unavailable). Although easy in principle, this may be difficult to implement in trial practice because of the problem in proving the defendant's culpability in rendering the child witness unable to testify (R. D. Friedman, 2002).

In conclusion, although the discussion in this section provides some guidance as to whether videotaped investigative interviews can be used in criminal cases, it is expected that the law will continue to emerge with conflicting decisions. The result is that many videotaped investigative interviews will not be allowed at trial, and other modifications (e.g., CCTV and court preparation programs) not affected by *Crawford/Davis/Hammon/Bockting* will be sought to prepare children for in-trial testimony. Another area left unsettled after *Crawford* includes whether the Sixth Amendment right to confrontation applies to preliminary hearings because state statutes and case law differ on this issue (Phillips, 2005c). Also, *Crawford* typically does not affect expert witness opinions (Phillips, 2005c). Because courtroom modification hearings may be considered a preliminary or evidentiary hearing, it is important for MHPs to seek legal consultation about the likelihood of using such videotaped evidence when testifying as an expert.

Child Hearsay Exception

What Is the Child Hearsay Exception?

Hearsay is defined as an "[oral or nonverbal] statement, other than one made by the declarant while testifying at the trial or hearing, offered in evidence to prove the truth of the matter asserted" (Fed. R. Evid. 801(c)). An adult (e.g., parent, police officer, MHP) offers hearsay testimony when he or she testifies in court about what a child said to him or her outside of the courtroom regarding an event (e.g., alleged abuse) to prove the truth of the child's assertion.[6]

An example might clarify the definition of hearsay:

Let's imagine that a child, Mary, has been seeing a therapist, Dr. Smith, because lately, Mary has become very violent. Mary has an uncle named John. One day, while Mary and Dr. Smith were having a therapy session, Mary told Dr. Smith that John, "hurts me where I go pee." Dr. Smith reported this statement to the police, who investigated and arrested John. John denies that he ever touched Mary.

The trial against John for sexually abusing Mary has now begun. The judge questions Mary and decides that she is not competent to testify because she does not understand the difference between the truth and a lie. Since Mary cannot testify, the prosecutor calls Dr. Smith as a witness to testify about what Mary said to Dr. Smith that day in therapy. Dr. Smith wants to tell the court that Mary told her that John hurts Mary where she "goes pee."

---

[6]Sometimes, a child's out-of-court statement is not hearsay if it is offered to prove something other than the truth of the matter asserted, such as proving (a) that the child has precocious sexual knowledge, (b) the effect of the child's statement on the listener, (c) the timing and circumstances of a report or investigation, (d) that the child was linked to the defendant, and (e) that the child could verbalize at the time of the utterance (APRI, 2004).

Remember our definition of hearsay: hearsay is a statement made by someone outside of court that is repeated by a witness testifying in court. The witness is repeating the statement so that it can be used as evidence in the trial. If Dr. Smith repeats Mary's statement in court, it would be considered hearsay because Dr. Smith is repeating to the court something that Mary told her outside of court. The prosecutor wants Dr. Smith to repeat Mary's statement so that Mary's statement can be evidence that John sexually abused Mary. Therefore, if Dr. Smith repeats Mary's statement, it would be hearsay. (Kaufman & Perry, 2000, ¶ 34–36)

Hearsay testimony is typically not admissible in court because of the fear that the truthfulness of the assertion cannot be tested through cross-examination in court. For hearsay testimony to be admitted, it must meet one of the exceptions to the hearsay rule (e.g., Fed. R. Evid. 803). Some exceptions rest on a historical "firmly rooted" basis and thus are presumptively reliable and trustworthy (*Idaho v. Wright*, 1990). For example, the "excited utterance" exception to the hearsay rule refers to a person's statement about a startling event or condition made while the person was under stress or excitement relating to the event or condition (Fed. R. Evid. 803; McGough, 1994; J. E. B. Myers, 1992a, 1992b). Although some of these exceptions have been found to apply to child witnesses (e.g., excited utterance exception[7]; statements for purposes of medical diagnosis or treatment exception[8]; *White v. Illinois*, 1992), hearsay statements about what the child asserted may not fall under one of the traditional hearsay exceptions. Some attorneys argue that when this occurs, it should be admitted under what is known as the *residual exception to the hearsay rule* (e.g., Fed. R. Evid. 807). Special exceptions specifically for alleged child victims of abuse were adopted in the 1980s. These special child

---

[7]The excited utterance exception allows statements to be admitted in child abuse cases when three elements are satisfied: (a) the child experienced a startling event that excited him or her, (b) the child made a statement relating to the startling event, and (c) the child's statement was made while he or she was still experiencing the excitement caused by the startling event (J. E. B. Myers, 1992b). When determining whether the child is still experiencing excitement, the modern trend in abuse cases is to examine more than just the length of time between the event and the statement (McGough, 1994). Courts consider all relevant circumstances under which the child disclosed the abuse, including the following factors (J. E. B. Myers, 1992b): the nature of the event, the type of questioning by adults, whether the statement was made at the first safe opportunity, the child's emotional condition at the time of the statement, the child's pattern of speech, the words spoken by the child, the child's physical condition, and the spontaneity of the child's statements. Excited utterances made to law enforcement, including 911 calls, are also examined under *Crawford* and *Davis/Hammon*.

[8]Hearsay comprising statements made for purposes of medical diagnosis or treatment refers to a person's statements to medical professionals about his or her medical history, past and present symptoms, pain and other sensations, and the perceived cause of his or her injuries or illness (J. E. B. Myers, 1992b). To be admitted under the firmly rooted exception, this information must be given to the professional for the purposes of diagnosis and treatment. Historically, this hearsay exception could only be applied to children who reported physical abuse to medical personnel. In addition, the physician or nurse could not report what the patient said about who caused the injury. The trend in child abuse cases has been to admit the child's report of emotional, psychological, and/or physical harm, including who the child named as the cause of the harm, to medical professionals and/or MHPs under this hearsay exception (McGough, 1994), but admission now also depends on whether the statement is testimonial (*Crawford v. Washington*, 2004; discussed earlier).

hearsay or residual exceptions (or both) apply in federal court and 40 state courts (Weinstein, Berger, & McLaughlin, 1998). Under these exceptions, the critical issues for the court are whether the hearsay testimony is relevant and reliable (i.e., trustworthy) and whether the statement is testimonial (see the legal section that follows for a more detailed discussion of this law). The special child hearsay exception is included in our list of modifications because it was designed specifically for child witnesses in abuse cases to facilitate the admission of their statements into evidence without the child witness being required to testify in court. For instance, one such statement could be Dr. Smith's recounting of Mary's statement that John "hurts me where I go pee."

What Is the Law Regarding the Child Hearsay Exception?

The majority of states have enacted special exceptions for child hearsay in criminal child abuse cases. These special child hearsay statutes vary by state and contain a number of prerequisite conditions.

- Type of proceeding: all states but Kansas require "special child hearsay exceptions" to be in child sexual or physical abuse cases only. Kansas also includes them for juvenile cases and proceedings to determine whether a child is in need of care (Kan. Stat. Ann. § 60-460(dd), 2006).
- Age requirements for the alleged child victim and/or witness: the majority of statutes require the child declarant to be aged 12 or younger (e.g., Ala. Code § 15-25-31, 2007 [Alabama]).
- Status of child as alleged victim and/or witness: the majority of states apply the exception only to statements by alleged victims, not to other witnesses (e.g., Minn. Stat. § 595.02, 2006 [Minnesota]); some allow statements by victims or witnesses (e.g., Colo. Rev. Stat. § 13-25-129, 2006 [Colorado]).
- Hearsay must go to a material element of the crime or identify the defendant (e.g., Kan. Stat. Ann. § 60-460, 2006 [Kansas]).
- The court determines that the child's statement as reported by the hearsay witness is reliable and trustworthy. This is typically based on factors surrounding the time, content, and circumstances of the child's statement (e.g., Haw. R. Evid. 804(b)(6), 2007 [Hawaii]).
- Sufficient advance notice must be given to the other party in the case about the intention to offer the statement and particulars about it (e.g., Del. Code Ann. tit. 11, § 3513, 2007 [Delaware]).
- The child either must (or can) testify during the trial or is found to be unavailable: the majority of states require the child to testify or be unavailable to testify at the proceeding (e.g., Mo. Rev. Stat. § 491.075, 2007 [Missouri]). A minority of states

require the child to be available (e.g., Alaska Stat. § 12.40.110, 2007 [Alaska]).

- Most states require corroboration if there is an assertion of unavailability (e.g., the defendant had the opportunity to commit the alleged offense; e.g., Colo. Rev. Stat. § 13-25-129 (2006) [Colorado]).

- Under the law of hearsay, unavailability generally includes situations in which the maker of the statement (the child): (a) is exempted by ruling of the court on the ground of privilege from testifying concerning the subject matter of the declarant's (child's) statement or (b) persists in refusing to testify concerning the subject matter of the declarant's statement despite an order of the court to do so; or (c) testifies to a lack of memory of the subject matter of the declarant's statement; or (d) is unable to be present or to testify at the hearing because of death or then existing physical or mental illness or infirmity; or (e) is absent from the hearing and the proponent of a statement has been unable to procure the declarant's attendance (or in the case of a hearsay exception under subdivision (b)(2), (3), or (4), the declarant's attendance or testimony) by process or other reasonable means (e.g., Fed. R. Evid. 804).

- In child hearsay exceptions, unavailability is sometimes also defined as cases in which the child would suffer significant emotional or psychological harm or trauma and/or could not reasonably communicate (e.g., Mass. Gen. Laws Ann. ch. 233, § 81, 2007 [Massachusetts]). Not all statutes specify that this showing should be due to the fear of testifying in the personal presence of the defendant at the time of the criminal proceeding, as in *Craig* (e.g., Cal. Evid. Code §§ 240 & 1228, 2007 [California]). A few statutes require expert testimony to show this type of unavailability (e.g., Va. Code Ann. § 63.2-1523, 2007 [Virginia]); others permit it (e.g., Ind. Code. Ann § 35-37-4-6, 2007 [Indiana]). The type of expert testimony may be specified:

  (i) From the testimony of a psychiatrist, physician, or psychologist, and other evidence, if any, the court finds that the protected person's testifying in the physical presence of the defendant will cause the protected person to suffer serious emotional distress such that the protected person cannot reasonably communicate. (ii) The protected person cannot participate in the trial for medical reasons. (iii) The court has determined that the protected person is incapable of understanding the nature and obligation of an oath. (Ind. Code Ann. § 35-37-4-6 (e)(2)(B), 2007 [Indiana])

- If found to be unavailable, the child may also be required to be available for cross-examination during the proceeding or when the statement or videotape was made (e.g., Ind. Code Ann. § 35-37-4-6 (f), 2007 [Indiana]).

As explained in the previous section on videotaped investigative interviews, a special child hearsay exception or a residual exception can be used without raising constitutional issues if the child testifies and is cross-examined (*California v. Green*, 1970). It is often the case, however, that these hearsay statements are sought to be introduced because the alleged child abuse victim is unable to testify because he or she fears the defendant. When this happens, Confrontation Clause issues are implicated if the child does not testify or has not previously testified.

As noted earlier, under the old law of *Idaho v. Wright* (1990) and *Ohio v. Roberts* (1980), hearsay could be admissible if the declarant was unavailable and there was a demonstration that the testimony possessed the required indicia of reliability (APRI, 2004; J. E. B. Myers, Redlich, Goodman, Prizmich, & Imwinkelried, 1999). To determine the indicia of reliability, the out-of-court statement must either fall under a firmly rooted exception or have particularized guarantees of trustworthiness drawn from the totality of circumstances surrounding the statement. Child hearsay statutes fall into the latter category. The U.S. Supreme Court in *Wright* declined to decide whether unavailability was required as a prerequisite to admissibility under a residual hearsay exception. *White v. Illinois* (1992), a case involving statements of a child victim to an investigating police officer, appeared to answer this question. *White* found that the unavailability requirement is a necessary part of the Confrontation Clause inquiry only when out-of-court statements were made in the course of a prior judicial proceeding. Thus it does not appear necessary to show unavailability to admit hearsay under a residual exception to the hearsay rule (e.g., Chase, 2003; S. J. Clark, 2003). Because most of the non–firmly rooted child hearsay statutes incorporated these reliability factors and because unavailability did not seem required, attacks on their constitutionality typically failed (Task Force, 2002).

Currently, however, *Crawford* holds that testimonial hearsay can only be admitted when a person is unavailable and if there was a prior opportunity for cross-examination; it does not matter whether a hearsay exception applies or whether the statement bears adequate indicia of reliability. Because *Crawford* overruled *Roberts* and cast doubt on *White*, special child hearsay statutes that relied on the old tests appear open to new constitutional attacks.

It is unclear whether nontestimonial hearsay needs to be examined under the Confrontation Clause. The U.S. Supreme Court left the issue open in *Crawford*: "It is wholly consistent with the Framers' design to afford the states flexibility in their development of hearsay law—as does *Roberts*, and as would an approach that exempted such statements from *Confronta-*

tion Clause scrutiny altogether" (p. 1374). At the time of this writing, some courts have held or assumed that *Roberts* governs the admission of nontestimonial evidence (e.g., *Commonweath v. Allshouse*, 2007). This means that admissibility for nontestimonial statements by child witnesses would follow state law requirements, which could still follow the requirements spelled out in the special child hearsay statutes (i.e., child witnesses' statements could be admitted under a special child hearsay statute if the child is unavailable, has never testified, and his or her statements meet the state's reliability test). It therefore appears appropriate that courts are applying the old reliability test of *Roberts* and *Wright* to nontestimonial statements made by an alleged child abuse victim (e.g., *People v. Geno*, 2004: admitting child's nontestimonial statement to child advocacy director under the residual exception to the hearsay rule because the trial court's findings supported the statement's "particularized guarantees of trustworthiness" as demonstrated by the "totality of the circumstances" under *Idaho v. Wright* and state case law standards; *People v. Vigil*, 2004, 2006: admitting child's nontestimonial statements to father and father's friend under the "firmly rooted" excited utterance exception to the hearsay rule even if the child does not testify).

Courtroom Design Changes

What Are Courtroom Design Changes?

Ordinary courtroom procedure involves the defendant sitting with his or her attorney at the defense table with a direct, unimpeded line of sight to the judge, jury, and witness stand. The witness sits in the witness box next to the judge and is questioned by attorneys who can walk around the courtroom, sometimes standing near the witness. Starting in the 1980s, some states specifically enacted laws to permit the courtroom layout to be modified to protect the child witness from coercion, intimidation, or undue influence, as well as to provide a more comfortable and safe environment for the child.

The three main ways to accomplish the task of shielding the child from a defendant in the courtroom involve placing a physical barrier or screen between the child and the defendant, rearranging the courtroom fixtures or personnel to shield the child from the defendant, or instructing the child to avoid eye contact with the defendant. It could be argued that instructing the child to avert his or her eyes from the defendant is not a modification because it does not change any aspect of the courtroom or its proceedings. Indeed, lawyers may advise child witnesses to do this without ever informing the court.

To help children feel more comfortable, a secure waiting area can be provided for them during court proceedings. When in court, they can be permitted to testify on child-sized furniture and may be allowed to bring a comforting item to court (e.g., stuffed animal, favorite toy, blanket). Some statutes specifically permit a judge not to wear a robe if, for example, the robe would intimidate the child witness (Cal. Penal Code § 868.8(b), 2007).

Statutes can also dictate whether attorneys may stand or sit when questioning the child and specify how far defendants must be seated from the child. Another recommendation that has been proposed is to have the attorneys "object silently by raising their hands instead of their voices" (APRI, 2004, p. 327). This practice is similar to what children see in school and will not be as distracting, disconcerting, or scary as an unpredictable, loud objection.

What Is the Law Regarding Courtroom Design Changes?

As explained in chapter 2 (this volume), the trial judge has inherent authority to make minor alterations to the courtroom environment and to the location of people within the courtroom to accommodate child witnesses (e.g., Fed. R. Evid. 611(a)). Of the various changes just discussed, four methods that shield the child from a defendant and therefore raise confrontation issues have been approved in statutes and case law.

First, screens or one-way mirrors are allowed in some states (Bulkley, Feller, Stern, & Roe, 1996; e.g., Alaska Stat. § 12.45.046, 2007 [Alaska]). The most influential case regarding this method involved the placement of a large screen between the defendant and two 13-year-old, female alleged sexual assault victims (*Coy v. Iowa*, 1988). The one-way screen allowed the defendant to see the girls' image on the screen but not vice versa while at the same time the judge and jury could see both the witnesses and the accused. The girls were cross-examined by the defendant's attorney. However, the U.S. Supreme Court in *Coy* reversed the defendant's conviction because the trial judge allowed the use of the screen without first determining whether each girl needed the specialized protection and because face-to-face confrontation was not provided. This finding was modified in *Craig* such that face-to-face confrontation is not required but merely preferred in such cases. In addition, the Court articulated the test for specialized protection by stating its three-part standard (as described previously), which means that screens can be permitted in certain cases.

For example, Alaska allows a child's testimony to be taken with the use of one-way mirrors "if the court determines that the testimony by the child victim or witness under normal court procedures would result in the child's inability to effectively communicate" (Alaska Stat. § 12.45.046 (a)(2), 2007). The judge must make this finding on the basis of clear and convincing evidence that the *Craig* criteria have been met (*Reutter v. State*, 1994). In addition, the statute requires that "the attorneys may pose questions to the child and have visual contact with the child during questioning, but the mirrors shall be placed to provide a physical shield so that the child does not have visual contact with the defendant and jurors" (Alaska Stat. § 12.45.046 (e), 2007).

The second shielding technique is to rearrange the physical courtroom to accommodate the child's fear of confrontation. The law does not set out any particular courtroom layout (J. E. B. Myers, 1992c, 1996a), and legal history supports such flexibility (Dziech & Schudson, 1991). Courts have approved a variety of courtroom alterations to shield child witnesses when these modifications do not infringe on the defendants' rights (J. E. B. Myers, 1996a, 1996b). In some cases, the witness's chair can be turned slightly away from the defendant as long as the defendant can still observe the child while testifying (*United States v. Thompson*, 1990; *United States v. Williams*, 1993) and hear the witness well enough to understand the answers and evaluate demeanor (*State v. Mannion*, 1899). The defendant should minimally have a full profile of the alleged victim's head, the trier of fact must see the child witness's face, and the witness should be able to look directly at the defendant by turning his or her head less than 90 degrees (APRI, 2004). Accordingly, a Georgia court of appeals approved the young witness's chair being placed at a 90-degree angle to the defendant (*Ortiz v. State*, 1988), and a Massachusetts court of appeals allowed a witness to sit at a 45-degree angle to the defendant, as long as the defendant could see the witness's profile and lips (*Commonwealth v. Conefrey*, 1991). However, another case by the Georgia Court of Appeals permitted alleged child victims to sit at a small table facing the jury with their backs to the defendants and attorneys and their foster father standing behind them while they testified, allegedly shielding them from the three defendants (*Boatright v. State*, 1989). The greater the infringement of the defendant's Sixth Amendment right, the greater the need to show the necessity of the modification (APRI, p. 467).

Prosecutors also have positioned themselves in the courtroom such that a child witness did not have to look at the defendant while testifying about alleged sexual abuse (e.g., *People v. Sharp*, 1994). The California Court of Appeals in that case found that the shielding action did not violate the defendant's confrontation right because the defendant did not have the right to "stare down or subtly intimidate a young child . . . [or have] a particular seating arrangement in the courtroom" (p. 123).

In a third shielding technique, prosecutors, MHPs, or other professionals may directly instruct the child to avoid eye contact with the defendant while testifying in court. The child could be encouraged instead to look at a supportive family member, friend, or professional (e.g., court-appointed special advocate, guardian *ad litem*). Eye contact between the child witness and the defendant is not required by the Constitution (*Coy v. Iowa*, 1988, "the Confrontation Clause does not, of course, compel the witness to fix his eyes upon the defendant; he may studiously look elsewhere, but the trier of fact will draw its own conclusions" [p. 1019]; J. E. B. Myers, 1992c).

Fourth, the "whisper procedure" has also been upheld (*United States v. Romey*, 32 M.J. 180 [C.M.A. 1991]; *Romey v. Vanyur*, 9 F. Supp. 2d 565 [D.N.C. 1998], declining to review the merits of the military court's finding). This case involved a mother who sat next to the alleged child victim and whispered to her the questions asked by attorneys; the child then whispered the answers to her mother, who repeated them out loud. In effect, the mother acted as an interpreter and was sworn in as such (*United States v. Romey*,

1991). It could be argued that this procedure shields the child from having to talk directly with the defense and may involve the child's avoiding eye contact with the defendant. It was upheld because the military court found the procedure to meet impliedly the necessity test of *Craig*.

DISCUSSION

Because these five modifications may have an effect on a defendant's Sixth Amendment rights, the law appropriately demands a more rigorous showing before they can be used compared with modifications that do not affect this right. Given the need to document the necessity for the use of a modification, and given that lawyers are not trained to evaluate the child's emotional needs, MHPs can be called to assist the court in this determination. Other expert witnesses can also be asked to testify regarding the need for a modification (e.g., other experienced attorneys who can describe various problems they have encountered when placing children in the courtroom to testify in the presence of the defendant) or the practical procedures for their implementation (e.g., an expert in the field of videotape equipment and closed-circuit technology can describe how the proposed procedures would operate or demonstrate them; Annotation, 2007).

What specifically is the court going to look for when MHPs testify? Trial judges will examine the MHP's assessment and testimony for relevant information pertinent to the legal standard regarding necessity in their jurisdiction. The following discussion therefore focuses on the four basic types of legal standards currently used across the five courtroom modifications that implicate the Confrontation Clause: (a) *Craig*'s minimum standard, (b) higher than *Craig* standards, (c) lower than *Craig* standards, and (d) no legal standard specified.

Craig's Minimum Standard

The U.S. Supreme Court's ruling in *Maryland v. Craig* (1990b) set forth the minimum standards with which state law must comply. As noted in chapter 1 (this volume), *Craig* standards only apply to modifications that could affect both the defendant's right to confront the witnesses against him or her and the defendant's right to due process. These modifications are limited to CCTV, videotaped depositions or preliminary hearing testimony, videotaped pretrial interviews introduced in trial, statements admitted under a special child hearsay exception, and other procedures that shield or remove the child from face-to-face contact with the defendant. These modifications may be permitted if a court finds that the procedure ensures the reliability of evidence and is necessary to protect the welfare of a particular child on the basis of an individualized assessment, shown by a finding that

- the child witness would be traumatized by the presence of the defendant and not the courtroom generally; and
- trauma or emotional distress that would be suffered by the child witness in the presence of the defendant would be more than *de minimis* (i.e., more than mere nervousness or excitement or some reluctance to testify) and "at least where such trauma would impair the child's ability to communicate" (*Maryland v. Craig*, 1990b, p. 857).[9]

In *Craig*, the Court upheld Maryland's statute, which provided, in part, that "'testimony by the child victim in the courtroom will result in the child suffering serious emotional distress such that the child cannot reasonably communicate.' Md. Cts. & Jud. Proc. Code Ann. § 9-102(a)(1)(ii) (1989)" (*Maryland v. Craig*, 1990b, p. 841). The statute set out higher standards than the U.S. Supreme Court's minimum standard. First, "serious emotional distress" reflects a greater degree of distress than a "more than de minimis" amount. Second, the statute's communication requirement (i.e., "cannot reasonably communicate") appears higher than the U.S. Supreme Court's description (i.e., impair the child's ability to communicate"). For these reasons, the lower bounds of constitutional acceptability were not tested, and the Court left open the question of "the minimum required showing of emotional trauma" (*Maryland v. Craig*, p. 856) required by the Confrontation Clause. For example, it did not specify whether *fear*, a word used in some statutes (e.g., 18 U.S.C.S. § 3509(b)(1), 2007 [United States]), was equal to or less than *emotional distress* or *trauma*, nor did it define these terms. Indeed, it appeared to use them (i.e., emotional distress and trauma) interchangeably. *Craig* also left open the question of whether impairment in communication ability is required. Although the communication issue is one in which states continue to appear almost equally divided, the U.S. Supreme Court decided not to hear a case on this question (*Vogelsberg v. Wisconsin*, 2007). This information will obviously be critical to MHPs who need to know exactly what they are looking for in their forensic assessments of children.

No new case has been heard by the U.S. Supreme Court to clarify the *Craig* test. However, at least two cases have been appealed to the Court that explore the lower reaches of the *Craig* minimum finding of distress (e.g., *Danner v. Kentucky*, 1998; *Marx v. Texas*, 1999). Because certiorari was denied in these two cases (i.e., the U.S. Supreme Court decided not to accept the case for review; it is not a ruling on the merits of the case), they are good law.[10]

---

[9]There is disagreement in the literature and among courts as to the components of the *Craig* test. First, some find that there are three parts to the test (i.e., necessary to protect the particular child witness, trauma from confronting the defendant, and emotional distress must be more than *de minimis*), whereas others set it out as we have done. It also is unclear whether the criterion regarding the level of emotional distress includes its effect on the child's communication ability, because the quoted phrase was included only in the U.S. Supreme Court's dicta (i.e., discussion) relating to the test. We include it under a conservative approach to case interpretation.

[10]Justice Scalia, joined by Justice Thomas, filed a dissenting opinion in both cases. His dissent is worth

In *Danner v. Kentucky* (1998), an alleged victim of rape and sodomy was permitted to use CCTV when testifying against her father. The case was appealed on two grounds: the age provision of the modification statute and the trial court's finding of compelling need for the modification. The alleged victim was between the ages of 5 and 10 years old when the abuse allegedly occurred and 15 years old at the time of trial. The court of appeals found the statute to be ambiguous about whether it pertained to the age of the child when the alleged act was committed or the age when the testimony was given. Relying on the "broad protective purpose of the statute" (p. 634) and the tradition of special treatment for child witnesses in the Kentucky courts, the appellate court allowed the 15-year-old to avail herself of the modification.

The court of appeals also upheld the trial court's finding of compelling need, which found that "due to the nature of the testimony and the age of the witness that face-to-face arrangement would inhibit the witness to a degree that the jury's search for truth would be clouded" (*Danner*, p. 635). In making this determination, the trial court asked the minor a number of questions. Although she responded that she was not afraid of the defendant, she said that she could not be near him and did not know whether she could testify even if she took breaks. The trial court felt that this indicated factors that "go much further than anxiety or nervousness, as referred to the various cases that have been cited, that compelling need exists" (p. 1010). The court of appeals agreed that the case was similar to those in which "the child would not testify as to the offense and was reluctant to testify in the presence of the accused" because open court testimony would "denigrate the reliability of her testimony" (p. 635).[11]

---

noting because (a) Justice Scalia has been successful in arguably restricting the use of child witness hearsay in *Crawford v. Washington* (2004), (b) he "remains unrelenting in his quest to return the Confrontation Clause to what he believes to be its 'original intent'" (R. L. Friedman, 2002, p. 500), and (c) his philosophy and approach is approved by some legal commentators (e.g., R. D. Friedman, 2002; but see Blumenthal, 2001). Justice Scalia's philosophy is to follow the historical intent of the framers of the Constitution, which means to him adopting a literal interpretation of constitutional language. Regarding the Confrontation Clause, Justice Scalia adopts a categorical approach in which all "witnesses" (i.e., those who make testimonial statements regardless of age or condition) against the accused must give their testimony under prescribed conditions (i.e., under oath subject to cross-examination in the face-to-face presence of the defendant, and/or in open court at trial; R. D. Friedman, 2002; R. L. Friedman, 2002). He further believes that, ideally, no exceptions should be permitted, but currently certain ones are allowed (e.g., forfeiture rule). If Justice Scalia's comments are in any way predictive of how the Court might decide a future case, the bar would be set higher than those enacted by most states. In addition, other restrictions may also be put in place that would curtail the use of certain courtroom modifications to only the most serious of cases involving the youngest alleged child victims of abuse. This would be a departure from the trend in state legislatures that allow other people to benefit from modifications (e.g., older children, people with developmental disabilities).

[11]In his dissent, however, Justice Scalia countered that *Danner* "comes nowhere close to fitting within *Craig's* limited exception" (p. 440). He appeared to be recommending a much higher standard of emotional distress than "more than de minimis," when he remarked, "Far from being rendered mute with fear at the prospect of facing her father, Danner's daughter did not even rule out the possibility of testifying if she could take breaks from the witness stand" (p. 440). It should be noted that his com-

In *Marx v. Texas* (1999), a defendant was charged separately with sexually abusing his 13-year-old developmentally delayed granddaughter, his two daughters, his 6-year-old niece, and another girl. He confessed to the alleged acts. The trial court allowed the 6-year-old and 13-year-old to testify by CCTV. The case brought up two issues on appeal: (a) the category of witness covered under the modification statute and (b) the basis for the finding of necessity for CCTV.

Because the 6-year-old girl had allegedly witnessed the abuse of the 13-year-old at an area lake, she was asked to testify as to what she had witnessed. Because the niece, who had not yet been asked to testify in a separate proceeding about her own alleged abuse, was not the victim in this case, the statute did not permit CCTV (i.e., because it only applied to victim–witnesses). However, the Court of Appeals of Texas and the Court of Criminal Appeals upheld the ability of the child to testify using CCTV, noting the inherent power of the court to control procedural aspects of a case, which includes permitting CCTV.

The trial court made its finding of necessity for the special procedure on the basis of testimony from the girl's mother and her psychotherapist, Dr. Calvert. The mother said that she thought the girl would be traumatized by testifying in the defendant's presence but later clarified that she could probably testify in the case in which she was only a witness. She also said that the girl had been wetting her bed and having nightmares since the incident. Dr. Calvert told the court that the girl was a "wreck" and did not want to see the defendant. She could not say whether the child would suffer additional emotional distress as a result of confronting her uncle but did state that it would be better if she testified outside of his presence. In addition, Dr. Calvert testified that the niece "tells me she wants to [testify]. So unless she gets more frightened than I expect, that little girl would probably testify okay" (p. 1036). The Court of Appeals of Texas upheld the finding of necessity for CCTV but noted that the "conflicting testimony" and other evidence were "less compelling" (p. 328). It concluded that the trial judge "adequately balanced" the defendant's rights with the state's interest in protecting the children. The Court of Criminal Appeals agreed that that the evidence was "weakly supported . . . but [not] actually outside the zone of reasonable disagreement" (p. 581).[12]

---

ments differ from what was decided in *Craig*; the U.S. Supreme Court rejected the need to explore less restrictive alternatives as a prerequisite to ordering CCTV (*Craig*, p. 860).

Justice Scalia also appeared to take issue with the lower courts' decisions about the age requirements of the statute. In fact, he seemed to be recommending an age restriction on the use of CCTV: "Moreover, *Craig* hardly contemplates that the child-witness exception is available to 15-year-olds" (*Danner*, p. 440). Restricting these modifications to children "around the age" of the alleged victims in *Craig* (6 years old) was not contemplated in *Craig* and is a departure from the majority of states that allow Confrontation Clause modifications for teenagers, school-age children, and young children. No justification based on child development theory or other social science was given by Justice Scalia for this age restriction or in other articles written on this issue (e.g., S. J. Clark, 2003, arguing for an "age of confrontation" to determine when a child witness is required to confront the defendant).

[12]Two judges on the Court of Criminal Appeals filed dissents in the case because they felt that requisite

Thus, although *Craig* is "still the final word from the U.S. Supreme Court on alternative forms of testimony" (Harmon, 2005, p. 168), dicta in these cases and other decisions such as *Crawford* may signal a shift to more rigorous requirements. As Raeder (2005b) noted, "So far, there has been no direct judicial attack on *Craig* even though *Crawford* clearly has a vision of the Confrontation Clause that rejects the type of balancing approach that *Craig* applied" (p. 387).

Higher Than *Craig* Standards

As noted earlier, states are free to legislate tougher standards for their courts to use when deciding whether to allow modifications for child witnesses. Pre-*Craig*, the majority of states, such as Maryland, already had high standards. Other states raised their threshold for admitting modification evidence after the *Craig* decision. Most states require more than a minimal amount of emotional distress, harm, or strain to be demonstrated (e.g., "substantial," "at least moderate emotional or mental harm," "severe emotional or mental distress," "unreasonable and unnecessary mental or emotional harm"). Some states append other requirements to the *Craig* minimum. For example, a few states require that the use of the modification "provide a setting more amenable to securing the child witness's uninhibited, truthful testimony" (Minn. Stat. § 595.02, 2006 [Minnesota]). Other states require that the courts impose a modification only if the evidence of the need for the modification meets a particular standard of proof (e.g., clear and convincing, substantial likelihood, preponderance of the evidence, more likely than not) that is independent of the standard used in the civil or criminal case the child is testifying in (Kan. Stat. Ann. § 22-3434, 2006 [Kansas]). When MHP testimony provides evidence that would satisfy a standard higher than that set in *Craig*, it is less open to legal challenge.

It needs to be highlighted that admissibility of hearsay testimony is guided by a set of standards different from those regarding remote testimony and courtroom design changes, even though hearsay is affected by the Confrontation Clause. As noted earlier, hearsay testimony (e.g., admission of a videotaped investigative interview in trial, admission of a child's out-of-court drawings that identify the alleged perpetrator) is not technically considered a courtroom modification. It is a standard part of evidence law and everyday courtroom practice. It is included in this book as a modification because special hearsay exceptions were created specifically for child witnesses who occasionally may be able to have their statements heard in court without having to testify during trial if they are found to be unavailable.

---

degree of harm had not been shown or linked to the anticipation of testifying before the defendant. Justice Scalia agreed, stating: "If the lower court's opinion in this case is in the ballpark, the 'minimum showing' required is no showing at all, and in all abused-child-witness cases this Court's exception has swallowed the constitutional rule" (*Marx*, p. 1035).

Finally, the law regarding unavailability of child witnesses overlaps with *Craig* in some states. As previously explained in the section on child hearsay, a few states have added a factor that can be used to demonstrate unavailability, which reflects a higher standard than that presented by *Craig*. For example, Indiana's hearsay exception for the child victim's or witness's out-of-court statement of abuse allows the child to be found unavailable to testify on a number of grounds, including if

> (i) [f]rom the testimony of a psychiatrist, physician, or psychologist, and other evidence, if any, the court finds that *the protected person's testifying in the physical presence of the defendant will cause the protected person to suffer serious emotional distress such that the protected person cannot reasonably communicate.* (ii) The protected person cannot participate in the trial for medical reasons. (iii) The court has determined that the protected person is incapable of understanding the nature and obligation of an oath [emphasis added]. (Ind. Code Ann. § 35-37-4-6 (e)(2)(B), 2007)

In other words, as previously noted, the states that require a showing that confrontation would impair a child witness's ability to communicate are using a higher standard than required by *Craig*.

Lower Than *Craig* Standards

When states create laws, they have flexibility in their choice of language as long as it comports with state and any federal constitutional law. However, at times state law uses language that does not appear on its face to fit federal standards. Until such laws are legally challenged for being inconsistent with U.S. Supreme Court jurisprudence, their status remains uncertain. This section reviews these issues as applied to the courtroom modifications reviewed in this chapter.

Some remote testimony and hearsay laws involving psychological unavailability are written to allow courts flexibility in decision making by using standards such as "good cause shown" (e.g., Ala. Code § 15-25-2, 2007 [Alabama]), "compelling need" (e.g., Ky. Rev. Stat. § 421.350, 2006 [Kentucky]), or "substantial likelihood" (e.g., N.J. Stat. § 2A:84A-32.4, 2007 [New Jersey]). The standard in *Craig* was necessity, which appears higher than the cited three standards. Also, as noted earlier, the words cited in the *Craig* test, such as "emotional distress" and "trauma," are not always included in state statutes; instead, "strain" (e.g., N.H. Rev. Stat. Ann. § 517:13-a, 2007 [New Hampshire]) or "harm" are used (e.g., Fla. Stat. ch. 92.54, 2007 [Florida]). In the latter case, one legal commentator recommended that to "comport with *Craig*, the fear must cause emotional distress and the fear must be of the accused" (E. J. O'Brien, 2000, p. 67). In fact, the 8th Circuit Court of Appeals held unconstitutional the sections of the 1990 Child Victims' and Child Witnesses' Rights federal statute that permit CCTV if the court finds (a) the child is unable to testify because of fear; (b) there is a substantial likelihood, established by expert testimony, that the child would suffer emotional trauma from testifying in open court; or (c) the child suffers from a mental or other infirmity (*United States v. Bordeaux*, 2005).

Another problem with these laws is that they may create a problem for MHPs who serve as experts because they differ from, and appear to require less than, the *Craig* language, of "necessity," "more than de minimis emotional distress," and "trauma." For instance, one state provides for CCTV or videotaped testimony if a child "would be so intimidated, or otherwise inhibited, by the physical presence of the defendant that a compelling need exists to take the testimony of the child outside the physical presence of the defendant in order to insure the reliability of such testimony" (Conn. Gen. Stat. § 54-86g, 2007 [Connecticut]). Although the emphasis on the impact of the defendant is vital (*United States v. Bordeaux*, 2005), it is uncertain whether intimidation would qualify as emotional distress, whether inhibition means more than mere reluctance to testify or difficulty in reasonably communicating, and whether an MHP or a law enforcement investigator would be the appropriate expert on intimidation and/or inhibition.

Moreover, because Maryland's statute (reviewed in *Craig*) required a showing of both emotional distress and a communication difficulty, the legal status of statutes under the U.S. Constitution that do not include both of these components is unclear. For example, one state allows CCTV testimony taken during the trial or proceeding if

> testimony by the child victim or the moderately, severely, or profoundly mentally retarded victim in the courtroom will result in the child or moderately, severely, or profoundly mentally retarded person suffering serious emotional distress such that the child or moderately, severely, or profoundly mentally retarded person cannot reasonably communicate or that the child or moderately, severely, or profoundly mentally retarded person will suffer severe emotional distress that is likely to cause the child or moderately, severely, or profoundly mentally retarded person to suffer severe adverse effects. (725 Ill. Comp. Stat. 5/106B-5, 2007 [Illinois])

Similarly, Delaware's hearsay exception for the child victim's or witness's out-of-court statement of abuse statute (Del. Code. Ann. tit. 11 § 3513, 2007) allows the child to be found unavailable to testify on a number of grounds, including "[s]ubstantial likelihood that the child would suffer severe emotional trauma from testifying at the proceeding or by means of a videotaped deposition or closed-circuit television." Because these laws can be triggered without the showing of a communication difficulty, it is unknown whether they would be upheld under appeal to the U.S. Supreme Court. State supreme courts are split on the issue. Some require a showing that trauma would impair the child's ability to communicate (e.g., *State v.*

Deuter, 839 S.W.2d 391 (Tenn. 1992) [Tennessee]) or testify reliably (e.g., *State v. Bronson*, 779 A.2d 95 (Conn. 2001) [Connecticut]). Other courts find that requiring such impairment would run counter to *Craig's* three-part test (e.g., *State v. Vogelsberg* (2006) [Wisconsin]) and that a finding of significant emotional trauma is sufficient (e.g., *Marx v. State* (Tex. Crim. App. 1999) [Texas]).

Finally, courtroom design changes can be viewed on a "continuum of confrontation" (J. E. B. Myers, 1997, p. 46). An individualized showing of necessity is still required for any alteration to the courtroom that implicates the Confrontation Clause; however, a lesser showing of necessity may be permissible "when the infringement is minor," such as turning the child's chair away from the defendant by less than 90 degrees (J. E. B. Myers, 1997, p. 46). For example, *Commonwealth v. Spear* (1997) noted, "Even where special seating arrangements are warranted in a particular case, . . . they are permissible, 'only on a showing by the Commonwealth, by more than a preponderance of the evidence, of a compelling need for the [implementation] of such procedure'" (p. 1043). Similarly, in the case involving the "whisper procedure," the Court of Military Appeal found that the trial judge impliedly made a necessity finding in the case to support its use (*United States v. Romey*, 1991). J. E. B. Myers (1997) argued that the mother's actions as an interpreter or conduit of information for the child did not interfere with direct or cross-examination and therefore did not implicate the Sixth Amendment.

No Legal Standard

Finally, state statutes may provide no or minimal guidance about modifications when no applicable state statute exists or when statutes do not specifically detail standards for application or admissibility of evidence. Even without a state law specifically permitting or requiring a modification, local practices may allow for the use of certain modifications, as long as the modification comports with reasonable standards of trial practice. In these cases, one would need to consider whether other sources of law, such as the rules of court promulgated by the state's supreme court and court cases that interpret state and federal law, address or more fully explain required procedures for child witness modifications. This step is important because in a few cases, courts have held that in the absence of explicit statutory authority, the trial court lacked the inherent power to authorize CCTV (e.g., *Hochheiser v. Superior Court*, 1984; *State v. Nutter*, 1992).

CONCLUSION

The information discussed in this chapter illustrates the variety and complexity of laws regarding the use of modifications for child witnesses that implicate the Confrontation Clause. Given the more recent changes in the law of modifications, and specifically *Crawford v. Washington* and its progeny, alternative procedures for presenting children's testimony (e.g., CCTV, videotaped testimony, shielding) may become more common (Lyon, 2004; S. McMahon, 2006). Moreover, legal techniques less frequently used in child witness cases, such as the forfeiture rule (R. D. Friedman, 2002; S. McMahon, 2006; Vieth, 2004), may have occasion to be raised more frequently if certain modifications, such as the child hearsay exception, are not available. This rule allows testimony, which might otherwise violate the Confrontation Clause, to be used if the witness was made unavailable by the defendant's wrongdoing.

Given the challenges of meeting the legal requirements in child sexual abuse cases, MHPs may be asked more often to serve as expert witnesses. MHPs must be familiar with the differing legal standards that govern the use of various modifications to be competent to practice in this area. More specifically, MHP evaluators should not only be aware of the range of practices that may be permitted in their jurisdiction but also be able to tailor their assessments appropriately to address the specific legal standards regarding the proposed modifications for a particular child.

MHPs may also serve as consultants to MDTs or CACs or be involved in conducting forensic interviews. The information presented in this chapter can be used to assist those responding to reports of child abuse, so that their practices take the laws of courtroom modifications for child witnesses into consideration.

Because one volume cannot cover all of the nuances of local practice, the rest of the book proposes an analytical approach for conducting modification evaluations and providing expert testimony based on the legal standards of a "typical" jurisdiction (and on the model Child Witness Act, which is discussed in chap. 11). In doing so, we consider the "higher" standards for modifications that implicate the Confrontation Clause, including assessing for communication impairments, although the recommendations presented in the rest of this book should serve as a way to approach the conduct of all courtroom modification evaluations. Chapter 4 further assists the MHP in preparing for this assessment by reviewing the relevant social science regarding courtroom modifications that involve confrontational issues.

4

SCIENCE OF COURTROOM
MODIFICATIONS

Once aware of the legal issues regarding courtroom modifications, mental health professionals (MHPs) who are interested in conducting evaluations of child witnesses for the purpose of providing evidence to the court about the need for such modifications must examine the science supporting the use of these modifications. In other words, do social and behavioral science data demonstrate that modifications are needed with certain child witnesses? If so, can a given modification do what it purports to do?

The process of evaluating the empirical support for a courtroom modification should begin with an examination of the clinical, scientific, and professional literatures to determine the need for the modification and the availability of social–behavioral science and/or legal research on the modification and its effects in the courtroom. If available, these resources should be scrutinized to determine whether they will help address the issues presented by a proposed courtroom modification.

The law minimally requires that a modification be protective and that its need does not unduly affect or outweigh the defendant's right to confront the witnesses against him or her and the defendant's right to due process. As noted in chapter 3, the five courtroom modifications that affect the defendant's right to confront the witnesses against him or her include allowing children to testify by remote testimony (closed-circuit television [CCTV]), substituting live appearances in court with videotaped depositions or testimony, presenting videotaped statements or interviews of the child as evidence in addition to or instead of the child's in-court testimony, having hearsay witnesses testify in addition to or instead of a child's live testimony, and using courtroom design changes to shield, screen, or block the child from seeing the defendant.

Accordingly, this chapter begins with a brief discussion of research highlighting the need to protect some children from testimonial stress. It then considers whether science exists to prove that these five modifications can work as intended and are nonprejudicial to the defendant. The chapter ends with recommendations regarding the use of these modifications.

EMPIRICAL RESEARCH REGARDING NEED FOR MODIFICATIONS

Courtroom modifications were established as a result of legal reform initiatives without the benefit of substantial empirical research (Sandler, 2006; Whitcomb, 2003). This occurred because of concerns about the welfare of allegedly abused children and the desire to protect them from "secondary victimization" (Quas, Goodman, & Ghetti, 2005, p. 1). This "protection school approach" (Davies & Westcott, 1995, p. 201) to children's testimony continues in legal and lay arenas. For example, England and Scotland have enacted laws that make children automatically eligible for certain courtroom modifications (Crawford & Bull, 2006a), and 74% of North Carolina pediatricians who were surveyed reported feeling that court is harmful or distressing for children involved in allegations of abuse (Theodore & Runyan, 2006).

Since the 1980s, a small but increasing number of U.S. and international studies have examined the effects of children's involvement with the law, including testimony in criminal cases. This research paints a "nuanced picture of children's legal involvement [that] may reveal both positive and negative effects" of such involvement (Edelstein et al., 2002, p. 262; Haugaard, 2005). This section reviews the research on distress related to the anticipation of court testimony and of the actual in-court testimony.

Research on Anticipatory Distress

At least eight published studies and technical reports have demonstrated that the *anticipation* of testifying in criminal court is related to increased anxiety and distress in some children. First, Goodman and colleagues (1992) compared 60 children who testified in criminal court with a matched group of children who did not testify (e.g., matched on age, severity of alleged abuse, precourt behavioral adjustment) and found that many children expressed pretrial fears of testifying and, in particular, of facing the defendant. These researchers then followed up with some of these children 12 to 14 years later. Quas et al. (2005) reported that "greater distress while waiting to testify was associated with mental problems years later" regardless of whether they actually testified (p. 100). The researchers did not examine the specific role of fear of facing the defendant in the longitudinal follow-up, however. In a third study, Berliner and Conte (1995) found that the anticipation of testifying was related to U.S. children's reports of increased distress in their study of 82 children and families, 3.5 years after they had been interviewed regarding alleged sexual abuse. Fourth, in a sample of criminal trials in Berlin, Germany, approximately one third of the children experienced distress before court, with sleep disturbances, fever, and diarrhea (Busse et al., 1996, cited in Köhnken, 2002). Fifth, Sas, Hurley, Hatch, Malla, and Dick (1993) similarly noted that Canadian parents reported an increase in behavioral and emotional problems as the court day approached, and children reported they had problems going to sleep and not eating much the day before court. Sas et al. concluded, "going to court was very, very scary for the majority of these children" (p. 107). Sixth, Wade (2002) conducted a qualitative study in the United Kingdom of 26 child witnesses' reactions to their testimonial experiences. Wade felt that the children's pretrial anxieties were heightened by misperceptions of the criminal justice system that they had learned from the media. These symptoms may be caused by feelings of uncertainty, helplessness, and anxiety, especially as the length of the legal process increases (Edelstein et al., 2002).

Finally, two technical reports revealed results from studies in which British child witnesses in Crown Court proceedings were interviewed about their experiences. Hamlyn, Phelps, Turtle, and Sattar's (2004) study for the British Home Office surveyed "vulnerable and intimidated" adult and child witnesses (VIWs) before and after "special protections" (i.e., modifications) were put in place. Of those reporting that their experience of being a witness or the court environment made them feel "really anxious or distressed," 16% to 17% of them reported that it was a result of precourt experiences (Hamlyn et al., p. 83). More than two thirds feared or experienced intimidation, which was "mainly a result of fear that they would see the defendant outside of the courtroom (31%) or a more general fear of the defendant or his or her family/friends (21%)" (Hamlyn et al., 2004, p. 21). Similarly, Plotnikoff and Woolfson (2004) interviewed 50 young witnesses in England, Wales, and Northern Ireland about their experiences in court. More than half (35 of 50) described themselves as "very nervous or scared in the pretrial period. Nine had felt intimidated. Twenty described symptoms of anxiety" (Plotnick & Wolfson, 2004, pp. 2–3).

For children awaiting trial, therefore, modifications that target anticipatory stress and provide support (e.g., court schools, victim assistance programs) can be helpful. For example, a Canadian court preparation program was found to reduce children's anxiety about testifying and improve their knowledge about the court process (L. M. Jones, Cross, Walsh, & Simone, 2005, citing Sas, n.d.). Similarly, the majority of English and Welsh witnesses having contact with Victim Support and Witness Service reported satisfaction with the services (Hamlyn et al., 2004). For child witnesses in the courthouse on the day of trial, providing a less stressful environment could also be beneficial. Haugaard (2005) provided a compelling visual to support this proposed change:

> I could picture these children sitting in the hallway of a courthouse, surrounded by activity and sure that everyone who looked at them knew why they were there and what had been done to them (or worse, what they had done). My heart went out to them. It must be like sitting in the school office waiting to see the principal because of some rule infraction, with teachers and students wandering through and knowing you had been "bad," only more intense. Separate rooms where children and their families could wait, with activities for the child or even a radio playing, would be easy to construct and may be of long-term benefit to children who must testify in court . . . [and] could be implemented without concern for the effect that they might have on a defendant's rights. (p. 134)

However, separate waiting rooms did not protect witnesses from seeing the defendant outside of the courtroom, which was a major source of pretrial anxiety (Hamlyn et al., 2004). Separate entrances or having a child appear by CCTV from a separate building have been offered as solutions to this dilemma (Applegate, 2006; Cashmore & Trimboli, 2006; Hamlyn et al., 2004). In addition, consulting with the child about what would most help him or her to testify has been recommended to give children some sense of control over the process (Sandler, 2006; Wade, 2002). Finally, Crawford and Bull (2006a) presented a sound rationale for involving the child's family (excluding the alleged perpetrator) in all child witness support and preparation programs. Each approach is consistent with the "empowerment tradition" (Davies & Westcott, 1995, p. 201) that aims to strengthen children's coping and testimonial abilities (Crawford & Bull, 2006a).

Research on Testimonial Distress

Moving from the research on anticipation of testimony to research on children's testimony, the majority of studies indicate that criminal court testimony *itself* is related to short-term distress in some, but not all, children (Edelstein et al., 2002). Children have the potential to be negatively affected by a number of aspects of traditional courtroom testimony, including the setting, the need to testify multiple times, the lack of social support, inadequate protections from the stress of cross-examination or other harsh courtroom treatment, a lack of legal knowledge, developmentally inappropriate interviewing techniques, and confrontation (Edelstein et al., 2002; Ghetti, Alexander, & Goodman, 2002; Goodman et al., 1998; Wade, 2002).

Regarding setting, Saywitz and Nathanson (1993) studied thirty-four 8- to 10-year-old children who all watched a staged event in their school library in which they were taught about the parts and functions of the human body. Two weeks later, the children were interviewed in either the courtroom at a law school or an empty classroom at their school. The children interviewed in the courtroom rated courtroom experiences as more stressful than those in the school condition. They also displayed impaired memory performance compared with those in the more familiar, less stressful setting. Although the topic of the interviews was not about alleged abuse, the study is useful because it described the importance of considering the effect of environmental variables on children's experience of distress and their ability to give accurate testimony.

In another study of short-term effects, Goodman et al. (1992) found that children in sexual abuse cases who testified exhibited more behavioral problems than nontestifiers after 7 months, particularly those who testified multiple times, who lacked maternal support, and whose allegations were not corroborated. Similarly, Whitcomb and colleagues (Whitcomb, 1991; Whitcomb et al., 1994) studied 256 children and adolescents aged 4 to 17 years and found that testifying multiple times and lack of social support were factors associated with children's distress.

Whitcomb and colleagues (1994) also found that long and difficult cross-examination predicted older children's distress. Child and adolescent witnesses themselves also reported "unhappiness" with cross-examination (Westcott, 2006, p. 181, citing Plotnikoff & Woolfson, 2004), with 1 in 5 mentioning crying, feeling sick, or sweating during testimony (Plotnikoff & Woolfson). Geared to discredit the (unreliable) witness, cross-examination contains elements that may increase child witnesses' stress, including complex and specific language, large numbers of questions, and questions that are unconnected and thus difficult to follow (Brennan & Brennan, 1988; Cashmore & Trimboli, 2006; Ghetti et al., 2002; Zajac, Gross, & Hayne, 2003). Cross-examination also may decrease the accuracy of the child witnesses' reporting (Perry et al., 1995; Zajac et al., 2003; Zajac & Hayne, 2003). Plotnikoff and Woolfson (2004) found that 10 of the 50 young witnesses they interviewed felt they had been forced into saying things they did not mean or had words put into their mouth or twisted around. Some attorneys intentionally inflict such stress during confrontation (Henderson, 2002). In the words of one attorney, referring specifically to child witnesses,

> [y]ou want to get them to sweat a bit. . . . My technique is to . . . extend the time for cross-examination . . . you're deliberately making it as long as possible. . . . Tactically you want to put them under as much pressure as possible. I want them to crack. (Henderson, 2002, p. 286)

Other attorneys noted that some colleagues deliberately use non-age-appropriate language to confuse child witnesses. This tactic is also prone to play on children's vulnerabilities and emotions because children report feeling fearful of not understanding questions in court (Sas, Austin, Wolfe, & Hurley, 1991). Of course, not all attorneys deliberately intend to confuse children or cause them undue stress. Also judges and child witnesses may ask that defense attorneys' questions be clarified (Cashmore & Trimboli, 2006).

Some children become emotionally disturbed in the courtroom because of the need to face the offender (Goodman, Levine, Melton, & Ogden, 1991; Kermani, 1993). In fact, "the phenomenon of confrontational stress experienced by children is amply supported by social science evidence" (Marsil, Montoya, Ross, & Graham, 2002, p. 213). Confronting the defendant has been found to be the most prominent fear, concern, and source of stress for child witnesses (Brannon, 1994; Dezwirek-Sas, 1992; Flin, 1990; Goodman et al., 1992; Murray, 1995; Sas et al., 1993). Stress may be intensified when the child has to testify "against an abuser, who may have been a parent, another relative, or a trusted friend or teacher" (Lusk & Waterman, 1986, p. 109).

It is not just the child witness who can suffer from confrontation with the defendant; the truth-finding process of the trial can also be diminished. Confrontation with and fear of the defendant in such cases can impair the child's ability to testify (Montoya, 1999). Confrontation has been found to affect negatively the quality (e.g., completeness), reliability, and accuracy of children's testimony (Goodman et al., 1998; Marsil et al., 2002, citing both Bussey et al., 1993, and Peters, 1991). In one study, children who appeared most frightened of the defendant were able to answer fewer of the prosecutors' questions (Goodman et al., 1992). That is, children who were most intimidated by face-to-face confrontation with the defendant provided less complete testimony, which undermined the truth-seeking purpose of the trial.

Emotional sequelae of testimony may also last for some time after the completion of the case. As noted earlier, Goodman et al. (1992) found that children in sexual abuse cases who testified face-to-face or in front of the defendant without modifications exhibited more behavioral problems than nontestifiers after 7 months, but it was unclear from that study how long psychological distress lasts. In the earliest study on this topic, Oates and Tong, 1987 (see also Tong, Oates, & McDowell, 1987), interviewed the nonoffending caregivers of 46 children an average of 2.5 years after they had been referred to a hospital for alleged sexual abuse. The parents of children whose cases went to court rated 86% of their children as upset immediately after the hearing, and 57% as still upset 2.5 years later (compared with 12% of children who did not go to court rated as still being upset). This study was limited in its generalizability by a poor response rate and small sample size (i.e., only 20% of the original sample of 229 could be contacted for follow-up), as well as the retrospective nature of the design.

A subsequent long-term prospective study examined parents' reports, as well as those of their children and their clinicians, of child functioning 3 years after completion of the child's testimony and the case (4 years after charges were brought; Sas et al., 1993). As in the Oates and Tong (1987) study, about half of the Sas et al. parents identified long-term repercussions of court involvement in their children (two thirds of parents in intrafamilial abuse cases and 41% of parents in extrafamilial cases). This finding did not match those of the children's and therapists' reports. A minority of children expressed having long-term problems as a result of the prosecution. Similarly, clinicians rated a small group of children as having long-term psychological problems (e.g., "worrisome levels of depression and emotional distress"; p. 172). However, when comparing clinicians' ratings with the type of court-room stressors, clinical problems were more related to precourt symptomology and/or court outcome than to whether the children testified or not. In other words, if the defendant was acquitted in a case or if the charges were dropped, the child was more likely to be rated as emotionally troubled at follow-up. It is important to note that the findings for the follow-up part of the Sas et al. study are limited by a 61% response rate, with it being unknown how the "missing" children (39%) fared.

More recently, Goodman and her colleagues followed up with the participants from their 1992 study. Their research reveals that testifying was sometimes, but not always, linked to psychological problems more than 10 years later (Quas et al., 2005). For example, adverse outcomes later in life were found in the sample of children who exhibited distress while testifying (i.e., cried during direct examination), even after statistically controlling for age and preprosecution behavioral adjustment scores. More specifically, those who cried during their testimony had higher caregiver-reported internalizing problems and more self-reported sexual problems and externalizing symptoms later in life. The researchers also found that higher testimonial distress was associated with participants endorsing more negative feelings about the effects that the legal case had on their lives.

Also in line with prior research on short-term effects, the follow-up study found that testifying a number of times was associated with long-term self-reported trauma symptoms (e.g., sexual problems and defensive avoidance), especially when the abuse was intrafamilial and categorized as more severe (Quas et al., 2005). Similarly, a higher number of interviews was associated with higher levels of self-reported dissociative tendencies and internalizing symptoms. Yet *not* testifying was also related to greater problems:

> when the abuse was less invasive or when the cases ended in a not guilty or lenient sentence. . . . Feeling that they could have done more to affect

the outcome of the case may have led participants to experience greater frustration, anxiety, and concerns about not being believed, all of which might cause them later to avoid thinking about negative events or to evince other behavioral problems. (Quas et al., 2005, p. 72)

Also, not testifying was related to perceptions later in life that the legal system is less fair (Quas et al., 2005).

Thus, this research shows that symptoms of trauma and emotional distress can persist well after legal involvement and testimony have been completed. In some cases, however, maternal and other forms of support can serve as buffers (Edelstein et al., 2002). Children who are provided with support (especially maternal support) show decreased suggestibility during questioning and are rated as better adjusted in the short and long term than children without maternal support (Edelstein et al., 2002; Goodman, Bottoms, Schwartz-Kenney, & Rudy, 1991; Goodman et al., 1998, citing Carter, Bottoms, & Levine, 1996; Quas et al., 2005; Moston & Engelberg, 1992; Sas et al., 1993).

Social support can also come from courtroom modifications. Wade (2002) described how children were surprised and impressed with the kindness shown by members of the Witness Support Service in the United Kingdom (i.e., volunteer support people who accompanied the children and waited with them in separate waiting rooms with games and toys). Participants in the Quas et al. (2005) follow-up study who were younger when they testified also recounted experiences of support; in the words of one who was a preschooler at the time of her case, "'We went to the courthouse, and a room had toys. The legal district attorney came, and everyone was gentle and caring'" (p. 108). Research also finds that social support provided by investigating interviewers enhances accuracy of reports by increasing resistance to misleading questions (S. L. Davis & Bottoms, 2002; Jones et al., 2005).

Of course, not all children are negatively affected by courtroom confrontation in the short term (Goodman et al., 1992 [studying criminal court testimony]; Runyan, Everson, Edelsohn, Hunter, & Coulter, 1988 [studying juvenile court testimony]) or long term (Quas et al., 2005 [studying criminal court testimony]). In studies by Goodman et al. (1992), Berliner and Conte (1995), and Wade (2002), the actual experience of testifying was not found to be related to increased feelings of distress in the children. Wade noted that all but one of the children with the most anxiety and greatest fear of retribution said that their nervousness diminished when they began answering questions. Some youth may find the experience positive and empowering (Henry, 1997; Melton & Limber, 1989; Walton, 1994), and others may be resilient if they experience stress (Wade, 2002). For example, one child witness to a murder case said the following:

I just felt so vulnerable . . . I was very aware [the defendant] was near me and he was there. Because even though [he] was behind, you could still see out of the corner of your eye. You know, I could feel him. I could feel him watching me. And I didn't like that at all. . . . But if anything, I think it helped . . . because I thought, I'm not letting you get away with it, kind of thing. I'm going to say what I've got to say. (Wade, 2002, pp. 225–226)

The fact that not all child witnesses will experience trauma from face-to-face confrontation does not obviate the value of using modifications that might help some children, including those modifications that implicate the Confrontation Clause (e.g., CCTV; Hall, 1995). The U.S. Supreme Court declared in *Craig* (*Maryland v. Craig*, 1990b) that the state has an obligation to protect such children, although their ruling is not generalizable to all children who must testify (Goodman, Quas, Bulkley, & Shapiro, 1999). The *Craig* opinion and its progeny, in conjunction with state laws, provide for a case-by-case individualized determination of emotional distress, not a blanket presumption of trauma/emotional distress and need. This legal approach is consistent with the research findings and what children are requesting (Plotnikoff & Woolfson, 2004; Wade, 2002).

EMPIRICAL RESEARCH ON THE EFFECT OF COURTROOM MODIFICATIONS

To maintain the integrity and truth-seeking purposes of the criminal justice system, the court, at a child witness modification hearing, will want to ensure that the proposed modification will serve and balance the court's protective and probative functions. For the former, there must be adequate empirical evidence that the modification can protect a child by ameliorating his or her more than *de minimis* level of emotional distress. For the latter, the modification should promote accurate statements by the child witness by increasing his or her ability to communicate with the court and promote fair proceedings by finding that the modification does not unduly prejudice the courtroom proceedings against the defendant. Each determination is important because the truth can only be discovered and justice provided when proceedings are fair and when the court balances its duty to protect children with protecting the rights of the defendant to confront the witnesses against him or her.

This section therefore reviews whether evidence exists that the modifications (a) reduce the child's more than *de minimis* level of emotional distress and facilitate his or her ability to communicate with the court (i.e., protective and probative regarding the child's testimony) and (b) do not unduly prejudice the courtroom proceedings against the defendant (i.e., juror bias against the defendant, more guilty verdicts). Because research on two-way CCTV applies to videotaped testimony (i.e., they both involve trial testimony that has been or will be cross-examined with the defendant present in the room or in close proximity at the time of the testimony), it is considered under the category of remote testimony. Similarly, the category of shielding techniques covers one-way CCTV, one-way mirrors, screens, and other means to block the child's view of the defendant. Finally, the category of hearsay evidence combines admission of videotaped investigative interviews as a child's out-of-court statement and statements by a child that are admitted by a special child hearsay exception.

Remote Testimony (Closed-Circuit Television and Videotaped Testimony)

Is Remote Testimony Protective and Probative Regarding the Child?

Studies of remote testimony using field research on actual cases and mock trial situations confirm that children are less distressed about testifying and more willing to do so when allowed to testify by CCTV or videotaped testimony. In addition, such testimony generally results in the child witness being better able to communicate, but jurors may find child witnesses who use these modifications to be less credible.

International research has been conducted with actual cases involving remote testimony and mock trial studies. In the United Kingdom, Live Link is the term for a two-way CCTV procedure that allows children or teenagers in maltreatment cases to give evidence during trial from another room within the court building but away from the courtroom. Its use is widespread and routine with this population; in 2003, more than 83% of facilities had Live Link capability, with 87% of those who were offered it using it and 90% of them reporting it "helpful to give evidence in this way . . . because they appreciated the ability to give evidence without having to see the defendant or anyone else in court" (Hamlyn et al., 2004, p. 70; Westcott, Davies, & Spencer, 1999). Similarly, of the 50 children interviewed by Plotnikoff and Woolfson (2004), 44 gave evidence through Live Link. Although more than half felt safe in the court complex, many were upset that they saw the defendant on the monitor or by the thought of being seen by the defendant, because "the major issue for most of them was to avoid seeing the defendant" (Applegate, 2006, p. 184). Because the Youth Justice and Criminal Evidence Act of 1999 (YJCEA) was "mostly implemented in the Crown Court in July 2002," Live Link and other special measures (e.g., screens, removal of wigs and gowns) are also available to other vulnerable and intimidated child and adult witnesses, but use of Live Link by adults is less common (Burton, Evans, & Sanders, 2006; Hamlyn et al., 2004).

Research on Live Link possesses ecological validity because it involves courtroom observations and interviews with actual child witnesses and their nonoffending parents and surveys of courtroom personnel and other criminal justice system professionals. However, a disadvantage of such research is its inability to determine the accuracy and completeness of a child's testimony. Only the legal decision makers' *perception* of the child witness's credibility, accuracy, and testimonial completeness can be tested in real cases. Because mock trial studies can test for these three variables, as well as many other issues, under controlled situations, MHPs should also consider their results.

Live Link was studied at 100 criminal trials in England and Wales, and findings supported the advantages of children testifying in this manner (Davies & Noon, 1991, 1993). Children who gave evidence by CCTV were rated as less unhappy (e.g., fewer tears shed), more confident, more consistent, and more resistant to leading questions compared with those children who testified in open court. However, CCTV testimony was found to have less immediacy and emotional impact on the jury. A favorable or very favorable impression of Live Link's effectiveness was given by 83% of barristers, with no significant differences in attitude found between prosecutors and defense. This level of rating was mirrored by 74% of judges, who noted that the main benefit of Live Link was the reduction in the child's stress, which, in turn, was beneficial for the child's well-being and the fact-finding function of the court. A comparison study of English and Scottish children found that the English children who testified by Live Link were more forthcoming and more audible than the Scottish children who testified in the traditional way (Davies & Westcott, 1995). These findings may be qualified by other differences in the samples, including the nature of the offense (sexual vs. physical abuse) and child's role (as a victim or witness; McAuliff & Kovera, 2002).

Live Link was introduced in Scotland because pre- and posttrial interviews with parents confirmed that the majority of children "before the trial are haunted by fear of confronting the accused in the courtroom" (Murray, 1995, p. ii). Furthermore, both prosecution and defense lawyers agreed that by using Live Link, a number of children gave evidence who otherwise would have been unable to speak. A 1991–1993 study of 65 child witnesses in Scotland found that the children using Live Link were less likely to be in tears during cross-examination than were the children in the courtroom (Murray, 1995). However, the evidence given by children using Live Link was significantly less detailed and complete; they were perceived as less audible, less fluent, less effective, and less credible. This may be because the children who were qualified to use Live Link were younger and met vulnerability criteria (Cashmore, 2002).

More recent evaluations of Live Link in courts in England, Wales, and Northern Ireland found that criminal justice personnel rated it highly (Applegate, 2006; Burton et al., 2006; Hamlyn et al., 2004). For example, Live Link was rated as

> the most effective measure by far . . . [due] to the fact that witnesses did not have to enter the courtroom and come into contact with other participants in the trial, and that this increased their confidence and reduced their level of fear and intimidation. (Burton et al., 2006, p. 56)

Similar to past English studies, although no formal comparison groups were used in the study, Applegate (2006) found that

> [a]lthough a minority felt that there were advantages to the child appearing in court, all accepted that these came at a heavy price. Child victims and witnesses were intimidated at the prospect of giving evidence in court and as a result the quality of their evidence suffered. Using a video link provided a marked improvement in both respects, albeit some of those we interviewed were less than entirely confident about using the new technology, and senior judges tended to rely on court officers. (pp. 190–191)

Results from mock studies appear more in line with the results from the English studies (Davies & Noon, 1991, 1993; Davies & Westcott, 1995) than with the Scottish study reported earlier (Murray, 1995). In the United Kingdom, Westcott, Davies, and Clifford (1991) studied children aged 7 and 8 and 10 and 11 who had watched a visiting theater act at their school. One week later, they were questioned about the event either face-to-face or by CCTV. The older children provided more information than the younger children, but no differences appeared in the quality or accuracy of testimony for either age group across the conditions of questioning. Similarly, Clifford, Davies, Westcott, and Garratt (1992, as cited in Davies, 1999) studied 10-year-old children questioned live or by CCTV about a classroom incident. The mock jurors did not rate the children who "testified" by CCTV differently in overall accuracy, completeness, or believability compared with those who "testified" in person. Mock jurors' perceptions of the witnesses' accuracy, completeness, or believability also did not differ by the age of the child witnesses.

Despite the discrepancy between the English and Scottish studies, the Scottish study revealed a finding that is worthy of consideration. The children who testified using Live Link were significantly more likely than children in the courtroom to report that the mode of presenting their evidence was fair (see also Small & Melton, 1994). This finding implies the need to consider the views and wishes of the child who is going to testify. A choice about the means of testifying may affect a feeling of control over the process, which can affect perceptions of the fairness and justice of the legal system (Quas et al., 2005). This would be consistent with the YJCEA (Hamlyn et al., 2004) and the United Nations Convention on the Rights of the Child, Article 12, which states that children will be given an opportunity to express their views "in any judicial or administrative proceedings" affecting them (Murray, 1995, p. 34).

In addition, giving children a voice in the choice of procedure may affect the quality of their testimony (Cashmore & De Haas, 1992). In Australia, where CCTV is the norm in some jurisdictions (Yeats, 2004), a study involving 37 witnesses, which was designed similarly to those in the United

Kingdom, found that the children testifying by CCTV appeared significantly less anxious that those testifying in the traditional way (Cashmore & De Haas, 1992). Although no significant differences were reported in the quality of the children's evidence when comparing these two groups of children, differences were found when the control group data were reexamined. When the researchers compared children who had chosen to give evidence in open court rather than Live Link (called the "refusers" group) with children who had not been allowed to use the Link (termed the "deprived" group), the deprived children were rated as significantly more stressed and less competent than the refusers or those who used Live Link. Although the findings are limited (because of the relatively small sample size and the fact that the refusers testified in less serious cases in which they were less likely to be related to the defendant), this research lends some support for the need to consult with children about their needs and wishes (Cashmore, 2002).

In the United States, such research is more difficult to conduct given differences in legal standards and practices that make CCTV use less frequent than in the countries just discussed. That said, however, research on remote testimony has been conducted in the United States. It has consisted of a survey of child witnesses and of four court simulation (mock trial) studies. Goodman and her colleagues (1992) conducted a survey of participants in actual cases, which revealed that children and parents most often mentioned use of videotaped testimony or CCTV when they were asked how the legal process could have been made less stressful.

One early courtroom simulation study used mock jurors who watched a videotape of an 8-year-old child testifying in court or a tape of the child's videotaped deposition (Swim, Borgida, & McCoy, 1993). Mock undergraduate jurors rated the child's credibility (i.e., accuracy, consistency, confidence) at various points during the proceedings, and no significant differences were found when comparing the two groups of child witnesses. There were some significant findings, however. Mock jurors in the videotaped testimony condition reported that they believed using the videotape enhanced the child's ability to testify and enhanced her psychological well-being. Conversely, mock jurors in the in-court condition believed that testifying in court was harmful both to the child's ability to testify and to her psychological well-being. Unfortunately, this study may only have tested mock jurors' beliefs about the effects of the two presentation conditions on the child witness rather than their beliefs after deliberation, and the college student participants may not have been representative of actual jurors from the community (e.g., age, race or ethnicity, socioeconomic status). Another weakness of this study was that the mock jurors viewed both conditions on videotape.

A second study used this same design to examine the impact of remote testimony (and protective shields) on conviction rates in a simulated sexual abuse trial (Ross et al., 1994). These researchers presented mock jurors with a videotaped simulated sexual abuse trial in which a 10-year-old child gave testimony in one of three ways: in court, with use of a shield, or by CCTV. This study found that the modality of children's testimony had little impact on the perceived credibility of the child witness or the defendant.

The third study overcame the weaknesses of the previous two studies by presenting a live mock trial to jurors. Goodman et al. (1998; Tobey et al., 1995 [reporting findings about the jurors' impressions of the child witnesses in the Goodman et al. study]) conducted 88 simulated trials with 186 (85 5- and 6-year-olds and 101 8- and 9-year-olds) child witnesses and 1,201 mock jurors. The study involved the children participating in two play sessions, one of which involved making a movie with a babysitter. The confederate babysitter asked the children to place stickers on their clothes ("defendant not guilty" condition) or nonclothed body parts (e.g., arms, toes, bellybutton; "defendant guilty" condition). After a 2-week delay, each child participated in a separate mock trial in a real courtroom. Before they were questioned, either in a courtroom or by CCTV from a separate room, they answered questions about their legal knowledge, anxiety level, and memory for the event; were given a court tour; engaged in role-plays about the process; and met some of the actors playing the role of judge and attorney. During the initial questioning, the children were told that the babysitter was "*perhaps* not supposed to make the movie and *might* be in trouble because of it [original emphasis]" (p. 178) and then were asked to testify. Of the 186 children, 47 refused to testify. Mock jurors from the community viewed the trials, made ratings about the child witness and defendant, and deliberated to reach a verdict.

Goodman et al. (1998) found that children who were more anxious had lower verbal ability and poorer memory for direct questions and were more likely to refuse to testify. In addition, those children who were asked to testify in open court were more likely to refuse than those asked to testify by CCTV, even with the court preparation activities. The authors noted that refusal to testify "could arguably be considered one form of inability to reasonably communicate" under *Craig* (p. 198). In other words, those children preparing to testify by CCTV had lower levels of anxiety than those children who were going to testify in open court. Jurors also perceived the CCTV children as less stressed.

In addition, the actual testimony was found to be more accurate for those children who testified by CCTV rather than in open court: "[CCTV] generally promoted more accurate testimony in children" (Goodman, Batterman-Faunce, Schaaf, & Kenney, 2002, p. 197). Older children were more accurate than younger children, but younger children who testified by CCTV made fewer errors in response to misleading questions compared with those who testified in open court. Even though the child witnesses were more accurate when testifying by CCTV, jurors generally *perceived* them to be less accurate (in some cases), less believable, less attractive, less intelligent, more likely to be making up a story, and less likely to be basing their testimony on fact versus fantasy compared with those who testified in court (Goodman et al., 1998; Tobey et al., 1995). An indirect finding of the study, however, qualifies this direct finding. When the CCTV children provided more actually accurate answers to direct questions, the mock jurors also correctly perceived them as more believable and accurate. In addition, jurors' accuracy ratings were sometimes, but not always, correlated with ratings of believability, consistency, and completeness. Summarizing their findings, Goodman et al. stated: "[j]urors tended to base their impressions of witness credibility on perceived confidence and consistency, rather than on accuracy, although in some cases actual accuracy and confidence and consistency ratings were significantly related" (1998, p. 198). However, it is difficult to reach conclusions on this issue because the study did not appear to define these concepts to the mock jurors before they were asked to rate their perceptions of the child witnesses, and it did not examine how jurors themselves defined and used these concepts when rating the child witnesses.

In sum, current mock and field research supports the use of CCTV with some child witnesses not only to lessen their emotional distress but also to improve their ability to communicate and to testify in court. It appears that more complete, more accurate, and more detailed reports are generally expected from less stressed children when they testify in private, informal settings, which was found in cases in which children testified by videotape or CCTV compared with those who testified in the traditional courtroom. However, the evidence is mixed regarding jurors' perceptions of child witnesses' accuracy, completeness, confidence, believability, and credibility when testifying by remote testimony.[1] More research is needed to test the assumption that remote testimony has less impact on jurors (e.g., Saywitz, Goodman, & Lyon, 2002) and explore the differing factors jurors use when deciding whether to trust or mistrust the testimony of child witnesses who use these modifications (e.g., child age, child verbal or nonverbal cues, juror gender, juror experience with children, juror expectancies; McAuliff & Kovera, 2002). Finally, studies also provide support for asking children (and their parents or caretakers) about their preference for this type of modification.

Is Remote Testimony Prejudicial to the Defense?

Given the importance in child maltreatment cases of balancing the needs of the child witness with the rights of the defendant, the modification should not unduly prejudice the courtroom proceedings against the defendant. In other words, does it increase the perception that the defendant is guilty or impair the presumption of innocence? (Kohlmann, 1996). One

---

[1]Although attorneys and judges would consider credibility and believability as a single construct, the empirical literature considers them to be separate factors. Unfortunately, however, this latter literature does not posit distinct criteria for defining each term.

way to determine this is to ask jurors whether they believe trials are fair if modifications are used or whether they think modifications bias trials against defendants. Perceptions of procedural fairness (Lind & Tyler, 1988) may vary according to how or which modifications are used (Feigenson & Dunn, 2003; Lindsay, Ross, Lea, & Carr, 1995; Quas et al., 2005). A second method is to compare case outcomes when remote testimony is used with outcomes when it is not. A finding of more guilty verdicts in cases in which a child testifies by remote methods compared with traditional ones might indicate a prejudicial effect of the modification.[2] A third way is to assess whether juries are biased toward the child witnesses, such that the child is seen as more credible or truthful if he or she testifies by remote means compared with regular in-court testimony, and to determine whether this has an effect on increasing guilty verdicts. Studies of CCTV and videotaped testimony have addressed these approaches using both mock case designs and field research on actual cases.

First, Goodman et al. (1998) asked mock jurors whether they thought the trial was fair to the defendant and whether it was fair overall. They found that jurors did not view CCTV trials as more or less fair to the defendant. Although fairness ratings were positive, female jurors found the trials to be less fair to defendants and less fair overall than did male jurors. Similarly, in a study of actual jurors in real trials in western Australia, O'Grady (1996) found that the majority of jurors in CCTV cases did not believe it would have been easier to reach a decision in the case if the child witness had testified live in court. In addition, judges and attorneys (for the defense and prosecution) in these cases felt that CCTV was fair to the accused. However, one study found a pro-defense bias. A videotaped mock trial study in Australia asked undergraduates to rate the degree to which the mode of child testimony (i.e., in court, video deposition, video link) affected the defendant's case and whether it had an impact on their beliefs about how justice was met during the trial (Eaton, Ball, & O'Callaghan, 2001). The student jurors rated the defendant's case as stronger when the child testified by Live Link compared with video deposition or in court. There was no significant difference in comparing the justness of the testimonial procedures. In sum, when jurors are asked about their perceptions of trials using modifications, results indicate that, on average, they are considered fair.

Second, no reliable differences have been found in the conviction rate when studies have compared CCTV with non-CCTV cases (Task Force on Child Witnesses of the American Bar Association Criminal Justice Section, 2002; Murray, 1995). In some cases, innovations such as CCTV are associated with fewer rather than more guilty outcomes (Goodman et al., 1999).

---

[2]Of course, higher conviction rates might also be an indication that the child was able to give more effective testimony as a result of using the modification. However, this approach is commonly used in the social science literature to examine bias against the defendant. The logic is that if the use of a modification increases conviction rates, it is because it changed the presumption of innocence on the part of the legal decision maker (e.g., Eaton, Ball, & O'Callaghan, 2001; Lindsay et al., 1995).

For example, O'Grady's (1996) study of actual trials from September 1993 to December 1994 showed that CCTV was less likely to result in a guilty verdict compared with trials in open court or using screens (see also Cashmore, 2002). By adding trials from 1995 to these numbers, however, there were no differences between guilty and not guilty verdicts. Likewise, when VIWs were asked about the verdict in their cases before and after special procedures, including Live Link, were introduced, there was no significant change in guilty (35%/38%) or acquittal (21%/24%) rates (Hamlyn et al., 2004). However, some mock studies do not show this finding, revealing that the differences in guilt determinations depend on when the mock juror is asked to reach a decision (i.e., before or after mock jury deliberation). In these studies, fewer guilty verdicts are made before the mock jury deliberations, but no differences are found after the jury deliberates (Goodman et al., 1998; Ross et al., 1994).

Third, negative stereotypes of children's abilities may result in a general bias against child witnesses, and thus bias the proceedings (Eaton et al., 2001). As discussed in the previous section, research is mixed as to whether jurors are biased against child witnesses who use remote testimony. The studies by Goodman et al. (1998), Tobey et al. (1995), and Murray (1995) found that real and mock jurors viewed children less favorably when CCTV was used, whereas Cashmore and De Haas (1992), Davies and Noon (1991, 1993), Sigal et al. (1993), Swim et al. (1993), and Ross et al. (1994) did not find significant differences in the perceived quality of evidence provided. Even when jurors find children more credible, however, this does not result in an increase in conviction rates or guilty verdicts (Davies, 1999). In some mock studies, the use of remote testimony has a pro-defense bias rather than a pro-prosecution bias (Eaton et al., 2001; Orcutt, Goodman, & Tobey, 2001; Ross et al., 1994; Swim et al., 1993), but this result might be a product of the particular experimental conditions. For example, some pro-defense findings have occurred when jurors were questioned after the child's testimony or before deliberation, but not after deliberation (but see Orcutt et al., 2001, who found no difference on postdeliberation verdict). In a real trial, the pro-defense bias (i.e., defendant is seen as more innocent when a child uses a modification) will probably be eliminated over the course of the trial, just as was shown in the studies' postdeliberation ratings.

Another aspect of research involves the impact of televised alternative procedures on jurors' perceptions of the child's truthfulness. In one study, mock jurors rated the truthfulness of children who were videotaped as they gave factual statements about a real-life event in which they were actively involved and which lasted a long time (Westcott et al., 1991). Consistent with other studies that presented live testimony to observers, this study found that adults were able to detect deception in videotaped children at a rate significantly higher than chance but that was still unimpressive (59%). Orcutt (1995, cited in Goodman et al., 1998; Orcutt et al., 2001) found that jurors' abilities to detect overt deception were no different when viewed over CCTV or in open court. These findings therefore suggest that remote testimony will not significantly enhance or impede jurors' decision-making processes regarding child witnesses' truthfulness or deception.

Thus, on the basis of empirical research, remote testimony does not appear to prejudice cases against the defense. Research indicates that remote testimony is viewed as fair and does not appear to prejudice verdicts in favor of or against either side in the litigation. Also, even when research findings in remote testimony studies conflicted, by showing child witnesses to be less credible or nonsignificantly different from in-court testifiers, these same studies showed that the mode of presentation did not have a prejudicial effect on case outcome. It is important to note, however, that the presentation mode appears to lessen a child's emotional distress level and improve his or her ability to communicate accurately when testifying. Consequently, there appears to be sufficient evidence that CCTV can be used as a protective, probative, and nonprejudicial modification for child witnesses.

Shielding Techniques

Are Shielding Techniques Protective and Probative Regarding the Child?

The two main issues that are relevant to this inquiry are whether one-way CCTV and courtroom design changes decrease the child's emotional distress during testifying and whether it increases a child's ability to communicate to the court. Unfortunately, little research is available on one-way CCTV, screens, or other altered courtroom arrangements that block the child's view of the defendant. Use of screens has rarely been found in studies of courtroom modifications in some countries (e.g., Flin, Bull, Boon, & Knox, 1992 [Scotland]; Sas et al., 1993 [Canada]) but not others (Pipe & Henaghan, 1996 [screens and other procedures have become the norm rather than the exception in New Zealand]). In England and Wales, the YJCEA produced an increase in the use of screens among VIWs (i.e., from 3%–13%), but one third of users at Time 2 were children and adolescents (Hamlyn et al., 2004). As with CCTV and videotaped testimony with child witnesses, shielding modifications are not often used in the United States. In a national survey of U.S. prosecutors' perceptions of child modifications, most reported never using screens to hide the defendant from the child witness (B. Smith, Elstein, Trost, & Bulkley, 1993). Similarly, a survey of prosecutors found that screens to shield children were never or rarely used, and rearranging the courtroom was never, rarely, or only sometimes used (Goodman et al., 1999).

The most frequent reasons cited by U.S. prosecutors for not using one-way CCTV, screens, or altered arrangements were fear of defense challenges (31%, 40%, and 34%, respectively) and not being permitted to use them by the court (45%, 49%, and 38%, respectively; Goodman et al., 1999). Only a minority of prosecutors said that these modifications were not needed (20%, 23%, and 23%) or felt they would hurt their case (16%, 14%, and 13%). No one reported that these measures would add trauma to the child witness. When asked to rate the modifications, prosecutors reported that one-way CCTV, screens, and rearranging the courtroom would be moderately useful in reducing the child's trauma (mean scores of 2.11, 2.19, and 2.28, respectively, on a 4-point scale where 0 = *never useful*, 1 = *rarely useful*, 2 = *useful*, and 3 = *very useful*), and sometimes useful in enhancing guilty outcomes (1.46, 1.35, and 1.74, respectively).

Similarly, in England and Wales, the traditional objection to screens was that they would be unduly prejudicial to the defendant (Burton et al., 2006). Despite changes in judicial instructions to the jury after the ACT, courtroom observations found that some defense attorneys suggested that its use had implications for the witnesses' truthfulness (Burton et al., 2006). Although the majority of judges in Burton et al.'s study regarded screens as only partially effective in supporting witnesses, prosecutors and police officers in interviews and in surveys felt that they were effective, gave confidence to witnesses, and were often unobtrusive. Also, the majority of witnesses who used them found them helpful (22 of 27, 9 of whom were under 17 years old; Hamlyn et al., 2004).

Two mock studies that examined the use of a shielding technique on the child's ability to testify resulted in different findings. On the one hand, Hill and Hill (1987) compared nonabused children testifying in a simulated courtroom in front of a defendant with a group that testified in a private room, as in one-way CCTV arrangements. The researchers found that testifying in front of the defendant resulted in less complete and somewhat less accurate testimony than testimony taken in a more sheltered environment. Children who testified in a simulated courtroom in front of the defendant were more likely to omit information by saying "I don't know" and were somewhat more likely to recall information less correctly than children who testified in a private room. Questioning a child outside the defendant's presence was found to enhance the reliability of the testimony. This study, however, was limited by a small sample size and the fact that they were not testifying about abuse.

On the other hand, as described in the section on remote testimony, Ross et al. (1994) assessed the impact of protective shields (and CCTV) on child credibility in two simulated sexual abuse trials with a 10-year-old alleged child victim–witness. Aspects of credibility that were measured included accuracy of memory, consistency, intelligence, suggestibility, truthfulness, and general credibility as a witness. The first study found that the modality of children's testimony had little impact on the perceived credibility of the child witness. However, female mock jurors rated the child witness as more credible than did male jurors. The second study involved the child as the first and only witness, with similar results. There were no differences in credibility when the child testified with a shield than when she testified in court or by CCTV, and women rated the child as more consistent, intelligent, and able to answer lawyers' questions than did the men.

As with the Hill and Hill (1987) study, however, it is difficult to have confidence in the Ross et al. study (1994). Other researchers have concluded that testimony in a supportive atmosphere may decrease commission errors (Goodman et al., 1991), with the result that studies such as these may "therefore actually under-predict how shielding improves children's accuracy" (Marsil et al., 2002, p. 222). As is the case with two-way CCTV (discussed earlier), complete and detailed reports are more likely to be expected in familiar, private, informal settings (as is used with one-way CCTV in states in which the defendant is not present in the room with the child witness) than in testimony given in the more formal courtroom.

No research has been done on whether instructing the child to avert his or her eyes from seeing the defendant, turning the child witness's chair, or otherwise blocking the child's view of the defendant is protective or whether it promotes effective testimony. Some commentators have hypothesized that this instruction will lessen the trauma of in-court confrontation (Whitcomb, 1992a). In addition, children may also be instructed to tell the judge whether the defendant is "making faces" or otherwise doing something to scare them (Whitcomb, 1992a). Although these tactics probably will not do as much as other modifications to eliminate the child's emotional distress, they may improve the child's feelings of control during the process of testifying, which may be protective (Small & Melton, 1994).

Thus, limited direct research on shielding techniques and indirect empirical research (i.e., from research on CCTV and videotaped testimony and depositions) exist to support the use of shielding techniques to lessen the emotional trauma of confrontation and to improve the child's ability to testify in court. Further direct research is needed on children using screens and other shielding techniques to explain more fully the manner and the degree to which they are (or are not) protective and whether they affect the probativeness of the testimony.

Are Shielding Techniques Prejudicial to the Defense?

The last issue in assessing shielding techniques is to determine whether they unduly prejudice the courtroom proceedings against the defendant. Most of the research in this area involves the use of screens or protective shields and one-way CCTV.

First, one study examined whether jurors felt that proceedings using the modifications were fair or biased against the defendant. Lindsay and his colleagues (1995) showed mock jurors a videotaped child sexual abuse trial in which the alleged child victim–witness's testimony was presented using one of three methods: in open court, from behind a protective shield, or by one-way CCTV. In some cases, the jurors were given instructions that the modification was not to be used as evidence of the defendant's guilt; in other cases, they were not given the instructions. Another study manipulation had the jurors take the perspective of different people in the case: a juror, a sibling of the defendant, or a sibling of the victim's mother. The results showed that the use of the screen or one-way CCTV did not affect jurors' perceptions of the trial's fairness. However, the instructions and the participants' roles did affect perceptions of fairness. Jurors who were given the jury instruction were significantly more likely to find that the modifications were fair than those who did not receive the instruction. Participants who played the role of the defendant's sibling rated the modifications as more biased and the proceedings unfair than those who played the role of juror or victim's mother. These results are consistent with those found in other mock studies involving remote testimony, especially when the jurors are given instructions not to allow the modification to imply or suggest defendant guilt (Marsil et al., 2002).

Next, four studies examined whether the use of shielding techniques is associated with a greater number of guilty verdicts. First, as noted earlier, Burton et al. (2006) did not find any difference in guilt or acquittal verdicts when special procedures, including screens, were used in English and Welsh Crown Courts. Second, in a national study of U.S. prosecutors described earlier, one-way CCTV screens or rearranging the courtroom was reported to be *sometimes* useful (in between *rarely useful* and *useful*) in enhancing guilty outcomes (Goodman et al., 1999). However, it is not known on what basis these statements were made or whether the modification was the only reason for the report of an increase in guilty verdicts. When the researchers examined general relations between the frequency that district attorneys' offices rated using the modifications with case outcomes per office, they did not find a relationship between one-way CCTV, screens, or rearranging the courtroom to shield the child related to guilty pleas, verdicts, or convictions.

Third, O'Grady (1996) studied actual trials in western Australia, where screens and CCTV are frequently used. She interviewed judges, attorneys, child witnesses, and their parents; conducted a survey of jurors; and coded observations of trials. In interviews with judges who had used both CCTV and removable screens, the judges reported preferring CCTV because screens did not remove as many sources of stress for the witness and were more likely to be interpreted as prejudicial to the accused (Yeats, 2004). However, most attorneys who had experience with removable screens had a positive opinion of them (10 of 12; O'Grady). Still, when screens were used in actual district court trials, the court outcome was more likely to involve a guilty verdict than a not-guilty verdict.

Fourth, one empirical study examined the impact of shields and one-way CCTV on conviction rates in two mock trials (Ross et al., 1994). The researchers found that the modality of children's testimony had no impact on the perceived credibility of the child witness or the credibility of the defendant. There was also no difference in guilty verdicts when the child testified with a shield, with one-way CCTV, or in court. However, when the child was the first and only witness, there was a difference in guilty verdicts according to when the dependent measure was assessed. Specifically, the conviction rate for in-court testimony was higher (compared with in-court shield testimony or one-way CCTV) when ratings occurred right after the child testified and before deliberation. In other words, shielding reduced the likelihood of conviction before deliberation occurred (Marsil et al., 2002), but there was no difference in conviction rates for testimony in court, in court with a shield, or by one-way CCTV when ratings occurred postdeliberation (Ross et al., 1994).

Therefore, limited research on one-way CCTV and screens in child abuse cases indicates that these forms of shielding modifications do not affect credibility judgments of the child or the defendant. They are also perceived as fair, especially when jury instructions are used. However, it is unclear whether screens or one-way mirrors have an impact on verdicts. Mock research suggests that they may potentially or temporarily bias the proceedings in favor of the defendant, but one Australian study showed that screens resulted in more guilty verdicts. For these reasons, shielding techniques might be prejudicial to the defense, and more research is needed from actual child abuse cases to reach a more firm conclusion.

Other shielding procedures (e.g., turning the witness's chair, having the prosecutor stand to block the child's view of the defendant, instructing the child to avert his or her gaze) only minimally impair the ability of the defendant to face his or her accuser directly and as a result are unlikely to prejudice jurors against the defendant. Only one study examined the impact of the witness's gaze on jurors' perceptions, and it involved a mock videotaped study with an alleged adult rape victim (Willis & Wrightsman, 1995). It found that the jurors perceived the woman's gaze avoidance as indicative of less truthfulness rather than emotional distress. Thus, at this time, a determination cannot be made as to whether these shielding procedures would be found to be prejudicial, protective, or probative. More research needs to be conducted on these types of in-court modifications, particularly because they are legally easier to implement.

Hearsay Testimony

As noted earlier, two types of hearsay evidence need to be considered in this chapter. First, videotaped investigative interviews (which can include the tapes themselves, written transcripts of the tapes, and interviewers' testimony about the content of the taped interview) can be introduced during trial under various hearsay exceptions (e.g., prior consistent statement, special child hearsay exception) if they meet the *Crawford* (*Crawford v. Washington*, 2004) test. Some commentators and evaluators feel that videotape is the best way to preserve a child's statement and to make a complete record of the interview (e.g., Hamlyn et al., 2004; Warren & Woodall, 1999; Watters, Brineman, & Wright, 2007). Some commentators go so far as to recommend that videotaping interviews become standard practice (Bruck, Ceci, & Principe, 2006; Kaushall, 1999; Kehn, Grey, & Nunez, 2007; McGough, 2002). As described in the previous sections, a neutral, private environment is less stressful and is likely to be more conducive in securing honest and complete answers than are adversarial courtroom settings (Mayer, 1990). Videotaped interviews may also assist children with limited language skills (Hamlyn et al., 2004). Cherryman, King, and Bull (1999) reported that the majority of videotaped interviews they studied in England contained relevant evidence that could be used in court. When interviews are recorded, multiple interviews can be avoided, which is one way to reduce harm to a child (Quas et al., 2005; Whitcomb, 2003), and the likelihood of statement contamination is (Ceci & Bruck, 1995; Lanning, 2002) prevented or minimized (Ghetti et al., 2002).

Second, in the United States, a variety of court statements that are made by a child can be admitted as evidence under the special child hearsay exception (e.g., statements or drawings made during videotaped investigative interviews, statements made to the child's therapist). Of course, out-of-court statements by children may also be admitted under other types of hearsay exceptions (e.g., excited utterance, statement for purpose of medical examination or treatment), but these are not the focus of this book because they can be used by people other than child witnesses in abuse cases.

If a hearsay statement is testimonial, the child witness would need to appear for cross-examination before the statement could be admitted into evidence, unless he or she was found to be incompetent as a witness or unavailable by the defendant's conduct (i.e., forfeiture rule; *Crawford v. Washington*, 2004). It appears likely that videotaped investigative interviews will be considered testimonial (see chap. 3, this volume). If the videotaped interviews or other out-of-court hearsay statements are considered nontestimonial, however, then they can be admitted if found to be sufficiently reliable and trustworthy for use in court. It is unclear whether the nontestimonial statement can be admitted in lieu of the child's cross-examined testimony if the child is found to be unavailable as a witness. However, children's hearsay is typically admitted in addition to, rather than in lieu of, their in-court testimony (Marsil et al., 2002).

Is Hearsay Testimony Protective and Probative Regarding the Child?

From a child protection perspective, one might prefer hearsay testimony to be given instead of a traumatized child being called to testify in court. Introduction of a videotaped investigative interview or a report of abuse made to an adult, for example, allows the court to hear the child's early account of the alleged abuse, which may be more fresh and accurate than when the trial is held (e.g., 1 year after the initial report). Thus, the courtroom proceedings do not affect the child because she or he does not participate in them. As a result of not testifying, the child is spared the potential stress of testifying in front of the defendant, and his or her information is communicated to the court through the hearsay witness (declarant) or videotape.

This approach is followed in some Western countries. In continental European countries that use civil–inquisitorial law procedures (e.g., Belgium, Germany, the Netherlands, France), hearsay is liberally admitted, and the defense is never allowed to confront child witnesses directly in child sexual abuse cases (Cordon, Goodman, & Anderson, 2003, citing Crombag, 1997). A modified approach takes place in England, Canada, and New Zealand. In England, videotaped investigative interviews are shown at trial in place of the child witness's live direct testimony, and CCTV can be used to cross-examine the child (Cordon et al., 2003; Hamlyn et al., 2004). In Canada and New Zealand, prosecutors may use the videotaped investigative interview in lieu of, or as part of, the child's direct testimony (Davis, Hoyano, Keenan, Maitland, & Morgan, 1999). Although substitution of the videotaped interview for testimony can happen in the United States, it rarely does because hearsay is typically used in conjunction with children's live testimony in court (J. E. B. Myers, Redlich, Goodman, Prizmich, & Imwinkelried, 1999; J. E. B. Myers, Cordon, Ghetti, & Goodman, 2002). On the other extreme, videotaped investigative interviews are inadmissible in Scotland (Davis et al., 1999).

Considering the different issues these practical scenarios raise, our discussion of the social science evidence on the protective and probative functions for hearsay testimony begins with studies on videotaped investigative interviews in cases in which they have been substituted for the child's in-court testimony. Next, research is examined regarding hearsay testimony involving videotaped investigative interviews in cases in which they were given in conjunction with the child's in-court testimony. The section concludes with a discussion of studies on the protective and probative functions of the child hearsay exception that, among other things, allows adult testimony about the alleged child-victim's statements.

Some research is available that directly assesses the validity of the child protective rationale for hearsay testimony involving videotaped investigative interviews that are substituted for the child's in-court testimony. In an English study, Davies, Wilson, Mitchell, and Milsom (1995) compared children testifying live versus the children during a videotaped interview. Observational ratings in the courtroom suggested that children testifying live were more anxious than those interviewed on videotape. This finding is similar to the results of another study of actual videotaped interviews in which children were described as relaxed in 70% of interviews (Westcott et al., 1999).

A U.S. study compared children who had their initial investigative interview videotaped with those who did not (Henry, 1999). Those whose interviews were videotaped were less likely to testify in court. Of those who were videotaped, the majority of children (86%) found the videotaping to be supportive or nonintrusive. Eleven (38%) found it helpful, and four (14%) found it worrisome (e.g., "Being on camera made me nervous"; "It made me a little leery. I knew more than one person would be watching it"; Henry, 1999, p. 43).

Regarding the ability to communicate, Davies et al. (1995) did not find significant differences in the effectiveness (e.g., clarity of communication) of the children's testimony (79% effective in court vs. 84% effective by video-tape). These figures are similar to those reported by Westcott and her colleagues (1999) in which a clear account of the alleged abusive event was obtained in 75% of actual videotaped interviews. Thus, when videotaped investigative interviews can be admitted as a hearsay statement in lieu of the child's testimony, videotaped forensic interviews can reduce the child's emotional distress but may not significantly improve his or her ability to communicate.

Videotaped investigative interviews admitted as hearsay evidence may provide a more complete and accurate (verbatim) account of the child's out-of-court statement(s) (Cashmore, 2002). Videotaping allows the actual questions and answers to be heard and the child's demeanor to be viewed by the trier of fact. MHPs should be aware of other issues that may affect the reliability of the videotaped evidence, including the circumstances under which the videotaped interview took place (e.g., When did the taping start? Was this the first interview with the child? Who questioned the child before the interview?) and the interviewer's qualifications and techniques (Was the interviewer trained? Did the interview involve suggestive techniques? Did the interviewer follow a recognized protocol? see generally Ceci & Bruck, 1995).

When an investigative interview cannot replace testimony, a child who has participated in a videotaped investigative interview will probably be required to testify and be cross-examined. This modification on its own therefore does not specifically protect all children against in-court emotional distress. Yet when the videotape is admitted, the child may receive some benefit. For example, the child may feel some support or less stress because the court's decision does not rest solely on his or her in-court testimony; the court will also use the videotape(s) and other evidence. In addition, the child may not have to testify for as long a period (Davis et al., 1999). Indeed, some courts have recognized the protective benefits of videotaped interviews even when the child testifies. For example, the Supreme Court of Canada noted that admitting videotaped evidence (Bala, 1999, p. 332, citing *R. v. D. O. L.*,

1993) "not only makes participation in the criminal justice system less stressful and traumatic for the child and adolescent complainants, but also aids in the preservation of evidence and the discovery of truth." These purported protective benefits have not been empirically tested, however.

The issue of videotaped investigative interviews in conjunction with a child's in-court testimony and their effect on a child's ability to communicate was tested in one study of jurors who served in actual child abuse criminal trials in two U.S. counties. Fifty-one jurors in nine trials (out of the total 248 jurors in 42 cases) watched a videotaped interview of the main child victim–witness as well as the child's in-court testimony (J. E. B. Myers et al., 1999). Although the protective aspect was not investigated in this study, jurors' perceptions of communication were studied. The researchers found that presentation at trial of a videotaped forensic interview was not associated with enhanced perceptions of child or hearsay witness credibility when compared with child witnesses for whom a videotape was not shown.

Also, regardless of whether a videotaped investigative interview was shown in court, child witnesses, on average, were rated as honest, accurate, consistent, and not likely to have reason to lie (J. E. B. Myers et al., 1999). However, when the researchers created a composite scale of believability (i.e., combining determinations about the child's testimonial consistency, certainty, and reason to lie), results indicated that the videotaped interview was more believable than the in-court testimony. Jurors also felt that the videotaped interviews were important for believing the child's in-court testimony. Thus, the introduction of videotapes as hearsay when a child testifies does not impede and may improve perceived communication ability.

In another study of actual trial participants, child witnesses reported that videotapes helped them feel less stress and more able to communicate. In a survey of 111 mainly child witnesses in England and Wales who gave their evidence-in-chief by videotape, 91% rated it as helpful for the following reasons (Hamlyn et al., 2004, p. 67):

- not having to appear in court (43%),
- easier to say things (22%),
- less scared (13%),
- helped witness to remember (12%), and
- friendly/comfortable environment (9%).

Although prosecutors, judges, and victim–witness personnel rated videotaping effective as a protection device, concerns were expressed about the technical quality of some of the tapes, delays between direct and cross-examination, the stress experienced by children viewing their tapes before trial, as well as tapes having less impact on the jury than live evidence (Burton et al., 2006).

Some evidence from a mock trial supports the concern about differences in impact. Goodman et al. (2006) conducted a study in which children aged 5 to 7 years either experienced a mock nonstressful "crime" involving touching/"battery" or were coached to say that they had experienced it and then took part in a forensic interview conducted by a social worker. Some children appeared at a mock trial with community member jurors in a law school courtroom; the testimony of others was presented by videotape or by the social worker (i.e., hearsay). Results showed that the accuracies and inaccuracies of the child's statements during the forensic interview and at trial did not differ. However, consistent with previous research on adults' inability to tell the difference between children telling truths or lies (e.g., Goodman et al., 1998; Talwar, Lee, Bala, & Lindsay, 2006), jurors were not able to discern the difference between accurate and inaccurate live or videotaped testimony.

Turning to the special child hearsay exception, no direct studies exist on the protective effects of special child hearsay exceptions. However, because videotaped investigative interviews are often admitted under this exception, the Davies et al. (1995) and Goodman et al. (2006) studies reviewed earlier are applicable. Some indirect support also exists. In addition to the British studies reported in this chapter, surveys have been conducted regarding the use of child hearsay exceptions in actual U.S. cases. In one national survey of state court judges, 72% reported using the special hearsay exception for allegedly abused youth (Hafemeister, 1996). Of these judges, more than 90% reported they were effective in reducing the trauma to children.

Similarly, in Goodman et al.'s (1999) survey of prosecutors, the child hearsay exception was ranked the eighth most frequently used of all modifications and the second highest when only those specific to in-court testimony were included (Warren, Nunez, Keeney, Buck, & Smith, 2002). The exception received an average rating of 2.24 by district attorneys' offices in child sexual abuse cases, where 2 = *sometimes used* and 3 = *frequently used* (on a scale from 0–4; Goodman et al., 1999). It also was ranked by prosecutors as being moderately useful for reducing trauma to the child witness (average rating of 2.34, with 2 = *useful* and 3 = *very useful*).

Regarding the issue of the child's ability to communicate and the child hearsay exception, jurors have the "doubly difficult task" of examining both the child's original account as well as adult hearsay witness's (i.e., the declarant's) version of the child's out-of-court statement (Warren et al., 2002, p. 846; see also McAuliff & Kovera, 2002). Determining the reliability of a child's hearsay statement therefore depends on how accurately and completely the adult obtained information from the child, recalled the interaction (Warren & Woodall, 1999), and related that information in court. Research indicates that hearsay testimony (even by trained investigative interviewers) is likely to be incomplete or degraded. Hearsay witnesses (i.e., declarants) are not able to relay verbatim what a child said, may leave out information, may lie or relay a child's lie, and may not be accurate about how they questioned a child; however, they are likely to be accurate about the gist of what was said (Bruck, Ceci, & Francoeur, 1999; Bruck et al., 2006; Buck, 2006; Cordon et al., 2003; Warren & Woodall, 1999; Watters et al., 2007).

Notes used by interviewers are also potentially problematic. Although interviews should be documented using exact language (Berliner & Lieb, 2001), notes have been found to misrepresent "the information elicited from child interviewees and the methods used to elicit that information" (McAuliff & Kovera, 2002, p. 428, citing Lamb, Orbach, Sternberg, Hershkowitz, & Horowitz, 2000). Although "summaries of interviews based on interviewers' notes and memories may be inaccurate for a number of reasons" (Bruck et al., 2006, pp. 798–799), interviewer hearsay testimony is more often admitted into evidence than are records of, or from, the original interview (e.g., videotapes, audiotapes, transcripts, notes; J. E. B. Myers et al., 1999).

To summarize, in the rare U.S. case in which a videotaped investigative interview is admitted under a hearsay exception in lieu of the child's testimony, social science research appears to support the modification as protective and probative for the child witness. Yet some jurors may still find in-court testimony more credible than videotaped testimony (Goodman et al., 2006). If the child must testify along with the introduction of the videotape or other out-of-court statements, indirect evidence supports a finding that it can protect a child witness from harm. Although a videotaped interview can improve perceptions of a child's ability to communicate in court in this condition, it is unclear whether the same is true for other out-of-court statements. This is because the child must testify and be subject to the stresses of confrontation, which can affect communication in some children. In addition, a number of factors can affect the clarity in which a hearsay witness (i.e., declarant) can present the child's out-of-court statement to the trier of fact.

Is Hearsay Testimony Prejudicial to the Defense?

Despite the law allowing videotaped investigative interviews and other out-of-court statements by alleged child abuse victims to be introduced through a special child hearsay exception, such hearsay is controversial for many reasons. As is true for all types of hearsay, child hearsay is a second-hand account, subject to questions about its accuracy and reliability, which does not allow for testing of the statement maker's credibility (Warren et al., 2002). Courts have traditionally not allowed hearsay for fear that jurors will be biased by and overvalue such testimony. In addition, it could be argued that the nonfirmly rooted child hearsay exception is unfair and that the introduction of videotaped investigative interviews at trial could be considered prejudicial to the defense. One reason it may be considered unfair is because the jury could reason that if this evidence was necessary instead of the child appearing, the alleged abusive event must actually have happened to cause the child not to testify (Ross, Lindsay, & Marsil, 1999). However, such hearsay testimony may imply that the child's testimony is less credible, needs bolstering, and thus would lead to fewer guilty verdicts (Ross et al., 1999). A number of studies have examined these issues.

First, although hearsay testimony is often admitted in child abuse cases, no studies have directly tested its fairness to the proceedings. One indirect study, a national survey of state court judges, found that 39% did not perceive it as fair (Hafemeister, 1996), even though 72% of the judges reported using the special hearsay exception. It appears, therefore, that judges do not consider this hearsay exception as categorically unfair. Because this study was carried out before *Crawford*, judges would only have admitted the videotaped testimony and other out-of-court statements by the child if they were reliable and trustworthy. Post-*Crawford*, this analysis appears only to apply to nontestimonial statements. With testimonial statements, the standard is different and thus could change the judges' perception of fairness.

Another reason that hearsay might not be considered fair is when multiple hearsay witnesses are used in criminal child abuse cases, which is a common practice (Marsil et al., 2002; J. E. B. Myers et al., 1999; Ross, Warren, & McGough, 1999). Repetitive, "multiple hearsay accusations through several adult witnesses presents the very real possibility of placing the person accused . . . at an unfair disadvantage . . . when much of th[e] evidence was merely cumulative and unnecessary" (Marsil et al., 2002, citing *Felix v. State*, 849 P.2d 220 (Nev. 1993), pp. 245–255). In other words, the problem of overvaluing hearsay testimony may be compounded when multiple hearsay witnesses are allowed to testify, especially when the child testifies (Montoya, 1999). Even though one study found that jurors may be able to evaluate child hearsay appropriately when multiple witnesses are not involved (Pathak & Thompson, 1999), no studies have examined the effect of multiple hearsay witnesses on perceptions of trial fairness or on case outcomes (Montoya, 1999; J. E. B. Myers et al., 1999; Watters et al., 2007).

The second way to examine the prejudicialness of hearsay testimony is by looking at guilty verdicts when the modification is used. Because hearsay is so commonly used in trials in which the child also testifies (e.g., parent testifying about a child's statement to him or her), it is not likely that jurors would infer guilt when it is used. However, because videotaped forensic interviews are visually compelling, it is possible that this modification might affect jurors' views of the defendant. Therefore, the rest of this section examines studies regarding the effect of videotaped investigative interviews on guilty verdicts.

Three studies involving actual trial practice addressed this topic. In Goodman et al.'s (1999) survey of prosecutors, most respondents felt that videotaped interviews were occasionally useful (1.55, where 1 = *rarely useful* and 2 = *useful*) and "videotaped statements as trial evidence" were useful (2.00) in enhancing guilty outcomes (p. 269). However, videotaped evidence was not found to be related to higher guilty pleas, verdicts, or convictions.

Another study involved actual child abuse cases in which some jurors watched a videotaped interview of the main child victim–witness as well as the child's in-court testimony. Although these jurors found the forensic interview helpful in making decisions both in favor of and against believing the child, the videotaped interview was not associated with guilty verdicts (J. E. B. Myers et al., 1999).

Similarly, no difference was found in English court verdicts when comparing children who participated in trials with videotaped interviews or in-court testimony (Westcott et al., 1999). Prosecutions were successful in 49% of cases in which videotaped evidence was presented, compared with 44% of cases in which the children testified live, a nonsignificant difference. Thus, research on actual cases supports the finding that videotaped investigative interviews do not prejudice the proceedings against the defendant either when they are offered to supplement the child's in-court testimony or to supplant it.

Finally, some studies have begun to evaluate jurors' and mock jurors' perceptions of the effect of videotaped investigative interview hearsay testimony on child and hearsay witnesses' credibility and on verdicts. J. E. B. Myers et al. (1999) conducted the one study of actual jurors' assessments of hearsay in child sexual abuse trials. There was no significant difference between jurors' *overall* ratings of the credibility for the child and adult hearsay witness. In addition, no age differences for child credibility were found (which contrasts with mock jury research findings discussed earlier). However, the adult witnesses were rated higher in certain aspects of credibility. Adult hearsay witnesses were rated more accurate, consistent, confident, and resistant to suggestions than the child witnesses. When favorable credibility ratings (i.e., accurate, consistent, honest) increased for both child and adult hearsay witnesses, the likelihood of guilty verdicts increased. However, when examining the effect of videotaped investigative interviews on credibility and verdicts, no significant results were found.

Similar findings have been found in some of the mock juror studies conducted in this area. Goodman et al. (1996) studied mock jurors from a community sample. They viewed children less favorably when children's live testimony was replaced with a hearsay witness (Goodman et al., 1996), but neither the credibility judgment nor testimony source (i.e., child in court, child's videotaped investigative interview, hearsay witness) was associated with increased guilty verdicts. This study is limited, however, because the simulated experiment did not involve allegations of abuse.

Next, Tubb, Wood, and Hosch (1999) compared the credibility of a 9-year-old child during a sexual abuse interview with the police officer hearsay witness who conducted the interview. Mock jurors read transcripts of the interview or of the police officer's verbatim version and were assigned to three conditions (child testified, police officer testified in lieu of the child, or police officer testified in lieu of the child and said that he believed the child was credible). No difference in credibility or verdicts was found among the conditions. However, this study is limited because jurors read a transcript of the interview rather than seeing a videotape.[3]

A more recent study overcame some of the limitations of the previous two mock studies. Redlich, Myers, Goodman, and Qin (2002) compared community mock jurors who saw a child's (4–7 years of age) videotaped investigative interview about alleged abuse with those who heard a police officer repeating the child's statements during that interview. Consistent with the previous studies, there was no direct effect of the type of hearsay on witness credibility or perceptions of guilt either before or after deliberation. Before deliberation, believability was the strongest direct predictor of guilty verdicts. A path analysis showed that participants who watched the videotape were more likely to believe that the child fully disclosed the abuse during the forensic interview, which influenced ratings of the child's believability. In turn, greater believability increased predeliberation ratings of the defendant's guilt. Postdeliberation, however, there were no differences in ratings. There are two main limitations to this study, however. First, the authors caution that their postdeliberation analyses were limited by a lack of statistical power. Second, the study did not contain a condition in which the child testified in court.

In another mock trial study on this topic, Warren et al. (2002) examined undergraduate participants' reactions to videotaped or transcribed interviews about a staged play event. Mock jurors were exposed to three formats of hearsay testimony (i.e., the interview with the child, the interviewer's "verbatim" account of the interview, and the interviewer's "gist" account of the interview) and were then asked to fill out a questionnaire about believability, accuracy, and credibility of the witness, as well as the guilt of the "defendant." Similar to the J. E. B. Myers et al. (1999) study reviewed earlier, the adult "gist" witness was rated as more accurate than the child witness in the videotape condition and more related to guilty verdicts. However, this result is limited because the interview was highly suggestive and conducted with a 4-year-old child, and no in-court testimony condition was included.

Warren et al.'s (2002) follow-up study attempted to address these limitations by using less suggestible ("moderately leading") sexual abuse interview transcripts (not videotapes). Although the child's believability ratings increased, the adult hearsay witness was rated as significantly more truthful and as having better memory ability than the child. In contrast to their first study, the verdict did not vary by hearsay condition. Guilty verdicts increased only as the interview quality was perceived to increase.

---

[3]Some researchers argue that transcripts and videotaped presentation of material can be interchangeable in studies (e.g., Warren et al., 2002), whereas others state that seeing the child results in higher believability of the child's statement (e.g., Goodman et al., 1996).

In the mock study described previously, Goodman et al. (2006) attempted to overcome some of the limitations of their 1996 and 2002 studies by involving an abuse case in which the child testified by videotape or during the trial or an adult hearsay witness testified. They found that jurors' perceptions of the witness's credibility affected their predeliberation confidence ratings of the defendant's guilt (or innocence). Jurors had more sympathy toward the children who testified at the mock trial and perceived them as more credible; these perceptions affected their confidence in the defendant's guilt. In contrast to Warren et al.'s (2002) study, the child testimony was perceived as more credible than the adult hearsay witness testimony. However, no difference in actual verdicts was found; 33 of the 35 were hung juries, and the remaining 3 were not-guilty verdicts involving the social worker hearsay condition.

The results from these six studies present a fairly consistent but incomplete picture regarding the prejudicial impact of videotaped investigative interviews as hearsay testimony on child abuse cases. The concern that hearsay testimony implies defendant guilt has not been empirically tested (Watters et al., 2007). Despite the confusion that exists about the components of credibility (there is no standardized analysis or test for it; McGough, 1999), videotaped interviews do not consistently appear to affect the credibility of the child or hearsay witness or to have a prejudicial effect on verdicts. Still, existing studies do not fully address whether or when children's live testimony, single or multiple adult prosecution and defense hearsay witness testimony, videotaped investigative interview hearsay testimony, or a combination thereof influence guilty verdicts in child abuse criminal and civil cases (Buck, 2006; Montoya, 1999). Other factors influencing verdicts, such as juror gender (e.g., Golding, Bradshaw, Dunlap, & Hodell, 2007) and ways to improve credibility assessments (e.g., Hershkowitz, Fisher, Lamb, & Horowitz, 2007), deserve continued attention. Although Goodman et al.'s (2006) study found some indirect impact of testimony type on predeliberation judgments, they concluded that "our findings suggest that the defendant's right to a substantially fair trial is not necessarily impaired by the introduction of hearsay in place of a child testifying live in court" (p. 394).

In summary, existing direct and indirect research indicates that the child hearsay exception is fair. Also, videotaped investigative interviews offered as hearsay evidence are not categorically prejudicial against the defendant in that they are not related to an increase in guilty verdicts, although more research is needed on this issue. Videotaped pretrial interviews, compared with adult hearsay about what the child witness said to them, "may be the most 'trustworthy' representation of a child's description of an abusive event" (Kehn et al., 2007, p. 65; see also Buck, 2006). Although all forms of hearsay testimony have their critics, its benefits arguably outweigh the costs of other alternatives for child witnesses in child sexual abuse cases (Watters et al., 2007).

SUGGESTIONS FOR USE

Some attorneys may believe that some or all of the courtroom modifications described in this volume are ineffective ways to reduce stress in child witnesses or that the modifications may negatively affect their cases (e.g., Goodman et al., 1999). The information presented in this chapter should help to correct these and other misperceptions (Cashmore, 2002; Saywitz et al., 2002; Welder, 2000) and provide MHPs with a more firm empirical basis for recommending their use.

Of the three categories of modifications reviewed in this chapter (i.e., remote testimony, shielding techniques, hearsay testimony), remote testimony has the strongest support in terms of its being protective and probative for the child witness and nonprejudicial to the defendant. Remote testimony is also generally supported by those who have experience using it, including attorneys, judges, court administrators, and child witnesses and their families (Burton et al., 2006; Davies, 1999; Hamlyn et al., 2004).

Although some support exists for shielding modifications (e.g., screens, one-way mirrors), children in abuse cases have expressed a preference for CCTV compared with screens (e.g., Sas et al., 1993), and research has shown that paying attention to children's concerns can affect their performance (e.g., Wade, 2002). Concerns were reported about being able to see around or under the screen, with fears about entry and exit from the courtroom also being noted. These factors were not found with remote testimony when conducted in a building separate from the courtroom. In addition, in some states remote testimony may allow the child to be in an atmosphere that is more supportive than the courtroom.

Other courtroom design changes do not implicate the Confrontation Clause to the same degree as the previously mentioned modifications. Although they may be less logistically complicated to implement in a case and operate under a less stringent legal standard for use, little is known about their protective, probative, or nonprejudicial effects. Therefore, MHPs would not know whether turning the child witness's chair, for example, would be likely to make a difference to the child's testimonial abilities.

Social science evidence supports admitting videotaped investigative interviews as hearsay in lieu of the child's testimony under our protective, probative, and nonprejudicial analysis. Given that this scenario rarely occurs in the United States and is unlikely to occur in the future if these interviews are found to be testimonial under *Crawford v. Washington* (2004), MHPs will need to proceed carefully before recommending that a videotape be admitted in conjunction with a child's testimony, for three reasons.

First, research is slim on the well-being of child witnesses when using the special child hearsay exception and on videotaped investigative interviews that are offered in conjunction with the child's in-court testimony. Logic, however, suggests that these modifications should be beneficial. Second, although research is needed to confirm this hypothesis, multiple sources of hearsay are common and might be prejudicial. Third, factors regarding the reliability of the videotape and the consistency of videotaped and in-court statements will need to be scrutinized. Decisions about the reliability and credibility of such testimony are left to the trier of fact, and jurors may give videotapes extra weight when deliberating (Redlich et al., 2002). For example, a more suggestible interview may result in more guilty verdicts (Warren et al., 2002), even if the majority of the interviews studied (reported earlier) did not reveal an impact of videotapes on guilty verdicts. Notwithstanding the need for more empirical research on this issue, such relevant but potentially biasing (e.g., suggestible, inconsistent) evidence will be tested through cross-examination and the adversary process. A minority of states also require corroboration before admitting hearsay testimony under a special child statute or residual exception (Montoya, 1999); corroboration has been found in one study to be associated with increased juror confidence in predeliberation judgments about defendant guilt (Goodman et al., 2006).

If they are not used as hearsay evidence, videotaped investigative interviews also have uses outside the courtroom. The prosecution can use them to refresh the child's memory before trial and facilitate an out-of-court settlement or plea bargain by the accused individual. The defense can use the videotape to prepare an effective cross-examination of the child (Whitcomb, 1992b). The videotapes can also be used in the child's therapy sessions, can be shown to a skeptical nonoffending parent, and can be used as an educational device to train child interviewers on skills that will be effective in eliciting information from the child that will withstand judicial scrutiny (J. E. B. Myers, 1992b, 1993; Welder, 2000, citing Wilson, 1997).[4]

Whatever modification is considered, juror expectations of how a child witness is to act also need to be taken into account when a modification is used. Preliminary work in this area indicates that jurors think that children using modifications "would be more confident, provide more consistent and detailed testimony, and maintain greater eye contact with the questioner than children testifying in a traditional manner" (McAuliff & Kovera, 2002, p. 439). On the basis of the research reviewed in this chapter, these expectancies may not hold true. Nonetheless, MHPs could advise the court that jury instructions (Lindsay et al., 1995) or expert testimony (Kovera, Gresham, Borgida, Gray, & Regan, 1997) might help jurors evaluate the evidence in a more informed manner.

Finally, because all of the empirical studies are nomothetic (i.e., they test group data), it is important to recognize that MHPs cannot know with certainty whether a given modification will work for a given child (i.e., an idiographic prediction, or one that is based on the study of individuals).

___

[4]Interested readers can find more complete descriptions of the uses, advantages, and disadvantages of videotaped investigative interviews in a number of sources (e.g., American Prosecutors Research Institute, 2004; Kaushall, 1999; Lanning, 2002; Meisenheimer, 1993; J. E. B. Myers, 1997; Welder, 2000).

Empirical research can only guide us in how a modification has affected a sample or group of children, jurors, and defendants. MHPs need to connect this information to their knowledge about the particular child whom they are evaluating.

CONCLUSION

This chapter examined the available social science research on each courtroom innovation or modification that impinges on the defendant's confrontation rights (i.e., CCTV, videotaped testimony or depositions, shielding techniques and courtroom design changes, child hearsay exceptions, videotaped investigative interviews or statements). A modification should only be recommended for use if it is legal in one's jurisdiction. In addition, it makes most sense to use those modifications that have been empirically shown to be protective, probative, and nonprejudicial. In particular, the modification should reduce the child's more than *de minimis* level of emotional distress and facilitate the child's ability to communicate with the court. In addition, the modification should not unduly prejudice the courtroom proceedings against the defendant, as shown by determinations of its fairness and lack of bias for or against the child witness, and should result in no change in case outcome or guilt determinations.

The analyses in this chapter found the most empirical support for courtroom use of remote testimony (CCTV, videotaped testimony or depositions), and videotaped investigative interviews and statements offered as hearsay testimony in lieu of the child's testimony. Recommendations for use of all five modifications were also provided. MHPs should link this analysis with a thorough understanding of the steps that should be taken when conducting an evaluation of the child witness for courtroom modification purposes. Chapter 5 presents the framework for conducting these evaluations.

5

ANALYTICAL APPROACH TO COURTROOM MODIFICATION EVALUATIONS

Preparing to conduct a courtroom modification forensic evaluation requires (a) familiarity with the law (chaps. 2 and 3, this volume) and social science regarding modifications (chap. 4, this volume); (b) becoming competent to conduct child witness modification evaluations including adopting an appropriate role in the case; (c) understanding the child's communication abilities, psychological condition, and the connections between any trauma-related communication or psychological problems and the defendant; and (d) providing an analytically sound evaluation through the ethical and clinically sound use of multiple sources of relevant and reliable information. This chapter addresses these clinical and ethical issues by first focusing on the knowledge required to become an expert on courtroom modifications and then considering the content of the evaluation and testimony in a case. Because this chapter provides an analytic approach, chapters 6 through 10 then flesh out this approach with important details for implementing it.

REQUISITE KNOWLEDGE

Before undertaking a courtroom modification evaluation, a mental health professional (MHP) must ensure that he or she has the requisite knowledge to provide competent services. Such knowledge derives from and is needed in four domains: professional standards; education, training, and experience; the relevant law; and the MHP's role in the case.

Adhering to Professional Standards

MHPs engaging in forensic practice (e.g., psychologists, psychiatrists, social workers, counselors, marriage and family therapists) should provide services that comport with the highest standards of their profession and ensure that the results of their services are used in a responsible way ("Specialty Guidelines for Forensic Psychologists," Committee on Ethical Guidelines for Forensic Psychologists, 1991). These professional standards are found in the general code of ethics of one's professional organization (e.g., "Ethical Principles of Psychologists and Code of Conduct," American Psychological Association [APA Ethics Code], 2002a; "ACA Code of Ethics," American Counseling Association, 2005), and in professional specialty guidelines for forensic practice generally (e.g., "Specialty Guidelines for Forensic Psychologists," Committee on Ethical Guidelines for Forensic Psychologists, 1991; *Ethical Guidelines for the Practice of Forensic Psychiatry*, American Academy of Psychiatry and the Law, 2005), as well as in a specific area of practice (e.g., "Guidelines for Child Custody Evaluations in Divorce Proceedings," APA, 1994).[1] MHPs also need to consult specific guidelines that are relevant to assessing children or adolescents who may have been maltreated, including the following:

- *Psychosocial Evaluation of Suspected Sexual Abuse in Young Children* (American Professional Society on the Abuse of Children [APSAC], 1990, 1998);
- *Psychosocial Evaluation of Suspected Psychological Maltreatment in Children and Adolescents* (APSAC, 1997);
- "Practice Parameters for the Forensic Evaluation of Children and Adolescents Who May Have Been Physically or Sexually Abused" (American Academy of Child and Adolescent Psychiatry [AACAP], 1997b);
- *Investigative Interviewing in Cases of Alleged Child Abuse* (APSAC, 2002); and
- Guidelines on the use of anatomical dolls as discussed in chapter 2 (this volume; e.g., APSAC, 1995; American Psychological Association Council of Representatives, 1991; Koocher, Goodman, White, Friedrich, Sivan, & Reynolds, 1995).

---

[1]For evaluations of child witnesses in civil cases, see "Guidelines for Psychological Evaluations in Child Protection Matters," American Psychological Association Committee on Professional Practice and Standards (1998). Attorneys also need to follow appropriate standards for practice in these cases (e.g., American Bar Association Standards of Practice for Lawyers Representing Children in Abuse and Neglect Cases, 1996).

Finally, APA and other professional organizations issue reports and policy statements on the topic that should be consulted, such as the following:

- *Professional, Ethical and Legal Issues Concerning Interpersonal Violence, Maltreatment, and Related Trauma* (APA Ad Hoc Committee on Legal and Ethical Issues in the Treatment of Interpersonal Violence, 2008); and *Twenty-Four Questions (and Answers) About Professional Practice in the Area of Child Abuse* (APA, 1995).

In sum, MHPs should follow the standards of practice, codes, and other relevant guidelines of their professional organization but should also consult relevant guidelines and publications from related organizations. Following this approach, this chapter includes information from guidelines for the forensic psychologist and from other professional organizations (e.g., forensic psychiatry).

Education, Training, and Experience

To help the court determine whether to allow the MHP's testimony as an expert witness, the MHP will need to present the factual basis (known in law as the *foundation*) for his or her expertise. This involves a description of one's professional accomplishments and competencies (e.g., J. E. B. Myers, 1998, pp. 458–459):

- educational attainments and degrees;
- specialization in a particular area of practice;
- specialized training in subject matter of the testimony;
- extent of experience with subject matter of the testimony;
- familiarity with relevant scientific and professional literatures;
- membership in relevant professional societies and organizations;
- publications relevant to subject matter of the testimony; and
- whether the MHP has qualified as an expert on the subject matter of the testimony in prior court proceedings.

Although a judge may permit the testimony of MHPs, not all psychologists, psychiatrists, social workers, or counselors who perform clinical evaluations in other topical areas should serve as an expert witness or as an evaluator on courtroom modification given the competencies desired by law and ethical practice (see generally Sales & Shuman, 2005).

To be competent as an expert in courtroom modification for allegedly maltreated children, the MHP needs the requisite knowledge, skills, experience, training, and education relevant to child abuse and courtroom modification, specifically including knowledge of the following:

- child development, children's communication and memory abilities, normative sexual behaviors of children, individual and family dynamics, caregiver and family competencies and risk factors, and sociocultural differences;
- trauma, child maltreatment, the disclosure process, symptoms of sexual abuse, eyewitness testimony, and coached and fabricated abuse allegations;
- child interviewing techniques, including familiarity with the various interviewing protocols and developmentally appropriate and inappropriate interviewing practices;
- the use and limits of psychological tests and other assessment methods with children, in accordance with accepted clinical and scientific approaches to performing such evaluations (involving knowledge of effects of base rates);
- legal standards and processes relevant to courtroom modifications for child witnesses (discussed in next subsection); and
- the evaluation (and treatment of) maltreated and nonmaltreated children.

Mastery of these topics is an ongoing process. Ethics codes require MHPs to "undertake ongoing efforts to develop and maintain their competence" (APA, 2002). Thus, the MHP must continue to keep current on the ever-evolving clinical and empirical research and work by relevant professional organizations (e.g., APSAC; APA Division 37 [Society for Child and Family Policy and Practice], Section on Child Maltreatment) in this field (Berliner, 1998). When needed, being competent also requires seeking out appropriate consultation to ensure one is competent to conduct the assessment and testify about one's findings. Such self-awareness is critical to ensure the ethicality of one's practice.

Relevant Law

As with all MHP services, courtroom modification assessments require that the expert be familiar and comply with the law and ethical obligations related to informed consent to services, confidentiality, privileged communications, and other professional obligations that will apply before, during, and after service provision (see, e.g., APA, 2002; Sales, Miller, & Hall, 2005). MHPs also must have a "fundamental and reasonable level of knowledge and understanding of the legal and professional standards that govern their participation . . . in legal proceedings," and "understand the civil rights of parties in legal proceedings in which they participate, and manage their professional conduct in a manner that does not diminish or threaten those rights" (Committee on Ethical Guidelines for Forensic Psychologists, 1991, p. 658). Finally, MHP evaluators in modification cases must know the legal standard for the requisite showing of necessity for the modification and the need to protect the defendant's Confrontation Clause rights. This is why a critical step in preparing for a courtroom witness modification evaluation involves a review of the law in the jurisdiction where the case is being tried. Indeed, courtroom modification evaluations, similar to all forensic evaluations, can be defined as "evaluations that are intended to address a legal issue or question" (AACAP, 1997b, pp. 37S–38S; Sales et al., 2005).

Role in the Case

Given a requisite level of education, training, experiences, and knowledge of the relevant law governing the case under consideration, MHPs have the potential to perform many roles when working with a child who is to be a witness in a child abuse case. The MHP has an ethical duty to be aware of his or her role or roles in a case and to inform the child, parents or caregivers, court personnel, and others about the nature of his or her functions and responsibilities.

Although MHPs can be therapists, advocates, consultants, researchers, expert witnesses, or forensic evaluators in these cases, ethical guidelines and rules discourage multiple- or dual-role relationships when they would negatively affect the MHP's objectivity, effectiveness, or his or her client (e.g., APA, 2002, 3.05, 3.06). Dual roles can be professional–personal (e.g., a therapist's client is also her neighbor) or therapeutic–forensic (e.g., a therapist is asked to consult with an attorney in the client's case). Some commentators have advocated an even more strict separation of roles, arguing that therapists should never serve as evaluators of their own clients given the difficulties in maintaining an impartial stance (e.g., S. A. Greenberg & Shuman, 1997; Shuman, Greenberg, Heilbrun, & Foote, 1998).

If the MHP cannot avoid a dual role in a case, he or she should take steps to minimize the potential negative effects on the client (e.g., Committee on Ethical Guidelines for Forensic Psychologists, 1991). One way this can be accomplished is by informing the client through the informed consent or notification of purpose process (Heilbrun, 2001). However, in many cases, this is difficult or impossible to do, especially in practice with children. For example, the MHP often starts out in the role of therapist but does not anticipate a future forensic role and thus does not discuss these issues with the child during the assent process (if assent is even obtained) or with the parents during informed consent to treatment. If the MHP later adopts a forensic evaluator role in the case in which the child is to testify, this choice, even if well intentioned, can lead to negative outcomes (L. R. Greenberg & Gould, 2001; Schetky, 2003). It can derail therapy, create confusion, divide loyalties, and even increase liability complaints (Heilbrun, 2001; one of the most frequently reported sources of dissatisfaction is with clinicians in child custody cases because they are perceived as biased in favor of the parent who was in therapy with the clinician over the other parent who was not; Schetky, 2003). Such problems may occur even if the MHP properly discussed the forensic procedures before starting the forensic evaluation.[2]

However, not all dual roles create conflicts for the MHP. For example, if the MHP chooses to be a therapist, he or she can serve many important functions in support of the child witness (e.g., the therapist helps a child prepare for the court experience by offering education about the court process in combination with anxiety reduction techniques). A court may also ask the child's MHP therapist to testify in the case as a lay or fact witness. A lay or fact witness is "someone with personal knowledge of relevant facts" who tells the court what he or she saw or heard (e.g., J. E. B. Myers & Stern, 2002, p. 379). For instance, an MHP therapist may be called to testify as to what the child disclosed to him or her in a therapy session (assuming privileged communications were waived by the client and, when possible, assented to by the child). Such information might be relevant to a courtroom modification hearing if, for example, a therapist serving as a lay witness testified that the child told him or her that she did not want to go to court because she was afraid of the defendant.

However, even when a second role is potentially nonconflicting, it might become conflicting (e.g., testimony violating patient confidentiality, privileged communication, or trust). In addition, as opposed to simply offering a recount of firsthand observations (lay witness role), a "treating expert" witness may end up relating specialized treatment knowledge about the child to the court, which would create a conflict if the client had not consented to the release of information or if the patient had not assented (e.g., S. A. Greenberg & Shuman, 1997). This is possible because MHP treating experts are qualified to offer expert opinions on a range of treatment-related issues, including a child's diagnosis, behavior patterns observed in treatment, coping skills, treatment progress, and changes in the child's family relationships that could be detrimental or supportive to the child (L. R. Greenberg & Gould, 2001). Although some MHP treating experts may testify as to their knowledge of the literature (e.g., inform the jury about research that recantation occurs among allegedly abused children; J. E. B. Myers & Stern, 2002), their primary reason for testifying would likely be to discuss their clinical assessments and treatment progress with the child, which is confidential and privileged.

Even if the parent agreed (and the child assented) to the release of the information, the MHP treating expert would need to guard against providing incompetent testimony because he or she did not have a competent grasp of the literature on the symptoms and behaviors of nonabused and abused children, as well as the effect of base rates (J. E. B. Myers, 1997, 2000; J. E. B.

---

[2]For a more in-depth consideration of these issues (as applied to child custody cases), see L. R. Greenberg and Gould (2001).

Myers & Stern, 2002). Even if the MHP was fully prepared with the requisite knowledge of the literature, his or her testimony would not address all of the legal issues under *Craig* (*Maryland v. Craig*, 1990b) and state law relating to use of a modification (e.g., is the child likely to suffer more than *de minimis* emotional distress from confrontation with the defendant, which would impair his or her ability to communicate in the courtroom?). The treating expert would only be able testify about the child's diagnosis and treatment progress while in therapy. How the child would respond in the courtroom is an issue the treating expert is unlikely to have assessed. Finally, if the therapist is brought to the witness stand to establish that the child is likely to suffer more than *de minimis* emotional distress (e.g., *Marx v. Texas*, 1999), the therapist is not likely to provide the most reliable evidence (e.g., because of bias or testimony based on pure clinical opinion) and consequently may not be viewed as credible a witness as would an independent forensic evaluator of the child. Thus, Saunders (1993) recommended that therapists take the following steps if they are asked to serve as experts:

1. Directly inform all parties of pertinent facts (e.g., the therapist has no opinion in the matter before the Court; formulation of such an opinion may jeopardize the treatment relationship; the parties have had no opportunity for informed consent).
2. Suggest an independent evaluation of all parties and make referral if necessary.
3. Invoke the privilege communication statute, if applicable in that state.
4. Have the existing record redacted by a trial judge, to exclude potentially destructive clinical material.
5. File a motion to quash a subpoena.
6. If called as a witness, withhold any expert opinion. (p. 55)

Although Saunders was writing about therapists in child custody cases, his recommendations are applicable to all MHPs in courtroom modification cases.

In contrast to the treating expert, the role of the MHP forensic evaluator is more focused on neutral, independent fact-finding for the court than with helping child clients (APA Ad Hoc Committee on Legal and Ethical Issues in the Treatment of Interpersonal Violence, 2008).[3] Forensic MHPs must strive to remain conscientiously objective in their science and practice to avoid the common criticism that their opinions can be bought (Ogloff, 2002). They also must admit to any personal biases and set them aside, so as to not take sides in the case (Vandenberg, 1998) or adversely affect their findings (Bruck & Ceci, 2004). MHPs' forensic evaluations will be

[3]Although the purpose of the MHP investigation is to provide an objective opinion to the court, forensic interviews may be therapeutic for the child (Sattler, 1998).

significantly more time-limited than is treatment in therapeutic practice but broader in scope than treatment evaluations because evidence is gathered from multiple sources to "determine objective reality" (Askowitz & Graham, 1994, p. 2091; L. R. Greenberg & Gould, 2001). For these reasons, the more objective MHP evaluator is in the best position to address the psycholegal questions regarding courtroom modifications by offering an expert opinion about the likelihood of trauma to the child, its source and intensity, and its effect on the child's ability to communicate.

CONTENT OF COURTROOM MODIFICATION EVALUATION AND TESTIMONY

To conduct a competent courtroom modification evaluation, MHPs must apply their professional knowledge to the specific legal questions specified in the law in the jurisdiction where the case is being tried. Accomplishing this entails adherence to principles that should guide the content of the evaluation and testimony (i.e., freedom from bias, multicultural appropriateness, use of objective and defensible methods, use of multiple sources of information and multiple methods, and selection of reliable and valid assessment instruments). This section addresses these issues and their application to the specific content of a courtroom modification evaluation.

Principles Guiding the Content of Courtroom Modification Evaluation and Testimony

Freedom From Bias

The MHP should not begin an evaluation with predetermined conclusions about the case (Feindler, Rathus, & Silver, 2003), such as "all child witnesses are in need of courtroom modifications." The MHP must examine his or her personal biases, as well as those of other professionals involved in the case, throughout the assessment process (AACAP, 1997b). For example, if MHPs see their role as protector or advocate for the child, they are unlikely to be able to perform their evaluation objectively. When interviewers hold certain a priori beliefs and do not test alternative competing hypotheses during interviews, such interviewer bias has been found to increase the suggestiveness of an interview and therefore the risk of eliciting false information during interviews (Bruck & Ceci, 2004). MHPs' choice of assessment instruments may also lead to problems in forensic work. Goodman and Melinder (2007) cautioned that "there may be a risk of over interpretation and confirmation bias with the use of projective and related clinical techniques" such as "play sessions, drawings and dolls" (p. 4). Other potential sources of bias include interviewers: having likes, dislikes, and biasing values; misunderstanding the interviewee's language or physical impairments;

using a physical environment that might affect the child's responses (e.g., a police station); having selective perceptions and expectancies; working with a child of differing ethnicity, culture, or socioeconomic status; using inadequate recording techniques; inappropriately interpreting the data; and applying a rigid theoretical perspective when conducting the interview (Sattler, 1998). Such biases, including countertransference reactions, can affect how MHPs see a child and his or her presenting problem, choose assessment methods, evaluate the assessment findings, and present recommendations to the court (AACAP, 1997b).

To remain as objective as possible and minimize bias, Mart (2006) suggested adopting the attitude of a good detective or forensic pathologist (i.e., similar to a crime scene investigator) who suspends judgment and proceeds in a methodical manner gathering data while continually asking questions and developing and testing alternative hypotheses. He correctly cautioned MHPs that "if you are the kind of person who places a great deal of importance on your hunches, guesses, and intuition, it is possible that forensic work is not for you" (p. 47). Other ways to guard against bias include the following (AACAP, 1997b; Sattler, 1998):

- developing, improving, and monitoring self-awareness;
- using a plan for the assessment;
- creating alternative hypotheses;
- assessing the child's strengths;
- checking notes for accuracy after meeting with the child;
- cross-validating information;
- remaining open to different explanations for results;
- writing reports that substantiate one's conclusions and opinions;
- preserving records for others to review; and
- consulting with colleagues, which might involve including other professionals in the assessment process.

Multicultural Appropriateness

We also recommend the use of culturally sensitive and contextually appropriate assessment practices because MHPs are increasingly assessing ethnically, racially and culturally diverse populations. For example, the *Diagnostic and Statistical Manual of Mental Disorders, Fourth Edition, Text Revision* (*DSM–IV–TR*; American Psychiatric Association, 2000, pp. 897–898; see also APA "Guidelines for Multicultural Education, Training, Research, Practice, and Organizational Change for Psychologists," 2002b) advised that clinicians supplement the five standard diagnostic axes with a five-part cultural formulation when working in multicultural environments:

1. Cultural identity of the individual. Note the individual's [self-identified] ethnic or cultural reference groups. For immigrants

and ethnic minorities, note separately the degrees of involvement with both the culture of origin and the host culture (where applicable). Also note language abilities, use, and preference (including multilingualism).

2. Cultural explanations of the individual's illness [or problem]. The following may be identified: the predominant idioms of distress through which symptoms or the need for social support are communicated (e.g., "nerves," possessing spirits, somatic complaints, inexplicable misfortune), the meaning and perceived severity of the individual's symptoms in relation to norms of the cultural reference group, any local illness category used by the individual's family and community to identify the condition (e.g., culture-bound syndromes), the perceived causes or explanatory models that the individual and the reference group use to explain the illness, and current preferences for and past experiences with professional and popular sources of care.

3. Cultural factors related to psychosocial environment and levels of functioning. Note culturally relevant interpretations of social stressors, available social supports, and levels of functioning and disability. This would include stresses in the local social environment and the role of religions and kin networks in providing emotional, instrumental, and informational support.

4. Cultural elements of the relationship between the individual and the clinician. Indicate differences in culture and social status between the individual and the clinician and problems that these differences may cause in diagnosis and treatment (e.g., difficulty in communicating in the individual's first language, in eliciting symptoms or understanding their cultural significance, in negotiating an appropriate relationship or level of intimacy, in determining whether a behavior is normative or pathological).

5. Overall cultural assessment for diagnosis and care. The formulation concludes with a discussion of how cultural considerations specifically influence comprehensive diagnosis and care.

As a result, MHPs should scrutinize their assessment measures and processes. A scale that is developed and normed on one cultural group cannot necessarily be used with a child from another cultural group (Arnold & Matus, 2000). Gee (2004), therefore, recommended that until a scale is normed on that child's cultural group, the MHP should supplement the measure with a structured or semistructured interview. Using this approach, the culturally competent MHP would ask the child follow-up questions to

(a) explain items that may not be culturally equivalent; (b) include questions about symptoms, conditions, or events that may not be covered in the scales (e.g., *ataque de nervious*—attack of nerves, "widely utilized by Hispanic American adults of Mexican, Caribbean, and Central American origins to describe a wide range of negative emotional conditions, troubling states, and somatic distress" [Varela et al., 2004, p. 237]; *taijin-kyofoshu*—a Japanese term for "an individual's intense fear that his or her body, its parts or its functions, displease, embarrass, or are offensive to other people in appearance, odor, facial expressions, or movements" [American Psychiatric Association, 2000, p. 903]; acculturation stress); and (c) make more valid interpretations of the child's behaviors as observed during the assessment (Gee, 2004).

Using Objective and Defensible Methods

An MHP's evaluation and proposed testimony should be based on sufficient facts or data, be the product of reliable principles and methods, reflect that those principles and methods were reliably applied to the facts of the case, be relevant to the courtroom modification issue in the case, and be helpful to the judge. In other words, the opinion should be "logical, consistent, explainable, objective, and defensible" (J. E. B. Myers & Stern, 2002, p. 382). To be able to render an expert opinion with "reasonable certainty" on a subject, the MHP therefore should be able to answer the following questions affirmatively:

1. In formulating an opinion, did the expert consider all relevant facts?
2. How much confidence can be placed in the facts underlying the expert's opinion?
3. Does the expert have an adequate understanding of pertinent clinical and scientific principles?
4. To the extent the expert's opinion rests on scientific principles, have the principles been subject to testing?
5. Have the principles or theories relied on by the expert been published in peer-reviewed journals?
6. Are the principles or theories relied on by the expert generally accepted as reliable by experts in the field?
7. Did the expert use appropriate methods of assessment?
8. Are the inferences and conclusions drawn by the expert defensible?
9. Is the expert reasonably objective? (J. E. B. Myers & Stern, 2002, p. 382)

Although these guidelines would suffice for getting the MHP's testimony admitted at trial, the evidence the expert presents in a courtroom modification hearing may not have to comply with the evidentiary rules for admissibility of expert evidence at trial (e.g., Sales & Shuman, 2005) because it is offered pretrial (e.g., Fed. R. Evid. 1101). However, MHPs should follow their ethical duty to present only information that is based on reliable methods and procedures (Shuman & Sales, 2001), and thus the recommendations just noted should still be used. Finally, because the expert's opinions are based on probabilistic judgments, opinion testimony should be given with a clear statement about the level of uncertainty the expert has about his or her opinion (Melton & Limber, 1991; Melton, Petrila, Poythress, & Slobogin, 1997).

Using Multiple Sources of Information and Multiple Methods

One way to improve objectivity and reliability in the courtroom modification evaluation is to use, whenever possible, multiple sources of information and multiple methods of data collection, including clinical and structured or semistructured interviews; self-, parent-, and teacher-report measures; more objective forms of assessments such as psychophysiological measures (Dubner & Motta, 1999; McNally, 1996); and direct observation in various settings (Kratochwill, 1996; Nader, Stuber, & Pynoos, 1991). The flexible use of various methods and sources of information is a recommended part of existing clinical and forensic assessment protocols (e.g., AACAP, 1997b; Sattler, 1998; Schetky, 2003; Simon, 2003), with the incremental value added by each piece of information being carefully monitored to ensure that costly and unnecessary procedures are not used (Mash & Terdal, 1997b).

For example, when assessing whether a child shows any current symptoms of emotional distress/trauma, the triggers of such symptoms, and how the child individually expresses distress and posttraumatic symptoms, MHPs should balance their observations with reports from the child and others. First, multiple sources and methods are needed because it may be easier to observe externalizing symptoms than internalizing symptoms, and internalizing problems such as depression and anxiety may be missed. Second, multiple raters can yield different perspectives about a child's functioning across different settings. Relying on one source "may lead to an incomplete or inaccurate picture of the problem" (Fonseca & Perrin, 2001, p. 137). For instance, the child's family members may provide information about the meaning of certain symptoms within his or her culture (Gee, 2004). Furthermore, studies of various raters of child behavior (e.g., parents, teachers, clinicians, children) have found that observers "do not agree very well in their evaluations of child functioning" (Kazdin, 2005, p. 549; De Los Reyes & Kazdin, 2005). For example, children's self-reports indicate more distress compared with adult reports of the child's internal distress (Lonigan, Phillips, & Richey, 2003). Third, obtaining multiple perspectives can assist the MHP in detecting false reporting (Allen, 1994), malingering (Schetky, 2003), and underreporting (Canino & Bravo, 1999). Another way to address underreporting, which at times may be due to children's tendency to want to present themselves in a positive or socially desirable way, is to frame instructions carefully (Silverman & Rabian, 1999). Underreporting because of ethnic and cultural differences should also be considered and approached through ethnographic or other culturally responsive approaches (Canino & Bravo, 1999; P. Cohen & Kasen, 1999; Dana, 2005).

Although discrepant findings can be confusing, integrating multisource data is widely recognized as necessary in child assessment (Achenbach, 2005). When attempting to aggregate information from different sources or that is gathered by different methods, MHPs must remember that clinical judgment (based on informal, unstructured methods) is often not as good as statistical or actuarial methods in making predictions about a person's future behavior (Meehl, 1954). This is especially true "when a domain of research is sufficiently advanced to permit identification and reliable measurement of key variables useful for prediction" (Westen &Weinberger, 2004, p. 609). Although clinical judgment can be valid (clinical prediction may match actuarial predictions; Grove & Meehl, 1997), we may not be able to ascertain whether it is accurate. Therefore, when an actuarial approach is not available, as in the case of some of the clinical judgments required in courtroom modification cases, the best way to improve clinical decision making is through the multisource, multimethod approach to assessment.

Selecting Reliable and Valid Assessment Instruments

Some of the clinical judgments needed in these types of cases can be made using existing assessment instruments (e.g., whether the child is experiencing a specific form of trauma). For these decisions, another way to improve the objectivity and evidentiary reliability of the MHPs evaluation and testimony is to incorporate assessment instruments for which validity and reliability have been established for use with members of the population tested. Indeed, the APA Ethics Code (2002a, Section 9.02(b)) requires this of psychologists.

From the perspective of psychological assessment and research, reliability is best understood as consistency. It is used as one indication of how good a particular assessment or measure is because it tells us how consistently we are measuring whatever we are measuring. Reliability has at least four important domains:

> (1) whether information obtained on one occasion is comparable to information obtained on other occasions from the same [person] (e.g., stability [consistency across time]); (2) whether information obtained from the . . . [person] is comparable to information obtained from another informant—for example mother versus father (i.e., interobserver agreement . . .); (3) whether the information reported by the . . . [person] is consistent with other information given by the . . . [person] in the same interview (i.e., internal consistency); and (4) whether the information

obtained by one interviewer is comparable to that obtained by another interviewer with the same [person]. (Mash & Terdal, 1997a, p. 35)

For psychological research and assessments, *validity* refers to the ability of a particular measure to give the assessor accurate information, to make an accurate prediction within specified limitations about the subject of interest, or both. In other words, validity indicates to what extent an assessment measures some aspect of what it purports to measure.

The term *reliability* is used differently in evidence law. Although it is commonly understood to mean dependability or trustworthiness (Trochim, 2006), its specific definition depends on the type of information being offered to a court. For scientific information, most courts define evidentiary reliability to mean scientific validity. For nonscientific expert testimony, the definition for evidentiary reliability is less specific because information to establish its validity is not available. In this latter situation, courts therefore typically look to whether the expert's opinions and conclusions, and the procedures used to derive them, are generally accepted in her or his profession (see, e.g., Sales & Shuman, 2005).

Briefly, reliability in science is typically tested through measures of internal consistency (the degree to which items on a scale are related to one another), interrater–interexaminer reliability (the degree to which different examiners rate a person's answers on a test), and test–retest reliability (the degree to which people who take the test two times under the same circumstances have the same scores both times). Although test–retest reliability is important for more stable constructs such as personality, it may not be as important or relevant for assessments of more malleable conditions such as depression (Kazdin, 2005). There are two main types of *validity*: construct validity (the degree to which an instrument is useful in testing hypotheses about a psychological condition based on theory) and predictive validity (the degree to which an instrument identifies people who, in the future, will or will not engage in some behavior or develop a condition that the measure is designed to test). Construct validity is typically assessed through face validity (the test contains items that look like they cover the condition or construct measured) and measures of concurrent, discriminant, convergent, and divergent validity (see, e.g., Carmines, 1979; Nunnally & Bernstein, 1994).

Although there is no minimum requirement set by professional standards in judging the psychometric adequacy of a test, higher standards should be applied in making reliability and validity judgments when decisions of higher import and of greater consequence are at stake (Grisso & Underwood, 2004). Prior reviews of child trauma measures (K. Myers & Winters, 2002, citing Andrews, Lewinsohn, Hops, & Roberts, 1993; Ohan, Myers, & Collett, 2002) summarize general guidelines for evaluating psychometric properties as *excellent* (> 0.90), *good* (0.80–0.90), *moderate* (0.50–0.70), *low* (0.30–0.50), and *poor* (< 0.30). A more sophisticated approach to evaluation is provided by Brooks and Kutcher (2003); see Table 5.1 summarizing statistics commonly used to indicate psychometric properties of measures and suggested interpretations of coefficient values. Arguably, forensic evaluations merit the use of high standards, with properties in the good to excellent range.

Our recommendations for the selection of trauma instruments in chapters 7 through 9 (this volume) follow those discussed by the emerging literature on evidence-based assessment, a movement to develop a scientifically supported clinical child and adolescent psychology (e.g., Achenbach, 2005; Kazdin, 2005; Mash & Hunsley, 2005).

Beyond meeting the criteria for reliability and validity, for an assessment instrument to be acceptable and useful in courtroom modification cases involving alleged child abuse, it must also be developed for children. Specifically, professionals should ensure that (a) the language used in the instrument is developmentally and culturally appropriate, (b) its length and complexity are matched to the child's level, and (c) its content is appropriate to the child's age, experiences, level of insight, and cultural background (Canino & Bravo, 1999; E. B. Carlson, 1997; Cohen & Kasen, 1999; Dana, 2005). The instrument should be used in such a manner as to limit or otherwise address the occurrence of children answering questions in a socially desirable manner; this is typically achieved through the use of culturally sensitive practices and "carefully worded instructions, such as 'All children have different feelings,' 'We are interested in how you feel about things,' and 'There are no right or wrong answers'" (Silverman & Rabian, 1999, p. 133). The instrument should have been validated on youth who have allegedly been subjected to abuse rather than on other groups (e.g., adults who have survived rape or on children who have survived war) and who are from the same ethnic or cultural background as the child to be assessed. This is because "the reliability and validity of a test used with individuals from different cultural or linguistic groups who were not included in the standardization sample are questionable" (Padilla, 2001, p. 6). It also is desirable if the instrument comports with recognized diagnostic criteria (e.g., *DSM–IV*) so that the MHP can discuss these criteria in her or his testimony. By using standardized measures and assessment approaches, MHP evaluators can avoid the common clinician pitfall of ignoring or overriding statistical data (Dawes, Faust, & Meehl, 1989). Such a comprehensive approach is likely to improve the validity of the information that the MHP can provide to the court (e.g., Grove & Meehl, 1997).

When such validity or reliability has not been established, psychologists describe the strengths and limitations of test results and their interpretation of them. Broadly speaking, the MHP evaluator should use the most reliable and valid methods available and follow ethical, clinically sound, generally accepted practices before offering an opinion in a courtroom modification hearing. Although the law does not require a particular

TABLE 5.1
Common Statistics Used as Indexes of Instruments' Psychometric Properties and Suggested Interpretations of Coefficient Values

Statistic (abbreviation)	Measure	Interpretation of values			
Cronbach's alpha (α)[a]	Internal consistency	α < 0.70 is questionable[b]	$0.71 \leq \alpha \leq 0.80$ is moderate[b]	α > 0.80 is good[r]	
Pearson's correlation coefficient (r), and Spearman's rho or Kendall's tau-b	Association between continuous (and ordinal) variables	As reliability measure: r < 0.60 is questionable[b,d]	As a reliability measure: $0.61 \leq r < 0.80$ is potentially fair[b,d]	As a reliability measure: $r \geq 0.80$ is potentially good[b,d]	
		As a validity measure, r < .40 is poor[b]	As a validity measure, $0.41 \leq r \leq 0.60$ is moderate[b]	As a validity measure: $0.61 \leq r < 0.80$ is good[b]	As a validity measure: $r \geq .80$ is excellent[b]
Intraclass correlation coefficient (ICC)[e]	Agreement (rank ordered and absolute) between continuous variables	ICC < 0.70 is questionable[f]	$0.70 \leq$ ICC is good[f]		
Cohen's kappa (k)[g,h]	Agreement between categorical variables	k < 0.40 is poor[i]	$0.40 \leq k \leq 0.58$ is fair[i]	$0.59 \leq k \leq 0.75$ is good[i]	k > 0.75 is excellent[i]
Area under receiver-operating characteristic curve (AUC)[j]	Diagnostic accuracy	AUC ≤ 0.70 is low[k]	$0.70 <$ AUC ≤ 0.90 is moderate[k]	AUC > 0.90 is high[k]	

Note. From "Diagnosis and Measurement of Anxiety Disorder in Adolescents: A Review of Commonly Used Instruments," by S. J. Brooks and S. Kutcher, 2003, Journal of Child and Adolescent Psychopharmacology, 13, p. 353. Copyright 2003 by May Ann Liebert, Inc. Reprinted with permission.

[a]Cronbach (1951). [b]The authors'(Brooks & Kutcher, 2003) own suggested interpretation. [c]Brymer and Cramer (1994). [d]Low values of Pearson's r indicate poor reliability. However, high values do not prove good reliability unless additional tests indicate that mean scores do not tend to increase or decrease across tests. [e]Bartko and Carpenter (1976). [f]Bedard et al. (2000). [g]Cohen (1960). [h]Kappa is an appropriate statistic where the base rate for the disorder is at or above 5% (Shrout et al. 1976; and also not more than 95%). This condition was met in all of the studies for which k values are cited in this review (Brooks & Kotcher, 2003). [i]Landis and Koch (1977). [j]Metz (1978). [k]Henderson (1993).

level of absolute validity or perfect evidence from the MHP expert witness (Melton, 1994), psychology as a science seeks to advance the most accurate information and knowledge possible about human behavior. Because in many forensic evaluations it is difficult if not impossible to conclude that one's assessment is accurate, it is critical that evaluators use the best developmentally and contextually appropriate assessment techniques and instruments available that are relevant to the legal question in the case and follow prescribed clinical procedures to improve the comprehensiveness and evidentiary reliability of the assessment.

Subject Matter of Courtroom Modification Evaluation and Testimony

In some states, the legal question in a courtroom modification hearing generally concerns the future likelihood of a child witness experiencing a certain level of emotional distress/trauma that would negatively affect his or her communication ability in the courtroom setting (*Maryland v. Craig*, 1990b; see chap. 3, this volume). For a courtroom modification to be needed to protect the welfare of the particular child witness, it must be shown that the child witness would be traumatized by the presence of the defendant, not by the courtroom generally, and that the trauma/emotional distress suffered by the child witness in the presence of defendant would be more than *de minimis* (i.e., mere nervousness, excitement, or reluctance to testify). The specific legal standard in one's jurisdiction might be higher than that required in *Craig* (e.g., a substantial level of emotional distress), requiring further information and conclusions.

Most courts would therefore look for evidence regarding the child's condition (including coping abilities and any problems or psychological disorders), the communication impairments or disorders caused or affected by the condition, how the impairments are likely to affect the child's ability to testify in court (Halleck, Hoge, Miller, Sadoff, & Halleck, 1992), and whether the defendant is the cause of or exacerbates the existing clinical condition and/or communication disorder. Thus, the MHP evaluator should address the following forensic issues in his or her courtroom modification evaluation:

- the *presence* of current, and the likelihood of continuing, emotional distress or trauma and, in some states, expressive communication problems;
- the *severity* of the emotional distress/trauma and communication difficulties (i.e., to help the court determine whether the distress or trauma is likely to be more than *de minimis*); and
- the *nature and source* of the emotional distress/trauma (i.e., to help the court determine whether the defendant is a likely future source of the distress/trauma).

Information regarding these areas can come from both idiographic (i.e., case-specific) and nomothetic (e.g., results from psychological tests) evidence. Using this information, the MHP should be able to help the court determine whether the evidence gathered from the child, significant others in the child's life, the child's file, and a critical review of the literature meets the minimum standard articulated in *Maryland v. Craig*, its progeny, and controlling state law. These three areas (i.e., presence, severity, and nature and source) form a focus for the courtroom modification assessment.

Before examining the three areas in detail, it is appropriate to question whether appropriately trained MHPs can validly assess and diagnose trauma, emotional distress, and an inability to communicate in children. Briefly, this first involves determining whether these three constructs are recognized by the relevant clinical professional communities (e.g., psychology and psychiatry) and, if so, whether they are valid. Although the use of the *DSM–IV*'s official diagnostic nomenclature is one way to address professional recognition, these constructs are only partially addressed in the *DSM*. In addition, there is recognition that a *DSM–IV* diagnosis reflects only "a general consensus that some patients may be described meaningfully by the established criteria and further study should occur, but it may not tell us much more" (Halleck et al., 1992, p. 495). Because *DSM–IV*'s status does not reflect the scientific validity of a construct, reviewing the empirical literature is the only way to determine the validity of the constructs. We undertake this task in chapters 6 through 10.

Presence of Legally Relevant Problems

The MHP first needs to determine whether the child witness is experiencing emotional distress/trauma and, in some states, whether a communication problem is likely to occur in the courtroom because of the distress/trauma. This requires that we examine how an evaluation to determine the presence of these problem areas should be conducted. Following the dictates of professional ethics and common sense, "no method of evaluation should be used in a forensic setting unless the evaluator can present good evidence, that would satisfy the most demanding of his or her professional peers" (Shuman, 2003, p. 13). This requires MHP evaluators to use reliable and valid assessment procedures and obtain information from multiple sources (e.g., the child abuse investigation process, case file, the child, and third parties such as a parent, therapist, and guardian *ad litem*) with multiple methods (e.g., interviews, structured assessment instruments). The MHP will also need to examine the child's functioning (strengths and struggles) before the alleged abuse event(s), during the criminal justice process, and at the present time (Filbert, 1997). Although the child's current level of functioning is not the primary focus of a courtroom modification evaluation, current behaviors and past history are used as the foundation for the predictive assessment about the child's likely functioning in the courtroom. This is because history is often a good predictor for future behavior (J. E. B. Myers, 1992b; Saywitz, 1997).

Past History. To gain information about the history of the child's behaviors, the MHP should begin his or her assessment with a review of the existing case file and interviews with and reports from collateral sources (e.g., parents, teachers, doctors, police, therapists, attorneys). Such information can help the MHP to determine whether and how a child has coped with the alleged experiences, if the child is struggling or not coping well, and when and in what contexts the child has displayed any emotional distress/trauma and communication problems. Furthermore, because the court will also be concerned with the child's condition at the time of trial, a courtroom modification evaluation should and typically does occur right before trial (e.g., *Hoverstein v. Iowa*, 1993). This is particularly important because trials often occur more than a year after the case is first filed. If the evaluation occurred before or at the time of filing the case, it may miss important information about the child's functioning up until, and at the time of, the trial.

For example, by the start of trial, law enforcement and child protective officials will have investigated the alleged abuse incident and completed their findings. Interviews with the child witness conducted by these professionals (including videotaped investigative interviews) are often a key part of this process and are an important source of data for the MHP evaluator. These data include the records of law enforcement, child protective service workers, medical personnel, and other participating multidisciplinary professionals who were involved in the preparation of the prosecution's case. There may also be information corroborating the alleged victim's claims of the abuse report (e.g., the child's disclosure to a nonoffending parent). Finally, the child and his or her family may have been referred for therapy to deal with the alleged event(s). All of this information should be reviewed by the MHP for evidence regarding the child's emotional reactions to, and communication abilities when, discussing the alleged abuse. Although reviewing these records and interviews are important cost-effective sources of data, MHPs must scrutinize such information carefully because it may be incomplete, contain biased information, and reflect a nonstandardized data collection process (Feindler et al., 2003).

When evaluating the quality of the collateral sources of information, MHPs should be knowledgeable about the recommended, empirically supported ways of interviewing children, especially regarding alleged abuse. This will help MHPs assess whether the information gathering process corrupted the accuracy of the collateral information. Although there are no "single proper methods for interviewing child victim witnesses that can be held out as the standard by which all questioning should be conducted" (Saywitz, Goodman, & Lyon, 2002, p. 369), there is "substantial consensus among researchers regarding the most desirable investigative interview techniques" (Sternberg, Lamb, Esplin, Orbach, & Hershkowitz, 2002, p. 410). Knowledge about these methods should be referenced when assessing the interviewing techniques that were used in a specific case (e.g., Bruck, 1998), because it is well documented that investigative interviews with children alleged to have been abused can be tainted (e.g., *State v. Michaels*, 1993/1994) by bias (Lawlor, 1998) and/or suggestive or leading questioning (Bruck & Ceci, 1995; Ceci & Bruck, 1993b). In turn, this can cause the child's recollections to be contaminated (C. B. Fisher, 1995; Haugaard & Repucci, 1988; White & Edelstein, 1991).

To assess such questioning problems (and to avoid them when conducting their own interviews with child witnesses), MHPs should consult guidelines produced by professional or governmental organizations and researchers for interviewing children about alleged abuse (e.g., AACAP, 1997b; APSAC, 1990, 1998; Memorandum of Good Practice, 1992; Sattler, 1998; Walters et al., 2003). Moreover, as noted earlier, some interviewing techniques have been subject to scientific scrutiny, including the Cognitive Interview (a set of interviewing guidelines shown to be effective for children aged 7 or older; for review, see R. P. Fisher, Brennan, & McCauley, 2002), and the National Institute of Child Health and Human Development protocol (effective with children older than preschoolers; Lamb, 1994; Sternberg et al., 2002), and the Stepwise Interview (Lindberg, Chapman, Samsock, Thomas, & Lindberg, 2003; Yuille, Hunter, Joffe, & Zaparniuk, 1993), which was one of the first child interview protocols developed for forensic purposes (Goodman & Melinder, 2007). More formalized protocols and extended scripts (e.g., better organized, increased use of open-ended questions) can improve the quality and quantity of information obtained from children in forensic interviews (N. E. Walker, 2002). Furthermore, to "respond effectively to the complexity and diversity of actual cases," it is best to learn more than one approach (Olafson & Kenniston, 2004, p. 11). Still, MHPs must keep in mind that

> none of the protocols that exist necessarily eliminates completely the influence of the interviewer's own characteristics, the interviewer's potential need for disclosure that can force him or her to press the child, or social and emotional factors within the individual child that often contribute to the child's vulnerable position in the legal system. As with even the best of tools, how they are used, on whom, by whom and the circumstances involved all need to be taken into consideration. (Goodman & Melinder, 2007, p. 13)

In general, these interviews should have started with an introduction or rapport-building phase before initiating questioning about alleged criminal abuse (Sternberg et al., 2002). This phase typically involves asking the child about neutral topics, such as school, so that the child can feel as relaxed and comfortable as possible (A. G. Walker, 2002). Although some aspects of rapport building have not been empirically studied, research has shown that supportive practices (e.g., varied voice tone, increased eye contact, frequent smiling, and relaxed sitting position with an open body posture) enhance recall and decrease suggestibility in young children (Carter, Bottoms, & Levine, 1996; Davis & Bottoms, 2002; but see Imhoff & Baker-Ward, 1999). Supportive practices can also include sitting at the child's eye level and at right angles to the child and engaging in drawing with the child (Olafson & Kenniston, 2004).

In addition, the introduction phase should have allowed the interviewer to assess the child's developmental level, evaluate his or her understanding of the difference between truth and lies, explain and practice the ground rules of the interview (e.g., ensuring the child that it is OK to correct the interviewer if she or he makes a mistake), and give the child practice with narrative elaboration techniques (NET; APSAC, 2002; Sternberg et al., 2002, citing Geiselman, Saywitz, & Bornstein, 1993; Warren & McGough, 1996). Narrative elaboration techniques prepare children to be questioned and provide an interviewing format that is an "interim step between free recall and leading questions" (Saywitz et al., 2002, p. 362; Saywitz & Snyder, 1996). NET involves a session in which children are first given instructions about the importance of being complete and accurate (without guessing or making up anything) when talking about something that they remembered. Children are then trained to use four cue cards that remind them to talk about the key areas in a forensic interview (i.e., the participants, the setting, the actions, and the conversation and feelings associated with the event; D. Brown & Pipe, 2003). Finally, they are given opportunities to practice and are given feedback and reminders about using the strategies (D. Brown & Pipe, 2003; Saywitz & Snyder, 1996).

It is also generally recommended that such forensic interviews be conducted using a "funnel" approach in which the interview begins with open-ended questions (e.g., "Do you know why you are here today?"; "Tell me all about what happened") and then uses more direct or focused (but not leading or suggestive) questions (e.g., "Did he or she touch you there?") "as little and as late in the interview as possible" (Sternberg et al., 2002, p. 411). Using an "hourglass" approach, any focused or direct question should be followed by an open-ended probing question to elicit the child's free responses (e.g., "Tell me more about that"). An open prompt may facilitate more information than if a more specific "where, how, when" question is used (Olafson & Kenniston, 2004). The interview should close with discussion of a neutral topic to end on a positive note, as well as by thanking the child and giving him or her an opportunity to ask questions (APSAC, 2002).

Current Functioning. The next step in a courtroom modification evaluation is to obtain a current picture of the child's functioning as related to the domains of interest for courtroom modification—namely, any emotional distress/trauma experienced by the child, the child's stated feelings or concerns about the defendant, and his or her receptive and expressive communication abilities. If information contained in the file or historical sources does not fully address the domains required to be covered in a courtroom modification determination, the MHP evaluator will need to assess the child directly and interview his or her parents and other people who know the child well and are familiar with his or her present functioning (e.g., therapist, teachers). As noted earlier, capitalizing on the use of multiple observers in a multisource evaluation can maximize the reliability of one's findings (Westen & Weinberger, 2004).

Although MHP opinions may be admitted into testimony even when those opinions are based solely on a review of records, a clinical interview with the child, or both, this is not the ideal approach in this forensic context. Current assessments of the child should include a structured or semistructured interview, observations, and the use of appropriate assessment instruments. Although not commonly used by MHPs in courtroom modification evaluations, instruments, if shown to be valid and reliable, will enhance the accuracy of the assessment process. Research has shown that

> when using a well-understood, well-validated instrument with known psychometric properties, experienced clinicians do not show the kind of biases and errors often attributed to them. Instead, they provide data with reliability and validity comparable to that of other informants, and their data show similar factor structure. (Westen & Weinberger, 2004, p. 604)

In chapters 7 through 10 (this volume), we place attention on specific measures that should be integrated into the forensic assessment process. Without such guidance, MHPs may fall back on flawed methods (e.g., relying solely on an unstructured clinical interview of a child; failing to consider disconfirmatory data). As Peterson (2004) noted, "For many of the most important inferences professional psychologists have to make, practitioners appear to be forever dependent on incorrigibly fallible interviews and unavoidably selective, reactive observations as primary sources of data" (p. 202). The discussion in those chapters emphasizes the reliability and validity of the available child trauma measures. This is important because "blanket recommendations to use reliable and valid measures . . . are tantamount to writing a recipe for baking hippopotamus cookies that begins with the instruction 'use one hippopotamus' without directions for securing the main ingredient" (Mash & Hunsley, 2005, p. 364). In addition, instruments vary widely in terms of research on their psychometric properties (i.e., the quantitative measurement of psychological data) and their cultural appropriateness.

Finally, because children who are referred for courtroom modifications may be particularly vulnerable, the MHP should take care to be sensitive to the child's needs in this assessment process. Although individual interviews and testing with the child will provide valuable, direct information about the child's thoughts, feelings, symptoms, communication abilities, and perceptions of the defendant and courtroom testimony, such comprehensive sessions may not be feasible (e.g., because developmentally, culturally, and linguistically appropriate measures are not available) or reasonable (e.g., because the child is too distressed to participate and the current therapist appears unable to address the relevant issues) in all cases. Such limitations should be communicated in the MHP evaluator's report. However, the MHP should keep in mind that assessment difficulties may be demonstrative of the child's modification need in the case.

Severity of Legally Relevant Problems

The second clinical assessment issue in these cases is to evaluate the severity of the child's emotional distress, trauma, or communication problems (e.g., is the trauma substantially likely to be more than *de minimis*?). As noted in chapter 3 (this volume), the major difficulty posed by this assessment question is that the U.S. Supreme Court (*Maryland v. Craig*, 1990b) has not defined the minimum showing of emotional trauma required by the Constitution to allow for courtroom modifications that implicate the Confrontation Clause. The Court only stated that "mere nervousness or some reluctance to testify" (a *de mimimis* showing) fell below the required level. What about children who when asked to testify are found to be barely above "mere nervousness" or who are more reluctant to testify than not? Presumably, the severity of trauma issue is left for each state to decide either statutorily or through case law.

Although a few states use a "more than *de minimis*" standard, most states have set higher thresholds, using phrases such as "serious emotional distress," "severe mental or emotional harm," "at least moderate emotional or mental harm," "psychological or emotional trauma," and "traumatic emotional or mental distress."[4] This is in part because Maryland's requirement of "serious emotional distress such that the child cannot reasonable communicate" clearly met constitutional requirements. Therefore, it appears that, in Mary-

---

[4]Of course, the statutory requirements alone do not dictate what is permitted in a given case. Child witnesses have been allowed to use courtroom modifications despite less than compelling evidence in states with high state statutory standards (e.g., *Danner v. Kentucky*, 1998, in which a 15-year-old adolescent reported not being afraid of her father who allegedly raped and sodomized her but stated that she could not be near him and did not know if she could testify against him in the same room; *Marx v. Texas*, 1999).

land and other states with similar legal requirements, part of this severity determination should include a finding that the nature of the emotional distress/trauma must adversely affect the child's ability to communicate in the courtroom. As the U.S. Supreme Court indicated, the trauma level would meet Constitutional standards "at least where such trauma would impair the child's ability to communicate" (p. 857).

Given the lack of legal clarity regarding the bounds of the severity finding, MHP evaluators should (a) keep in mind that the constructs of emotional distress (more than mere nervousness), trauma, and ability to communicate (more than reluctance to testify) each exist on a continuum; (b) determine where the particular child witness falls along those continua; and (c) understand what the law requires in the jurisdiction he or she is being asked to testify. When determining whether current levels of emotional distress/trauma (if there is any) would be likely to impair the child's ability to testify in front of the defendant, MHP evaluators should try to incorporate tests and measures as part of their assessment of child witnesses (as noted earlier). Ideal assessment instruments contain cut points that enable MHPs to determine varying stages of clinical distress along a continuum. When such ideal instruments do not yet exist for use in this context, MHPs should choose other appropriate assessment instruments or techniques (e.g., structured or semistructured interviews) to evaluate the frequency, intensity, duration, and course of the child's symptoms as well as their precipitating circumstances (Nader, 1997). Measuring the child's variation in each level will provide the MHP with information about the severity of the child's symptomology. The child's severity level should then be put in societal context by comparing the level to normative data (e.g., data taken from samples of "normal" children as well as data taken from samples of clinically referred and allegedly abused children). This approach can be used to distinguish normal child symptoms of stress from clinically elevated symptoms of traumatization (Nader, 1997). It also should be used to identify qualitative and quantitative differences in responses to assessment questions from children in different groups and from different cultural backgrounds. By comparing a child's responses to appropriate group norms, more potentially valid conclusions can be made about the severity of a child's problem.

On the basis of this information, the MHP evaluator might conclude that a certain child currently meets criteria for a DSM–IV diagnosis. In such cases, the child could be said to be presently experiencing more than a *de minimis*, or even a severe, amount of emotional distress because a number of troubling symptoms have been occurring for a relatively long duration that cause the youth to experience clinically significant distress or impairment in a number of important areas of functioning, such as school and home. However, MHPs should remember that the usefulness of DSM–IV diagnoses to predict the child's behavior in future courtroom testimony will depend on at least two factors: (a) the timing of the assessment (i.e., assessments conducted 1 week before the child's testimony will be more helpful than those conducted 1 year before it) and (b) the course of the child's disorder (i.e., those disorders with a known, persistent course are more informative for modification evaluation purposes than are those disorders with less known courses). On their own, diagnoses are not predictive of future behavior. In addition, risk and protective factors need to be taken into account.

As an alternative, MHP evaluators may form an opinion about the severity of a child witness's current and future functioning that does not contain a *DSM–IV* diagnosis. The most important information to gather for this purpose is the frequency, intensity, duration, and course of any symptoms along with the triggers or context of those problem behaviors.

Nature and Source of Legally Relevant Problems

The final major assessment issue in courtroom modification cases is to determine whether the child's emotional functioning and communication abilities would likely be negatively affected by future courtroom testimony in the physical presence of the defendant (as opposed to the presence of other factors relating to in-court testimony). When performing these evaluations, MHPs should consider how the child's present emotional functioning and communication skills (a) were likely affected by the prior alleged traumatic event and alleged abuser—the defendant and (b) might be affected in the future by testifying in front of the defendant.

Grisso (2003) correctly reminded MHPs working in forensic settings to consider the specific environmental and social context in which the child will be expected to function. This is because children's skills performance and abilities (e.g., attention, motivation, resistance to suggestion, stress tolerance and coping) can be influenced by context (Saywitz, 2002). For example, in a case about alleged abuse, the child may be asked to relate his or her recollection of the alleged maltreatment in the context of a courtroom. To examine the child's emotional state and his or her ability to talk about the alleged abusive experience(s) in that context, MHPs should review any prior records involving interviews or discussion about the alleged abuse and evaluate others' impressions of the child's emotional state and ability to communicate at those times. MHPs who conduct interviews with the child for a courtroom modification evaluation should note whether any trauma symptoms are produced by the child when he or she discusses possible courtroom-related issues, including talking about the alleged abuse incident(s), thinking about the defendant, and reflecting on past, current, and future interactions with criminal justice or child protective personnel. As further described in chapter 6 (this volume), posttraumatic symptoms may include displays of increased autonomic arousal levels (e.g., tension, jumpiness, flinching, attempts to flee the situation), attempts to avoid reminders of the trauma (e.g., refusing to answer questions, emotionally shutting down or acting out, recanting allegations), and numbing (e.g., appear to show no emotion or "spacing out" during discussions about the traumatic incident or incidents). In addition, the child's general communicative ability could be affected. Without considering context, "adults who see children functioning in familiar situations may overestimate their abilities in unfamiliar settings like the courtroom" (Steward, Bussey, Goodman, & Saywitz, 1993, p. 28).

It is important to reiterate that this assessment process does not attempt to prove whether the defendant was a person who abused the child witness and, as such, was the source of the child's trauma if he or she is found to be experiencing traumatic symptoms. In sexual abuse cases especially, clear documentation indicates that there is currently no way to prove a child has been sexually abused on the basis of the child's self-report, behaviors, or emotions (Ceci & Hembrooke, 1998). In such cases the MHP's assessment should therefore not be used to attempt to substantiate the occurrence of child sexual abuse (C. B. Fisher & Whiting, 1998) or its source (i.e., the defendant; Berliner & Conte, 1993; Conte, 1992; Heiman, 1992). This reasoning would also apply to allegations involving other types of abuse (e.g., physical abuse, emotional abuse) that were based solely on the child's self-report.

For these reasons, MHPs should only offer appropriately limited opinions on how the child's current level of functioning may be affected by future confrontation with the defendant. Although the child's current level of functioning is not the focus of a courtroom modification evaluation, it is used as a foundation for the MHP's predictive assessment. The MHP will render an opinion as to the likelihood of the individual child experiencing trauma symptomology in the future in the courtroom as a result of seeing the defendant rather than from being in the general courtroom environment.

Unfortunately, MHPs are limited in their abilities to make predictions about future human behavior (Melton et al., 1997). Actuarial instruments can improve predictive accuracy, but such tools are lacking on this topic. Recognizing these limitations, MHPs in these cases should attempt to gather as much objective information as possible about the child's interactions with the defendant, examine competing hypotheses, and reframe predictions as estimated probabilities.

Specifically, assessments of a child witness should include a review of how the child reacted after interactions with the defendant and with any legal actors or experiences because, as already noted, history is often a good predictor for future behavior (J. E. B. Myers, 1992b; Saywitz, 1997). This assessment will entail investigating whether the child has faced the defendant in other settings, especially after abuse allegations have been made. If so, the MHP should try and obtain information about both the child's and the defendant's language and behaviors during and after those encounters. This will entail the MHP evaluator addressing such questions as the following:

1. How did the defendant act in the presence of the child?
2. How did the child act when in the presence of the defendant?
3. How did the child react when out of the defendant's presence before and after the interaction?
4. How did the child's responses change over time or in different settings?
5. What has the child said about the defendant to others?

If the child displays or expresses fear of the defendant, the MHP can assess the sources and severity of the child's feelings and can describe the effect of any threats made by the defendant (J. E. B. Myers, 1992b). Myers further notes that threats an adult would not take seriously might paralyze a young child. Reasons for and against the child being likely to continue expressing symptoms and communication problems should also be explored.

Next, to guard against confirmatory bias (Mart, 2006), the MHP evaluator must explore and explain possible competing explanations about what *other than the defendant* might have caused the child's negative reactions. For example, the child might fear that if he or she discloses the sexual abuse, the defendant may physically harm him or her, another person, or an animal or object to which he or she is deeply attached. In addition, the child may fear being sent to live in a foster home or having the defendant removed from the home as a result of disclosure.

The MHP should also compare the child's reactions to the defendant with the child's reactions to other people (i.e., other adults, legal actors) or settings. Ideally, information about a child's emotional reactions and communication abilities would be gathered across a variety of environmental variables, some similar to the courtroom and some not. For instance, observing or gathering knowledge about the child across settings (e.g., interviews conducted in a police station, school, attorney's office, courtroom) can help the MHP to determine whether the child's emotional reactions might be due to the setting or other variables. If a child appeared distressed during discussions about the defendant across each setting, the MHP might be able to opine that the setting did not appear to be a particularly controlling variable in the child's distress in the past. In such a case, future distress in the courtroom when testifying might not be solely due to the courtroom setting. It might be due to other factors, including but not limited to being separated from a loved one, discussing the defendant, being asked to talk about the alleged abuse, or anticipating testifying in front of the defendant.

Finally, the MHP should form his or her opinion in the form of a probability. This approach is appropriate because decision making in psychiatry and psychology generally involves "working with degrees of uncertainty and turning them into estimates of probability" (Bursztajn & Brodsky, 1998, p. 268). The MHP should also describe the level of uncertainty in their conclusions and their reasoning process and not turn probabilities into facts (e.g., this child will be traumatized by having to face the defendant in court; Melton et al., 1997). Thus, the expert MHP should use a categorical as opposed to a numeric format to communicate probabilities, using terms such as *probable, substantial probability,* and *little probability,* along with the appropriate parameters or situations in which the behavior is likely or less likely to occur (Grisso, 1998; Shapiro, 1991, p. 219; Slovic, Monahan, & MacGregor, 2000). This information and the MHP's conclusion would then be used by the court, along with any other information it deems appropriate, to reach its legal conclusion about whether a courtroom modification is needed.

CONCLUSION

To become competent to conduct a courtroom modification evaluation, the MHP evaluator needs to review carefully the law and social science in this area and consider his or her role in the case. Adopting the role of an impartial evaluator, the MHP will plan an independent investigation that will include examining the child's history before and after the alleged abuse (including the alleged abusive event or events and the defendant's alleged role in the event or events; Filbert, 1997). The MHP can then proceed with his or her multisource, multimethod evaluation guided by our analytical approach.

The MHP evaluator's approach can begin with an examination of whether the child is currently experiencing any emotional symptoms or communication difficulties. If so, the MHP evaluator will then explore the triggers of the child's current symptoms or problems and examine how the child individually expresses them. MHPs should take particular care to document any current and past observable behaviors, or reports of behaviors, that affect the child's ability to communicate. Because it may be easier to observe externalizing than internalizing symptoms, MHPs should integrate observations with reports from the child and others, the case file, and psychological testing. In addition, MHPs should review the frequency, duration, and intensity of such symptoms to assess their severity, as well as the likelihood that such emotional disturbances or communication impairments will continue.

To make a prediction about the child's likely testimonial behavior in the presence of the defendant, the MHP needs to determine how the individual child's emotional state and communication skills might be affected by future courtroom testimony, particularly in the presence of the defendant. For example, in court, the child will probably be asked to relate his or her recollection of the alleged maltreatment. To examine the child's emotional state and his or her ability to talk about the alleged abusive experience(s), the MHP should review any prior records involving interviews or discussion about the alleged abuse and evaluate others' impressions of the child's emotional state and ability to communicate across settings. In addition, if the child's trauma is in doubt, the MHP should consider meeting with the child in various settings, including a courtroom, to perform his or her assessment.

To obtain the most valid and reliable responses from a child, the MHP should apply the recommended principles of child interviewing described earlier in the chapter. For example, when exploring the content of the reported traumatic events and the role of the alleged abuser (Norris & Riad, 1997), children tend to answer questions about these issues more accurately when a skilled interviewer asks the appropriate probing question and when the children can ask questions of the interviewer (Nader, 1997). Professionals should select assessment measures that describe the event behaviorally rather than more generally (i.e., they must describe the specific type of conduct involved instead of using the general term *abuse*; Boeschen, Sales, & Koss, 1998). This distinction is developmentally important because terms that are concrete and visually salient elicit more accurate reports from children (e.g., "How many times did he *hit* you?" is better than "How many times were you *abused?*"; Saywitz & Camparo, 1998, p. 831). MHP evaluators should note the emotional and communicative behaviors or symptoms produced by the child when he or she discusses possible courtroom testimony-related issues, including talking about the alleged abusive incident(s) and past, current, and future interactions with the defendant, criminal justice personnel, and child protective services personnel. Finally, the assessment should pay specific attention to areas of strength and coping that may protect the child from trauma and/or communication problems and disorders.

Psychological tests can be helpful to determine whether a child is currently experiencing any difficulties and, if so, to provide information about the severity of such emotional problems or communication difficulties. However, because the rates of sensitivity and specificity are not perfect, no psychological test has a 100% hit rate (Boeschen et al., 1998) or avoids Type I or Type II errors (i.e., false positive or false negative). Thus, expert witnesses who testify on the basis of assessment instruments must discuss the limitations of these tools and their testimony and explore competing explanations for their findings. Before conclusions are drawn, findings from assessment instruments must always be integrated with other collateral information and the information gathered during other parts of the evaluator's investigation.

The analysis would conclude with the MHP's determination of whether the child's future ability to communicate in a courtroom setting would be impaired by a certain level of emotional distress because of the defendant's presence. The MHP would communicate the future likelihood of such emotional or communication difficulties to the court in the form of an estimated categorical probability.

Finally, to implement our analytic approach for courtroom modification evaluations, the MHP evaluator must be competent in assessing the content areas of trauma and how it affects the child's ability to communicate in the courtroom. The next chapter therefore discusses the concepts of trauma and emotional distress in children. Chapters 7 through 9 discuss clinical posttraumatic conditions, and chapter 10 focuses on communication abilities and disorders.

6

TRAUMA, EMOTIONAL DISTRESS, AND COURTROOM MODIFICATION EVALUATIONS

Emotional distress and *trauma*, terms that the law uses (see chaps. 2 and 3, this volume), are widely used but ill-defined and somewhat overlapping concepts. Because these constructs are often misunderstood, and consistent with our recommendations for reducing bias in chapter 5, mental health professional (MHP) evaluators should test their assumptions about emotional distress and trauma before proceeding with a courtroom modification assessment. This chapter reviews and discusses the definitions of these two constructs, with specific reference to information relevant to courtroom modification evaluations. Because this book concerns assessing how child witnesses deal and cope with the potential trauma of confronting the defendant in a case of alleged maltreatment, we also discuss the factors that influence how children cope with traumatic experiences.

EMOTIONAL DISTRESS

Emotional distress is a term that is used in the psychological and psychiatric literatures to refer to a broad range of negative psychological states in adults, adolescents, and children. Most commonly, this umbrella term is used as a proxy for internalizing symptoms, such as anxiety and depression (e.g., Roberts & Strayer, 1987; Steele, Phipps, & Srivastava, 1999). In other research, it also includes externalized symptoms. For example, one study with adolescent girls defined emotional distress as including depression, anxiety, and hostility given the overlap of these emotional states in this developmental stage (Milan et al., 2004). In still other cases with traumatized youth, emotional distress was equated with posttraumatic stress (e.g., McDermott & Palmer, 2002) or posttraumatic stress disorder (PTSD), as well as with depression, and/or anxiety (Mohlen, Parzer, Resch, & Brunner, 2005; Sabin, Zatzick, Jurkovich, & Rivara, 2006).

Emotional distress is typically measured using general symptom checklists, screeners, and inventories. An example of a child screening measure that defines emotional distress as anxiety, depression, and anger or acting out is the widely used and psychometrically sound Child Behavior Checklist (CBCL). The CBCL is a 120-item measure of the global constructs of internalizing and externalizing problems as well as social competencies over the past 6 months. Child, parent, and teacher forms are available, and problems are rated on a 3-point scale: 0 = *not true*, 1 = *somewhat or sometimes true*, 2 = *very true or often true*. For teenagers, the adolescent version of the CBCL (Youth Self Report) and the Brief Symptom Index (BSI; Derogatis, 1993) are often cited in the literature. The BSI is a 53-item scale used to assess overall emotional distress, which asks participants to rate how much various symptoms bothered them during the previous week on a 5-point Likert scale ranging from 0 (*not at all*) to 4 (*extremely*)—for example, "Tell me how much this problem has bothered you: feeling easily annoyed or irritated."

An example of a screening measure that equates emotional distress with PTSD, anxiety, and depression is the Pediatric Emotional Distress Scale (PEDS; Saylor, Swenson, Reynolds, & Taylor, 1999). Developed specifically for children and youth exposed to trauma, the PEDS is a 21-item scale completed by parents about their children age 2 to 10 years. Tapping into internalizing and externalizing symptoms, factor analyses on the 17 general behavior items in a sample of 475 children ages 2 to 10 years (exposed to traumatic events and nontraumatic events) yielded three reliable factors: Anxious–Withdrawn, Fearful, and Acting Out (Saylor et al., 1999). Continued development of the scale is needed, however, because work on the PEDS with a more diverse sample found support for only two factors (Act Out and Internalize; Spilsbury et al., 2005), whereas the four trauma-specific–PTSD items were not examined in the factor analyses.

Moreover, clinicians may use general measures of emotional distress before selecting a more specific trauma inventory (see next section) on the basis of the results of the screening. Given cross-cultural differences in some emotional distress measures, the measures should be scrutinized before interpreting scores (e.g., Norasakkunkit & Kalick, 2002). Although emotional distress measures give an indication of the severity of a child's condition, the MHP in a courtroom modification evaluation can, and arguably should, obtain more in-depth information about the child's symptoms of anxiety, depression, and posttraumatic stress, which we discuss in the next section. In addition, a *Diagnostic and Statistical Manual of Mental Disorders, Fourth Edition, Text Revision* (DSM–IV–TR; American Psychiatric Association, 2000) diagnosis can only be made with more specific measures. For this reason, the MHP in child modification cases should not rely solely on emotional distress screening assessments but should also directly evaluate for the conditions and disorders related to trauma.

TRAUMA

The concept of trauma is poorly and variously defined. Some sources refer to trauma as an event (e.g., Monahon, 1997; Terr, 1991). Others describe it as an individual's reactions to an event (e.g., Sparta, 2003) or the effects of an event or events, including symptoms, disorders, and syndromes. Still other sources appear to equate trauma with PTSD (e.g., Briere, 1996b; Piers, 1998), with more recent work critiquing such an approach (e.g., van der Kolk, 2007). This section discusses these three definitions in more detail.

Trauma Defined as an Event

Event-based definitions of trauma typically describe the nature of an event or experience in such a way that it is differentiated from normal or ordinary stressors, such as moving or undergoing a routine medical procedure. Children are commonly exposed to traumatic events; 25% to 40% of children in general population studies have reported exposure to at least one traumatic event in their lives (Costello, Erkanli, Fairbank, & Angold, 2002; Kassam-Adams & Winston, 2004, citing Boney-McCoy & Finkelor, 1995; Schwab-Stone, Fallon, Brigs, & Crowther, 1994). Event-based traumas can be grouped into two categories: noninterpersonal and interpersonal (Sparta, 2003). Noninterpersonal traumas include the following:

- accidental injuries, such as from motor vehicle accidents, especially those "that result in repeated or painful medical procedures, hospitalizations, or disfiguring injuries . . . lengthy rescue operations . . . [and those that] have claimed the lives of others" (Monahon, 1997, p. 11; see also Landolt, Vollrath, Ribi, Gnehm, & Sennhauser, 2003);
- chronic or severe illnesses, such as cancer, when accompanied by invasive and radical medical procedures (Monahon, 1997, citing Nir, 1995) and the child's or parent's appraisal of serious risk of harm from the illness (Stuber & Shemesh, 2003); and
- catastrophes and environmental disasters, including fires,

floods, tornados, earthquakes, hurricanes, volcanic eruptions, tsunamis, and nuclear accidents (Monahon, 1997; Renick, 2001).

The interpersonal category of trauma includes physical or sexual maltreatment; witnessing domestic violence or spousal murder; hate crimes, community violence, war, or school shootings; kidnapping; and traumatic losses ("[d]eaths which are sudden, violent, or expose a child to horrifying scenes or mutilation"; Monahon, 1997, p. 15). Intergenerational trauma (e.g., discrimination, forced assimilation, genocide) and internalized oppression should also be considered as historical and ongoing stressors that can co-occur with other types of interpersonal trauma in some minority groups, such as American Indian and Alaskan Native populations (Deters, Novins, Fickenscher, & Beals, 2006). This has been referred to as "compounded community trauma" (Deters et al., 2006, p. 336, citing Horowitz, Weine, & Jekel, 1995). Because intentional, interpersonal cruelty and evil tend to disrupt a person's ability to trust others, intentional events (e.g., kidnapping, murder) can result in more severe PTSD symptoms compared with natural disasters and accidents (Al-Mateen, 2002; American Psychiatric Association [DSM–IV–TR], 2000; Gabarino, Dubrow, Kostelny, & Pardo, 1998). Defined this way, therefore, noninterpersonal and interpersonal event-based trauma, "by its very nature, is unexpected . . . rare" (Renick, 2001, p. 30), "unusual, unpredictable, and outside the range of a child's typical experience" (Monahon, 1997, p. 10). However, ethnic minorities may experience traumatic events, especially the interpersonal trauma of community violence, more frequently than Caucasians (e.g., Avilas et al., 2006; Deters et al., 2006; J. M. Jones, 2007).

Often connected with event-based definitions of trauma are descriptions of its sequelae. In this way, the traumatic event is seen as a cause of an individual's difficulties. For example, psychological trauma has sometimes been described as "an overwhelming experience that can result in a continuum of posttrauma adaptations and/or specific symptoms" (Sparta, 2003, p. 209), and as "events that are so sudden, uncontrollable, and extremely negative that they produce overwhelming fear" (E. B. Carlson & Dutton, 2003, p. 133). DeBellis (1997) noted that interpersonal traumas may lead to symptoms that are more severe and of longer duration than symptoms of noninterpersonal traumas. However, researchers suggest that there is a direct relationship between the dose of exposure to disasters and transportation accidents (noninterpersonal traumas) and the severity of traumatic reactions (Pynoos, Steinberg, & Wraith, 1995).

Similarly, Terr (1990, 1991, 1994) proposed that two types of trauma lead to PTSD in children: Type I and Type II. Type I traumatic conditions involve unanticipated single events that result in the child experiencing full, detailed memories, "omens," and misperceptions. When such an event occurs suddenly, the child does not have the benefit of being able to mentally or physically prepare for it (Monahon, 1997). In such cases, the child may perceive the event as overwhelming, experience feelings of helplessness and despair (Terr, 1991), and demonstrate sleep difficulties and physiological hyperarousal (Famularo, Fenton, Kinscherff, & Augustyn, 1996). If acute symptoms occur, however, most resolve spontaneously without therapeutic intervention (Sparta, 2003). Unifying characteristics of both types of childhood trauma include (a) strongly visualized or otherwise repeatedly perceived memories; (b) repetitive behaviors; (c) trauma-specific fears; and (d) changed attitudes about people, aspects of life, and the future (Terr, 1991). Common symptom presentations are important to note because "no extant studies have indicated differing sequelae depending on type I versus type II distinction" (Lonigan, Phillips, & Richey, 2003, p. 174).

Type II traumas involve long-standing or repeated exposure to external events (e.g., ongoing sexual or physical abuse). Consequently, victims often come to expect them and may not experience the events as rare or abnormal. Some researchers note that children who have experienced Type II trauma show symptoms of denial, numbing, dissociation, rage (Terr, 1990, 1994), restricted affect, sadness, detachment (Famularo et al., 1996), and increased PTSD symptoms (Kaysen, Resick, & Wise, 2003). Repeated exposure to traumatic experiences may lead to problematic symptoms if the child is not able to benefit from moderating variables such as social support and positive coping skills (Sparta, 2003). As previously described, many event-based definitions of trauma do not adequately reflect the Type II traumatic experience. They also do not directly take into account the child's subjective experience of the event, which is an important factor in determining emotional distress (Weaver & Clum, 1995). Thus, event-based definitions should be expanded to account for the existence, nature, and child's experience of Type II traumas, including compounded community trauma and "polyvictimization" (Finkelhor, Ormrod, & Turner, 2007).

Even so, event-based definitions that imply a causal relationship between an event and an outcome are flawed. There is "no clear and simple cause-and-effect relationship between a traumatic experience and subsequent psychological symptoms. Two people can have the same traumatic experience yet show very different responses" (E. B. Carlson, 1997, p. 5). Some people recover from traumatic events with no behavioral, psychological, or physical effects (Konner, 2007; Renick, 2001). This is why examining a child's response to stressors is vital (Haugaard, 2005) and why trauma might be better understood from a broader developmental, multicultural, and biopsychosocial perspective.

Trauma Defined as Responses or Effects

The second and third approaches to defining trauma focus more on the responses of the individual in his or her context. For example, psychologists and lawyers have been said to define trauma "interchangeably" as "a qualitative degree of suffering within the child (an effect) or as a psychological consequence related to a forensically relevant event (cause)" (Sparta, 2003, p. 209). Traumatizing effects are those that potentially can shatter or change the expectations, worldviews, and even the nature of a person (Monahon, 1997). Others find that traumatizing effects can impair a child's future ability to "process information, regulate affect and adapt socially (Berliner, 1997)" (Sparta, 2003, p. 212; see also van der Kolk, 2007). Such effects may be due to neurological changes and impairments (Cook, Blaustein, Spinazzola, & van der Kolk, 2003), such as increased sympathetic nervous system activity, smaller brain size, and increased cortisol levels in children who have been maltreated or diagnosed with PTSD compared with control children (Pervanidou & Chrousos, 2007; Putnam, 2006). Sometimes the literature discusses the effects in descriptive terms that attempt to describe individuals' character or unconscious processes. For example, working from a psychoanalytic approach, Mills (2004) described clients with structural traumas as having a "damaged core, dislocated and polluted" who see themselves as "hopelessly damaged, maimed, flawed, and defective" (¶ 3).

Other professionals refer to them in the form of symptoms, emotions, disorders, and syndromes. The two most common symptoms of traumatic events are reexperiencing (e.g., the presence of intrusive thoughts or images of the event, flashbacks, nightmares, physiological reactions) and avoidance (E. B. Carlson, 1997). Although the emotion of fear has been described as the "essence of trauma," other emotions experienced by childhood trauma victims include "[h]elplessness, depression, shame, grief, and mental collapse" (van der Kolk, 2007, p. 225).

A number of psychological disorders are frequently observed following trauma, including adjustment disorder (qualified by possible features of anxious or depressed mood, disturbance of conduct, sleep disorders, academic inhibition, mixed emotional features, or mixed disturbance of emotions and conduct; Meyer, 1993), bereavement, acute stress disorder, PTSD, other anxiety disorders, dissociative disorders, depression, and substance abuse (Renick, 2001). Attention-deficit/hyperactivity disorder is also common in children with maltreatment histories (Ackerman, Newton, McPherson, Jones, & Dykman, 1998). For children who have experienced "the death of a loved one as unexpected, shocking, and frightening," a condition known as childhood traumatic grief may develop if they also experience subsequent traumatic symptoms that interfere with "their ability to negotiate the normal grieving process" (J. A. Cohen, Mannarino, Padlo, Greenberg, & Seslow, 2005, p. 7-2; see also Brown & Goodman, 2005). Thus, Sparta (2003) cautions that MHP evaluators should not limit assessments of childhood trauma to traditional diagnostic classification systems, such as *DSM–IV*, because

important areas of legally relevant information related to the child's response to traumatic events may be overlooked. Some children experience problems not detectable on standardized tests. Some have few symptoms; those who do not reach thresholds of clinical concerns may yet be at risk for "sleeper" effects, experiencing significant problems later in the developmental sequence. (p. 212)

As noted previously, some equate trauma and posttraumatic symptomology with the *DSM–IV* disorder of PTSD. This disorder is a helpful and relevant diagnosis to consider in courtroom modification assessments. As described in more detail in chapter 9 (this volume), the *DSM–IV* definition for PTSD takes into account the traumatic event as well as the individual's response to it (notably, reexperiencing and avoidance). It also is in accordance with the developmental model of stress, which conceptualizes trauma as having objective and subjective components (Pynoos et al., 1995).

However, the objective Criterion A of the *DSM–IV* definition of PTSD does not appear broad enough to cover all of the events that could produce traumatic symptoms. In addition, many of the subjective symptoms of PTSD cannot be reliably assessed in young children (Friedrich, 2002). At least 8 of the 18 criteria require verbal descriptions of the child's experience and internal states, which is an impossible task for infants, toddlers, preschoolers and some early elementary-school-age children (Friedrich, 2002; Scheeringa, Zeanah, Drell, & Larrieu, 1995). As noted earlier, the PTSD diagnosis also does not capture the wide range of traumatic responses in children (Sparta, 2003; van der Kolk, 2007) nor the factors that mediate its impact on developing children.

Recognizing that PTSD does not include all domains of impairment in some children exposed to maltreatment, researchers associated with the National Child Traumatic Stress Network have developed the concept of complex trauma (Cook et al., 2003) and proposed a "new diagnosis provisionally called 'developmental trauma disorder'" (van der Kolk, 2007, p. 233). Complex trauma has been used to describe "the dual problem" of children's exposure to multiple traumatic events (i.e., "simultaneous or sequential child maltreatment") and the "impact of this exposure on immediate and long term outcomes" (Cook et al., 2003, p. 5). Outcomes include symptoms that include but are not limited to PTSD symptoms, and span seven domains of impairment, including "(I) Attachment; (II) Biology; (III) Affect regulation; (IV) Dissociation; (V) Behavioral regulation; (VI) Cognition; and (VII) Self-concept" (Cook et al., 2003, p. 6). Similarly, developmental trauma disorder is said to develop out of multiple interpersonal traumatic events that (a) trigger a pattern of affective, somatic, behavioral, cognitive, and relational dysregulation in response to trauma cues; (b) result in altered attributions and expectancies about the self, others, and the world; and (c) are expressed in dysfunction in multiple domains of functioning (e.g., school, home; van der Kolk, 2007). Given the introduction of these constructs, they are in need of further study before MHPs can rely on them in a forensic context such as courtroom modification evaluations. For example, the National Child Traumatic Stress Network Complex Trauma Task Force noted that "[v]alid diagnostic classification of complex trauma sequelae in children awaits formal epidemiological research" (Cook et al., 2003, p. 6).

Finally, various syndromes have been established to help MHPs understand children's reactions to and ways of coping with various types of trauma, particularly abuse and its disclosure, including but not limited to

- battered child syndrome (Kempe, Silverman, Steele, Drogemueller, & Silver, 1962),
- child sexual abuse accommodation syndrome (Summitt, 1983; also known as the *child abuse syndrome* or the *sexually abused child syndrome*),
- child sexual abuse syndrome (Sgroi, 1982), and
- traumagenic dynamics (Finkelhor & Browne, 1985).

These syndromes describe a variety of physical, psychological, and behavioral effects that are said to be typically experienced by children after they have been abused. However, they are not clinical diagnoses or mental disorders. As with PTSD, these models of understanding reactions to trauma do not "provide an adequate description of the full ranges of responses to these events [child sexual abuse]" (Sbraga & O'Donohue, 2003, p. 323). Despite their inefficiency, lack of specificity, and questionable empirical support, some MHPs have included syndromes in their expert testimony in child maltreatment cases. Regarding the courtroom modification assessment, syndromes do not appear to be of functional assistance because they do not assess the relevant *Craig* issues of the severity or likely future cause of emotional distress in a courtroom setting. Therefore, although they may have a place in research and clinical settings, syndromes should not be used for courtroom modification purposes.

In sum, trauma is best understood in a way that is similar to descriptions of sexual abuse. As Friedrich (2002) put it, "[u]nlike depression or anxiety disorders in children, sexual abuse is not a disorder characterized by a discrete cluster of symptoms. Rather, it is an experience with widely diverse manifestations" (p. 56). Likewise, trauma can be described as a biopsychosocial experience of stress from historical and current sources that manifests itself in a variety of sequelae, and not all sequelae are emotionally distressing. As Konner (2007) noted, Hans Selye's classic stress model or "general adaptation syndrome" includes some stress experiences that are "negative and can impair future functioning, whereas other stress is positive, producing effective coping and enhancing the organism's long-term function" (p. 308).

COPING

A child's responses to a traumatic event or series of events are affected by a number of variables, including but not limited to the following (Briere, 2004; E. B. Carlson, 1997; Chandy, Blum, & Resnick, 1996; Meiser-Stedman, 2002; Rosen, Milich, & Harris, 2007; Rutter, 2007; Saywitz, Mannarino, Berliner, & Cohen, 2000; Silverman & La Greca, 2002; Sparta, 2003; Vernberg, La Greca, Silverman, & Prinstein, 1996):

- the characteristics of the stressor or events(s) (e.g., severity; duration; Type I or II, complex trauma, combined community trauma);
- the characteristics of the child (e.g., age, gender, race, ethnicity, culture, personality, predisposition for autonomic arousal, coping abilities, comorbid or premorbid developmental–psychological conditions);
- the child's subjective cognitive processes, including appraisals or perceptions of the stressor or event(s) as negative;
- responses of the child's support system to the stress and the child; and
- the characteristics of the child's environment.

Because these risk and protective factors "account for significant variability among children who experience what appears to be equivalent stressors . . . it is essential for forensic evaluators to view each child's situation as unique" (Sparta, p. 212). When viewing a child, MHPs are reminded that "not everyone exposed to even severe stressors develops PTSD" and "the typical response to acute psychological trauma is recovery over time" (Konner, 2007, pp. 319–320). Indeed, most are resilient to trauma (Feeny, Foa, Treadwell, & March, 2004; Salzer & Bickman, 1999).

For this reason, MHPs should examine a child's coping and resilience, which occurs across evolving, multifaceted, and interacting domains of competency in the child's individual, familial, and sociocultural environments (Hjemdal, Friborg, Stiles, Martinussen, & Rosenvinge, 2006; Masten & Coatsworth, 1998; Waller, 2001). Although a few studies revealed that avoidance coping is commonly used by adolescent survivors of sexual abuse, this emotion-focused type of coping is associated with greater levels of distress in adolescents (Whiffen & MacIntosh, 2005) and PTSD in children (Kaplow, Dodge, Amaya-Jackson, & Saxe, 2005). Constructs related to coping and resilience such as posttraumatic growth, hardiness, and thriving have come under increased attention in part because of the positive psychology movement, but studies with children and adolescents are still limited (e.g., Ickovics et al., 2006).

Factors found to be "most critical for promoting resilience" include (a) positive attachment (Bowlby, 1988) and connections to emotionally supportive and competent adults within a child's family or community, (b) development of cognitive and self-regulation abilities, (c) positive beliefs about oneself, and (d) motivation to act effectively in one's environment (Cook et al., 2003, p. 20, citing Luthar et al., 2000; Masten, 2001; Werner

& Smith, 1992; Wyman, Sandler, Wolchik, & Nelson, 2000). In sexually abused children, social support, and particularly maternal support, plays a key role in determining outcome (Cook et al., 2003; Finkelhor & Kendall-Tackett, 1997). Similarly, kinship supports as well as spirituality were sources of resilience against developing complex trauma PTSD for a sample of African American children living with poverty and chronic community violence (J. M. Jones, 2007).

CONCLUSION

Because the goal of the courtroom modification assessment is to gauge a child's level of emotional distress and trauma when in the presence of the defendant, MHP evaluators should be familiar with assessing the most common posttraumatic reactions in children. Trauma symptoms for which the "principal manifestation is emotional distress include fear, anxiety, low self-esteem, and sadness/depression" (Kolko & Swenson, 2002, p. 11). Also, as noted earlier, two of the most common posttraumatic symptoms are re-experiencing and avoidance (E. B. Carlson, 1997; Meiser-Stedman, 2002). With specific attention to childhood sexual abuse, in a review of the research on the most common types of emotional distress related to this experience, Whiffen and MacIntosh (2005) cited posttraumatic stress disorder, dissociation, depression, and anxiety.

Therefore, the next three chapters discuss the generally recognized clinical conditions most frequently associated with trauma and emotional distress (chap. 7: "Posttraumatic Stress Disorder"; chap. 8: "Dissociation"; chap. 9: "Fear, Anxiety, and Depression"). Although "considerable similarity has been found in both the patterning and prevalence of problems among children from many very different cultures (Ivanova et al., 2005; Rescorla et al., 2005)" (Achenbach, 2005, p. 545), the chapters highlight ethnic or cultural differences as reported in the literature so that the MHP is reminded to take into account the child's context during assessment. An examination of factors related to a child's vulnerabilities as well as resilience should be part of that contextual view (Konner, 2007).

Our discussion takes a wide view of diagnostic possibilities because "relying only on *DSM–IV* criteria can result in an evaluation in which a tail of symptoms wags a diagnostic dog, thus finding only that for which one is looking" (Drake, Bush, & van Gorp, 2001, p. 4). *DSM–IV* criteria and instruments designed to assess for its disorders also may not apply to children across and within ethnic groups and may not fully take into account culture-bound syndromes (Gee, 2004; see *DSM–IV–TR*, 2000, Appendix I, for a glossary of culture-bound syndromes). Specific attention is given to the population of allegedly abused children because they are often the subject of courtroom modification requests. After defining each condition, we discuss available assessment measures and explore whether (and which) measures provide information that would be helpful (relevant and reliable) in a courtroom modification assessment (i.e., the severity of the emotional distress and its nature and source).

7

POSTTRAUMATIC STRESS DISORDER AND COURTROOM MODIFICATION EVALUATIONS

Posttraumatic stress disorder (PTSD), one of the two most distinctive posttraumatic responses (E. B. Carlson, 1997) and a "core manifestation of sexual abuse trauma" (Kaplow, Dodge, Amaya-Jackson, & Saxe, 2005, p. 1305), is an accepted way to conceptualize traumatic and posttraumatic stress and emotional distress symptoms in adults and children. It is included as a *Diagnostic and Statistical Manual of Mental Disorders, Fourth Edition, Text Revision* (*DSM–IV–TR*; American Psychiatric Association [APA], 2000) diagnosis applicable to children and adolescents, including alleged victims of abuse who are the subject of courtroom modification assessments. This chapter reviews diagnostic issues related to PTSD in children and adolescents and the available assessment instruments that are appropriate for use in the courtroom modification evaluation.

DIAGNOSIS OF POSTTRAUMATIC STRESS DISORDER

According to the current edition of the *DSM* (*DSM–IV–TR*; APA, 2000), PTSD is an anxiety disorder that may be diagnosed when an individual feels horror, intense fear, or helplessness (children may also display disorganized or agitated behavior) after having been exposed to a traumatic event that involved a violation of physical integrity or actual or threatened serious injury or death. Then, for at least 1 month, the person persistently reexperiences the event, displays symptoms of increased arousal, tries to avoid stimuli associated with the traumatic event, and shows a numbing of general responsiveness. These symptoms may be defined in various ways and with various expressions by "people of different cultural, national, linguistic, spiritual, and ethnic backgrounds . . . (e.g., flashbacks may be 'visions,' hyperarousal may be 'attacque de nerves,' dissociation may be spirit 'possession'"; Cook, Blaustein, Spinazzola, & van der Kolk, 2003, p. 18). Last, these four disturbances cause the person to experience clinically significant distress or impairment in a number of important areas of functioning, such as school, work, and home.

There is "extraordinary variability in the onset and course of PTSD" (Rosenberg, 2001, p. 36; see also Blank, 1993). The onset and duration of symptoms may affect the type of PTSD that is diagnosed in a number of ways. If symptoms last 1 to 3 months, the child may receive a specification of acute PTSD; if symptoms persist longer than 3 months, specification of chronic PTSD is appropriate. Delayed-onset PTSD may be specified when symptoms do not appear for at least 6 months after the traumatic event. Blank (1993) also noted that symptoms can be intermittent or recurrent.

Predictors of initial PTSD symptoms include negative coping strategies, such as blame and anger (Lonigan, Phillips, & Richey, 2003). Other factors that mediate the development of PTSD in children include parental distress related to the trauma, parental support, and the child's temporal proximity to the stressor (J. A. Cohen & Mannarino, 2000; Foy, Madvig, Pynoos, & Camilleri, 1996; Lubit, Hartwell, van Gorp, & Eth, 2002; Ostrowski, Christopher, & Delahanty, 2007; Schetky & Guyer, 2002). Cultural, racial, and ethnic variables can serve as risk (e.g., Ko, 2005) as well as protective factors (e.g., Rabalais, Ruggiero, & Scotti, 2002).

On the basis of data from research with adults, it has been hypothesized that dissociative (chap. 8, this volume) and depressive symptoms (chap. 9, this volume) predict chronic PTSD in children (Laor et al., 2002), but "to date we have little understanding as to whether children manifest dissociative symptoms in a similar manner to adults following trauma, and whether such symptoms are associated with the development of PTSD in this population" (Kenardy et al., 2007, p. 457). However, Kaplow et al. (2005) found that dissociation symptoms reported by children after forensic interviews for suspected sexual abuse directly predicted parent report of PTSD symptoms 7 to 36 months later. Kaplow et al. also found that life stress and anxiety–avoidance predicted PTSD symptoms. Similarly, another prospective study following a community sample of first-grade children into young adulthood found that early childhood depressive and anxiety problems "predicted an increased risk for PTSD following exposure to traumatic events" (Storr, Ialongo, Anthony, & Breslau, 2007, p. 124).

Finally, acute stress disorder (ASD) is a separate *DSM–IV* diagnosis used to describe stress reactions that occur in the first month after a traumatic event, with special emphasis on the presence of dissociative symptoms (chap. 8, this volume), but do not persist longer than 1 month. ASD was first introduced in the *DSM–IV* (APA, 1994) without empirical support but with the goal of identifying acutely traumatized people who would go on to develop chronic PTSD (Bryant, 2003). In other words, ASD is often treated in the literature as a "provisional PTSD" diagnosis, with the diagnosis being changed to PTSD if symptoms are present for at least 1 month. Unfortunately, ASD has limited predictive power in subsequent studies of adults (Bryant, 2003) and children (e.g., Kassam-Adams & Winston, 2004). "Acute stress disorder has limited usefulness as a screening criterion because most people who develop PTSD never meet diagnostic criteria for ASD, and very little scientific information pertains to children" (Friedman, Foa, & Charney, 2003, p. 766). In addition, diagnostic distinctions between PTSD and ASD "were made with little evidence from children" (Saxe et al., 2003, p. 973). Furthermore, although ASD has been studied in a handful of studies with child and adolescent trauma survivors, empirical support for the diagnosis in this population is limited (March, 2003; Meiser-Stedman, Dalgleish, Smith, Yule, & Glucksman, 2007). There are no assessment measures specific to ASD in children, although screening measures are in development (Saxe et al., 2003; Winston et al., 2002) and supplemental items to an existing anxiety interview schedule (i.e., Anxiety Disorders Interview Schedule for *DSM–IV*: Child and Parent Versions [ADIS–IV: C/P]; Silverman & Albano, 1996; reviewed in chap. 9, this volume) have been created (Meiser-Stedman, Dalgleish, et al., 2007; Meiser-Stedman, Smith, Glucksman, Yule, & Dalgleish, 2007). For these reasons, at least at this time, we caution against using ASD as the sole way to predict a child's future emotional condition during courtroom testimony without validated assessment measures.

PTSD is a relatively new disorder in the psychological and psychiatric literatures. Although various forms of posttraumatic responses have been recognized for hundreds of years (L. S. O'Brien, 1998), PTSD was not formally recognized as a distinct diagnostic entity until it was included in the third edition of the *DSM*. After PTSD was incorporated into the *Diagnostic and Statistical Manual of Mental Disorders, Third Edition* (*DSM–III*) in 1980 (APA), initial research on this diagnosis focused on adults, primarily combat veterans and rape victims. At that time, it was thought that the diagnosis was not applicable to children and adolescents (Dyregrov & Yule, 2006). One result is that studies of children diagnosed with PTSD (including theory, assessment, and treatment issues) are in their infancy, but it "is the subject of a burgeoning corpus of research" (Meiser-Stedman, 2002, p. 217).

Notwithstanding calls for changes to the *DSM–IV*,[1] PTSD is recognized as a diagnosis applicable to many children who have suffered different traumatic experiences (e.g., Famularo, Fenton, Kinscherff, & Augustyn, 1996; Famularo, Fenton, Kinscherff, Ayoub, & Barnum, 1994; Jaycox et al., 2002; Linning & Kearney, 2004; Qouta, Punamäki, & Sarraj, 2003; Saigh, 1987, 1989; Saigh, Yasik, Oberfield, Halamandaris, & McHugh, 2002; Ta-ïeb, Moro, Baubet, Revah-Lévy, & Flament, 2003; Wolfe, Sas, & Wekerle, 1994). The *DSM–IV* commentary regarding PTSD states that the disorder can occur at any age, and as a result, the diagnostic criteria specifically provide for children. *DSM–IV* recognizes that children may reexperience the trauma through repetitive play, trauma-specific reenactment, and frightening dreams without recognizable content. Regarding the symptom domain of increased arousal, the *DSM–IV* notes irritability and anger outbursts as diagnostic symptoms of the disorder. For example, in a study of traumatized children and adults, those with PTSD reported higher anger estimates than did children without PTSD and children in a control group (Saigh, Yasik, Oberfield, & Halamandaris, 2007).

Research has also found other differences in children's PTSD symptom expression and reporting. When compared with adults with PTSD, children with PTSD are more likely to have sleep disturbances (Schetky & Guyer, 2002) but less likely to show emotional numbing and report avoidance reactions (Dyregrov & Yule, 2006; Eth & Pynoos, 1985; Scheeringa, Wright, Hunt, & Zeanah, 2006). In addition, when asked directly, children are more likely to report PTSD symptoms than when their parents are asked about their child's symptom presentation (Dyregrov & Yule, 2006; Meiser-Stedman, Smith, et al., 2007; Scheeringa et al., 2006). Dyregrov and Yule (2006) offered three reasons for this finding. First, they suggested that children may not discuss traumatic events and their consequences with their parents because they recognize that it would upset their parent(s), and as a result, their parent(s) may not be aware of their need to process their experience. Second, parents who struggle with their own traumatic symptoms may have reduced abilities to support their children. Third, parents may intentionally limit discussions with their children to protect them or to maintain

---

[1]For example, some controversy exists regarding application of the existing *DSM–IV* criteria for PTSD in children because it does not fully address the diagnostic distinctions proposed by Terr (1991) as discussed in chapter 6 (this volume) and may not be appropriate for young children (e.g., Scheeringa, Zeanah, Drell, & Larrieu, 1995; Scheeringa, Zeanah, Myers, & Putnam, 2003), as discussed later. Others debate whether PTSD should be placed in its current classification system with the anxiety disorders; alternative nosology include the dissociative disorders, a new broad stress response systems category, or the disorders of extreme stress not otherwise specified (Brett, 1993; L. S. O'Brien, 1998). Still others argue that PTSD is a normal reaction to stress and not a disorder or illness (e.g., Blank, 1991; for a review of the issue, see Yehuda & McFarlane, 1995).

cultural norms, or unintentionally use a more restrictive narrative communication style. Although problems with parent–child agreement has been well established with other anxiety disorders, it has received little attention in the PTSD and ASD literature (Meiser-Stedman, Smith, et al., 2007) and deserves future research.

Debate exists in the field, however, about the need to develop new diagnostic criteria for PTSD in young children. Some argue that the *DSM–IV* criteria are not sensitive enough to make the diagnosis in infants and preschoolers (Kaplow, Saxe, Putnam, Pynoos, & Lieberman, 2006; Scheeringa et al., 1995, 2006; Scheeringa, Zeanah, Myers, & Putnam, 2003; Yorbik, Akbiyik, Kirmizigul, & Söhmen, 2004). In a study of children aged 2 to 16 years after the 1999 earthquake in Turkey, age-related differences were found in the perception of and responses to trauma (Yorbik et al., 2004). Some young children may not have the cognitive or verbal skills to describe their experiences and articulate their emotions (Friedrich, 2002; Quinn, 1995). As a result, Scheeringa and his colleagues (1995, 2003, 2006; Scheeringa, Peebles, Cook, & Zeanah, 2001) have been developing alternate criteria for PTSD for preschool children. Their proposed changes include reducing and modifying the number of required existing PTSD criteria and creating new criteria (i.e., loss of previously acquired developmental skills, new separation anxiety, new aggression, new fears that seem unrelated to traumatic stimuli). Yorbik et al. (2004) agreed that new criteria recognizing regressive behaviors and newly developed fears should be part of the diagnostic criteria. However, Lonigan et al. (2003) noted that there is little data concerning the validity of these variations. In fact, Scheeringa et al.'s (2003) validation study of their proposed criteria found that the "four novel symptoms did not substantially add to the diagnostic validity of the criteria" (p. 561). Thus, although MHPs should take a developmentally sensitive approach when assessing for PTSD in young children (March, 1998, 2003; Pynoos, 1994; Pynoos et al., 1995), further research using well-validated measures of PTSD is needed before changing the *DSM–IV* criteria for PTSD (Dyregrov & Yule, 2006; Lonigan et al., 2003) given the differing levels of agreement in the field about the range and severity of posttraumatic stress reactions in this population (Dyregrov & Yule, 2006).

For children who are abused or allegedly abused child witnesses, research suggests that PTSD is an appropriate clinical construct for describing and understanding the reactions and clinical conditions that some of them may experience. Some investigations have shown that child maltreatment is a significant risk factor for short- and long-term PTSD, especially for those children who have suffered severe or chronic abuse (Dubner & Motta, 1999; Famularo et al., 1994; Foy et al., 1996; Linning & Kearney, 2004; Widom, 1999). An epidemiological review of clinical studies found estimates of child and adolescent PTSD that ranged from 18.2% to 53.8% for sexual assault and abuse and from 11.1% to 70.8% for physical assault and abuse (Saigh, Yasik, Sack, & Koplewicz, 1999). One study of sexually and physically abused youth aged 7 to 13 years found that children who had been subjected to both forms of abuse had higher prevalence rates of PTSD than the children who had been only physically or only sexually abused (Ackerman, Newton, McPherson, Jones, & Dykman, 1998). When comparing sexually maltreated children with those in general clinical child populations, sexually abused children show a higher frequency of PTSD (Becker et al., 1995; Kendall-Tackett, Williams, & Finkelhor, 1993; McLeer, Callaghan, Henry, & Wallen, 1994). Whereas earlier PTSD studies examined children receiving treatment in psychiatric hospitals or outpatient clinics, more recent work has looked at abused children in a wider variety of settings, such as court-referred services, shelters, and foster care placements (e.g., Brosky & Lally, 2004; Dubner & Motta, 1999; Linning & Kearney, 2004).

Child maltreatment and exposure to domestic violence are highly co-morbid (Dickstein, 2002; Edelson, 1999; Fantuzzo & Mohr, 1999; Shipman, Rossman, & West, 1999). Exposure to domestic violence can include "watching or hearing the violent events, direct involvement (e.g., trying to intervene or calling the police), or experiencing the aftermath (e.g., seeing bruises or observing maternal depression)" (Fantuzzo & Mohr, 1999, p. 22). Because children may also acquire PTSD through means other than direct experience, such as observation and verbal mediation (Osofsky, 1995; Saigh, 1991), children who have been exposed to the abuse of loved ones may develop PTSD (L. S. Carter, Weithhorn, & Behrman, 1999) among other negative effects and conditions (Dickstein, 2002; Johnson et al., 2002; Margolin & Gordis, 2000). Given the negative effects of witnessing domestic violence, some states have expanded their definitions of emotional maltreatment to include exposure to domestic violence.

Several methodological considerations limit the validity of these prevalence studies and statistics, however. The studies all involved children about whom a report of child maltreatment had been made or confirmed. This may result in inaccurate estimates of the incidence rates of PTSD as a result of maltreatment because children often do not report traumatic events to anyone (Bruck & Ceci, 2004; Lyons, 1988). In addition, older studies may underestimate rates because PTSD has only recently been recognized as an important diagnosis to consider when evaluating children. Other methodological concerns that may alter the prevalence rates include, but are not limited to, the use of retrospective reports and cross-sectional designs, selection of study samples from settings that are highly likely to have skewed prevalence rates for PTSD (e.g., inpatient facilities), samples containing co-morbid physical and sexual abuse, the use of different assessment instruments with varying sensitivity and specificity, differing sources for symptom reporting (e.g., self-reports, teacher opinions), and the use of different diagnostic criteria (i.e., *DSM–III*, *Diagnostic and Statistical Manual of Mental Disorders, Third Edition, Revised* [*DSM–III–R*], *DSM–IV*; APA, 1980, 1987, 1994).

In addition to methodological difficulties in studying this population, little is known about the role of risk and protective factors (mediating and moderating variables) and their interactions in the development of PTSD symptoms in young persons exposed to trauma (Amaya-Jackson & March, 1995). In the past 10 to 15 years, research has attempted to identify the effects of such variables, including demographic factors, cultural factors, neurobiological conditions, preexisting psychological conditions or disorders, the presence of psychiatric comorbidity, other life events, prior trauma, social support, social cognition (e.g., threat appraisals, metacognitions, rumination), and parental and familial functioning and reactions to the traumatic event. For example, Tolin and Foa's (2006) meta-analysis of articles spanning the past 25 years found that girls and women were more likely to meet criteria for PTSD than boys and men. Last and Perrin (1993, as cited in Austin & Chorpita, 2004a) found "higher lifetime prevalence of posttraumatic stress disorder [based on *DSM–III–R* criteria] among African American versus White children even when controlling for the effects of socioeconomic status" (p. 217); other studies show no difference in PTSD symptoms by race or ethnicity (Dubner & Motta, 1999; Mennen, 1995). Regarding child maltreatment, although the severity of exposure to abuse affects PTSD symptomology (Foy et al., 1996), the effects of trauma may be mediated by the child's initial psychological reaction (e.g., cognitions, attributions) to the abuse (Daigneault, Tourigny, & Hébert, 2006; Dalgleish, Meiser-Stedman, & Smith, 2005; Valle & Silovsky, 2002; Wolfe et al., 1994), his or her locus of control (Amaya-Jackson & March, 1995), the parent's response (Schetky, 2003), the parent's own posttraumatic stress symptoms (Ostrowski, Christopher, & Delahanty, 2007), and family support and parental monitoring (Tyler, 2002).

Finally, trauma and maltreatment have been associated with psychological consequences other than PTSD, and PTSD is often comorbid or intercurrent with other disorders (Hawkins & Radcliffe, 2006; March, 1998; Saigh, Sack, Yasik, & Koplewicz, 1999; Yasik, Saigh, Oberfield, & Halamandaris, 2007). Abused children with PTSD have been found to experience comorbid problems, including mood and anxiety disorders (chap. 9, this volume; Ackerman et al., 1998; Dykman et al., 1997; Kilpatrick et al., 2003), dissociative symptoms (chap. 8, this volume; Lipschitz, Winegar, Hartnick, Foote, & Southwick, 1999), externalizing problems (Tyler, 2002), and adverse neurobiological development (DeBellis et al., 1999, 2002; Kaplan, Pelcovitz, & Labruna, 1999; Perry, 1996; van der Kolk, 2003, 2007). Nevertheless, it is important to remember that there is no single item or cluster of items, including posttraumatic responses, that can say definitively whether or not a child has been abused (Campbell, 1997; Friedrich, 1995).

POSTTRAUMATIC STRESS DISORDER ASSESSMENT MEASURES

As part of a multidimensional evaluation (Kendall-Tackett et al., 1993), the assessment of PTSD in children should involve extensive record reviews and history taking, clinical interviews with the child and important adults (e.g., parents), diagnostic interviews with the child, direct observations (Kratochwill, 1996; Nader, Stuber, & Pynoos, 1991), and psychological testing with the child. A consensus exists that a combination of parent and child reports is "most likely to yield the most accurate assessment of internalizing symptomatology" (Scheeringa et al., 2006, p. 645).

Because incorporating the child's developmental context is an essential part of the assessment process, general psychological testing of the child's cognitive (including intelligence, memory, language, and executive functioning), emotional, adaptive, and academic functioning may be needed along with specific trauma and PTSD measures (American Academy of Child and Adolescent Psychiatry, 1997b; Drake et al., 2001; Sparta, 2003). Psychophysiological measures may also be considered, such as the Stroop test (Dubner & Motta, 1999; McNally, 1996). Unlike more transparent structured interviews or self-report measures, physiological measures are the "only tests which appear to have the likelihood of being robust against dissimulation" (L. S. O'Brien, 1998, p. 259). But research evidence showing greater physiological arousal in the context of traumatic stimuli has come from only adult samples (Tolin & Foa, 2006), and the predictive validity of measures such as resting heart rate is limited (Bryant, Salmon, Sinclair, & Davidson, 2007). Further research connecting physiological and behavioral measures is warranted (Hawkins & Radcliffe, 2006).

More specifically, cognitive testing should be considered because clinical research has shown that "youths with intelligence scores in the deficient and borderline range find it difficult to understand the questions that are needed to formulate a PTSD diagnosis. We have also repeatedly noticed that such youths provide inconsistent answers" (Saigh & Yasik, 2002, p. 623). As a result, findings are mixed on the relationship between trauma, PTSD, and IQ in children and adolescents, and the directionality of results is unclear. For example, low IQ at age 5 was found to predict PTSD in adulthood (Koenen, Moffitt, Poulton, Martin, & Caspi, 2007), and PTSD associated with interpersonal trauma may negatively affect verbal IQ scores (Saltzman, Weems, & Carrion, 2006). In addition, learning and memory problems have been found in a sample of traumatized children and adolescents with PTSD but were not found in traumatized youth without PTSD or control children (Yasik et al., 2007).

Broader psychological (and neuropsychological) testing will help the MHP assess for PTSD symptoms not contained in the *DSM–IV* and for comorbid conditions, such as attention-deficit/hyperactivity disorder, conduct disorder, oppositional–defiant disorder, depression, anxiety, and substance-related disorders (for reviews, see Barkley, 1997; Pelcovitz & Kaplan, 1996; Perrin, Smith, & Yule, 2000; Pfefferbaum, 1997; Saigh et al., 1999). The most reliable method of evaluating for PTSD, therefore, is to use a comprehensive assessment process in which the MHP relies on convergent information from different types of appropriate instruments and sources of information.

Assessment tools designed specifically to assess PTSD in children are essential in this regard (March, 1998) and are integral to the MHP's courtroom modification assessment. There are two general categories of specific PTSD measures: clinician-administered structured or semistructured interviews with the child, parent, or both and child self-report or parent-report measures (Allen, 1994; Drake et al., 2001; Miller & Veltkamp, 1995; Ohan, Myers, & Collett, 2002). More recently, there has been increased interest in child PTSD coupled with the development of many new PTSD assessment instruments for clinical and research use with this population. Given the relatively new and specialized nature of these instruments, most of the tools may not have been a part of an MHP's general clinical training. For some excellent review articles on various measures for assessing PTSD and other trauma-related disorders, see Hawkins and Radcliffe (2006, reviewing 7 measures); March (1998, reviewing 16 measures); Nader (1997, reviewing 12 measures); Ohan et al. (2002, reviewing 15 measures); Strand, Sarmiento, and Pasquale (2005, reviewing 35 measures).

Unfortunately for courtroom modification assessment purposes, and despite the lengthy list of existing measures, the field still lacks psychometrically validated and standardized tools for assessing PTSD and other trauma-related symptoms in children (Briere, Elliott, Harris, & Cotman, 1995; Drake et al., 2001; Hawkins & Radcliffe, 2006; Saxe et al., 2003). Although progress is being made, "[d]espite thirty years of research, assessment tools for pediatric PTSD leaves a lot to be desired with respect to breadth of symptom coverage, developmental sensitivity, ability to inventory the stressor as well as PTSD symptoms, and basic psychometric properties" (March, 1998, p. 214). Also, the validity of using instruments normed on Caucasian youth with "multiethnic, multinational youth" is "another open question" (Hawkins & Radcliffe, 2006, p. 422). Obviously, as new validation studies are published, these concerns and conclusions could change. Thus, MHPs must keep current with the literature, choose such instruments wisely, and be prepared to address the strengths and weaknesses of the chosen instruments in their reports and on the witness stand.

When choosing methods for the courtroom modification assessment, MHPs should rely on the best available measures. The ideal assessment tool for PTSD according to the National Institute of Mental Health consensus panel on the assessment of pediatric PTSD is one that should

(1) provide reliable and valid ascertainment of symptoms across multiple domains; (2) identify objective and subjective responses to divergent

traumatic events; (3) evaluate symptom severity; (4) incorporate and reconcile multiple observations, such as parent and child ratings; and (5) be sensitive to treatment-induced change in symptoms. (March, 1998, p. 199)

In the forensic context, the need to demonstrate symptom reliability and validity across methods (Criteria 1 and 4) is especially important (Drake et al., 2001). Structured and semistructured interviews with children and important adults are preferable to unstructured clinical interviews because they tend to provide more reliable data, but the measures still must be psychometrically sound. Of course, the validity of the interview data also depends on factors such as interviewer bias (also see discussion in chap. 5, this volume), interviewer training and cultural competence, establishment of positive rapport, and adherence to the interview structure. Reliability and validity data of self- and parent-report measures and observational techniques should also be scrutinized.

When using various techniques and reporters, MHPs should be aware of and assess for inconsistencies and inaccuracies (Steward & Steward, 1996), false reporting (Allen, 1994), underreporting, and malingering (Schetky, 2003). When examining inconsistencies, MHPs should be aware that parent and child reports of internal symptoms do not always correspond; children's self-reports tend to indicate more distress compared with adult reports of the child's internal distress (Lonigan et al., 2003).

MHPs will be examining whether and how a child is experiencing any of the four major categories of posttraumatic symptoms (i.e., persistently reexperiencing the event, displaying symptoms of increased arousal, trying to avoid stimuli associated with the traumatic event, and showing a numbing of general responsiveness) if the child has been exposed to a traumatic event that involved a violation of physical integrity or actual or threatened serious injury or death. For example, a child who reexperiences a traumatic event can experience involuntary flashbacks or other negative stimuli associated with the incident(s). In reaction to intrusive and negative stimuli, children with PTSD may respond to such stimuli with avoiding symptoms.

Triggers of such symptoms should also be explored because they might include settings or individuals, such as the courtroom or defendant. Common triggers of intrusive symptoms and flashbacks in sexual abuse victims include disclosures of one's abuse experiences and abusive behavior of other adults (Briere, 1992). In physical abuse victims, flashbacks are often triggered by overt conflict with others or by being in the presence of someone who is in some way physically frightening.

In addition, MHPs should review the frequency, duration, and intensity of PTSD symptoms to assess the likelihood of future continuation of such posttraumatic symptomology in the courtroom setting. Frequency and intensity can be seen to be measures of severity because they measure the qualitative differences among children's abuse responses. In forensic settings, measures that assess "frequency and severity of each PTSD symptom as well as inquiring about specific examples would be better than a brief self-report measure that yields only one rating of frequency per symptom" (E. B. Carlson & Dutton, 2003, p. 135). In addition, the duration and course of the child's posttraumatic stress need to be assessed as part of a severity determination. In cases of substantiated abuse, whether a child was subjected to a single incident of abuse or multiple incidents over a period of time may affect the nature and the duration of their reactions to the abuse (Nader, 1997). Furthermore, the child's posttraumatic stress reaction may vary over time. The course of PTSD symptoms is affected by the child's developmental stage and the cyclical nature of PTSD (Realmuto et al., 1992). Children from ethnic minority populations may often experience more severe symptomology for longer periods of time than do children from the majority group (J. A. Cohen, Deblinger, Mannarino, & de Arellano, 2001; Ko, 2005; but see Mennen, 2004).

Of the currently available PTSD assessment instruments, only two psychometrically sound tools (psychometric properties in the good to excellent range, as discussed previously) include ratings of frequency and intensity: the Childhood PTS Reaction Index (CPTS–RI; Frederick, Pynoos, & Nader, 1992) and the Clinician-Administered PTSD Scale for Children and Adolescents for *DSM–IV* (CAPS–C/CAPS–CA; Nader et al., 1998, 2002; Nader, Kriegler, Blake, & Pynoos, 1994).

The CPTS–RI is a widely used and heavily studied 20-item scale that can be used with children aged 8 to 18. Appearing suitable across a variety of traumatic experiences, the CPTS–RI has been translated for use in Armenia, Bosnia, Cambodia, Herzegovina, and Kuwait and with Spanish-speaking students in Los Angeles (Strand et al., 2005). The clinician can administer the CPTS–RI as a semistructured interview to children or give it as a self-report measure for older children and adolescents. Most often it is used as a self-report measure (Hawkins & Radcliffe, 2006). Administration is estimated to take between 20 and 45 minutes with American children (Nader, 1997). Parallel parent questionnaires are also available.

Children are asked to rate the frequency of posttraumatic symptoms on a 5-point Likert scale with items ranging from *none of the time* to *most of the time*. Although it does not map directly on *DSM–IV* criteria, the CPTS–RI factor structure partially overlaps with the three *DSM–IV* factors of reexperiencing, arousal, and avoidance (Ohan et al., 2002). It also provides a scoring system that establishes a "level of 'PTSD'" (Nader, 1997, p. 310), with symptom cutoff scores ranging from mild (12–24), moderate (25–39), severe (40–59), and very severe (more than 60). Because it has been used "most effectively in studies of children in the acute phase or first few years after a single incident," it is unclear how well it captures information about prolonged exposure to trauma or delayed reports (Nader, 1997, p. 311). An updated version, the UCLA PTSD Reaction Index (Pynoos, Goenjian, &

Steinberg, 1998), is currently under development (A. M. Steinberg, Brymer, Decker, & Pynoos, 2004).

The CAPS–CA is a semistructured clinical interview designed for use with children aged 8 to 15 years. On the basis of the adult *DSM–III* and *DSM–II–R* Clinician-Administered PTSD Scale (CAPS), the CAPS–C was created for children on the basis of *DSM–IV* criteria in 1994 and has been revised in 1998 and 2002.

After a life events checklist is completed regarding the history of traumatic events the child reports having experienced, the CAPS–CA is used to measure the frequency and intensity of symptoms associated with the *DSM–IV* diagnosis of PTSD and found in the literature, including those for ongoing traumas and regression and the impact of symptoms on the child's school and social functioning. The CAPS–CA provides rating sheets with scales using pictures to "depict more abstract concepts, including frequency (calendars marked with Xs), intensity-problems (cartoon figures with facial and somatic expressions), and intensity-feelings (facial expressions)" (Drake et al., 2001, pp. 7–8). Frequency and intensity of each symptom are rated on a 5-point Likert scale (0–4 for frequency and 0–4 for intensity) and then summed. A frequency score of 2 (*some of the time, once or twice a week*) or greater is required to be considered to meet criteria for having the symptoms when making diagnostic decisions. Clinicians then provide subjective global ratings for the validity of the responses, overall severity of symptoms, and overall improvement. The CAPS–CA concludes with asking children three questions regarding their coping: How the trauma has affected their lives, what has helped them feel better, and what they do to feel better when they are feeling bad. It is estimated that 30 minutes to 2 hours are needed to complete the interview (Strand et al., 2005).

The CAPS–CA has been criticized because "it provides leading questions. In particular, it helps a child who seeks to be seen as having symptoms to know exactly what to say" (Lubit et al., 2002, p. 836). Thus, it should be used after a screening measure has been administered and in conjunction with other reports. Although data on the validity and reliability of the CAPS–CA is limited, the CAPS and CAPS–C "are [already] widely accepted because of their sound psychometric properties" (Strand et al., 2005, p. 65). They have primarily been studied in the United States with multiethnic youth (Hawkins & Radcliffe, 2006). (See Table 7.1 for more information about these tools.)

Other psychometrically promising scales that provide symptom frequency or severity scores but are in need of additional development include the Angie–Andy Cartoon Trauma Scales (Praver, 2002; Praver, DiGiuseppe, Pelcovitz, Mandel, & Gaines, 2000), the Child PTSD Symptom Scale (Foa, Riggs, Dancu, & Rothbaum, 1993; Foa, Treadwell, Johnson, & Feeny, 2001), the My Worst Experience Survey (Hyman, Berna, Snook, DuCette, & Kohr,

TABLE 7.1

Posttraumatic Stress Disorder (PTSD) Instruments for Use in Courtroom Modification Evaluations With Children and Adolescents

PTSD and trauma measures with severity indicators	Age range	Reliability data	Validity data	Severity level/ cutoff scores	Features and summary	Weaknesses
The Childhood PTS Reaction Index (CPTS–RI; Frederick et al., 1992); New title: UCLA PTSD Reaction Index for *DSM–IV* (Pynoos et al., 1998) Contact Information: Robert S. Pynoos, National Center for Child Traumatic Stress, 11150 W. Olympic Blvd., Suite 770, Los Angeles, CA 90064 rpynoos@mednet.ucla.edu	8–18 years	Internal consistency: .68–.80 (in a sample of traumatized children) Interrater reliability: .88–.94 total (in samples of traumatized adolescents) Test–retest reliability: .93 over 1 week (in a sample of traumatized adolescents)	Convergent validity: .91 total with PTSD (in sample of traumatized youth); .69–.80 subscales with extent of trauma, depression; .29–.44 with trauma exposure; .38 total with trauma exposure (in a sample of traumatized children)	*Mild* (12–24), *moderate* (25–39), *severe* (40–59), and *very severe* (> 60)	This is one of the best-studied scales. This 20-item scale (child, adolescent, and parent versions) considers main *DSM–IV* symptoms of PTSD, including questions related to reexperiencing trauma, numbing and avoiding, and physiological arousal. Sensitivity and specificity for PTSD diagnosis are moderate to good (Goenjian et al., 1995). Other strengths include suitability with youth of different ages, diverse cultures, and various traumatic experiences.	There is some inconsistency between the items on the scale and the symptoms listed in the *DSM–IV*, including some items asked more than once and some symptoms not addressed by the scale. No normative data. Psychometric data on new scale are not yet published. Training is available and recommended.
The Clinician-Administered PTSD Scale for Children and Adolescents for *DSM–IV* (CAPS–CA; Nader et al., 2002); (CAPS–C; Nader et al., 1998) To obtain: National Center for PTSD (116D), VA Medical Center, 215 N. Main St., White River Junction, VT 05009 ncptsd@ncptsd.org http://www.ncptsd.org	8–15 years	Internal consistency of CAPS–CA: .81, .75, and .79 for the Criteria B, C, and D symptom cluster (sample of incarcerated adolescents) Interrater reliability (in a sample of traumatized adolescents using CAPS-C): .64 (lifetime diagnosis); .84 (current diagnosis)	Concurrent correlations of r = .51 with the CPTS–RI and r = .64 with the Child PTSD Checklist	None	This instrument assesses all *DSM–IV* criteria for PTSD. Frequency and intensity of each of the symptoms are rated (0–4 for frequency and 0–4 for intensity) and then summed. Pictorial scales, opportunities to practice before questions, and a standard procedure for identification of time frames increase the usefulness of the scale with young people (Weems, Silverman, Rapee, & Pina, 2003).	The validity measure is subjective. The scale has been criticized as a "long and involved and complicated interview that tries to do everything . . . a challenging task for most teens (and some adults), let alone younger children" (Fletcher, 2005, ¶17). There are no normative data. Training is available and recommended.

(continues)

TABLE 7.1
Posttraumatic Stress Disorder (PTSD) Instruments for Use in Courtroom Modification Evaluations With Children and Adolescents   *(Continued)*

PTSD and trauma measures with severity indicators	Age range	Reliability data	Validity data	Severity level/cutoff scores	Features and summary	Weaknesses
The Children's PTSD Inventory (CPTSDI; Saigh, 2003a, 2003b; Saigh, Yasik, & Oberfield, 2000) To obtain: The Psychological Corporation, 19500 Bulverde Rd., San Antonio, TX 78259-3701, Tel: (800) 872-1726, Fax: (800) 232-1223, http://www.PsychCorp.com Contact information: Dr. Saigh, CUNY, Graduate Center, 33 W. 42nd Street, New York, NY 10036 e-mail: pasaigh@aol.com	7–18 years	Internal consistency: alpha = .95 (overall diagnosis); .53–.89 (subscales) Interrater reliability: Cohen's kappa = .96 (overall diagnosis) Intraclass correlation coefficient = .91 (overall diagnosis) Test–retest reliability at 2 weeks: kappa = .91 (overall diagnosis) (stress-exposed and non-stress-exposed hospital sample of children and adolescents)	Convergent validity: .80–.92 with PTSD structured interview (stress-exposed and non-stress-exposed sample of children and adolescents) .32–.70 with measures of anxiety and depression (sample of clinical and nonclinical youth) Divergent validity: –.07–.21 with externalizing scales (stress-exposed and non-stress-exposed sample of children and adolescents) Discriminant validity: PTSD from other clinical groups (Ohan et al., 2002)	The instrument yields the following diagnoses: negative PTSD, acute PTSD, chronic PTSD, delayed onset PTSD, and no diagnosis (i.e., information).	This structured interview is considered the gold standard of PTSD diagnosis (Fletcher, 1996). Quick to administer, it is also one of the best researched in terms of psychometric properties. Sensitivity and specificity are reported to be moderate to excellent (Ohan et al., 2002). The interview gives duration information and can be scored for severity.	Some consider this inventory costly for many treatment and research contexts (manual: $66; pack of 25 test protocols: $43). No normative data are available. Training is available and recommended.
The Trauma Symptom Checklist for Children (TSCC; Briere, 1996a, 1996b) To obtain: Psychological Assessment Resources, Box 998, Odessa, FL 33556, Tel: (800) 331-8378 http://www.parinc.com Contact information: John Briere, PhD, Associate Professor, Psychiatry and Psychology, USC School of Medicine, 2020 Zonal Ave., Los Angeles, CA 90033 e-mail: jbriere@usc.edu	8–16 years	Internal consistency: alpha = .89 total; .66–.89 for clinical scales (standardization sample)	Reasonable convergent (.75–.82), discriminant, and predictive validity in normative and clinical samples (Briere, n.d.; http://www.johnbriere.com/tscc.htm)		This is a self-report, 54-item measure of posttraumatic stress and related psychological symptomatology (anxiety, depression, dissociation, anger) with a normative sample of 3,008. There are two validity scales and eight critical items. A computer scoring program is available.	The checklist does not map to *DSM–IV* criteria. The Sexual Concerns and Hyperarousal scales show moderate internal consistency (manual: $43; pack of 25 test booklets: $50; pack of 25 profile forms: $27).

Note.   DSM–IV = Diagnostic and Statistical Manual of Mental Disorders, Fourth Edition (American Psychiatric Association, 1994).

2002), and the Pediatric Emotional Distress Scale (discussed in chap. 6, this volume).

The duration and course of PTSD symptoms should also be examined as part of the courtroom modification assessment. There are two measures with good psychometric properties, also seen in Table 7.1, that assess symptom duration and course: the Children's PTSD Inventory (CPTSDI; Saigh, 1998, 2003a, 2003b; Saigh et al., 2000) and the Trauma Symptom Checklist for Children (TSCC; Briere, 1996a, 1996b).

The CPTSDI is a well-researched, clinician-administered scale for children aged 7 to 18 years. On the basis of the *DSM–IV* criteria, the scale examines the presence and absence of symptoms, and scores estimate the following diagnoses: PTSD Negative, Acute PTSD, Chronic PTSD, Delayed Onset PTSD, and No Diagnosis (Saigh & Yasik, 2002). Scores can also be "examined dimensionally to indicate severity" (Ohan et al., 2002, p. 1406). Its administration is estimated to take between 5 and 20 to 45 minutes, depending on the child's reported history of trauma.

The interview begins with examples of traumatic ("scary") experiences, and then the child is asked whether he or she has ever experienced a scary event. If yes, the child is asked if (a) the event scared the child, (b) the child felt upset when it happened, and (c) the child felt he or she could do nothing to stop it from happening. If answers indicate either a traumatic stressor did not occur or if the child did not react negatively to it even if it did happen, the interview ends, and "No Diagnosis" is given. Otherwise, additional yes–no questions are asked in subtests for reexperiencing symptoms (11 items), numbing and avoidance (16 items), hyperarousal (7 items), and significant distress (5 items). Questions related to duration of symptoms are also asked.

The TSCC is a self-report measure appropriate for use with children aged 8 to 16 years. A unique strength of this instrument is that it was normed on 3,008 nonclinical ("normal") children aged 7 to 17 from diverse racial and socioeconomic backgrounds, providing norms based on age and sex. The TSCC may be administered in two forms, the full 54-item TSCC, which contains a section of questions addressing sexual issues, and a 44-item or 40-item TSCC-A, which makes no reference to such symptoms. Each item is scored on a 4-point Likert scale ranging from 0 (*never*) to 3 (*lots of times*). It yields six clinically derived scales (Anxiety, Depression, Anger, Posttraumatic Stress, Dissociation, and Sexual Concerns), which do not overlap directly with *DSM–IV* criteria. Although it cannot be used to make diagnoses, the TSCC is useful in estimating symptom course following reported trauma. Another unique facet of the TSCC is its two validity scales (Underresponse [denial] and Hyperresponse [faking; "cry for help"]). The TSCC takes approximately 15 to 20 minutes to administer and 5 to 10 minutes to score by hand (computer scoring is also available).

A 90-item parent or caretaker report Trauma Symptom Checklist for Young Children (aged under 7 years) has also been made available. Although it appears promising on the basis of initial reliability and validity data in one published study (Briere et al., 2001), additional work is needed to support its validity (Strand et al., 2005).

Another instrument, the Child and Adolescent Psychiatric Assessment: Life Events Section and PTSD Module (Costello, Angold, March, & Fairbank, 1998) distinguishes among acute, chronic, and delayed diagnoses, but its psychometric properties are variable.

Finally, one comprehensive semistructured interview, the Schedule for Affective Disorders and Schizophrenia for School-Age Children—Present and Lifetime Version (K–SADS–PL; J. Kaufman et al., 1997), contains a module that can be used to assess the presence and severity of current and lifetime diagnoses of PTSD. Because the K–SADS–PL is also used for the other anxiety disorders (PTSD is classified as an anxiety disorder) as well as depression, it is reviewed more thoroughly in chapter 9 (this volume).

CONCLUSION

Predicting a child's functioning in courtroom testimony is a challenging task. Ratings of current symptom frequency, intensity, duration, and course gathered from reliable and valid instruments can provide some evidence of future symptoms and behaviors. However, most measures do not assess for multiple, chronic, or complex trauma (Hawkins & Radcliffe, 2006), and their appropriateness in different ethocultural contexts warrants additional investigation (Cook et al., 2003). Therefore, multiple measures are needed given the limitations of current interviews and PTSD instruments. Because measures are not available to address all of these domains adequately, the MHP should "conduct posttesting interviews about symptom duration, frequency, and intensity" (Sparta, 2003, p. 226, citing Nader, 1997), as well as clarify the child's perceptions and experiences, especially as "related to proximate cause, secondary traumatic effects and comorbid or premorbid factors" (Sparta, 2003, p. 225, citing Nader, 1997).

8

DISSOCIATION AND COURTROOM MODIFICATION EVALUATIONS

Another distinctive reaction to trauma is dissociation (E. B. Carlson, 1997). Dissociation is said to be most common in individuals with a trauma history, especially early, severe, and chronic maltreatment (Cardena & Weiner, 2004; Cromer, Stevens, DePrince, & Pears, 2006; Diseth, 2006). At the same time, debate exists as to the extent to which dissociative symptoms are culturally shaped (Dalenberg & Palesh, 2004). This chapter reviews definitional and diagnostic issues related to dissociation in children and adolescents and the available assessment instruments that mental health professionals (MHPs) should examine before use in a courtroom modification evaluation.

DEFINITION AND DIAGNOSIS OF DISSOCIATION

Although widely recognized, dissociation is challenging to define (Ohan, Myers, & Collett, 2002). Definitions cited in the literature often confuse description with etiology and provide multiple, inconsistent approaches to defining it. Dissociation is variously described as an isolated symptom, a process, a disorder or syndrome, "an autohypnotic disorder, a skill, an altered state of consciousness, a neurobiological phenomenon, and a means of resolving psychological conflict" (Carrion & Steiner, 2000, p. 353). Etiological definitions may be misleading because no consensus exists regarding the developmental pathways of dissociative symptoms or the disorder (International Society for the Study of Dissociation [ISSD], 2004).

According to the ISSD (2005), dissociation can be defined as "[a]n ongoing process in which certain information (such as feelings, memories, and physical sensations) is kept apart from other information with which it would normally be logically associated" (p. 74). In children, dissociation is considered "a malleable developmental phenomenon [p. 120] . . . a developmental disruption in the integration of adaptive memory, sense of identity, and the self-regulation of emotion" (ISSD, 2004, p. 123). A review of case studies regarding adolescents with dissociative conditions showed that all cases involved "loss of consciousness, amnesia, identity confusion, and most involve[d] conflicts in the family, frequently regarding sexuality and the expression of anger" (Silberg, 2000, p. 120). In accordance with the ISSD adult definition, the *Diagnostic and Statistical Manual of Mental Disorders, Fourth Edition, Text Revision* (*DSM–IV–TR*; American Psychiatric Association [APA], 2000) describes the essential features of dissociative disorders as disruptions in a person's "usually integrated functions of consciousness, memory, identity, or perception" (p. 519), but it does not reference problems with emotional regulation said to be found in children and adolescents. Currently, "we have little understanding as to whether children manifest dissociative symptoms in a similar manner to adults following trauma" (Kenardy et al., 2007, p. 457). As a result, Dell (2001) rightly concluded that "[d]espite over a century of research, no generally accepted definition of *dissociation* or *pathological dissociation* exists" (p. 20).

Typically, aspects of dissociation (or its symptoms) are said to occur along a spectrum or continuum from normal to pathological (Ogawa, Sroufe, Weinfeld, Carlson, & Egeland, 1997; Putnam, 1997). For example, a person could proceed from occasional daydreaming to preferring fantasy over reality (Ohan et al., 2002). This dimensional or trait model envisions dissociation as a trait or continuous variable that everyone possesses to some degree and posits that pathological dissociative experiences are not qualitatively different from those experienced on the low end of the continuum (Putnam, 1997; Seeley, Perosa, & Perosa, 2004). Dissociative experiences are viewed as problematic when they are no longer functional in one's cultural context or when they become "chronic, recurrent, and uncontrollable and when they produce dysfunction and/or distress" (Cardeña & Weiner, 2004, p. 497). Some evidence exists for the cross-cultural validity of the continuum model, with differences in presentation (e.g., Umesue, Matsuo, Iwata, & Tashiro, 1996). For example, multiple personality disorder, a controversial and contested diagnosis, may be more visible in individualistic societies than in collectivistic societies (Martinez-Taboas, 1995) or may be "experienced, expressed or understood in culturally specific cognitive categories" such as spirit possession (Castillo, 1994, p. 141; Suryani & Jensen, 1992). Finding differences in self and identity is not surprising given that identity development is a culturally constructed process (Dion, 2006).

Other investigators, however, posit that there are distinctive types of dissociation, a psychological defense and a pathological symptom or disorder (Carrion & Steiner, 2000; Putnam, Hornstein, & Peterson, 1996). In this typological or taxonic model, pathological symptoms such as depersonalization, identity alteration, and amnesia for dissociative states are seen as categorically different from normal phenomena such as absorption and imaginative involvement (the ability to be lost in the task at hand) and experienced only by a small number of people (Farrington, Waller, Smerden, & Faupel, 2001; Seeley et al, 2004.). The typological model can be tested through taxometric analysis (Waller & Meehl, 1997), but such procedures did not find a stable taxon in a sample of Puerto Rican outpatient 11- to 17-year-olds (Martinez-Taboas et al., 2004). Development of a specific taxon scale (e.g., the Adult Dissociative Experiences Scale—Taxon) for children and adolescents would assist in this process.

Given the definitional confusion, it is not surprising to find that diagnostic weaknesses exist. Calls to modify significantly the DSM criteria for adults have been made to improve reliability and validity (Dell, 2001, 2006; Steinberg, 2001). Although it is generally agreed that children and adolescents may experience problems with dissociation, information about the condition in youth is still evolving (ISSD, 2004). The field is considered "in an early developmental stage" (ISSD, 2004, p. 121). Therefore, assessment and diagnosis of dissociative conditions in young people could be considered even more difficult and controversial than in adults.

Another reason for diagnostic difficulties with children is that no consensus exists regarding the diagnostic criteria for children and adolescents (ISSD, 2004). A diagnosis specifically designed for children was proposed (G. Peterson, 1991) but not accepted into the latest version of the DSM. Furthermore, the current DSM–IV distinctions among the dissociative disorder diagnoses do not appear to be applicable to children and adolescents (Silberg, 2000). Currently, the DSM–IV recognizes child cases in three of the five dissociative diagnoses (i.e., dissociative amnesia,[1] dissociative identity disorder [DID; formerly multiple personality disorder],[2] and depersonaliza-

---

[1]*Dissociative amnesia* is "characterized by an inability to recall important personal information, usually of a traumatic or stressful nature, that is too extensive to be explained by ordinary forgetfulness" (APA, 2002, p. 519).

[2]*DID* is "characterized by the presence of two or more distinct identities or personality states that recurrently take control of the individual's behavior accompanied by an inability to recall important personal information that is too extensive to be explained by ordinary forgetfulness" (APA, 2000, p. 519).

Five key DID symptoms include "amnesia, depersonalization, derealization, identity confusion, and identity alteration" (Steinberg, 2001, p. 60). This diagnosis remains one of the most controversial, however, and is not accepted in all parts of the world, although it is included in the 10th revision of the *International Classification of Diseases* (L. S. O'Brien, 1998).

tion disorder,[3] but not dissociative fugue[4] or dissociative disorder not otherwise specified [DDNOS][5]). However, younger children have been found not to fit the clear-cut *DSM–IV* definitions of DID and may be more correctly considered as DDNOS (Putnam, Hornstein, & Peterson, 1996). Even though it is not officially recognized in children by the *DSM* and does not have set diagnostic criteria, DDNOS is the most common diagnosis given in populations of dissociative children and adolescents (ISSD, 2004). Also, case reports of children and adolescents with dissociative amnesia, depersonalization disorder, and dissociative fugue show that the clinical presentation of dissociative symptomology is similar across different diagnoses (Silberg, 2000). Still, no consensus exists about the typical case, and prevalence rates are lacking for dissociative diagnoses in children (ISSD, 2004).

In addition, children and adolescents may experience a range of dissociative phenomena that are not included in the *DSM–IV*'s diagnostic criteria or that do not meet the threshold for diagnosis as a disorder. For example, Putnam (1993) listed dissociative symptoms and behaviors that have been found to appear in children that, considered alone, do not meet *DSM–IV* thresholds: amnesia or memory loss; disturbances in sense of self; absorption or trancelike states; rapid shifts in mood and behavior; perplexing shifts in access to knowledge, memory, and skills; auditory and visual hallucinations; and vivid imaginary companionship.

The wide range and differing severity levels of dissociative clinical symptomology in children and adolescents likely result from developmental factors that affect the way that dissociative symptoms are presented in children (Putnam et al., 1996). For example, some authors have suggested that dissociation may appear as memory fragmentation in some children. This may be normal for a child's developmental level because he or she may not yet have the ability to remember and integrate the various aspects of a traumatic experience (Pynoos, Steinberg, & Goenjian, 1996). Other types of fluctuations (e.g., identity, internal states) that are essential to making a diagnosis of dissociative disorders are also part of the normal developmental process (E. B. Carlson, 1997), such as daydreaming. Types of normative adolescent dissociative experiences, such as identity confusion and absorption in one's imagination lessen as the youth moves into adulthood (Armstrong, Putnam, Carlson, Libero, & Smith, 1997). Although some dissociation is normal, the pattern and course of these experiences are not well established (Haugaard, 2004). Furthermore, children may also present with somatic symptoms such as "sensory losses, loss of motor control, general paralysis, and

---

[3]*Depersonalization disorder* is "characterized by a persistent or recurring feeling of being detached from one's mental processes or body that is accompanied by intact reality testing" (APA, 2000, p. 519).

[4]*Dissociative fugue* is "characterized by sudden, unexpected travel away from home or one's customary place of work, accompanied by an inability to recall one's past and confusion about personal identity or the assumption of a new identity" (APA, 2000, p. 519).

[5]*DDNOS* is "included for coding disorders in which the predominant feature is a dissociative symptom, but that do not meet the criteria for any specific Dissociative Disorder" (APA, 2000, p. 519).

alterations of vision, hearing, taste, and smell" (Diseth, 2006, p. 234). Thus, although some children and adolescents may express dissociative symptoms in ways that are similar to adult patterns, many do not.

Another reason for diagnostic confusion may be that many child clinicians consider dissociation a controversial subject (Silberg, 2000). Some clinicians do not believe that dissociative disorders, especially DID, exist in children (Lewis & Yeager, 1994). Others fear that children are being over-diagnosed, in part because children may be more vulnerable to suggestion and adult influence (Silberg, 2000). Some believe that it is a culture-bound syndrome or media-induced phenomenon, although cross-cultural studies show otherwise (e.g., Zoroglu, Sar, Tuzun, Tutkun, & Savas, 2002). Others recognize that DID is controversial but advise clinicians that "the existence of less severe dissociative symptoms and behaviors among children is more generally accepted" (Haugaard, 2004, p. 151).

Finally, some clinicians may be uninformed about the issues. Because dissociation was first recognized by the *Diagnostic and Statistical Manual of Mental Disorders, Third Edition, Revised (DSM–III–R)* in 1987 and because severe dissociative symptoms are rare, some clinicians may not have received training or education in these disorders (E. B. Carlson, 1997; Haugaard, 2004). As a result, they may fail to ask children about dissociative symptoms or confuse children's dissociative symptomology with other issues that they more commonly expect or encounter with children, including inattention, anxiety, oppositional behaviors, or learning disabilities. Dissociative disorder can also be missed because the symptoms can occur with other disorders that are more frequently reported in allegedly abused children. For example, McLeer, Callaghan, Henry, and Wallen (1994) compared a group of abused children with a control group and found that attention-deficit/hyperactivity disorder (46% of the abused group compared with 30.4% of the control group) and posttraumatic stress disorder (42.3% of the abused group compared with 8.7% of the control group) were the most frequently diagnosed problem areas in their sample. People with dissociative disorders typically "present with a highly complex profile of comorbidity and extreme forms of distress" (Martinez-Taboas et al., 2004, p. 48). This may result in dissociative disorder not being diagnosed because its symptoms are misdiagnosed as attention, learning, or conduct problems or disorders; anxiety or mood disorders; psychoses; or personality disorders (Carrion & Steiner, 2000; Cromer et al., 2006; Putnam, 1993). Not asking is also problematic because children may not be troubled by or even aware of their dissociative experiences (Friedrich, Gerber, et al., 2001; Haaugard, 2004).

Despite diagnostic difficulties and controversy, dissociative experiences in children appear to be generally recognized in the United States as well as other countries as real clinical phenomena. If a focus on dissociative symptoms is chosen over diagnoses, symptoms can be organized around five categories (ISSD, 2004, p. 123):

1. inconsistent consciousness [which may be reflected by] symptoms of fluctuating attention, such as trance states or "black outs";
2. incoherence in developmental memory processes [which may be reflected by] autobiographical forgetfulness and fluctuations in access to knowledge;
3. difficulties in self-regulation [which may be reflected by] fluctuating moods and behavior, including rage episodes and regressions;
4. disorganization in the development of a cohesive self [which may be reflected by] the child's belief in alternative selves or imaginary friends that control the child's behavior; and
5. a subjective sense of dissociation from normal body sensation and perception or from a sense of self [which may be reflected by] depersonalization and derealization.

Such symptoms could potentially adversely affect a child witness's ability to pay attention, accurately recall information, and participate in a calm, age-appropriate manner during in-court testimony.

As clinically real and forensically relevant phenomena, dissociative symptoms are important to consider during courtroom modification assessments of allegedly maltreated children and adolescents. Because dissociation is strongly correlated with histories of trauma, many theorists posit that the most severe dissociative disorders are the direct result of early childhood traumatic events (Silberg, 2000), but causality has not been empirically confirmed (Diseth, 2006). Theoretically, dissociation is thought to protect the victim of abuse from being completely aware of event(s) and from the posttraumatic pain it would cause (Briere, 1992).

> A trauma may be so intense and complex that the child's mind is unable to process the events as a whole experience. The cognitive schemas are lacking, the level of affect is too high, and the traumatic experiences may become split off from consciousness. (Diseth, p. 234)

Supporting this hypothesis, studies with adults have found a relationship between dissociation and child sexual abuse (Briere & Runtz, 1990a; Chu & Dill, 1990; Farley & Keaney, 1997; Neumann, Housekamp, Pollock, & Briere, 1996; Roesler & McKenzie, 1994), physical abuse (Briere, Cotman, Harris, & Smiljanich, 1992; Chu & Dill, 1990), sexual and physical abuse (Draijer & Langeland, 1999), and psychological abuse (Briere & Runtz, 1988; Draijer & Langeland, 1999; Sanders & Giolas, 1991).

Dissociative symptoms have also been assessed in child and adolescent clinical populations with histories of sexual abuse, physical abuse, or both (Atlas & Hiott, 1994; Atlas, Wolfson, & Lipschitz, 1995; Friedrich, Gerber, et al., 2001; Friedrich, Jaworski, Huxsahl, & Bengtson, 1997; Kisiel & Lyons, 2001; Macfie, Cicchetti, & Toth, 2001; Trickett, Noll, Reiffman, &

Putnam, 2001), as well as those who suffered from psychological abuse and neglect (Brunner, Parzer, Schuld, & Resch, 2000; Carrion & Steiner, 2000; Sanders & Giolas, 1991). Although a history of abuse regardless of type appears associated with dissociation (Seeley et al., 2004), the literature is still divided as to whether dissociation is more frequently associated with sexual versus other types of abuse. In adolescents, Atlas and Hiott (1994) noted a trend for dissociation to be associated with sexual abuse rather than physical abuse. However, Putnam, Helmers, Horowitz, and Trickett (1995) found that physical abuse and physical coercion during sexual abuse were each more likely to be associated with dissociation than was sexual abuse. Similarly, in a study of delinquent adolescents, Carrion and Steiner (2000) found that a history of physical abuse and physical neglect, but not of sexual abuse, was significantly correlated with self-reported dissociation. Complicating matters further, Brunner et al. (2000) found that emotional neglect best predicted dissociative symptoms compared with sexual and physical abuse and stressful life events in a sample of German adolescents in inpatient treatment.

The few studies that focused on children under the age of 12 years reported similarly conflicted results. On one hand, Malinosky-Rummell and Hoier (1991) studied dissociative symptomology in 10 sexually abused girls compared with 50 same-age nonabused girls and found that the sexually abused girls scored higher on measures of dissociation. Similarly, Macfie et al. (2001) compared 45 maltreated preschool-age children with 33 nonmaltreated children and found that the sexually and physically abused children demonstrated more dissociation than the control group. On the other hand, Rhue, Lynn, and Sandberg (1995) studied 39 sexually abused, physically abused, and a clinical control sample of nonabused children and found that dissociative symptoms were not associated with the sexually abused children; dissociation was associated with the physically abused group.

In sum, the research in this area suggests that "there is not an exclusive or necessary association between sexual abuse and dissociation in children (Ogawa, [Sroufe, Weinfield, Carlson, & Egeland], 1997; Rhue et al., 1995)" or adolescents (Silberg, 2000, p. 124). In addition to abuse, other types of maltreatment or trauma are also associated with dissociative symptomology in young people, such as war, natural disasters, exposure to domestic violence, medical procedures, and emotional abuse (Diseth, 2006; ISSD, 2004). In addition, children may experience severe problems with dissociation even when there is no history of a traumatic event (Coons, 1996; Malenbaum & Russell, 1987; Silberg, 1998), and exposure to traumatic events does not always produce dissociation. Genetic factors, behavioral changes or difficulties, and other individual traits are being explored as predictors (ISSD, 2004; Seeley et al., 2004). Other individual and systemic variables found to play a role in the development of other trauma-related symptomology, such as socioeconomic status, race and ethnicity, culture, environment, and family and community support, should continue to be investigated as well. Further research is needed to explore the relationship between trauma and the expression of dissociation in children and adolescents before any definitive conclusions can be drawn.

DISSOCIATION ASSESSMENT MEASURES

Following the multidimensional assessment process described in chapter 5 (this volume), MHPs would include the following components in their evaluations for trauma-related dissociation in child witnesses: screening and other psychological tests, structured and nonstructured clinical interviews with the child and reliable third parties, and a medical evaluation to rule out general medical conditions that may present like dissociation, such as seizure disorders and other neurological conditions, allergies, exposure to toxins, and effects from legal or illegal substances (ISSD, 2004). MHPs should also examine whether and how a child is experiencing a dissociative disorder (one of the three dissociative diagnoses in the DSM–IV—dissociative amnesia, DID, and depersonalization disorder—that are said to apply to children and adolescents), its triggers, and the frequency, duration, and intensity of any dissociative symptoms. In addition, MHPs should note "whether the dissociative experiences reported are a normal part of the individual's cultural group and whether they produce dysfunction or suffering, no matter how unusual they may be" (Cardena & Weiner, 2004, p. 504). Complicating matters, however, is the doubt cast by writings in the field of dissociation on the appropriateness of using the DSM–IV for assessing dissociative problems in young people. The ISSD (2004) eschewed diagnosis and provided guidelines for assessment (primarily though clinical interviews) that are symptom-based. Similarly, as noted earlier, Silberg (2000) found that the diagnostic distinctions between the dissociative disorders are not applicable to children and adolescents. Instead of using diagnoses of dissociation in this population, Silberg recommended attempting to identify dissociative processes and symptomology in youth because she concluded that dissociative symptoms are clinically real phenomena. In line with this approach, Haugaard (2004) offered clinicians a list of behaviors associated with dissociation in children to use during the assessment process and reminded clinicians to ask about severity and frequency of these behaviors (which is also what would be done for a courtroom modification evaluation).

However, this approach should be regarded with caution in forensic settings. As previously noted, assessment and diagnosis of children and adolescents with dissociative problems and disorders is difficult and fraught with methodological problems. Haugaard (2004) correctly cautioned clinicians that "not enough information is currently available to provide specific guidelines regarding the number of behaviors or constellation of behaviors that must be present for interventions focused on dissociation to be indicated" (p. 150). For example, epidemiological information on dissociative disorders or symptoms is scarce (Martinez-Taboas, Canino, Wang, Garcia, & Bravo, 2006). There are no U.S. studies that examine the prevalence of dissociation in a general, "normal" sample of children and adolescents (ISSD, 2004; Silberg, 2000). Only one community sample is reported in the literature; Martinez-Taboas et al. (2006) found that 4.9% of youth between the ages of 11 and 17 years in Puerto Rico reported experiencing pathological dissociative symptoms on a Spanish version of the Adolescent Dissociative Experiences Scale (described subsequently). In addition, reliability is lowered when researchers use and report dissociative symptomology and not diagnoses of dissociative disorders, as is commonly the case (Halleck et al., 1992) and which is what is recommended by the ISSD (2004). Even with the *DSM–IV*, one researcher noted that "the everyday reliability of the diagnosis of DID [made by nonexpert clinicians] is abysmal" (Dell, 2001, p. 9). Finally, without reliable and valid diagnostic criteria (and it is not clear that the *DSM–IV* fits this need for children), MHPs are left to rely on their own clinical descriptions and judgments about cases.

Because no diagnostic standard exists for dissociative disorders in children (ISSD, 2004; Silberg, 2000), it is not surprising that assessment instruments have not yet been fully developed for childhood dissociation. The use of standardized measurement techniques would allow for reliable assessment and diagnosis of dissociative symptoms and disorders in young people (Steinberg, 1996). They would also allow for better understanding of the disorders in this population (Seeley et al., 2004). For example, Martinez-Taboas et al. (2006) commented how they would have liked to use the Diagnostic Interview Schedule for Children—Version IV to validate their Hispanic version of the Adolescent Dissociative Experiences Scale (A-DES); but were unable to because it does not include a dissociative disorders module. At this time, clinicians can only choose from adult diagnostic instruments, clinical judgment, and child screening instruments, none of which have been validated for use with allegedly maltreated children and adolescents.

Seven screening instruments address dissociative symptomology in children and adolescents (see Table 8.1). Regarding instruments that must be completed by people other than the child, there is a parent self-report measure, the Child Dissociative Checklist (CDC; Putnam, 1990), a checklist for clinicians (Child/Adolescent Dissociation Checklist [CADC]; Reagor, Kasten, & Morelli, 1992), and an instrument characterized by its authors as still in development that is to be used during psychological testing, the Dissociative Features Profile (DFP; Silberg, 1998). There are four child and/or adolescent self-report instruments: the Children's Perceptual Alteration Scale (CPAS; Evers-Szostak & Sanders, 1992), the Dissociative Experiences Scale (DES; E. M. Bernstein & Putnam, 1986), the A-DES (Armstrong et al., 1997, presented in Table 8.1 instead of the DES because the A-DES is based on the DES), and the Dissociative Questionnaire (Dis-Q; Vanderlinden, Van

TABLE 8.1
Dissociation Assessment Instruments for Use in Courtroom Modification Evaluations With Children and Adolescents

Dissociation measures	Age range	Reliability data	Validity data	Severity level/cutoff scores	Features/summary	Weaknesses
Adolescent Dissociative Experiences Scale (A-DES; Armstrong et al., 1997) A-DES is based on the DES; copies of the DES-II (in any available language) and the A-DES are in the public domain and may be reproduced and used without copyright restrictions. The A-DES can be found in Armstrong et al. (1997); an A-DES packet that contains 5 copies of the test (English only) and an article by the authors can be purchased from Sidran online or by phone ($12). Contact information: Sidran Institute, (888) 825-8249; http://www.sidran.org Judith Armstrong, 501 Santa Monica Blvd., Suite 402, Santa Monica, CA 90401; e-mail: jarmstrong@mizar.usc.edu	11–17/18 years Flesch–Kincaid reading grade level of 5.7 (Armstrong et al., 1997)	Internal consistency, Cronbach's alpha total scale: .92–.94 (Armstrong et al., 1997, inpatient and outpatients; Brunner et al., 2000, German inpatients; Farrington et al., 2001, U.K. secondary school; Muris et al., 2003, Netherlands secondary school; Smith & Carlson, 1996, U.S. junior and senior high school students; Zoroglu et al., 2002, Turkish outpatient and high school students); Cronbach's alpha for subscales: .64–.83 (Smith & Carlson, 1996); .72–.85 (Armstrong et al., 1997); split-half r (Spearman–Brown): .90–.944 (Armstrong et al., 1997; Brunner et al., 2000; Farrington et al., 2001; Smith & Carlson, 1996) Test-retest: .77 (Smith & Carlson, 1996); .91 (Zoroglu et al., 2002)	Convergent: $r = .77$ w/ DES (Friedrich et al., 2001, sex offenders in residential treatment; Smith & Carlson, 1996, college students) Discriminant: "supported" (Ohan et al., 2002) Known-groups validity: distinguished dissociative-disordered adolescents from a "normal" sample and from a patient sample with a variety of diagnoses (mean significantly higher than all but psychotic disorder group; Armstrong et al., 1997; Smith & Carlson, 1996; Zoroglu et al., 2002) A-DES means differed significantly by abuse status (sexual and physical, no abuse; Armstrong et al., 1997; Kisiel & Lyons, 2001; Seeley et al., 2004)	Normative data available but limited by small sample sizes Assesses frequency of symptoms Clinical cutoff on total score (range = 0–10) above 3 on total score: Diseth, 2006; Martinez-Taboas et al., 2004, 2006 (Spanish ADES-8); above 4 on total score: Kisiel & Lyons, 2001; above 4.8 on total score: Armstrong et al., 1997; Smith & Carlson, 1996	• Thirty-item, self-report instrument. A shorter, 8-item version (ADES-8) is also used in research. • "Designed for examining developmental trajectories of both normal and pathological dissociation during adolescence as well as for use as an efficient screen for pathological dissociation . . . [it] includes multiple constructs under the global construct of dissociation. This multidimensional approach was used to capture both normal and pathological dissociative phenomena." (Feindler, Rathus, & Silver, 2003, pp. 127–128) • Response format is a continuous 11-point Likert scale (0 = *never*, 10 = *always*), assessing six domains: dissociative amnesia (7); absorption and imaginative involvement (6); passive influence (5); depersonalization and derealization (12); dissociated identity (4); and dissociative relatedness (3). • 80% sensitivity and 74% specificity (dissociative disorders [DD] vs. nonclinical and DD vs. diagnoses; Ohan et al., 2002); 87% sensitivity and 68% specificity for 8-item version (clinical vs. nonclinical; Seeley et al., 2004) • High scores associated with verbal and procedural memory impairment in adolescent inpatients (Prohl et al., 2001) • Twenty minutes to administer • Versions available: French Canadian, Spanish, German, Turkish, Japanese (Umesue et al., 1996)	• This screening (not diagnostic) instrument is in a preliminary stage of validation. • Factor analysis yielded single factor in two studies of nonclinical youth but was designed with four scales. • Because the instrument was based on the adult DES, some language and scenarios are not appropriate or relevant to all youth. • Does not include checks for denial or symptom fabrication; fantasy-prone individuals may score high; follow-up interviewing essential. • Does not distinguish between dissociative and psychotic groups.

Instrument	Population	Reliability	Validity	Description	Comments
The Child Dissociative Checklist (CDC) A copy of version 3.0 can be found in Putnam & Peterson (1994) Contact Information: Frank W. Putnam, Cincinnati Children's Hospital Medical Center; e-mail: frank.putnam@cchmc.org	Parent or caretaker of 5- to 12-year-old child	Internal consistency: .78–.95 total scale (.78 in Malinosky-Rummel & Hoier, 1991, sexually abused and nonclinical nonabused girls; .95 for total sample in Putnam et al., 1993, clinical and nonclinical/mixed group of sexually abused/nonabused girls [.73 for control girls, .91 for sexually abused girls, .64 for girls with DDNOS, .8 for children with MPD]; .86 Putnam & Peterson, 1994, therapist ratings of children with MPD, DDoC, or other DD) Test–retest: .73 total over 204 weeks (Malinsky-Rummel & Hoier, 1999); .69 over 1 year; and .69–.92 individual item test–retest with median coefficient .735 (Putnam et al., 1993)	Convergent: "low to moderate" (Ohan et al., 2002), .33–.63 total score with other dissociation scales (Friedrich et al., 1997, sex offenders in residential treatment; Malinosky-Rummel & Hoier, 1991) Discriminant: supported (Ohan et al., 2002) Discriminated between psychiatric inpatients and nonabused children but not between sexually abused inpatients/nonabused inpatients. Discriminated between children with MPD and DDNOS (Feindler, 1997). Normative data available, with higher scores reported in inpatient study (Wherry et al., 1994). Score ≥ 12 is said to indicate a clinical level of dissociation (Putnam & Peterson, 1994).	• Twenty-item adult report; completed by someone familiar with the child's functioning during the previous 12-month period, usually a parent or other caretaker. • Ratings are on a 3-point scale (2 = *very true*, 1 = *sometimes true*, 0 = *not true*). • Ratings are summed to yield a total score ranging from 0–32. • Assesses several dissociative symptoms in the following domains: dissociative amnesia; rapid shifts in demeanor; access to information; knowledge; abilities; age appropriateness of behavior; spontaneous trance states; hallucinations; identity alterations; and aggressive/sexual behavior. • Instrument is brief and can be completed in short amount of time, often only 5–10 minutes to administer. • Easy to perform repeated assessments during different times and circumstances in the child's life.	• Screening (not diagnostic) instrument only • Does not systematically assess *DSM* criteria • CDC scores decline with child's age, indicating a decreased sensitivity of the scale for dissociative symptoms and behavior in older children or in younger children who experience more dissociation. • Veracity can vary with the accuracy of parent's perceptions. • No reliability and validity for children under age 6. • Self-report version not available but is in development; self- and parent-report scores differ (Ohan et al., 2002). • Atheoretical; items derived from professional experience with dissociative disorders.

(continues)

TABLE 8.1

Dissociation Assessment Instruments for Use in Courtroom Modification Evaluations With Children and Adolescents *(Continued)*

Dissociation measures	Age range	Reliability data	Validity data	Severity level/cutoff scores	Features/summary	Weaknesses
Child/Adolescent Dissociative Checklist (CADC; Reagor, Kasten, & Morelli, 1992) Available in Reagor et al. (1992)	3–18 years	Internal consistency: not reported Test–retest: readministered 1 year later, but small return rate precluded statistical analysis.	Convergent: not reported Divergent: not reported	Cutoff score of 10 (24 of 26 children accurately identified in Study 1; 11 of 14 in Study 2)	• Seventeen-item yes–no checklist completed by MHPs • Factor analysis revealed five factors: emotional overloading (5 items), psychological symptoms and illness and injury (5 items), physical and emotional abuse causing inconsistency (4 items), family history of dissociation (2 items), major traumatic history (3 items) • Summed total was found to be significantly associated with diagnosis of MPD/DD.	• Checklist reliability and validity not sufficiently examined. • Atheoretical; created from other symptom lists and clinical experience; five items consist of traumas • Tested with no control group; second follow-up study used small nonrandom sample with low return rate; those completing measure appeared to be doing so with intent of finding dissociative disorders and were the same people making diagnoses (not blind or independent).
Children's Perceptual Alteration Scale (CPAS; Evers-Szostak & Sanders, 1992) Contact information: Mary Evers-Szostak, PhD, 2609 N. Duke Street, Suite 1000 Durham, NC 27704-3048 Tel: (919) 220-8817	8–12 years	Internal consistency: .82 (clinical); .64 (Evers-Szostak & Sanders, 1992, normal sample of 53 children from pediatric practice) Test–retest: not reported	Convergent: .44–.60 with measures of fantasy and imagination (Rhue et al., 1995) and with parents' behavior reports (Achenbach Child Behavior Checklist & Eyberg Child Behavior Inventory; Evers-Szostak & Sanders, 1992, clinical abused and nonabused children)	Original cutoff score of 55 not supported by Rhue et al. (1995) study, which supported cutoff score of at least 66.	• Twenty-eight-item self-report instrument • Children are asked to rate their experience of each item on a 4-point scale: 1 = *never happens*, 2 = *sometimes*, 3 = *often*, 4 = *almost always happens*; higher ratings said to reflect higher levels of dissociation • Based on adult Perceptual Alterations Scale, with items rewritten to better suit children. • Dissociation conceptualized as having six aspects: automatic experiences, imaginary playmates, amnesia, loss of time, heightened monitoring, and loss of control over behavior and emotions. • Five to 10 minutes to administer	• No normative data • Reliability and validity not sufficiently examined. • Not tested on youth with dissociation and other clinical samples. • Items include behaviors not specific to dissociation (e.g., "I am hungry"); total scores may be misleading (Ohan et al., 2002) • Lack of association with sexual abuse • Factor analysis does not support six subscales; only total score is calculated,

Measure	Age	Reliability	Validity	Comments	Concerns
Children's Perceptual Alteration Scale (CPAS; Evers-Szostak & Sanders, 1992) (Continued)			Construct validity not supported for link between dissociation, fantasy-proneness, and sexual abuse (Rhue et al., 1995). Discriminant: supported (Ohan et al., 2002); Evers-Szostak & Sanders, 1992 (children with clinical problems vs. normal children); Rhue et al., 1995 (physically abused vs. nonabused children)		suggesting one factor • Small sample sizes used in the two studies (53 in Evers-Szostak & Sanders, 1992; 39 in Rhue et al., 1995) • Rarely used in the literature
Dissociative Features Profile (DFP; Silberg, 1998) Contact information (the Sidran Institute is the publisher and exclusive distributor of DFP): Sidran Institute, 200 E. Joppa Road, Suite 207 Towson, MD 21286; Tel: (410) 825-8888; Fax: (410) 337-0747; http://www.sidran.org	6–17 years	Internal consistency: not reported Test–retest: not reported Interrater reliability (two raters using percent agreement): 93% for behaviors; 82% for test response/markers (Silberg, 1998)	Convergent: not reported Divergent: not reported Measure was able to select 93% of dissociative target group (Silberg, 1996).	Not available	"The DFP was developed to be used with a typical psychological testing battery which might include the Rorschach, the TAT [Thematic Apperception Test], Drawings, Sentence Completion, and a Wechsler IQ Test. The DFP may be used if at least two measures were administered. . . . The DFP consists of two parts—Part I (Behaviors) and Part II (Markers). The Behaviors Section picks up unusual behaviors or presentations of the patient during the testing. Part II (Markers) describes actual test responses. Predictive validity improves when both parts of the measure are used, but Part II (Markers) may be used alone." (Sidran, n.d., ¶ 2–3)	• No normative data • Reliability and validity not sufficiently examined; Sidran Web site says that it is "currently under development." • Rarely used in the literature • Interrater reliability statistic does not control for chance agreement between raters. • Testing bias may have been present in test administration.

(continues)

TABLE 8.1

Dissociation Assessment Instruments for Use in Courtroom Modification Evaluations With Children and Adolescents *(Continued)*

Dissociation measures	Age range	Reliability data	Validity data	Severity level/ cutoff scores	Features/summary	Weaknesses
Dissociation Questionnaire (DisQ; Vanderlinden, Van Dyck, Vandereycken, & Vertommen, 1991) Available from Johan Vanderlinden, PhD, Universitair Centrum, St. Jozef v.z.w., Leuvense Steenweg 517, B-3070 Kortengerg, Belgium; e-mail: jvanderlin@online.be	10–60+ years 15–19 years (Svedin, 2004)	Internal consistency, Cronbach's alpha: .96 total scale (Vanderlinden et al., 1991, general population and small [n = 46] patient group with dissociative disorders: .96, Svedin et al., 2004, cited in this article on Swedish translation with normal adolescents in school and small clinical sample with trauma history); subscales: .67–.94 (Vanderlinden et al., 1991)	Convergent: .79 with Swedish translation of Youth Self Report problem scale (Svedin et al., 2004) Dissociative symptoms found more in traumatized clinical group than in the normal group (Svedin et al., 2004). Construct and congruent validity: generally satisfactory (Svedin et al., 2004) Divergent: not available	Cutoff score of 2.5 for general population, not specific to adolescents (91% sensitivity, 97% specificity; Vanderlinden et al., 1991).	• Sixty-three-item self-report measure • Five response categories: 1 = *not at all,* 2 = *a little bit,* 3 = *moderately,* 4 = *quite a bit,* 5 = *extremely* • Four subscales detected by item/ factor analysis (accounted for 77% of variance): identity confusion; loss of control over behavior, thoughts, and emotions; amnesia; absorption; however, study of U.S. college students found evidence for single-factor solution (I. H. Bernstein, Ellason, Ross, & Vanderlinden, 2001).	• Created from study of general population in Belgium and the Netherlands; translated for use with adolescents in Sweden; used with U.S. college students; unclear whether valid for use with U.S. adolescents. • Not clear whether psychometric data applicable to adolescents given lack of clear reporting of source in Svedin et al. (2004) study.
The Bellevue Dissociative Disorders Interview for Children (BDDI-C; Lewis, 1996) Contact Information: Dorothy O. Lewis, MD, A245, Old Bellevue, 2, A245, New York, NY 10016;	Not reported	Internal consistency: not available Test-retest: not available Interrater reliability (three raters): kappa = .78 (Lewis, 1996)	Convergent: not available Divergent: not available Protocol distinguished two pretested groups from each other (Lewis, 1996; 46 normal school	Not available	• Flexible interview protocol • Protocol modified (in response to concerns about children's attention span and interviewer's freedom to leave and return to subjects based on the child's reaction) to be a single-sheet listing the categories of topics to be explored, with cues to specific questions. • Summary sheet for unstructured	• No normative data • Reliability and validity not sufficiently examined • Not reported as used in other publications

	Age	Reliability	Validity	Description	Comments
The Bellevue Dissociative Disorders Interview for Children (BDDI-C; Lewis, 1996) (Continued) Tel: (212) 562-8653; Fax: (212) 263-6208; 100 York Street, New Haven, CT, 06510; Tel: (203) 777-0422				children and 23 abused children in residential treatment) interview covers states of awareness, problems with memory, moods, imaginative experiences, hearing experiences including hallucinations, visual and sensory experiences including hallucinations, temper and aggression, disciplinary experiences, medical issues, sexual experiences, identity disturbances and alterations, and alterations in skills and abilities.	
Child Interview for Subjective Dissociative Experiences (CISDE; Liner, 1989, unpublished manuscript)	6–14 years	Internal consistency, Chronbach's alpha: 0.67 (total sample), .34 (50 nonabused 7–12-year-old girls); .81 (10 abused 8–11-year-old girls), Malinosky-Rummell & Hoier, 1991; .85 for total sample (Diamanduros, 2004; 20 sexually abused boys, 20 nonabused clinical boys, 20 pediatric group) Test–retest: not available Interrater reliability: 96.7% (*n* = 44) Diamanduros (2004)	Convergent: CISDE correlated at .51 with CDC across informants (Malinosky-Rummell & Hoier, 1991); .54 (Diamanduros, 2004; Pearson, 2007) Abused girls scored higher on CISDE and CDC than nonabused girls when family risk/disruption controlled for (Malinosky-Rummell & Hoier, 1991). Sexually abused boys significantly different from pediatric group only on CIDSE (Diamanduros, 2004). Divergent: Abuse did not predict CISDE scores except when combined with CDC (Malinosky-Rummell & Hoier, 1991).	Not available • Twenty-six-item semistructured interview for children • Rated on presence or absence of symptoms • Four subscales: cognitive dissociation, fantasy absorption, depersonalization, miscellaneous	• Original measure not published; no psychometric or normative data available. • Reliability and validity not sufficiently examined. • Malinoksy-Rummell & Hoier (1991) used small nonrandom sample and modified the CISDE to 16 items. • Not reported as used in other publications since 1991 with the exception of Diamanduros's (2004) dissertation.

(continues)

TABLE 8.1
Dissociation Assessment Instruments for Use in Courtroom Modification Evaluations With Children and Adolescents   *(Continued)*

Dissociation measures	Age range	Reliability data	Validity data	Severity level/cutoff scores	Features/summary	Weaknesses
Structured Clinical Interview for *DSM–IV* Dissociative Disorders—Revised (SCID-D-R; Steinberg, 1994) Available from American Psychiatric Publishing, Inc. (package of five and interviewer's guide: $83.50); http://www.appi.org/set.cfm?id=8862 Contact information: Marlene Steinberg, MD, 64 Gothic St. #103, Northampton, MA 01060-3042; Tel: (413) 584-2929	For adults; has been used with youth as young as 11 years	Internal consistency: not available Test–retest in adults good to excellent for symptom severity and diagnosis (e.g., kappa = .88; Steinberg, 2000). Interrater: in adults, reported to be good to excellent (Steinberg, 1996, 2000) No information on reliability with adolescents (Steinberg, 2000)	No information on validity with adolescents Convergent: n/a Discriminant: with adults, "very good"; numerous studies show it can distinguish "between patients with clinically diagnosed dissociative disorders and other psychiatric disorders"; also distinguished "between patients with seizures and pseudoseizures" (Steinberg, 2000, p. 149)	Measures severity and presence of dissociative symptoms, as well as diagnoses. Severity of each of the five symptoms rated using an interviewer's guide to the SCID-D-R; evaluated in terms of distress, dysfunctionality, frequency, duration, and course of the symptom. Severity receives a numeric code: 1 = *absent/none*, 2 = *mild*, 3 = *moderate*, 4 = *severe* Total score ranges from 5 (*no symptomatology*) to 20 (*severe manifestations of all five dissociative symptoms*). Cutoff scores for adolescents not available.	• Semistructured interview with more than 250 items. • Measures five core dissociative symptoms: amnesia, depersonalization, derealization, identity confusion, identity alteration, as well as *DSM–IV* diagnoses of dissociative disorders and acute stress disorder. • Differential diagnosis: control subjects tend to score between *none* to *mild* (1–2); subjects with variety of nondissociative disorders score between *none* and *moderate* (1–3); people with dissociative disorders experience moderate to severe (3–4) symptoms (Steinberg, 2000). • Format elicits informative descriptions of dissociative experiences, not yes–no answers. • Designed to be filed with a patient's charts. • Descriptions required are thought to help evaluate malingering (Steinberg, 2000).	• Instrument needs to be further evaluated for reliability and validity with adolescents (Koopman et al., 2004) although it has been used in adolescents as young as 11 (Steinberg, 2000, citing Carrion & Steiner, 2000; Steinberg & Steinberg, 1995); also see Koopman et al., 2004 (study of 41 delinquent adolescents). • Officially supervised training is required. • Clinical sophistication on the part of the interviewer is necessary (Putnam, 1997). • Time intensive: requires 2–3 hours to complete (Putnam, 1997). • Atheoretical; derived from a critical synthesis of literature on trauma and dissociation as well as clinical experience.

Note. DD = dissociative disorder; DDoC = dissociative disorder of childhood; DDNOS = dissociative disorder not otherwise specified; *DSM–IV* = *Diagnostic and Statistical Manual of Mental Disorders, Fourth Edition* (American Psychiatric Association, 1994); MHP = mental health professional; MPD = multiple personality disorder; n/a = not applicable.

Dyck, Vandereycken, & Vertommen, 1991, 1993). An adolescent version of the Multidimensional Inventory of Dissociation (MID; Dell, 2006) was last reported as currently under development. Because it has not yet been published, it is not reviewed here. The Trauma Symptom Checklist for Children, which was reviewed in chapter 7 (this volume), also contains a dissociation scale. There are also three semistructured or structured interviews, also included in Table 8.1: the Child Interview for Subjective Dissociative Experiences (CISDE; Liner, 1989), the Bellevue Dissociative Disorders Interview for Children (BDDI-C; Lewis, 1996), and the Structured Clinical Interview for the *DSM–IV* Dissociative Disorders (SCID-D—Steinberg, 1994; Steinberg & Steinberg, 1995; SCID-D-R—Steinberg, Rounsaville, & Cicchetti, 1990; Steinberg, 2000). Because the adult Dissociative Disorders Interview Schedule (DDIS; Ross et al., 1989) has only been used with adolescents in Turkey with a Turkish version of the instrument (Sar, Yargic, & Tutkun, 1996; Sar, Tutkun, Alyanak, Bakim, & Baral, 2000; Tutkun et al., 1998), the DDIS is not reviewed here. For good review articles on various measures for assessing dissociation along with other trauma related disorders, see Ohan et al. (2002) reviewing the A-DES, CDC, and CPAS; Steinberg (1996) reviewing the CDC, CADC, A-DES, CPAS, and SCID-D; and Strand, Sarmiento, and Pasquale (2005) reviewing the A-DES and CDC.

Regarding applicability to the population of allegedly abused children and adolescents involved in courtroom modification assessments, the CDC is the most widely used child dissociation assessment instrument (Silberg, 2000), studied with caretakers of sexually abused girls (Malinosky-Rummell & Hoier, 1991; Putnam et al., 1995), boys (Diamanduros, 2004; Friedrich et al., 1997), and children in foster care (Cromer et al., 2006; Putnam, 1997). The CADC was created through clinician ratings of children and adolescents with trauma histories that included sexual, physical, and emotional abuse, as well as serious injury or illness and serious loss (Reagor et al., 1992). The CPAS and DFP were studied with sexually and physically abused children (Rhue et al., 1995; Silberg, 1998). The DES and A-DES have been studied on adolescents with histories of sexual, physical, or psychological abuse and neglect (or a combination of these histories; Atlas & Hiott, 1994; Brunner et al., 2000; Friedrich et al., 2001; Kisiel & Lyons, 2001; Sanders & Giolas, 1991). Likewise, the BDDI-C was pilot tested on a sample of abused children in residential treatment (Lewis, 1996). The Dis-Q's normative sample included adults and adolescents with a history of trauma, including sexual, physical, and emotional abuse; war experiences; and disease (Svedin, Nilsson, & Lindell, 2004). Regarding the interviews, the SCID-D was used with samples of adolescent inpatients, delinquent adolescents, and sex offenders with significant victimization histories (Carrion & Steiner, 2000; Koopman et al., 2004); the CISDE was used with sexually abused girls (Malinosky-Rummell & Hoier, 1991) and boys (Diamanduros, 2004); and the BDDI-C has not yet been used with this population.

The CDC is the "most well-developed and tested" instrument for childhood dissociative disorders (Hornstein, 1996, p. 143). Its developers recommend that the CDC only be used as a screening device and a research instrument for quantifying dissociation (Putnam & Peterson, 1994). It is a brief 20-item questionnaire that is administered to a person familiar with the functioning of a 5- to 12-year-old child in the last year, and so it can be completed by multiple raters across settings, including school, home, and play. The CDC was developed atheoretically on the basis of symptom lists developed from evaluations of children with dissociative disorders and those who had been maltreated and from those generated and modified by members of the child abuse treatment community (Ohan et al., 2002). Similarly, its six subscales (dissociative amnesia, rapid shifts in demeanor and abilities, spontaneous trance states, hallucinations, identity alterations, and aggressive or sexualized behavior) were developed rationally rather than statistically (e.g., by factor analysis). Caregivers are asked to rate child behaviors in the past 12 months on a 3-point scale, ranging from 0 (*not true*) to 2 (*very true*). Putnam (1997) offered some norms for total summed scores: 2 to 3 points for normal populations, mean 10.3 for 5- to 8-year-old maltreated children, and at least 20 for children with DID or DDNOS (Cromer et al., 2006). Although the CDC appears to be a reliable measure (Ohan et al., 2002; Putnam, Helmers, & Trickett, 1993; Putnam & Peterson, 1994), clarification is needed regarding its validity (Ohan et al., 2002; Steinberg, 1996). A solid child measure of dissociation would be necessary to establish the validity of its underlying construct (Friedrich et al., 1997).

Because the CDC loses sensitivity after age 12 (Putnam et al., 1993), an adolescent screening measure of dissociative symptoms is also needed. Although some clinicians consider using the DES, the DES was developed for use with adults and is not appropriate for use with younger people. In an attempt to address this problem, A-DES was created from the DES for specific use with 11- to 18-year-olds (Armstrong et al., 1997). It is a 30-item self-administered questionnaire that asks adolescents to designate the frequency of dissociative experiences on a continuous 11-point scale, ranging from 0 (*never*) to 11 (*always*). Items on the A-DES can be grouped into four categories, said to reflect the multidimensional approach to dissociation: amnesia, depersonalization and derealization, absorption and imaginative involvement, and passive influence (Armstrong et al., 1997). Versions for use in other countries (e.g., Sweden: Nilsson & Svedin, 2006; Turkey: Zoroglu et al., 2002) have also been developed.

On the A-DES, preliminary reliability data are excellent, and validity data are promising. However, extant research has not tested the underlying factor structure of the A-DES with clinical samples, which is important because studies with nonclinical samples reveal a one-factor structure that contrasts with the hypothesized four-factor structure (Farrington et al., 2001; Muris, Merckelbach, & Peeters, 2003; Nilsson & Svedin, 2006). Research also has not provided sensitivity or specificity data for the 11-item response format and has not reliably identified cutoff scores that could accurately predict whether an adolescent experiences extreme levels of dissociation (Seeley et al., 2004). A cut point of 3 with "good sensitivity and specificity as a screening instrument" has been noted for the 30-item measure (Diseth, 2006, p. 236), as well as for an 8-item format in development with youth in Puerto Rico (Martinez-Taboas et al., 2004, 2006). Furthermore, the A-DES does not solve the weaknesses of the DES, including developmentally inappropriate language and scenarios, not assessing dissociation in its entirety, and being susceptible to dissimulation and malingering (i.e., faking dissociative symptoms; Ohan et al., 2002; Steinberg, 1996). In addition, adolescents who are considered fantasy-prone (i.e., "excessively involved in daydreaming or in age-inappropriate fantasy") may score high on this measure (Ohan et al., p. 1414). Fantasy-proneness is a "relatively benign trait, but when given self-report scales or memory tasks, fantasy-prone persons will often display a response pattern that is characterized by overendorsement, exaggeration, and false alarms" (Muris et al., 2003, p. 23). For these reasons, although some consider the A-DES a valid and reliable measure, "additional studies are still needed to determine its usefulness for adolescents" (Seeley et al., p. 757), and caution is advised in using it as a part of a multimodal assessment in forensic settings.

Regarding other screening instruments and semistructured interviews for dissociation, the CADC, CPAS, DFP, Adolescent Multidimensional Inventory of Dissociation (A-MID), BDDI-C, and CISDE have not been fully validated and do not measure DSM–IV criteria (Cardeña & Weiner, 2004; Ohan et al., 2002; Silberg, 2000). In addition, given that "socio-cultural factors may play an important role in the experience of dissociative phenomena," the Dis-Q (developed in the Netherlands and Belgium) may not be valid for use with adolescents in the United States (Svedin et al., 2004, p. 350).

Finally, the SCID-D is a highly structured interview designed for adults that has been used clinically with adolescents "who can maintain adequate attention and have an average or higher level of cognitive functioning (Steinberg & Steinberg, 1995; Carrion & Steiner, 2000)" (ISSD, 2004, p. 126). Of all of the dissociation instruments previously reviewed, the SCID-D-R is the only one that can provide a DSM–IV diagnosis. When comparing it against other adult assessment tools, the SCID-D is widely recognized as the "'gold standard' for diagnosing of dissociative disorders" on the basis of its rigorous field testing of reliability and validity (Steinberg, 2001, p. 60). It was specifically designed to assess the presence and severity of five dissociative symptoms (amnesia, depersonalization, derealization, identity confusion, and identity alteration; Steinberg, 1996). Severity is evaluated "in terms of distress, dysfunctionality, frequency, duration, and course of the symptom" (Steinberg, 2000, pp. 156–157). However, "[n]o diagnostic interview schedules [including the SCID-D] have been validated for children and adolescents" (ISSD, 2004, p. 126). Although the SCID-D-R appears to be an accepted measure, only three published studies discuss its reliability and validity with adolescents (Carrion & Steiner, 2000, 65 delinquent adolescents; Koopman et al., 2004, 41 of the 65 adolescents in the Carrion & Steiner study; Steinberg & Steinberg, 1995, 3 case studies). Because further work is needed on its reliability and validity for use with adolescents (Koopman et al., 2004), use of the SCID-D-R in courtroom modification assessments is not recommended at this time.

CONCLUSION

Some MHPs may assert that instruments and structured interviews are not necessary for a clinical assessment of the presence and effect of dissociation in children and adolescents. For example, one review of dissociative disorders in children and adolescents concluded, "there is no available diagnostic substitute for the clinical interview and evaluation" (Hornstein, 1996, p. 143). Similarly, a more recent review ended noting that "[u]ltimately, the detection of dissociative phenomena will continue to depend first and foremost on informed and sensitive clinical interaction and observation and on a clear understanding of dissociative phenomena" (Cardeña & Weiner, 2004, p. 504). Such conclusions are unfortunate because standardized criteria and structured assessment tools should significantly raise the level of diagnostic accuracy for traumatic sequelae that are also major *DSM–IV* disorders, including dissociative disorders (Steinberg, 1996). The need for sound, culturally appropriate, reliable, and valid assessment procedures is especially important given the shaky basis of *DSM–IV* dissociative diagnoses in children and adolescents as well as the lack of consensus about which combination of symptoms necessitate treatment in this population. It must be concluded, therefore, that although MHPs can give a child witness a diagnosis of a dissociative disorder, the diagnosis does not rest on a strong scientific foundation.

Given this conclusion, our examination of the assessment instruments used to assess dissociative disorders in youth does not support the appropriateness of their use for courtroom modification evaluations at this time. Studies are needed that examine existing screening instruments and include a structured interview in multicultural child and adolescent populations (Martinez-Taboas et al., 2004, 2006). Further development of narrative procedures is also warranted (Kenardy et al., 2007). Although developmentally and culturally sensitive clinical interaction, observation, and knowledge of dissociation in children and adolescents are necessary components of making a dissociation diagnosis in this population (Cardena & Weiner, 2004), they are not sufficient for courtroom modification evaluations. Of course, this conclusion will, and should, change when the dissociation assessment instruments are more fully developed, validated, and tested in this population.

9

FEAR, ANXIETY, DEPRESSION, AND COURTROOM MODIFICATION EVALUATIONS

The final category of traumatic sequelae to be reviewed includes the internalizing problems and emotional distress symptoms of anxiety, fear, and depression. The first section in this chapter provides a brief introduction regarding the prevalence of anxiety and depression in young people and the assessment challenges that these constructs present. It is followed by sections containing significantly greater detail about the definitions of and assessment measures for fear, anxiety, and depression to inform courtroom modification evaluations.

BRIEF INTRODUCTION TO ANXIETY AND DEPRESSION

Anxiety has long been recognized as a significant problem in childhood. Epidemiological data show that anxiety disorders are among the most common forms of childhood psychopathology, with prevalence rates "between 2.5% and 9% in the general population, and between 20 and 30% among clinically referred children (Anderson, 1994; Costello et al., 1988)" (Fonseca & Perrin, 2001, p. 128). More recent studies estimate collective prevalence rates of 6% to 20% (Costello & Angold, 1995, cited by Langley, Bergman, & Piacentini, 2002; Costello et al., 1996, cited by Silverman & Lopez, 2004).

Similar overall prevalence rates are found in the emerging cross-cultural literature, with "significant ethnic group differences in the rates of specific anxiety disorders such as separation anxiety disorder, posttraumatic stress disorder and social phobia" (Austin & Chorpita, 2004a, p. 217). For example, samples of Chinese youth report higher levels of social anxiety symptoms than Western youth, even though they may not perceive them as distressing, which may be because of differences in parenting practices, greater sensitivity to or importance placed on social cues and relationships among those from collectivistic compared with individualistic cultures, or other factors (Hsu & Alden, 2007; Yao, Zou, Zhu, Abela, Auerbach, & Tong, 2007).

In contrast to the long-standing recognition of anxiety, the existence of depression in children and adolescents has only been accepted since the 1970s (Klein, Dougherty, & Olino, 2005); consensus now exists that depression in children and adolescents is similar to that in adults (Kaslow, Morris, & Rehm, 1998). Studies from various countries show that depression is found to be less common in children (6-month prevalence rates of 1%–3% in community samples and 8%–15% in clinic samples among school-age children) and more common in adolescents (6-month prevalence rates of 5%–6% and lifetime prevalence rates of 15%–20% in community samples; more than 50% in clinical samples; Essau, 2007; Klein et al., 2005, citing Garber & Horowitz, 2002; Lewinsohn & Essau, 2002; and Schwartz, Gladstone & Kaslow, 1998). Yet, as discussed later, depression may be defined and expressed differently across cultures.

Anxiety and depression are both recognized in the *Diagnostic and Statistical Manual of Mental Disorders, Fourth Edition, Text Revision* (*DSM–IV–TR*; American Psychiatric Association [APA], 2000) as general categories, each of which contains a number of disorders. Many mood and anxiety disorders are relevant to allegedly abused youth who may be asked to serve as child witnesses (i.e., major depression, dysthymia, bipolar disorder, separation anxiety disorder, generalized anxiety disorder [GAD], phobias, panic disorder, posttraumatic stress disorder [PTSD; discussed in chap. 7, this volume], and obsessive–compulsive disorder [OCD]). Specific mood and anxiety disorders in studies with abused children and adolescents with the most empirical support are PTSD, major depression, dysthymia, GAD, phobias, and separation anxiety disorder (J. Brown, Cohen, Johnson, & Smailes, 1999; Chaffin, Wherry, & Dykman, 2005; Kaplan, Pelcovitz, Salzinger, & Mandel, 1999; Saywitz, 1997). Longitudinal studies have also found childhood maltreatment to be associated with anxiety and depression in adulthood (e.g., Kaplow & Widom, 2007). It is important to remember, as noted previously, that abuse does not always result in these disorders given the influence of risk and protective factors, such as supportive relationships with mothers and peers (Adams & Burkowski, 2007).

Although the *DSM–IV* uses a categorical format, it does not assume that each disorder is a discrete entity. Controversy exists regarding whether mood and anxiety disorders are discrete or exist on a continuum, and extant research has not solved the question (Ferdinand, van Lang, Ormel, & Verhulst, 2006; Fonseca & Perrin, 2001; Klein et al., 2005). In addition, controversy exists regarding the boundary between normal variations in mood and anxiety and the disorders (Klein et al., 2005). Boundary lines are influenced by various cultural, social, economic, and developmental factors. Emerging cross-cultural research appears to suggest that fears and anxieties may be perceived and/or manifested differently in different countries (Fonseca & Perrin, 2001; Schroeder & Gordon, 2002) or in different contexts in the United States (Lambert, Cooley, Campbell, Benoit, & Stansbury, 2004; Varela & Biggs, 2006), just as it is for depression (Nezu, Nezu, McClure, & Zwick, 2002; Tsai & Chentsova-Dutton, 2002).

Another boundary issue that contributes to confusion, controversy, and assessment difficulties is the complex relationship between depression and anxiety. The current debate in the field centers around whether these are separate and unique disorders, variations of the same problem or a single disorder, or whether both exist along with a third category of anxious depression (Klein et al., 2005; Laurent, Catanzaro, & Joiner, 1999; Moffitt et al., 2007). The high comorbidity of depression and anxiety disorders in children and adolescents has been well documented (Achenbach, 2005; Angold, Costello, & Erkanli, 1999; Garber & Horowitz, 2002; Kendall, Kortlander, Chansky, & Brady, 1992; Klein et al., 2005; Laurent et al., 1999; Silverman & Ollendick, 2005). Comorbidity rates vary widely from 28% to 69% (American Academy of Child and Adolescent Psychiatry [AACAP], 1997a); across age groups rates vary from 12% to 69% in adolescents and 17% in preadolescents (Anderson, 1994).

It is difficult for the debate to be resolved given diagnostic inadequacies and uncertainty about the causes of these problems and their comorbidity. Current diagnostic criteria for depression and anxiety share some symptoms (e.g., irritability, difficulty concentrating), and assessment instruments generally have poor discriminant validity. This means that many assessment tools are not sensitive to differences between these internalizing disorders. Second, the cause of depression and anxiety has not been identified. Whereas some find that "anxiety problems in early childhood are often followed by depressive problems (Kovacs, Gatsonis, Paulauskas, & Richards, 1989; Roza, Hofstra, van der Ende, & Verhulst, 2003)" (Achenbach, 2005, p. 543) and others posit that they have a common cause (Klein & Riso, 1993; Merikangas, 1990), the empirical data do not yet support a causal link (Garber & Horowitz, 2002; Klein et al., 2005; Seligman & Ollendick, 1998). Current knowledge about etiology only points generally to a combination of genetic and environmental influences, such as parenting practices, support, and stressful life events including abuse and family conflict, on childhood and adolescent depression (e.g., Hankin, Mermelstein, & Roesch, 2007; Luby, Belden, & Spitznagel, 2006; Rice, Harold, Shelton, & Thapar, 2006) and anxiety (e.g., McLeod, Wood, & Weisz, 2007).

In addition, age and developmental changes may affect a child's ability to recognize and report some symptoms of depression and anxiety. For this reason, assessment measures must be sensitive to age and developmental changes (Fonseca & Perrin, 2001). Compared with adolescents, children are less reliable reporters of psychopathology (Edelbrock, Costello, Dulcan, Conover, & Kala, 1986), perhaps because of the emerging development of linguistic and metacognitive skills (W. M. Reynolds, 2006). They also have more difficulty reporting time-related information, such as "age of onset, previous episodes, and duration of current episodes" (Klein et al., 2005, p. 418).

Age is not the only variable that affects the ability to recognize internalizing problems, such as anxiety and depression, in youth. The source of evaluation information may affect the assessment of such problems in children, including those who have been allegedly maltreated. Parents tend to overestimate or underestimate depression in their children (Schroeder & Gordon, 2002). Depressed mothers, in particular, have been found to tend to overestimate, or be more sensitive to, their children's depressive symptoms. Also, Kinard (1998) compared depressive symptoms between a sample of sexually abused, physically abused, or neglected elementary-age children with a matched group of nonmaltreated children who were assessed by mother, teacher, and child ratings. The maltreated children were more likely to be rated as clinically depressed by their mothers and teachers but not by their own ratings. However, studies of parents and teachers generally show that they report lower levels of depression than their youth report themselves (Klein et al., 2005). For this reason, compared with their parents, children with depression are "likely to provide more accurate information on internal states which include mood and affect, sleep problems, changes in attention, energy level, guilt feelings, and suicidal thoughts and behaviors" (Orvaschel, 2004, p. 307). Differences between parent, teacher, and child reports are also found in studies of anxiety disorders, with parents reporting more anxiety symptoms than do youth (e.g., Doerfler, Connor, Volungis, & Toscano, 2007; Puliafico, Comer, & Kendall, 2007). These differences may be due to measurement error, lack of parent–child communication, or underreporting because of discomfort, social desirability (or "faking good"), developmental differences in cognitive abilities, or avoidant coping (Baldwin & Dadds, 2007; Schniering, Hudson, & Rapee, 2000; Schniering & Lyneham, 2007). Thus, clinicians should use multiple assessment sources and follow guidelines for weighing sometimes conflicting information when determining whether a child merits a diagnosis of anxiety or depression (Klein et al., 2005; Puliafico et al., 2007; Sternberg, Lamb, Guterman, & Abbott, 2006).

Another way to approach the problem of comorbidity in assessment is to apply L. A. Clark and Watson's (1991) tripartite model of anxiety and depression, which has been generally supported in studies with multiethnic children and adolescents (Austin & Chorpita, 2004a; Klein et al., 2005). The first dimension, generalized distress, notes that both depression and anxiety are characterized by a high level of distress with shared "negative affect" (NA), which includes symptoms of anxious or depressed mood, irritability, sleep and eating problems, and difficulty concentrating. The second dimension, anhedonia and low positive affect (PA; i.e., not experiencing pleasure in things that previously gave one pleasure, cognitive and motor slowing), is said to be what uniquely characterizes depression. The third dimension, physiological hyperarousal (PH), is said to be what uniquely characterizes anxiety. Some research evidence suggests that NA and PA "may be relatively unaffected by variations in the surrounding culture" (Austin & Chorpita, 2004a, p. 218). Although instruments developed from this model have been shown to discriminate between depression and anxiety in children (i.e., the Child Anxiety and Depression Scale [Chorpita, Yim, Moffitt, Umemoto, & Francis, 2000], the Positive and Negative Affect Scale for Children [Laurent et al., 1999], the Physiological Hyperarousal Scale for Children [Laurent et al., 2004], and the Affect and Arousal Scale [Chorpita, Daleiden, Moffitt, Yim, & Umemoto, 2000; Daleiden, Chorpita, & Lu, 2000]), physiological measures have not found elevated PH only in anxiety (Greaves-Lord et al., 2007). Also, additional cross-cultural research is needed (Yang, Hong, Joung, & Kim, 2006). Thus, further research is recommended to develop the model, the measures, and their clinical relevance (Silverman & Ollendick, 2005).

Comorbidity not only presents assessment and measurement problems, it also has significant clinical implications. Comorbidity is associated with greater impairment, persistence of problems, and poorer treatment outcomes compared with single-disorder cases (Klein et al., 2005; Laurent et al., 1999; Silverman & Ollendick, 2005). For example, depressed youth with comorbid disorders are at higher risk for suicide (Birmaher, Ryan, & Williamson, 1996). Thus, comorbidity should be considered when making courtroom modification assessments because the future mental and physical health of the allegedly abused child witness is of particular concern.

The four subsections that follow first define and then describe the assessment measures for fear and anxiety, followed by depression. As in previous chapters, we provide guidance for the multidimensional assessment process, including descriptions of relevant, valid, and reliable screening and psychological tests, as well as interviews that evaluate the frequency, duration, and intensity of any anxious or depressive symptoms, taking into account the individual context of the child. Again, it is important to refer the child to a physician to conduct a medical evaluation to rule out general medical conditions that may present like anxiety or depression. Physical conditions that might produce anxiety symptoms include the following:

1. reactions to caffeine, psychostimulants, sedatives and hypnotics, inhalants, and neuroleptics;
2. central nervous system problems, including partial seizures, lesions of the limbic system and frontal lobes, and postconcussion syndrome;
3. metabolic and endocrine disorders, including hypoglycemia, hyperthyroidism, carcinoid tumor, and hypocalcemia; and
4. cardiac problems, such as mitral valve prolapse, arrhythmias, and valvular disease causing palpitations. (Schroeder & Gordon, 2002, p. 284)

For examination of depression, "laboratory work should include a hematologic profile with differential to evaluate for thyroid disease, and an electrolyte panel (including liver and kidney function tests) to evaluate for potential metabolic abnormalities and kidney disorders . . . an EEG [electroencephalogram] to rule out seizures . . . a drug screen . . . [and] a thorough medication history" (Kaslow et al., 1998, p. 56). Other medical rule outs include "malignancies, chronic diseases, infectious mononucleosis, anemia, and vitamin deficiency (especially folic acid)" (Bhatia & Bhatia, 2007, p. 74).

WHAT ARE FEAR AND ANXIETY?

Fear and anxiety are generally seen as similar, related constructs. Accordingly, they have been equated with emotional distress (chap. 6, this volume) and described as individual symptoms as well as clusters of symptoms or disorders. As symptoms, both can be understood as "future-oriented emotion[s], characterized by perceptions of uncontrollability and unpredictability over potentially aversive events and a rapid shift in attention to the focus of potentially dangerous events or one's own affective response to these events" (Barlow, 2002, p. 104; see also Barlow, Allen, & Choate, 2004). In other words, fear and anxiety can be seen as normal emotional reactions that come from anticipating real or imagined threats to the self (Fonseca & Perrin, 2001). Subtle differences between the terms may be found. Whereas anxiety can be described as "a subjective feeling of tension; fear is a sense of dread or impending doom" (Silverman & Ollendick, 2005, p. 381).

All people experience these emotions. In fact, mild to moderate levels of fear and anxiety are a normal part of the developmental process (AACAP, 2007) and can be seen as adaptive (Marks, 1987). Normative and cross-cultural data exist regarding patterns of children's fears from infancy through adolescence (Fonesca & Perrin, 2001; Morris & Kratochwill, 1998; Schroeder & Gordon, 2002; see Table 9.1).

However, some differences in contextual variables have been found. For instance, girls report "higher prevalence and intensity of fears and anxi-

TABLE 9.1
Sources of Fears and Worries at Different Age Levels

Age level	Sources of fear or worry
0–6 months	Loud noises Loss of support Excessive sensory stimuli
6–9 months	Strangers Novel stimuli (e.g., masks) Heights Sudden or unexpected stimuli (e.g., noise, bright light)
1 year	Separation from caretaker Strangers Toilets
2 years	Auditory stimuli (e.g., trains and thunder) Imaginary creatures Darkness Separation from caretakers
3 years	Visual stimuli (e.g., masks) Animals Darkness Being alone Separation from caretakers
4 years	Auditory stimuli (e.g., fire engines, sirens, noises) Darkness Animals Parents leaving at night Imaginary creatures Burglars
5 years	Visual stimuli Concrete stimuli (e.g., injury, falling, dogs) "Bad" people Separation from caretakers Imaginary creatures Animals Personal harm or harm to others
6 years	Auditory stimuli (e.g., angry voices, thunder) Imaginary creatures Burglars Sleeping alone Personal harm or harm to others Natural disasters (e.g., fire, floods) Animals Dying or death of others
7–8 years	Imaginary creatures Staying alone Personal harm or harm to others

(continues)

TABLE 9.1
Sources of Fears and Worries at Different Age Levels   *(Continued)*

Age level	Sources of fear or worry
	Media exposure to extraordinary events (e.g., bombings, kidnappings) Failure and criticism Medical and dental procedures Dying or death of others Frightening dreams or movies Animals
9–12 years	Failure and criticism (e.g., school evaluation) Rejection Peer bullying or teasing Kidnapping Dying or death of others Personal harm or harm to others Illness
13–18 years	Social alienation Failure Embarrassment or humiliation Injury or serious illness Natural and human-made disasters (e.g., economic and political concerns) Death and danger

Note. From *Assessment and Treatment of Childhood Problems: A Clinician's Guide* (2nd ed., pp. 265–266), by C. S. Schroeder and B. N. Gordon, 2002. New York: Guilford Press. Copyright 2002 by Guilford Press. Reprinted with permission.

eties than males" (Li & Morris, 2007, p. 446). Also, evidence suggests that "the quantity, structure, and stability of African American children's fears may differ from children of other ethnic backgrounds, especially for those living in urban environments (Lambert et al., 2004, p. 248). In addition, some children experience anger as well as fear in situations that are anxiety-provoking (March et al., 1995), but not everyone experiences clinically significant problems with anxiety or fear.

Consensus generally exists regarding the distinction between normal and pathological anxiety in children. "In contrast to normal anxiety, pathological anxiety is seen as being beyond that expected for the child's developmental level, disproportionate to the threat posed (e.g., extreme fear of the dark), severe (e.g., causing distress to the child), persistent and impairing one or more areas of functioning (e.g., school and relations with family or peers)" (Fonseca & Perrin, 2001, p. 128). In contrast, there is confusion in the field about whether distinctions exist between fear, panic, and phobia, and no agreed-on definitions exist (Morris & Kratochwill, 1998). Some use the terms interchangeably (e.g., Fonseca & Perrin, 2001; Silverman & Ollendick, 2005), whereas others distinguish fear as a normal reaction from clinical fear or phobia. Clinical fear or phobia is seen as a subcategory of fear that has the following characteristics (Morris & Kratochwill, p. 93, citing Graziano, DeGiovanni, & Garcia, 1979; Marks, 1969; and Miller, Barret, & Hampe, 1974):

1. is out of proportion to the demands of the situation;
2. cannot be explained or reasoned away;
3. is beyond voluntary control;
4. leads to an avoidance of the feared situation . . .
5. persists over a period of time [over 2 years] or has an intensity that is debilitating to the child's routine lifestyle;
6. is maladaptive; and
7. is not age or "stage specific."[1]

When anxiety and fear responses reach the level of a disorder, they can be seen as a complex response pattern with three related components: cognitive–subjective–verbal, behavioral–motoric, and physiological–somatic. First described by Lang (1968) as the triple-response conceptualization, the tripartite model (L. A. Clark & Watson, 1991) provides the organization for the *DSM–IV* anxiety disorders (Zinbarg & Barlow, 1996). The cognitive system is often referred to as the *verbal* or *subjective response system* because it relies on the child's self-report to share its existence with others (Morris & Kratochwill, 1998). At this level, the child's anxiety is expressed through reports of danger, fearful apprehension, worry, distorted thoughts about his or her level of safety or performance, or a combination of these. In the behavior or motor response system, others can observe the child's overt behaviors. These can include escape or avoidance behaviors (e.g., running away) as well as signs of restlessness (e.g., pacing, hand wringing, foot tapping), nervousness (e.g., nail biting, trembling), clinging to loved ones, and stuttering (Fonseca & Perrin, 2001; Morris & Kratochwill, 1998). In the physiological or somatic response system, there can be heightened arousal of the autonomic system (heart rate, blood pressure, galvanic skin response perspiration) and a number of self-reported somatic complaints, such as headaches or stomachaches (Morris & Kratochwill, 1998; Silverman & Lopez, 2004; Silverman & Ollendick, 2005). Although somatic symptoms are "hallmark clinical features of anxiety disorders in children" and adolescents, more research is needed regarding specific types of somatic symptoms; how somatic symptoms vary across time, demographic, and clinical characteristics; and how somatic symptoms are assessed (Ginsburg, Riddle, & Davies, 2006, p. 1180; Hofflich, Hughes, & Kendall, 2006). For example, some evidence suggests that African American and Hispanic and Latino children may be more likely to focus on or report somatic symptoms than Caucasian children

---

[1]Items 1 through 4 from Morris and Kratochwill (1998, p. 3) citing Marks (1969). Item 5 from Morris and Kratochwill (1998, p. 3) citing Graziano et al. (1979). Items 6 and 7 from Morris and Kratochwill (1998, p. 3) citing Miller et al. (1974).

(Canino, 2004, citing Varela et al., 2004, and Pina & Silverman, 2004; Neal-Barnett, 2004; Varela & Biggs, 2006).

All anxiety disorders share these three responses but differ in the focus or the content of the worry or apprehension (Silverman & Ollendick, 2005). For example, children with social anxiety disorder (SAD)[2] worry about something bad that might happen to their caregivers, whereas children with panic disorder[3] are afraid that a panic attack will happen again and about what might happen if it does.

Anxiety and clinical fears are relevant to consider in courtroom modification assessments because some responses, especially those in the behavioral or motor system, can adversely affect a child's ability to communicate in court. Moreover, elevated anxiety levels have been found in child and adolescent victims of various forms of child maltreatment, some of whom may appear as child witnesses (e.g., Chaffin, Silovsky, & Vaughn, 2005; Gomes-Schwartz, Horowitz, & Cardarelli, 1990; Kolko, Moser, & Weldy, 1988; Somer & Braunstein, 1999). Abusive experiences can cause a child to experience overwhelming fear (E. B. Carlson, Furby, Armstrong, & Shales, 1997), including fear of impending death (Conte, Briere, & Sexton, 1989). Acute fear and terror have also been associated with the development of PTSD in adult survivors of child sexual abuse (Hanson et al., 2001). Maltreated children and adolescents, especially those who have been physically and sexually abused, appear to be at increased risk for anxiety disorders in the short- and long-term (Chaffin et al., 2005; Kaplan, Pelcovitz, & Labruna, 1999).

---

[2]SAD is "characterized by developmentally inappropriate and excessive anxiety concerning separation from home or from those to whom the child is attached" (APA, 2000, pp. 40–41).

[3]The essential features of panic disorder are "the presence of recurrent, unexpected Panic Attacks . . . followed by at least 1 month of persistent concern about having another Panic Attack, worry about the possible implications or consequences of the Panic Attacks, or a significant behavioral change related to the attacks" (APA, 2000, p. 433). A panic attack is defined as a "discrete period of intense fear or discomfort in the absence of real danger that is accompanied by at least 4 of 13 somatic or cognitive symptoms" that develops abruptly, reaches a peak rapidly (within 10 minutes), and is "often accompanied by a sense of imminent danger or impending doom and an urge to escape:
1. palpitations, pounding heart, or accelerated heart rate
2. sweating
3. trembling or shaking
4. sensations of shortness of breath or smothering
5. feeling of choking
6. chest pain or discomfort
7. nausea or abdominal distress
8. feeling dizzy, unsteady, lightheaded, or faint
9. derealization (feelings of unreality) or depersonalization (being detached from oneself)
10. fear of losing control or going crazy
11. fear of dying
12. parasthesias (numbness or tingling sensations)
13. chills or hot flushes." (APA, pp. 430–432)
Panic disorder can occur with or without agoraphobia, which is "anxiety about being in places or situations from which escape might be difficult (or embarrassing) or in which help may not be available in the event of having a Panic Attack . . . or panic-like symptoms" (APA, p. 432).

The *DSM–IV* diagnoses for anxiety that have been applied to allegedly abused and maltreated children include separation anxiety disorder, generalized anxiety disorder (GAD),[4] phobias,[5] panic disorder, obsessive–compulsive disorder (OCD[6]; e.g., Ackerman et al., 1998; Chaffin et al., 2005), and PTSD[7]. The reader should note that GAD has taken the place of the *Diagnostic and Statistical Manual of Mental Disorders* (*DSM–III–R*; APA, 1987) overanxious disorder of childhood, and social phobia has taken the place of the *DSM–III–R* avoidant disorder of childhood, because the older disorders have been referred to in some studies of abused children (e.g., Ackerman et al., 1998). The anxiety disorders most common in children generally are SAD, GAD, and phobias (Schroeder & Gordon, 2002). Whereas SAD and phobias are found more often in young children, GAD, social phobia–social anxiety disorder, and panic disorder are more common in older children and adolescents (Rao et al., 2007; Zahn-Waxler, Klimes-Dougan, & Slattery, 2000).

ANXIETY ASSESSMENT MEASURES

A wide range of assessment strategies are available to mental health professionals (MHPs) to assess anxiety disorders, including structured and semistructured diagnostic interview schedules; parent, teacher, child, and clinician rating scales; direct observations; self-monitoring procedures; and physiological measures. Because anxiety was one of the first childhood problem areas to be evaluated with rating scales, the number of available measures for this task is significant. In 1988, Barrios and Hartmann described 100 instruments that were available for the assessment of children's anxieties and fears; in 1997, they reviewed more than 160 (Barrios & Hartmann, 1988, 1997). New measures continue to be developed to examine specific types of disorders or aspects of anxiety (e.g., physiological measures) and to redress problems with measures developed in the 1950s to 1970s that were created from adult measures and as such are less developmentally appropriate. Over time, "a trend has arisen toward enhanced developmental sensitivity and greater specificity with respect to the assessment of anxiety and related

---

[4]GAD is "characterized by at least 6 months of persistent and excessive anxiety and worry" (APA, 2000, p. 429).
[5]Various types of phobias are recognized by the *DSM–IV*. Specific phobia is "characterized by clinically significant anxiety provoked by exposure to a specific feared object or situation, often leading to avoidance behavior" (APA, 2000, p. 429). Social phobia is "characterized by clinically significant anxiety provoked by exposure to certain types of social or performance situations, often leading to avoidance behavior" (APA, 2000, p. 429).
[6]OCD is "characterized by obsessions (which cause marked anxiety or distress) and/or by compulsions (which serve to neutralize anxiety)" (APA, 2000, p. 429).
[7]PTSD is also an anxiety-related diagnosis, but it is discussed in chapter 8 of this volume because it is a major component of the broader category of posttraumatic stress. The literature supports separating posttraumatic stress from anxiety as different effects of child abuse.

behavior in children" and a recognition of the need for culturally sensitive practices (Greco & Morris, 2004, p. 99).

When choosing a measure, MHPs should follow instrument selection criteria for anxiety assessment instruments for children and adolescents. For example, Stallings and March's (1995) often-cited recommendation states that clinicians should choose anxiety measures that "(1) provide reliable and valid ascertainment of symptoms across multiple symptom domains; (2) discriminate symptom clusters; (3) evaluate severity; (4) incorporate and reconcile multiple observations, such as parent and child ratings; and (5) be sensitive to treatment-induced change in symptoms" (p. 127). A choice is also influenced by the purpose of the assessment, developmental and cultural appropriateness of the measure, and other pragmatic issues, such as administration time and cost.

Because reviewing all measures is beyond the scope of this book, this section focuses on those interview- and self-report-based instruments that appear most relevant, reliable, valid, and consistent with empirically based assessment guidelines and selection criteria for use in courtroom modification assessments. Although behavioral observations and physiological measures could be helpful in the assessment process, they are not included at this time because standardized methodological approaches to implement these techniques have not yet been established in the child anxiety literature (Woodruff-Borden & Leyfer, 2006). Readers may also reference extensive reviews of many of the available measures for child anxiety disorders, including the following:

- Barrios and Hartmann's (1997) thorough review of more than 160 instruments, organized by anxiety-provoking stimuli;
- G. A. Bernstein, Borchardt, and Perwien's (1996) list of 14 types of anxiety assessment instruments for children and adolescents: Schedule for Affective Disorders and Schizophrenia for School-Age Children—Epidemiological version (K–SADS–E), Anxiety Disorders Interview Schedule (ADIS), Diagnostic Interview for Children and Adolescents—Revised (DICA–R), Diagnostic Interview Schedule for Children (DISC), State–Trait Anxiety Inventory for Children (S–TAIC), Revised Children's Manifest Anxiety Scale (RCMAS), Fear Survey Schedule for Children—Revised (FSSC–R), Visual Analogue Scale for Anxiety—Revised (VASA–R), Social Anxiety Scale for Children—Revised (SASC–R), Multidimensional Anxiety Scale for Children (MASC), Hamilton Anxiety Rating Scale (HARS or HAM-A), Anxiety Rating for Children—Revised (ARC–R), Personality Inventory for Children (PIC), and Child Behavior Checklist (CBCL);

- Brooks and Kutcher's (2003) detailed review of 15 "most commonly used instruments" for adolescents: K–SADS, Anxiety Disorders Interview Schedule for Children for *DSM–IV: Child and Parent Versions* (ADIS–IV: C/P), DISC, RCMAS, State–Trait Anxiety Inventory (S–TAI), S–TAIC, FSSC–R/II, CBCL Youth Self Report version of the CBCL (YSR), Screen for Child Anxiety Related Emotional Disorders—Revised (SCARED–R), MASC, Pediatric Anxiety Rating Scale (PARS), Child Anxiety Sensitivity Index (CASI), Social Phobia Anxiety Inventory (SPAI), Social Phobia Anxiety Inventory for Children (SPAI–C), SASC–R, and Social Anxiety Scale for Adolescents (SAS–A);
- Greco and Morris's (2004) discussion of "commonly used" (p. 99) measures, including the ADIS–IV: C/P interview schedule, three parent- and teacher-report measures (CBCL and Teacher Report Form [TRF], Child Symptom Inventory—Fourth Revision, SCARED–R), three global self-report measures (MASC, SCARED–R, Spence Children's Anxiety Scale [SCAS]), seven syndrome-specific measures (SASC–R, SPAI–C, Children's Yale–Brown Obsessive–Compulsive Scale (CY–BOCS), Leyton Obsessional Inventory–Child Version (LOI–CV), Child PTSD Reaction Index, Child PTSD Symptom Scale, CASI, and a general review of behavioral assessment tests, as well as school, peer, and family observations;
- Greenhill, Pine, March, Birmaher, and Riddle's (1998) review of 20 scales used in studies of controlled drug treatment studies, broken down by "diagnostic": DICA, ADIS, Child & Adolescent Psychiatric Assessment (CAPA), DISC-2.3, Schedule for Affective Disorders and Schizophrenia for School-Age Children: Present and Lifetime Version (K–SADS–PL), KSADS–Columbia; "self-report": STAIC, RCMAS, FSSC–R, VASA—Revised, SASC–R, SPAI–C, MASC, SCARED; and "clinician-based, other" measures: HAM–A, ARC–R, Children's Anxiety Rating Scale (CARS), PIC, CBCL, Clinical Global Impressions.
- Langley, Bergman, and Piacentini's (2002) review of five structured diagnostic interviews (ADIS–IV, K–SADS–PL, DISC–IV, DICA–R, CAPA), four clinician-administered measures (CY–BOCS, PARS, HARS, National Institutes of Mental Health Obsessive Compulsive Disorder [NIMH OCD] Global Scale), five self-report measures of global anxiety (MASC, SCARED, RCMAS, STAIC, CBCL/YSR/TRF), 12 self-report measures for specific anxiety disorders (SASC–R, SPAI–C,

School Refusal Assessment Scale [SRAS], LOI–CV, Child Obsessive Compulsive Impact Scale, Stress Management Questionnaire [SMQ], FSSC–R, PTSD Index for *DSM–IV*, PTSDRI, Coping Questionnaire, Negative Affect Self-Statement Questionnaire [NASSQ], CASI), and describes other methods (behavioral avoidance tests, psychophysiological measures, and investigating information processing biases);

- K. Myers and Winters's (2002) discussion of 10 widely represented anxiety scales in the child and adolescent literature: HARS, RCMAS, MASC, SCARED, PARS, STAI–C, SPAI–C, SASC–R, FSSC–R, CY–BOCS;
- Silverman and Lopez's (2004) presentation of brief summaries of "the most widely used" (p. 273) semistructured and structured interview schedules (ADIS–IV: C/P; K–SADS; NIMH DISC–IV; CAPA; DICA); child rating scales (Youth Self Report; RCMAS; STAIC; SAS–R; SPAIC; CASI; Test Anxiety Scale for Children (TASC); FSSC–R; MASC; SCARED; Spence Anxiety Scale); and parent and teacher rating scales (CBCL; Conner's Rating Scales—Revised [CRS–R]; Behavior Assessment System for Children [BASC]; Devereux Behavior Rating Scale [DBRS], School form). They also described procedures for using director observations, self-monitoring, and physiological measures;
- Silverman and Ollendick's (2005) review of the 31 most widely used interviews (ADIS: C/P, CAPA, DICA, DISC–IV, K–SADS) and rating scales (child-report: Affect and Arousal Scale [AAS], Anxiety Control Questionnaire for Children [ACQC], Children's Automatic Thoughts Scale, CASI, FSSC–R, MASC, NASSQ, Penn State Worry Questionnaire for Children [PSWQC], Physiological Hyperarousal Scale for Children [PHSC], Positive and Negative Affect Schedule for Children [PNASC], Revised Child Anxiety and Depression Scales [RCADS], RCMAS, SCARED, SASC, SPAIC, SCAS, STAI–C, TASC; parent and teacher report: BASC, CBCL, Conner's Rating Scales—Revised Parent/Teacher, DBRS [Teacher form], STAI–C–PR–T; clinician rating scales: CY–BOCS, PARS, ADIS: C/P);
- Silverman and Serafini's (1998) "evaluative descriptions" (p. 343) of a comprehensive set of methods, including interviews (K–SADS, DICA, Interview Schedule for Children [ISC], Child Assessment Schedule [CAS], DISC, ADIS: C, CAPA–C), behavior problem checklists (CBCL, Revised Behavior Problem Checklist [RBPC], CRS–R, Eyberg Child Be-

havior Inventory [ECBI]), self-rating scales (RCMAS, STAIC, SASC–R, TASC, CASI, FSSC–R), observational procedures (Preschool Observational Rating Scale [POSA], Behavioral Avoidance Test [BAT]), self-monitoring procedures ("daily diary," log sheets), and psychophysiological measurement (heart rate, galvanic skin response, cortisol levels); and

- Woodruff-Borden and Leyfer's (2006) review of various methods for assessing anxiety in children: diagnostic interviews (ADIS: C/P, DICA, DISC, K–SADS), self-report measures (MASC, RCMAS, STAIC, FSSC–R), behavioral observations, cognitive assessment, and physiological assessment.

Structured and semistructured interviews provide for more reliable diagnosis of disorders than unstructured clinical interviews, even if they are more time-consuming to administer. Of the five most commonly used interviews for assessing anxiety in children and adolescents (i.e., ADIS–IV: C/P, CAPA, DICA–IV, DISC–IV, and K–SADS–PL), the ADIS–IV: C/P and K–SADS–PL are considered the best (Brooks & Kutcher, 2003; Greenhill et al., 1998; Silverman & Ollendick, 2005) and follow the previously discussed recommendations of Stallings and March (1995). They are useful for modification assessments with a wide age range of children (as young as 6–8 years of age and as old as 16–18 years of age) because they provide valid and reliable *DSM–IV* diagnoses and address symptom frequency, severity, and duration.

- The ADIS–IV: C/P (Silverman & Albano, 1996; Silverman & Eisen, 1992; Silverman & Nelles, 1988; Silverman, Saavedra, & Pina, 2001) is one of the best known and most widely used measures (Fonseca & Perrin, 2001) designed specifically to provide differential *DSM–IV* diagnosis of anxiety disorders in youth. Considered the gold standard, the ADIS–IV possesses good psychometric properties and empirical support, and it assesses a child's "cognitive, behavioral and physiological functioning across a range of potentially anxiety-inducing situations" (Greco & Morris, 2004, p. 100), as gathered from semistructured interviews with the child and caregiver (1–1.5 hours for each interview). Adding to its developmental appropriateness, visual aids are provided to help the child and parent judge levels of worry, impairment, and frequency. For example, a 0- to 8-point Feelings Thermometer is used to rate how each disorder interferes with the child's functioning at school and with family and friends. Clinicians also use a 0- to 8-point scale (0 = *none* to 8 = *very seriously disturbing/impairing*) to assign a degree of distress and interference of functioning for each disorder, with ratings over 4 (4 = *definitely disturbing/impairing*) signaling a "clinical" diagnosis. Of additional interest to the child modification assessment is that diagnosis and severity scores (but not symptom scores) have been found to be sensitive to change. In addition to measuring severity and frequency, the ADIS–IV: C/P can also be used to gather information about precipitating events and the course of the anxiety problem and related problems, including mood disorders, disruptive disorders, and developmental delays (Greco & Morris, 2004).

- The K–SADS–PL (J. Kaufman et al., 1997) accommodates *DSM–IV* criteria and generates reliable and valid child psychiatric diagnoses for 32 disorders, including anxiety disorders. Extensively used in clinical and research settings, it has been translated into 16 languages (J. Kaufman & Schweder, 2004) and has been studied in populations of multiethnic youth (Hawkins & Radcliffe, 2006). Requiring extensive training, the K–SADS–PL begins with 10 to 15 minutes of unstructured general questions (e.g., demographic information, reason for referral, child's functioning across settings) and then moves to 82 questions about core symptoms of each diagnostic area covered, with questions answered on a 0- to 3-point scale (0 = *no information*, 1 = *not present*, 2 = *subthreshold*, 3 = *threshold*). Probes are made to determine timing and severity of symptoms. Supplemental sections, including one for anxiety disorders, are given if one threshold rating is made during the screening interview. For preadolescents, the parent is interviewed first; the order is reversed for adolescents. Each interview can take 35 to 45 minutes for those reporting little difficulties to an average of 1.25 hours for those in psychiatric settings. Its sensitivity to change has not been proven.

See Table 9.2 for more details about these interviews and their psychometric properties.

When weighing options of which assessment measures to choose, these interview schedules provide for reliable, but time-consuming, diagnostic assessment of various internalizing problems from a variety of sources. If time is a concern, MHPs could consider the use of a screening instrument before administering a semistructured interview (Silverman & Serafini, 1998). However, in the area of anxiety disorders, it is currently recommended that anxiety screening measures (e.g., the MASC for GAD in girls and anxiety comorbid conditions in girls and boys) be used in conjunction with other assessment measures—namely, diagnostic interviews (Silverman & Ollendick, 2005). The most parsimonious approach therefore appears to be to start with the diagnostic interview or with a more general valid and reliable screening

TABLE 9.2
Anxiety Assessment Instruments for Use in Courtroom Modifications With Children and Adolescents

Anxiety measures	Age range	Reliability data	Validity data	Severity level/cutoff scores	Features/summary	Weaknesses
Anxiety Disorders Interview Schedule for DSM–IV (ADIS–IV) for Children and Parent Versions (C/P) Available from Oxford University Press, http://www.oup.com/us/; Tel: (800) 445-9714; Fax: (919) 677-1303; e-mail: custserv.us@oup.com To order a book by phone, please contact the Orders Department at (800) 451-7556 or e-mail at custserv.us@oup.com. Contact information for primary author: Wendy K. Silverman, PhD, Professor of Psychology, Florida International University, University Park, Miami, FL 33199; Tel: (305) 348-2880; Fax: (305) 348-3879; e-mail: silverw@fiu.edu	6–18 years	Internal consistency: not reported Interrater reliability • Kappa coefficients (Lyneham, Abbott, & Rapee, 2007; Silverman & Lopez, 2004), child: .81/.78 (SAD), .87/.71 (SocP), .85/.80 (SP), .82/.63 (GAD); parent: .83/.88 (SAD), .83/.86 (SocP), .87/.65 (SP), .82/.72 (GAD); combined: .89/.84 (SAD), .82/.92 (SocP), 1.0/.81 (SpecP), .80/.80 (GAD) Test-retest: administered 7–14 days apart by same diagnostician ($n = 62$), 7–16-year-olds referred to anxiety clinic Combined diagnoses Kappa/Intraclass correlation coefficients = .84 (SAD), .92 (SOP), .81 (SpecP), .80 (GAD), 1.00 (ADHD), .62 (ODD; Silverman, Saavedra, & Pina, 2001).	Convergent validity: "strong correspondence" with MASC (Greco & Morris, 2004, p. 100) Discriminative validity: "fairly well established" (Brooks & Kutcher, 2003, p. 359) Sensitivity to treatment, induced change: "established for ADIS: C/P diagnoses and ADIS: C/P severity ratings" (Brooks & Kutcher, 2003, p. 392; Greco & Morris, 2004)	Severity and level of impairment rated on a 9-point scale ($0 = $ not at all, $4 = $ some, $8 = $ very, very much) by child, parent, and clinician. Rating ≥ 4 is required to give a diagnosis. Cut score of 4 parent-endorsed social fears distinguished children with SOP from those with SAD/GAD and nonanxious community youth aged 7–14 years (Puliafico, Comer, & Kendall, 2007).	• Semistructured interview • Parent, child, or combined versions • Specifically designed for differential diagnosis by trained clinicians of all DSM–IV anxiety disorders in youth: school refusal, SAD, SpecP, simple phobia, PD, PD with agoraphobia, agoraphobia without history of PD, OAD, GAD, OCD, or PTSD. • Structure: contains 300 yes–no items to assess cognitive, behavioral, and physiological functioning across a range of potentially anxiety-inducing situations. • Information can be collected on precipitating events, symptom course, and associated problems such as mood disorders, developmental delays, and disruptive disorders. • Provides recommended probe questions and visual aids to help with judging levels of worry, impairment, and frequency of symptoms. • Symptoms are assessed as present, absent, or other (if they cannot decide, even with more prompting). • Duration: each interview usually takes 1–1.5 hours	• Administration time • Does not include ICD–10 diagnoses • Reliable and valid for anxiety disorders only, with further investigation needed with children under 9–10 years old (Fonseca & Perrin, 2001) • More concordance data needed with other means of diagnosis and among child, parent, and combined diagnoses

(continues)

TABLE 9.2

Anxiety Assessment Instruments for Use in Courtroom Modifications With Children and Adolescents (Continued)

Anxiety measures	Age range	Reliability data	Validity data	Severity level/cutoff scores	Features/summary	Weaknesses
The Schedule for Affective Disorders and Schizophrenia for School-Age Children: Present and Lifetime Version (K–SADS–PL) Other K–SADS versions include the K–SADS–P (Present episode), K–SADS–E (Epidemiological version), K–SADS–L (Lifetime version), and K–SADS–IVR Available at http://www.wpic.pitt.edu/ksads/default.htm Restrictions on use are as follows: "This instrument is copyrighted. Usage is freely permitted without further permission for uses which meet one or more of the following: Clinical usage in a not-for-profit institution, Usage in an IRB [internal review board] approved research protocol. All other uses require written permission of the principal author, Dr. Kaufman, including but not limited to the following: Redistribution of the instrument in printed, electronic or other forms, Commercial use of the instrument." Original citation: J. Kaufman et al. (1997). Schedule for Affective Disorders and Schizophrenia for School-Age Children—Present and Lifetime version: Initial reliability and validity data. *Journal of the American Academy of Child & Adolescent Psychiatry, 36,* 980–988.	6/7–18 years	Internal consistency • Cronbach alpha .039 (K–SADS–P with 52 clinic-referred 6–17-year-olds); >.75 (OAD and SAD 25 anxious and/or depressed 6–17-year-olds); .80 (OAD in 108 13–18-year-olds in inpatient care; Brooks & Kutcher, 2003) Interrater and test-retest reliability • Kappa: combined .78 (OAD), .80 (SpecP; Silverman & Lopez, 2004) • Kappa = .80 (n = 11, present anxiety diagnosis), .67 (n = 8, PTSD), and .78 (n = 8, GAD) in nineteen 7–17-year-old psychiatric patients and 1 normal control subject assessed 2–38 days apart by two independent clinicians, found excellent kappa for present anxiety disorder diagnoses (Brooks & Kutcher, 2003) • Kappa = .84 (any anxiety disorder) for Spanish version (Ulloa et al., 2006)	Concurrent validity: youth meeting criteria for any AD on KSADS–P also had higher RCMAS, HAM-A (or HARS), and S–TAIC scores; on K–SADS–PL with SCARED and CBCL Internalizing scales (Brooks & Kutcher, 2003; J. Kaufman & Schweder, 2004) Discriminative validity, KSADS–PL: Sample (n = 66) of 7–17-year-olds who met criteria for current AD (n = 34) scored higher than those for other psychiatric disorders on the CBCL internalizing scale and on a 38-item version of the SCARED Sensitivity to change: "not proven, not intended for monitoring changes" (Brooks & Kutcher, 2003, p. 391)	Severity and timing of symptoms are scored with probes used during screening process with parent and child on 0–3 scale: 0 = *no information,* 1 = *not present,* 2 = *subthreshold,* 3 = *threshold.* Summary diagnoses for each disorder placed on a 1–4 scale: 1 = *no disorder,* 4 = *definite disorder.*	• Semistructured interview • Designed for trained clinicians qualified to make diagnoses to be used to assess 32 current or lifetime *DSM–IV* and *DSM–III–R* differential diagnoses, including the following anxiety diagnoses: GAD/OAD, SAD, OCD, PD, PTSD, simple phobia, avoidant disorder/social phobia, and agoraphobia. • Three-component structure: begins with a 10- to 15-minute unstructured introductory interview, followed by an 82-item screening interview in which core symptoms are rated on a 3-point scale and skip-out criteria are used and use of five diagnostic supplements based on need: affective disorders; psychotic disorders; ADs; behavioral disorders; and substance abuse, eating, or tic disorders; supplements are asked in time order or based on possible comorbid conditions. • Administered first to parents for preadolescents; with adolescents, the order is reversed. • Clinician integrates data from parent and child reports and outside data using judgment to produce summary diagnoses for each disorder on a 1–4 scale.	• Administration time • Requires extensive training, clinical experience, and *DSM–IV* familiarity. • Does not include *ICD–10* diagnoses. • No standardized procedure for combining data from multiple informants. • More concordance data needed with other means of diagnosis, and for diagnoses from single informants. • Most translated versions do not have published psychometrics data.

(continues)

Instrument / Source	Age	Reliability	Validity	Scoring	Description	Comments
The Schedule for Affective Disorders and Schizophrenia for School-Age Children: Present and Lifetime version (K–SADS–PL) (Continued)		• Test-retest kappa with 1- to 5-week interval in sample (n = 55) of psychiatric outpatients and 11 normal control subjects = .90 (MDD and/or dysthymia); .78 (GAD); .80 (any AD); .63 (ADHD); .74 (ODD) (J. Kaufman & Schweder, 2004) • Interrater reliability in use of skip-out across 20 diagnostic areas surveyed averaged 99.7% (range: 93%–100%; J. Kaufman & Schweder, 2004)			• Duration: 35–45 minutes per interviewee with control subjects, 1.25 hours per interviewee with clinical patients. • Translated into 16 languages.	• No computer versions currently available.
Multidimensional Anxiety Scale for Children (MASC)	8–19 years	Internal consistency (Brooks & Kutcher, 2003) • Original sample: 374 8–17-year-olds; total alpha = .90, main subscales > .70 • Normative sample, total scale: alpha ≥ .88 for 12–15-year-olds, 16–19-year-olds (male and female subjects); for male subjects, four main subscales had good alphas (.70 ≤ alpha ≤ .86, both age groups); For female subjects, both age groups, good for physical symptoms and social anxiety (.84 ≤ alpha ≤ .87); harm avoidance and SAD were less satisfactory	Concurrent validity (Brooks & Kutcher, 2003) • Sample of 108 subjects aged 9–13 years, r = .72 with original SCARED • Original sample: 374 subjects aged 8–17 years, r = .63 (with RCMAS), .19 (with CDI, for which RCMAS and CDI were r = .62); same pattern seen with the CES-D (although the correlation between MASC and CES-D is higher, about .5) • Clinical sample (Rynn et al., 2006) MASC total scores: r = .61 (with RCMAS), .14 (with STAIC-P), .60 (with STAIC), .69 (BAI), .34 (with HAMA [or HARS]); similar pattern with MASC-ADI and MASC-10	Items rated on a 4-point scale: 0 = *never*, 1 = *rarely*, 2 = *sometimes*, 3 = *often*	• Widely used 39-item child self-rated screening instrument for anxiety symptoms based on *DSM–IV* • Studied in clinical and community samples • Covers physical, cognitive, affective, and behavioral symptoms of anxiety • Yields: total score; four-factor structure validated in clinical and population samples—Physical Symptoms (6 tension–restlessness items, 6 somatic–autonomic arousal items), Harm Avoidance (4 perfectionism items, 5 anxious coping items), Social Anxiety scale (5 humiliation/rejection items, 4 public performance items), Separation Anxiety/Panic (9 items)	• Parent–child concordance is low in U.S. and Australian samples (Baldwin & Dadds, 2007). • Harm Avoidance scale may be a measure of perfectionism/social desirability (Baldwin & Dadds, 2007).

Available from Multi-Health Systems, Inc., https://www.mhs.com
MHS Inc., P.O. Box 950, North Tonawanda, NY 14120-0950; Tel: (800) 456-3003; Fax: (888) 540-4484; e-mail: customerservice@mhs.com

John S. March, MD, MPH, Division Chief, Child Psychiatry, DUMC 3527, Durham, NC 27710; Tel: (919) 416-2404; Fax: (919) 416-2420; e-mail: john.march@duke.edu

TABLE 9.2
Anxiety Assessment Instruments for Use in Courtroom Modifications With Children and Adolescents *(Continued)*

Anxiety measures	Age range	Reliability data	Validity data	Severity level/ cutoff scores	Features/summary	Weaknesses
Multidimensional Anxiety Scale for Children (MASC) *(Continued)*		($.62 \leq$ alpha $\leq .66$); AD subscale: less than ideal for both sexes, both ages ($.62 \leq$ alpha $\leq .64$); MASC–10, 12–15 years old: $.64 \leq$ alpha $\leq .65$; 16–19 years old, .71 (male), .68 (female) • Clinical sample (Rynn et al., 2006): 193 child and adolescent outpatients, randomly selected, 30% ethnic minority youth; total scale alpha = .87; subscales: Physical Symptoms = .84, Harm Avoidance = .72, Social Anxiety = .86, Separation Anxiety = .78; ADI = .62; MASC–10 = .67 • Community sample of 8–13-year-olds in Sydney, Australia (Baldwin & Dadds, 2007): child report total score alpha = .89; parent report total score alpha = .90 Test–retest • Population Sample (March et al., 1997): average ICC = .79 for 3-week interval; ICC = .93 for 3-month interval	• Convergent validity in Australian community sample (Baldwin & Dadds, 2007): MASC Social Anxiety with SCAS Social Phobia, child $r = .76$, parent $r = .74$; MASC Separation/Panic with SCAS Separation Anxiety, child $r = .68$, parent $r = .74$; MASC Harm Avoidance with SCAS Panic, child $r = .08$; MASC Harm Avoidance with SCAS Social Phobia, parent $r = .16$ Criterion validity • Clinical sample (Rynn et al., 2006): mean MASC total, subscale (except for Physical Symptoms), ADI, and MASC–10 scores for anxious children were significantly different in the desired direction (i.e., higher) than depressed children (age corrected) Discriminative validity (Brooks & Kutcher, 2003) • Sample ($n = 76$, with 36 matched control subjects): 87% were classified correctly (89% sen, 84% spe); with ADI ($n = 36$), found 88% were correctly classified (89% sen,		• Two shorter forms available: Anxiety Disorders Index (sum of the 10 items with the greatest diagnostic validity; 10-item version, MASC–10), and Inconsistency Index (items to identify careless or contradictory responses) • Duration: 15 minutes to complete, 10 minutes to hand score • Fourth-grade reading level • Normative scores established, by gender for 8–11-year-olds, 12–15-year-olds, 16–19-year-olds • Discriminative validity strong between anxiety and depression; anxiety and ADHD, and better than RCMAS (Baldwin & Dadds, 2007) • Translated into other languages (e.g., Chinese: Yao et al., 2007; Swedish: Ivarsson, 2006)	

Instrument	Age	Reliability	Validity	Format / Description	Comments
Multidimensional Anxiety Scale for Children (MASC) (Continued)		• Population Sample (March, Sullivan, & James, 1999): 142 8–18-year-olds, randomly selected, 3-week interval; ICC = .78 (total); subscales, Anxiety Disorders index, MASC-10, were all > .70, though Harm Avoidance was .62	84% spe) • Greenhill et al. (1998): ADI with patients with anxiety disorders relative to "normal" children (age and gender matched), sensitivity was 95%, false positive was 5%, false negative was 5%; overall correct classification rate was 95%		
Screen for Child Anxiety Related Emotional Disorders—Revised (SCARED–R) Contact information: Peter Muris, Institute of Psychology, Erasmus University, Rotterdam Woudestein, T13-37 P.O. Box 1738, 3000 DR Rotterdam, The Netherlands; Tel: (010) 408 8706; Fax: (010) 408 9009; e-mail: muris@fsw.eur.nl	8–18 years	Internal consistency • Large-scale study: 1,011 7–19-year-olds, total alpha = .94, 7 of the 9 subscales were > .70 (OCD and SpecP-Environmental were .66) • Clinical study: outpatient sample, 8–17-year-olds, ADs (n = 25), disruptive disorders (n = 23); full score was an alpha of .86 (AD), .92 (disruptive), .94 (total sample); total sample subgroups: GAD, SAD, PD, OCD, SocP, and TSD were adequate: $.70 \leq r \leq .86$ (AD: $.60 \leq r \leq .74$; disruptive: $.62 \leq r \leq .87$); for total and subgroups SpecP subscales ranged from < .6 to > .7 Test-retest reliability • Sample of 101 11–14-year-olds, 12-week	Concurrent validity (Brooks & Kutcher, 2003) • FSSC-R: $r = .64$ (48 outpatients aged 8–17 years); .67 (120 school children aged 8–13 years) • RCMAS: $r = .86$ (total), .78 (SAD vs. Worry; 75 subjects aged 9–12 years) • S-TAIC: $r = .73$ (Trait scale); .65 (State scale, 68 subjects aged 8–12 years; 198 subjects aged 8–13 years; $r = .85$ (Trait scale) • YSR: total score and Internalizing ($r = .77$) and Externalizing subscales ($r = .49$) • SCAS: 1,011 subjects aged 7–19 years, $r = .89$ between total scores, subscales; $r = .79$ (SAD), .71 (AD), .67 (OCD), .72 (PD); SpecP subscales SCAS Physical Injury Fears were moderate ($.60 \leq r \leq .68$); SocP subscale, .49	• Frequency/ severity rating • Symptoms reported on a 3-point scale: 0 = *almost never,* 1 = *sometimes,* 2 = *often* • Sixty-six-item self-report measure screens for the entire spectrum of *DSM-IV* anxiety disorders in children • Revision of the 38-item SCARED • Nine subscales: PD, 13 items; GAD, 9 items; SocP, 4 items; SAD, 12 items; OCD, 9 items; TSD, 4 items; SpecP—Animal type, 3 items; SpecP—Blood/ Injection/Injury type, 7 items; SpecP—Environmental/ Situational, 5 items • Scores are summed, range from 0–132 • Duration: 15 minutes • Parallel parent–child versions	• Psychometric properties established in Netherlands (Dutch translation) with diverse school children. • English version has not been validated, although the prior 38-item and 41-item versions continue to be tested and supported for use in North America.

(continues)

TABLE 9.2
Anxiety Assessment Instruments for Use in Courtroom Modifications With Children and Adolescents (Continued)

Anxiety measures	Age range	Reliability data	Validity data	Severity level/cutoff scores	Features/summary	Weaknesses
Screen for Child Anxiety Related Emotional Disorders—Revised (SCARED–R) (Continued)		Interval: ICC = .81 (total), .68 (GAD), .71 (SpecP—Animal), .77 (SpecP—Blood), .78 (SpecP—Environmental), .74 (SocP), .72 (PD), .64 (OCD), .40 (SepAD), .41 (TSD)	• SASC-R: 252 subjects aged 8–13 years, $r = .62$ correlation (SocP subscale) Discriminative validity (Brooks & Kutcher, 2003) • Study: higher total score and all subscales except SpecP in 8–17-year-olds with anxiety disorders ($n = 25$) compared with subjects with disruptive disorders ($n = 23$) • Study: Social Phobia subscale, those meeting DISC-2.3 criteria ($n = 28$) scored significantly higher than control subjects ($n = 224$; aged 8–13 years old) Sensitivity to change • Significant declines in scores following group or individual CBT for anxiety disorders (Greco & Morris, 2004)			
Screen for Child Anxiety Related Emotional Disorders (SCARED) Available at http://www.wpic.pitt.edu/research/ Boris Birmaher, MD, Professor of Psychiatry, University of Pittsburgh School of Medicine; Tel: (412) 246-5788;	9–18 years	Internal consistency • Outpatient sample of 341 9–18-year-olds: alpha coefficients range from .74 to .93 (Birmaher et al., 1997) Test–retest reliability: .70—.90 (Birmaher et al.,	Convergent validity • "Good" convergent validity with the KSADS-PL, CBCL, and STAIC (Brooks & Kutcher, 2003) Discriminant validity • "Good" divergent validity compared with disruptive	Severity of symptoms rated on a 3-point scale: 0 = not true/almost never; 1 = sometimes; 2 = often	• Child self-report screening inventory for DSM–IV anxiety disorders; parent version also available. • Original version contains 38 items, rated on a 3-point scale (Birmaher et al., 1997). • SCARED-41 contains 41 items on 3-point scale (Birmaher	Factor structure showed difference in some ethnically diverse samples but not others (Wren et al., 2007).

Measure	Ages	Reliability	Validity	Scoring/Utility	Comments
Screen for Child Anxiety Related Emotional Disorders (SCARED) (Continued) e-mail: birmaherb@upmc.edu		and depressive disorders and within anxiety disorders using KSADS–PL, CBCL, STAIC (Greenhill et al., 1998; Wren et al., 2007) 1997) Parent–child agreement • Outpatient samples (Greenhill et al., 1998): r = .47 • Community (ethnically diverse primary care) sample (Wren et al., 2007): R = 61 total score; .50 biracial; R = .67 white, Asian/Pacific Islander		For outpatient sample: "Optimal cutoff point (25) on the child SCARED with a sensitivity of 71% and a specificity of 67%, 61% and 71% when discriminating b/w anxiety and non-anxiety, anxiety and depression, and anxiety and disruptive disorders, respectively" (Wren et al., 2007, p. 334).	et al., 1999) • Five factors: GAD, SAD, SocP, somatic/panic, school phobia, although nonclinical diverse samples reveal four factor structure. • Developed for children and adolescents; not a downward extension of an adult scale (K. Myers & Winters, 2002). • Psychometric properties examined in Dutch, South African, Italian, and U.S. youth. • Takes 10 minutes or less to complete.
Revised Child Anxiety and Depression Scales (RCADS; Chorpita, Yim, Moffitt, Umemoto, & Francis, 2000) Contact information: Bruce F. Chorpita; Tel: (601) 984-5805; e-mail: chorpita@hawaii.edu	6–19 years	Internal consistency • Original sample of 1641 Hawaiian schoolchildren 6–18 years old (Chorpita et al., 2000) in Study 1: alphas SocP = .82, PD = .79, GAD = .77, MDD = .76, SAD = .76, OCD = .73; in Study 2: (n = 246) SP = .81, PD = .85, AD = .80, MDD = .76, SAD = .78, OCD = .71 • 513 Hawaiian outpatient 3–12-year-olds (Chorpita, Moffitt, &	Convergent validity • "Good" (Fonseca & Perrin, 2001) • Original sample (n = 125) RCDAS MDD subscale with CDI = .70; (n = 125), RCMAS total score with RCDAS subscales: SAD = .58, SocP = .62, OCD = .49, PD = .59, GAD = .68; MDD = .60 • Hawaiian outpatient sample RCDAS subscales with ADIS–IV–P/C and RCMAS, OCD = .22/.34/59,	Frequency of symptoms (how often these items apply to them) reported on a 4-point scale: 0 = never; 1 = sometimes; 2 = often; 3 = always. Girls tend to score higher than boys in	• The RCADS is a 47-item child self-report measure that was adapted from the SCAS; the FPI scale and agoraphobia items were removed, and a depression scale and GAD scale were added to better address DSM–IV criteria. • RCDAS covers 6 of the DSM–IV anxiety and depressive disorders: SAD, GAD, SocP, PD, OCD, and MDD. • Six-factor structure confirmed in Dutch longitudinal community sample of 10–12-year-olds. • More study with mainland U.S. samples is suggested (Chorpita et al., 2005). • Chinese and Filipino American children scored significantly higher on RCADS SocP than White

(continues)

TABLE 9.2
Anxiety Assessment Instruments for Use in Courtroom Modifications With Children and Adolescents (Continued)

Anxiety measures	Age range	Reliability data	Validity data	Severity level/cutoff scores	Features/summary	Weaknesses
Revised Child Anxiety and Depression Scales (RCADS; Chorpita, Yim, Moffitt, Umemoto, & Francis, 2000) (Continued)		Gray, 2005): SAD = .78, SpecP = .87, OCD = .82, GAD = .84, MDD = .87 • Dutch longitudinal community sample of 10–12-year-olds (n = 2210, Wave 1; 2,067, Wave 2); SAD = .66/.59, GAD = .80/.75, SpecP = .78/.88, PD = .75/.72, OCD = .68/.66 (Ferdinand, Dieleman, Ormel, & Verhulst, 2007) Test–retest reliability: • 125 Hawaiian schoolchildren 8–18 years old, 1 week, ranged from r = .65 (OCD) to .80 (SocP; Chorpita et al., 2000)	GAD = .26/.48/.65, SAD = .29/.52/.60, PD = .31/.42/.64, SocP = .43/.54/.72; with ADIS–IV–C/P and CDI, MDD = .45/.65/.70 • Dutch community sample of 10–12-year-olds (n = 2,935), RCDAS SAD scale with YSR/DSM–IV Anxiety Problems scales, r = .52; RCDAS MDD scale with YSR Affective Problems, r = .67; RCDAS SocP with YSR Anxious/Depressed, r = .59; RCDAS MDD with YSR Withdrawn, r = .55 (van Lang, Ferdinand, Oldehinkel, Ormel, & Verhulst, 2005) Discriminant validity • "Good" (Fonseca & Perrin, 2001) • Original sample RCDAS subscales with CDI, SAD = .18, SocP = 39, OCD = 29, PD = .45, GAD = .45 • Hawaiian outpatient sample RCDAS subscales with ADIS–IV–C/P oppositional behavior, MDD = .07/.09, OCD = −.04/.05, GAD = −.01/.01, SAD = −.02/−.01, PD = .05/.05, SOC = −.05/−.06	a clinically referred sample (Chorpita et al., 2005), except OCD in nonreferred school-age children and adolescents (Chorpita et al., 2000) Cutoff scores derived from ROC analyses (Chorpita et al., 2005), MDD = 11 (sen = .74, spe = .77), SOC = 10 (sen .59, spe 64); GAD = 7 (sen .69, spe .72); SAD = 5 (sen .73, spe 69); OCD = 5 (sen .70, spe 65); PD = 12 (sen .78, spe .92)	(Ferdinand, van Lang, Ormel, & Verhulst, 2006)	children (Austin & Chorpita, 2004a). • High correlation between the RCDAS MDD subscale and the RCMAS.

Measure	Age	Reliability	Validity	Description	Comments
Spence Children's Anxiety Scale (SCAS; Spence, 1998) Contact information: ellender@psy.uq.edu.au SCAS and psychometric information available at: http://www2.psy.uq.edu.au/~sues/scas/	6–19 years	Internal consistency • Original study of Australian 8–12-year-olds: for total score and 6 subscales, alpha = 6–.82 (Spence, 1998) • Study of 875 Australian 13–14-year-olds: total score = .92, subscales 60–80 (Spence, Barrett, & Turner, 2003) Test–retest reliability • Six-month interval for Australian 8–12-year-olds, r = 63 (Silverman & Lopez, 2004); 12 week for Australian 13–14-year-olds, r = .63 total score	Convergent validity • SCAS total score, r = .71/.75 with RCMAS total score (Spence, 1998; Spence, Barrett, & Turner, 2003) Discriminant validity • Total SCAS scores, r = .48/.60 with CDI (Spence, 1998; Spence, Barrett, & Turner, 2003)	Frequency of symptoms (how often these items apply to them) reported on a 4-point scale: 0 = never; 1 = sometimes; 2 = often; 3 = always	• The SCAS contains 45 items: 38 anxiety items, 7 social desirability items; there are 6 subscales: generalized anxiety, social anxiety, separation anxiety, panic/agoraphobia, obsessions/compulsions, and fear of physical injury. • Parent version available	• SCAS psychometric properties derive from community populations and may not be generalizable to clinical populations; limited support for GAD scale validity (Greco & Morris, 2004). • Newer version (RCDAS) is available.
Revised Children's Manifest Anxiety Scale (RCMAS) Available from Multi-Health Systems, Inc., https://www.mhs.com MHS Inc., P.O. Box 950, North Tonawanda, NY 14120-0950 Tel: (800) 456-3003; Fax: (888) 540-4484; e-mail:customerservice@mhs.com Western Psychological Services, 12031 Wilshire Blvd., Los Angeles, CA 90025-1251; Tel: (800) 648-8857 (U.S. and Canada); Fax: (310) 478-7838; http://www.wpspublish.com/; e-mail: help@wpspublish.com Order status: myorder@wpspublish.com.	6–19 years	• Summary: "good short- and long-term reliability in most samples" (Brooks & Kutcher, 2003, p. 292) Internal consistency • Extensively studied, alpha coefficients range from .6 to .8 • Subscale alphas: - Sample (1985) of 6–19-year-olds, .64–.76 - Sample of 503 11–13-year-olds, .68 (PA), .8 (wo), .66 (sc/c) - Sample of 544 14–16-year-olds: .60 (PA),	Concurrent validity • Strong correlations have been found with the S-TAIC (Trait scale) and the FSSC-R (Brooks & Kutcher, 2003; Fonseca & Perrin, 2001) Discriminative validity • Mixed evidence (Brooks & Kutcher, 2003) • 24 subjects aged 7–14 years, RCMAS distinguished subjects with ADs from normal control subjects (with KSADS–P), but other measures did not • Twelve subjects aged 9–14 years; RCMAS did not distinguish subjects with	Items rated using a yes–no format	• One of the most frequently used instruments to assess general symptoms of anxiety, depression, and emotional distress in youth. • Dominance in research (comparability across international studies) • Extensive normative data • 37-item child self-report • Scales: - 28 items: physical, affective, cognitive, behavioral manifestations of generalized anxiety, sum to obtain a total score (0–28); - Lie scale: 9 items, an index of the tendency to favorably misrepresent the self;	• Downward extension of an adult measure • Unclear utility of Lie scale • Poor discriminative validity; may indicate depression as much as an AD.

(continues)

TABLE 9.2

Anxiety Assessment Instruments for Use in Courtroom Modifications With Children and Adolescents   *(Continued)*

Anxiety measures	Age range	Reliability data	Validity data	Severity level/ cutoff scores	Features/summary	Weaknesses
Revised Children's Manifest Anxiety Scale (RCMAS) *(Continued)* Available from Psychological Assessment Resources, PAR, Inc., 16204 North Florida Ave., Lutz, FL 33549; http://www3.parinc.com/; Tel: (800) 331-8378; Fax: (800)727-9329		.78 (wo), .67 (sc/c) - Sample of 385 African Americans 11–14-year-olds, alphas close to .70 for all scales - Sample of 53 Mexican, 46 Mexican American, and 51 European American 10–14-year-olds: .75–.89 for total RCMAS; .44–.71 (Mexican), .65–.83 (Mexican American, .62–.78 (European American) for subscales (Varela & Biggs, 2006) Test–retest reliability • Group (*n* = 80), mean age = 12.2 years, 1-week interval: .88 (Pearson) and .60–.85 for subscales; all scores decreased • Group (*n* = 81), mean age = 12.0 years, 5-week interval: .77 (Pearson) and .60–.85 for subscales; all scores decreased • Group (*n* = 534), aged 9–12 years, 9-month interval: .68 total score, .58 Lie scale	ADs from healthy control subjects (as measured by ADIS–C), but other measures did Diagnostic accuracy • 72 ninth graders (aged 13–15 years), receiver operator characteristic curve analysis; poor for GAD in female subjects, SpecP and SocP in both sexes (AUC < .70); moderate accuracy for major depression (AUC .73), externalizing disorders Divergent validity (poor) • Subjects aged 8–17 years (*n* = 475), RCMAS correlated as strongly with the CDI (.62) as did the MASC (.63); correlated strongly with CES-D (.66, 284 boys; .76, 348 girls) in ninth graders		younger children and ethnic minorities score higher - Three subscales/ statistically derived factors: Physiological (10 items), Worry/Oversensitivity (11 items), Social Concerns/ Concentration (7 items) • Duration: 10–15 minutes • Normative data available by age and gender (in 1-year intervals), as well as by some different ethnicities/ nationalities. • Shows treatment sensitivity. • Versions in languages other than English available (e.g., Spanish).	

Revised Children's Manifest Anxiety Scale (RCMAS) *(Continued)*		• Group of African American adolescents (*n* = 385), 6-month interval; Pearson correlation coefficient was .74 for girls, .30 for boys (total score); subscale Pearson correlation coefficient was ≥ .60 for girls (whose scores all decreased), ≥ .35 for boys		• Five- and three-factor models are found in studies.
Social Phobia Anxiety Inventory for Children (SPAI–C): Parent version (SPAI–C–P; Beidel, Turner, Hamlin, & Morris, 2000)	8–14 years	Internal consistency (Brooks & Kutcher, 2003; Silverman & Lopez, 2004) • Total score alpha = .95 (*n* = 154, 8–17-year-olds), .92 (*n* = 148, 8–12-year-olds) • 158 Hawaiian 10–14-year-olds and their caregivers: total score child version alpha = .93; total score parent version = .93 (Higa et al., 2006)	Convergent validity, reviewing measures/studies (Brooks & Kutcher, 2003): • FSSC-R (*n* = 59), 8–17-year-olds: Failure and Criticism subscale, *r* = .53 • S-TAIC (*n* = 38), *r* = .50 Trait scale; .13 State scale • CBCL (*n* = 74), *r* = .45 Internalizing • SASC-R (*n* = 277) 9–12 year-olds, *r* = .63 • Hawaiian caregiver SPAI–C–P with CBCL Internalizing, *r* = .42 (Higa et al., 2006)	Frequency on 3-point scale: 0 = *never or hardly ever*, 1 = *sometimes*; 2 = *most of the time or always* • Potential to show which groups of people or situations cause more anxiety	• 26-item empirically derived child self-report measure assessing the range and frequency of social anxiety/phobia and anxiety. • Reflects *DSM–IV* criteria. • Good psychometric properties in diverse clinical and community samples: reliability; discriminative validity (children with and without SocP; between Soc P and other ADs, and externalizing disorders). • Measures cognitive, behavioral, and somatic aspects of anxiety. • Assesses a range of potential fear-eliciting scenarios, including anxiety experienced with familiar and unfamiliar audiences (peers and adults). • Caretaker version supported in an ethnically diverse community sample. • Yields total score and 3-factor scales: assertiveness/general conversation,
Available from Multi-Health Systems, Inc., MHS Inc., P.O. Box 950, North Tonawanda, NY 14120-0950; https://www.mhs.com; Tel: (800) 456-3003; Fax: (888) 540-4484 e-mail: customerservice@mhs.com Two principal coauthors: Samuel M. Turner, PhD, ABPP Professor, University of Maryland, Co-Director, Maryland Center for Anxiety Disorders; Tel: (301) 405-0232; Fax: (301) 405-8154; e-mail: turner@psyc.umd.edu Deborah C. Beidel, PhD, ABPP, Professor, University of Maryland, Codirector, Maryland Center for Anxiety Disorders; Tel: (301) 405-0232; Fax: (301) 405-8154; e-mail: beidel@psyc.umd.edu		Test–retest reliability • 2 weeks (*r* = .86, *n* = 62), 10 months (*r* = .63, *n* = 19) Parent–child agreement • 55 parent–child dyads, parent and child version, *r* = .31 (Beidel et al., 2000) • 158 Hawaiian caregiver–child dyads, *r* = .43	Discriminative validity • Three studies (sample size < 100) showing the ability to discriminate those with ADIS–C diagnoses of SocP from normal control subjects; cutoff score of 18 (70% sen, 67% spe, one study; 87% sen, 60% spe, another study; Brooks & Kutcher, 2003)	

(continues)

TABLE 9.2

Anxiety Assessment Instruments for Use in Courtroom Modifications With Children and Adolescents   (Continued)

Anxiety measures	Age range	Reliability data	Validity data	Severity level/cutoff scores	Features/summary	Weaknesses
Social Phobia Anxiety Inventory for Children (SPAI–C); Parent version (SPAI–C–P) (Beidel, Turner, Hamlin, & Morris, 2000) (Continued)		(Higa et al., 2006)	• Hawaiian caregiver SPAI–C–P with CBCL Externalizing, r = .19, Rulebreaking, r = .18, Aggressive, r = .18 (Higa et al., 2006)		traditional social encounters, public performance; 5-factor scales: assertiveness, general conversation, physical and cognitive symptoms, avoidance, public performance. • Third-grade reading level • Duration: 20–30 minutes • Shows treatment sensitivity. • Available in languages other than English.	
Social Phobia Anxiety Inventory (SPAI) Available from Multi-Health Systems, Inc., MHS Inc.., P.O. Box 950, North Tonawanda, NY 14120-0950; https://www.mhs.com; Tel: (800) 456-3003; Fax: (888) 540-4484; e-mail:customerservice@mhs.com Two principal coauthors: Samuel M. Turner, PhD, ABPP, Professor, University of Maryland, CoDirector, Maryland Center for Anxiety Disorders; Tel: (301) 405-0232; Fax: (301) 405-8154; e-mail: turner@psyc.umd.edu Deborah C. Beidel, PhD, ABPP, Professor, University of Maryland, Codirector, Maryland Center for Anxiety Disorders; Tel: (301) 405-0232; Fax: (301) 405-8154; e-mail: beidel@psyc.umd.edu	Adult (13–18 years; was designed for adults but can be used for this age range)	Internal consistency (Brooks & Kutcher, 2003) • Mixed clinical (n = 102) and community (n = 121) sample of 12–18-year-olds, alphas = .97 (SocP), .91 (agoraphobia), .97 (full scale) • Spain (translation): 3,000 14–17-year-olds, alphas of .96 (SocP), .84 (agoraphobia) Test-retest reliability (Brooks & Kutcher, 2003): 175 Spanish 14–17-year-olds (most meeting ADIS–IV SocP criteria), average interval 10 days, r = .86 (SocP), .77 (agoraphobia), .83 (difference)	Concurrent validity (Brooks & Kutcher, 2003) • Sample: 223 subjects aged 12–18 years • ADIS–IV social phobia score (n = 303), 14–17-year-olds: r = .78 • FSSC–R: r = .51 (failure and criticism subscale), .48 (unknown subscale) • SAS-A (n = 303), 14–17-year-olds: total score with SPAI SocP, r = .73 (n = 303, 14–17) • S-TAIC Trait: r = .48; Discriminative validity (Brooks & Kutcher, 2003) • Sample (n = 223) of 12–18-year-olds: group with SocP (K–SADS) (but not agoraphobia) had significantly higher SPAI SocP scores than subjects	• Seven-point scale for how often item matches the respondent: 0 = never, 6 = always • Potentially could be used to establish which types or groups of people cause the most anxiety	• Good psychometric properties: reliability; discriminative validity (between SocP and other ADs). • 45-item self-report measure • Two subscales: Social Phobia (32 items; 17 assess anxiety in situations with 4 types of people present; 4 assess anxiety in a particular situation or in anticipation of it) and Agoraphobia (13 items). • Range of scores: 0–192 (SocP), 0–78 (agoraphobia), SPAI difference score (SocP minus agoraphobia). • Duration: 30 minutes	• Not suited to younger adolescents. • No data on sensitivity to change in adolescents.

Social Phobia Anxiety Inventory (SPAI)
(Continued)

with other ADs or other psychiatric disorders and normal control subjects
• Similar findings in a Spanish sample of 303 Spanish 14–17-year-olds

Note. AD = anxiety disorder; ADHD = attention-deficit/hyperactivity disorder; AUC = area under the curve; CBCL = Child Behavior Checklist; CDI = Children's Depression Inventory; CES–D = Center for Epidemiologic Studies Depression Scale; DISC = Diagnostic Interview Schedule for Children; *DSM–IV = Diagnostic and Statistical Manual of Mental Disorders* (4th edition); FSSC–R = Fear Survey Schedule for Children—Revised; GAD = generalized anxiety disorder; ICC = interclass correlation coefficient; ICD–10 = *International Classification of Diseases*, 10th revision; MDD = major depressive disorder; OAD = overanxious disorder; OCD = obsessive–compulsive disorder; ODD = oppositional–defiant disorder; PA = physiological anxiety; PD = panic disorder; PTSD = posttraumatic stress disorder; Social Anxiety Scale for Children—Revised (SASC–R); SAD = separation anxiety; SCAS = Spence Children's Anxiety Scale; SC/C = social concerns/concentration; sen = sensitivity; SocP = social phobia; SOP = social phobia; spe = specificity; SpecP = specific phobia; State–Trait Anxiety Inventory for Children (S–TAIC); TSD = traumatic stress disorder; wo = worry/oversensitivy; YSR = Youth Self Report version of the CBCL.

measure (or both). Another benefit of starting with a general screening measure or interview is to avoid the pitfall of premature closure on a diagnostic label; in other words, an MHP assessing a child referred for anxiety problems should not use only anxiety measures lest he or she miss other important problems and strengths (Achenbach, 2005).

After a diagnosis is made, the MHP should consider exploring other ways to quantify anxious symptoms as well as their controlling or maintaining conditions through the use of rating scales. Although direct observations and self-monitoring procedures could also be used because they are excellent ways to determine "the frequency and severity of symptoms/behaviors and their antecedents and consequences" (Silverman & Serafini, 1998, p. 349), concerns about their reliability, validity, and feasibility (Silverman & Ollendick, 2005) limit their use in modification assessments. Quantifying symptoms involves an assessment of "the degree to which internalizing problems, such as anxiety or depression is relevant to a child, or the probability that the child will emit one of a class of behaviors (e.g., worry/oversensitivity) (Jensen & Haynes, 1986)" (Silverman & Serafini, 1998, p. 348). In addition to providing a relatively quick method for examining anxiety levels, rating scales allow MHPs to look at what is fueling and maintaining the anxiety. Presumably, therefore, a rating scale could help MHPs determine whether a child could show anxious symptoms in a future courtroom encounter and whether a defendant plays a part in a child's anxiety.

Of the available self-report rating scales, the MASC and SCARED–R are considered the best (Greenhill et al., 1998). Not only can they be used to make specific anxiety disorder diagnoses, they also show potential for differentiating those with anxiety disorders from those with other disorders (Brooks & Kutcher, 2003), with the MASC said to be "the most clinically useful self-report anxiety measure for children available" (Baldwin & Dadds, 2007, p. 253). If MHPs want to use a specific measure to distinguish anxiety from depression, the MASC (Rynn et al., 2006) and the RCADS (Chorpita, Yim, et al., 2000) have been recommended (Silverman & Ollendick, 2005). Reliable measures that are commonly used to assess severity of anxiety symptoms (RCMAS, STAI–C, FSSC–R) are downward extensions of adult measures developed before DSM–IV and therefore do not distinguish between anxiety disorders or between those with anxiety disorders and other disorders, including depression (Brooks & Kutcher, 2003; Greco & Morris, 2004). In addition, the commonly used Achenbach System of Empirically Based Assessment screening measures (e.g., CBCL, YSR) do not sufficiently map on DSM–IV diagnoses, despite attempts to create DSM–IV-specific scales, in part because they do not contain enough items, cover symptom duration, and assess the impact of symptoms on daily functioning (Ferdinand, 2007). However, given that severity is a component of the modification assessment, MHPs could consider these instruments for a general screening of level of distress and negative affect (Greco & Morris, 2004).

Other instruments deserve brief mention because they hold promise for courtroom modification assessments. Two self-report measures tap specifically into whether a child feels that his or her anxiety symptoms are controllable (the Anxiety Control Questionnaire for Children; Weems, Silverman, Rapee, & Pina, 2003); the Penn State Worry Questionnaire for Children (Chorpita, Tracey, Brown, Collica, & Barlow, 1997). Another looks at anxiety sensitivity, which is a construct believed to be a potential risk factor for the development of panic attacks and other anxiety disorders (the CASI; Silverman, Fleisig, Rabian, & Peterson, 1991). The Pediatric Anxiety Rating Scale (PARS; Research Units on Pediatric Psychopharmacology Anxiety Study Group, 2002) is an instrument that clinicians use to rate the frequency, severity, and impairment of anxiety symptoms in youth aged 6 to 17 years. Because these measures are in need of further research (Silverman & Ollendick, 2005), clinicians should monitor the literature for updated information about their reliability and validity.

The most appropriate self-report rating scales for courtroom modification assessments at this time are as follows:

- The MASC (March, Parker, Sullivan, Stallings, & Connors, 1997; March, Sullivan, & James, 1999) is a 39-item self-report measure that assesses anxiety in children aged 8 to 19 years. Given "robust psychometric properties" and clinical relevance (Hofflich, Hughes, & Kendall, 2006, p. 233), the MASC is considered a "preferred instrument" and is "one of the most widely used" (Greco & Morris, 2004, p. 104). In addition to providing a Total Anxiety Disorder Index, it also yields four empirically derived subscale scores (and subfactor domains in parentheses) that cover the various physical, cognitive, emotional, and behavioral domains: physical symptoms (tension–restlessness, somatic–automatic arousal), social anxiety (with performance anxiety, humiliation), harm avoidance (perfectionism, anxious coping), and separation anxiety. In addition, the MASC contains an Inconsistency Index derived from responses to 10 pairs of related items. Items are rated in terms of frequency of symptoms on a 4-point scale (0 = *never*; 1 = *rarely*; 2 = *sometimes*; 3 = *often*). It is written at a fourth-grade level and is estimated to take 15 minutes to complete and 10 minutes to score. The MASC has a parent-report form and is available in Afrikaans, Chinese, Dutch, English (U.S. and South African), French (Canadian and European), German, Hebrew, Hungarian, Italian, Icelandic, Lithuanian, Norwegian, Polish, Spanish (European and U.S.), Swedish, and Turkish.
- The SCARED (Birmaher et al., 1997) and the SCARED–R (Muris, Merckelbach, Van Brakel, & Mayer, 1999) are self-

report measures that assess the *DSM–IV* anxiety symptoms in children aged 8 to 18 and also provide a total anxiety score. Symptoms are reported on a 3-point frequency scale (0 = *almost never*, 1 = *sometimes*, 2 = *often*), and the instrument is estimated to take approximately 10 to 15 minutes to complete. The SCARED–R assesses the entire range of anxiety disorders and has been shown to be sensitive to treatment effects (Muris, Merckelbach, Gadet, Moulaert, & Tuerney, 1999). Parent versions of the SCARED–R and SCARED are also available, with moderate levels of parent–child agreement (Greco & Morris, 2004). Variations in the factor structure of the SCARED and SCARED–R in diverse samples reveal the need for continued research (Wren et al., 2007).

- The RCADS (Chorpita, Moffitt & Gray, 2005; Chorpita, Yim, et al., 2000), a revision of the SCAS (Spence, 1994), is a 47-item self-report measure that assesses the following disorders in youth aged 6 to 19 years: separation anxiety disorder, social phobia, GAD, panic disorder, OCD, and major depressive disorder (MDD). Ratings are made in terms of frequency, that is, how often each item applies to them (0 = *never*, 1 = *sometimes*, 2 = *often*, 3 = *always*).

- The RCMAS (Reynolds & Richmond, 1979, 1985), also known as "What I Think and Feel," is one of the most frequently used and researched self-report measures of anxiety in children aged 6 to 19 years. Taking about 15 minutes to complete, it contains 37 yes–no format items; 28 items represent the physical, emotional, cognitive, and behavioral aspects of anxiety and are reported in three empirically derived subscales: physiological, worry and oversensitivity, and social concerns and concentration. It has been shown to be sensitive to change in treatment outcome studies, and its structure has been replicated in other countries, as well as with Mexican and Mexican American youth (Varela & Biggs, 2006). Unique compared with all other child anxiety measures, some RCMAS items are used to produce a "lie" score, which can be used as an indication of the child's attempts to respond to items in a socially desirable manner. Potentially useful in a forensic setting, this Lie scale should be used carefully, given studies finding that younger children score higher than older children, African American and Hispanic American youth score higher than European American youth (Silverman & Ollendick, 2005), and Bulgarian children score higher than U.S. children (Bidjerano, 2006). In addition, because of concerns about discriminative validity, the RCMAS is recommended for assessment of general distress only and not of anxiety. Also, some researchers do not recommend this older measure when comparing it with the MASC or SCARED (K. Myers & Winters, 2002). Thus, MHPs who choose to use the RCMAS should be aware of its limitations.

- The SPAI–C (Beidel, Turner, Hamlin, & Morris, 2000; Beidel, Turner, & Morris, 1995, 1998) is a 26-item, empirically derived self-report measure for children aged 8 to 14 years. It assesses a range and frequency of *DSM–IV*-related cognitions, behavior, and bodily responses across a range of situations known to elicit fear in youth with social phobia. Of relevance to the courtroom modification assessment, the SPAI–C also "distinguishes among anxiety experienced in the presence of familiar peers, unfamiliar peers, and adults, with some items measuring anxious responding before and during social interaction and performance situations" (Greco & Morris, 2004, p. 107), such as "scared when I have to do something while others watch me." Items are rated on a 3-point scale measuring frequency (0 = *never or hardly ever*, 1 = *sometimes*, 2 = *most of the time or always*), and the instrument takes about 20 to 30 minutes to complete. The SPAI–C has also been tested for use with adolescents aged 13 to 17 years (Storch et al., 2003). Investigations of the psychometric properties of the parent version, the SPAI–C–P (Beidel et al., 2000), with racially diverse samples, revealed promising results (Higa, Fernandez, Nakamura, Chorpita, & Daleiden, 2006). Alternatively, the adult, 32-item SPAI (Turner, Beidel, Dancu, & Stanley, 1989), which takes about 30 minutes to complete, can be used with adolescents aged over 13 years. The measure has also been tested on adolescents in Spain (Garcia-Lopez, Olivares, Hidalgo, Beidel, & Turner, 2001; Olivares et al., 2002).

See Table 9.2 for more details about these measures and their psychometric properties.

Because these five measures only address frequency ratings, whichever measure is chosen should be supplemented by an evaluation of the degree and duration of impairment in functioning (Beidel et al., 2000; Epkins, 2002), as well as response biases inherent in such measures (Anastasi & Urbina, 1997), in courtroom modification assessments. In particular, when gauging social desirability, MHPs are advised to let children know at the start of the assessment that there are "no right or wrong answers" and that they should try to answer questions as "honestly and truthfully as possible" (Silverman & Lopez, 2004, p. 289).

WHAT IS DEPRESSION?

Depression has been variously described as referring to a single symptom, such as feeling sad or blue, and to a cluster of symptoms, such as those that the *DSM–IV* mood disorders comprise (Schroeder & Gordon, 2002). People often naturally experience depressed feelings or symptoms after negative life experiences, such as loss of a loved one or exposure to traumatic events (Nezu, Ronan, Meadows, & McClure, 2000). When such feelings increase in severity or intensity or persist over time, they may reach the level of a depressive disorder. Recognized as significant mental health problems, depressive disorders place children and adolescents at "high risk for suicidal behavior; substance abuse, including nicotine dependence; physical illness; early pregnancy; exposure to negative life events; and poor work, academic, and psychosocial functioning" (AACAP, 1998, p. 9; Essau, 2007; Klein, Dougherty, & Olino, 2005).

The most common and recurrent mood disorders in children and adolescents are MDD, subclinical MDD, and dysthymic disorder (DD; AACAP, 1998; Schroeder & Gordon, 2002). MDD is characterized by one or more major depressive episodes, defined as follows:

> a period of at least 2 weeks during which there is either depressed mood or the loss of interest or pleasure in nearly all activities. In children and adolescents, the mood may be irritable rather than sad. The individual must also experience at least four additional symptoms drawn from a list that includes changes in appetite or weight, sleep and psychomotor activity; decreased energy; feelings of worthlessness or guilt; difficulty thinking, concentrating, or making decisions; or recurrent thoughts of death or suicidal ideation, plans or attempts. (APA, 1994, p. 320)

MDD typically lasts 7 to 8 months in samples of young people in clinical populations, with high rates of relapse and recurrence (Klein et al., 2005).

DD is "characterized by at least 2 years of depressed mood for more days than not, accompanied by additional depressive symptoms that do not meet criteria for a Major Depressive Episode" (APA, 1994, p. 317). In children and adolescents, the required minimum duration of symptoms is 1 year. Studies show that the average duration of DD is 48 months in clinical samples of children and adolescents (Klein et al., 2005).

Because DD involves "greater chronicity, but lesser severity" of MDD symptoms (Nezu et al., 2000, p. 10), the two are viewed as related syndromes. DD is a risk factor for MDD and its recurrence in children and adolescents (Orvaschel, 2004). When MDD happens during the course of DD, this condition is referred to as *double depression*. Children with double depression may have "more extensive functional impairments," lower rates of recovery, and higher rates of relapse than children diagnosed with MDD alone (Orvaschel, 2004, p. 299; see also Nezu et al., 2000). Thus, untreated, both MDD and DD usually persist into adulthood and pose an increased risk for self-destructive behavior (e.g., suicide, substance abuse) and behavior problems (e.g., running away; Birmaher & Brent, 1998; Essau, 2007; Green, 1993; Kaplan et al., 1997).

Other diagnostic categories applicable to children and adolescents include bipolar disorders, SAD, substance-induced mood disorder, adjustment disorder with depressed mood, and bereavement (Kazdin & Marciano, 1998). Bipolar disorders are characterized by various combinations of recurrent depressive and manic episodes. A manic episode is characterized by "a distinct period during which there is an abnormally and persistently elevated, expensive, or irritable mood" (APA, 1994, p. 328).

The *DSM–IV* criteria for mood disorders are valid for use with children (Kazdin & Marciano, 1998), with a few noted modifications. As noted earlier, children and adolescents with depression commonly display symptoms of irritability (often instead of depressed mood). Depressed children also exhibit somatic complaints and social withdrawal (APA, 1994), as well as deficiencies in communicating with others and in expressing affect (Kendall, Cantwell, & Kazdin, 1989). Both depressed children and adolescents report feelings of helplessness and hopelessness, anticipate negative outcomes in various life experiences, and attempt suicide (Laurent et al., 1999). Depression is the "leading risk factor for youth suicide and may be a risk factor for the development of other disorders, such as substance abuse" (Klein et al., 2005, p. 416; O'Leary et al., 2006). However, depressed children are less likely than their adolescent counterparts to show other depressive symptoms such as psychomotor retardation (e.g., slowed speech, thinking, and body movements), hypersomnia (i.e., oversleeping), and delusions (APA, 1994).

Because young people are more labile in terms of mood than adults are, normative developmental issues can create difficulty in diagnosing or otherwise determining that a child or adolescent is depressed (Crowe, Ward, Dunnachie, & Roberts, 2006). For this reason, modifications to current *DSM–IV* criteria have been proposed. Orvaschel (2004) recommended that the time-frame criterion for depressive disorders ("most of the day nearly every day") be modified for children aged 5 to 11 years. To be developmentally appropriate, Orvaschel advised that "[f]or a 7 or 8 year old, 3 hours of consistent sadness in a day often qualifies as a minimal screen for depressed mood, while in an older child (e.g., 13 or 14 years old) a lengthier time depressed, approximating that of adults, may be expected" (p. 298). Despite resistance to applying mood disorders to preschoolers, Luby and colleagues (e.g., Luby, Mrakotsky, Heffelfinger, 2003; Luby, Mrakotsky, Heffelfinger, Brown, & Spitznagel, 2004) have been investigating modified *DSM–IV* criteria for children aged 3 to 5 years (Stalets & Luby, 2006). Their criteria shorten the required duration of symptoms and take into account preschool children's limited verbal skills and use of play as means of expression. These are reflected in the diagnostic criteria used for Birth to Three programs, which have yet to be empirically tested (Keren & Tyano, 2006).

In addition to considering age-related issues, the *DSM–IV* notes that these disorders may be affected by gender. Boys and girls are equally affected by MDD and dysthymia, the latter resulting in poor school performance and social interaction because children are often cranky, irritable, and depressed and have poor social skills and low self-esteem (APA, 1994, p. 347). In adolescents, however, depression is more commonly reported by girls than boys (Austin & Chorpita, 2004; Hankin, Mermelstein, & Roesch, 2007), with prevalence rates revealing differences in early adolescence and becoming approximately 2 to 3 times as common in girls than boys by age 15 (Hankin et al., 1998; Klein et al., 2005; Lewinsohn & Essau, 2002). Studies examining whether gender differences have been found with adolescents of color provide conflicting results (Casper, Belanoff, & Offer, 1996, who found gender differences regardless of race; Hayward, Gotlib, Schraedley, & Litt, 1999, who reported no gender differences for African American and Hispanic adolescents).

Although the *DSM–IV* considers depression a disorder found in all cultural groups, it may not be a universal construct (e.g., Dana, 2005). Increased attention is being given to how depressive symptoms are experienced, expressed, and interpreted in different ethnic and cultural contexts (Crowe, Dunnachie, & Roberts, 2006; Manson, 1995). For example, a lack of eye contact may not be a sign of dysphoric affect but one of respect (Takushi & Uomoto, 2001). Also, certain culture-bound or culturally related syndromes may include symptoms related to depression (e.g., *susto*; Tsai & Chentsova-Dutton, 2002). Furthermore, because people may use "specific vocabularies to describe the cultural meanings of the[ir] experience[s]" (Dana, 2005, p. 18), MHPs should be aware of the "modes of communication that both the assessor as well as the family bring to their interaction" (Cook et al., 2003, p. 18; Manson, 1996). This involves an examination of one's own biases in assessing depression in culturally diverse youth (Choi, 2002), including the instruments one chooses to use (Tsai & Chentsova-Dutton, 2002).

Depression is a relevant consideration in courtroom modification assessments because it is one of the most common sequelae of child maltreatment (Danielson, de Arellano, & Kilpatrick, 2005; Green, 1993; J. Kaufman & Charney, 2001; Kendall-Tackett, 2002; Kilpatrick et al., 2003; Koss, Bailey, & Yuan, 2003) and can have an impact on an allegedly abused child witness's ability to communicate in court. In general, depressive symptoms have been linked to all types of child maltreatment: childhood sexual abuse, physical abuse, and psychological abuse and neglect (Briere, 1992). Research has shown sexual and physical abuse to be risk factors for depression in the short term (Flisher, Kramer, Hoven, & Greenwald, 1997; Swanston, Tebbutt, O'Toole, & Oates, 1997) and the long term (Danielson et al., 2005; Stevenson, 1999). Witnessing interpersonal violence is also a risk factor for depression (Kilpatrick et al., 2003; Somer & Braunstein, 1999). Finally, being abused appears to put children and adolescents at higher risk for becoming suicidal (J. Brown, Cohen, Johnson, & Smailes, 1999; Danielson et al., 2005; Fergusson, Horwood, & Lynskey, 1996; Finzi, Har-Even, Shnit, & Weizman, 2002; Kaplan et al., 1999).

DEPRESSION ASSESSMENT MEASURES

The two main approaches to the assessment and diagnosis of depression in children and adolescents involve interviews and rating scales. At this time, there is insufficient evidence to support the use of observational measures and coding systems and a lack of physiological or biological laboratory measures (Klein et al., 2005). Valid and reliable structured and semistructured interviews have been developed to study childhood mood disorders (Birmaher, Ryan, & Williamson, 1996). Such interviews provide a reliable method that enables comprehensive and thorough diagnoses (Rabkin & Klein, 1987) that are superior to unstructured interviews (Angold & Fisher, 1999; Klein et al., 2005). A benefit of interviews over self-report measures is that interviewers, trained to be aware of cultural nuances in how symptoms are expressed and described, can clarify items and answers as they are given (Rourke & Reich, 2004). In fact, structured and semistructured interviews are the only accepted method for deriving a *DSM–IV* diagnosis of MDD or DD (Compas, 1997). As a result, they are typically used as the "gold standard" against which other measures are compared (Daviss et al., 2006, p. 927; Klein et al., 2005, p. 420), even though "there is little consensus in the field regarding what the 'gold standard' for diagnosis might be" (Wasserman, McReynolds, Fisher, & Lucas, 2005, p. 231; see also Silverman & Serafini, 1998).

For youth, the most widely used semistructured interviews include the revised versions of the Schedule for Affective Disorders and Schizophrenia in School-Age Children (K–SADS; Chambers et al., 1985; K–SADS–PL, J. Kaufman et al., 1997), the Diagnostic Interview Schedule for Children (DISC; Shaffer, 1989; DISC–IV, Shaffer, Fisher, Lucas, Dulcan, & Schwab-Stone, 2000), and the Diagnostic Interview for Children and Adolescents (DICA; Herjanic & Campbell, 1977; Reich, 2000; Reich, Shayka, & Taibleson, 1991). The Child and Adolescent Psychiatric Assessment (CAPA; Angold, Prendergast, et al., 1995) is also available. As explained earlier in the section on assessing anxiety, each interview is separately administered to the youth and his or her parent or caregiver.

Typically, the interviews are designed for use with children over 6 years of age, although concern has been raised with the administration of semistructured interviews and self-rating scales to children under 8 or 9 years of age (Angold & Fisher, 1999). For this reason, work is underway to modify instruments for use with younger children. Regarding interviews, the DISC–IV has been modified for children as young as 3 years (DISC–IV–YC;

Luby et al., 2006; Luby, Mrakotsky, Heffelfinger, Brown, & Spitznagel, 2004; Lucas, Fisher, & Luby, 1998), and a downward extension of the CAPA, the Preschool Age Psychiatric Assessment (PAPA; Egger, Ascher, & Angold, 1999) shows promise (Egger & Angold, 2004; Egger, Erkanli, & Keeler, 2006; Stalets & Luby, 2006).

Yet older age does not ensure reliability. For example, adolescents asked to give the date of onset for their depressive symptoms provided unreliable answers when they had to think back over 3 months (Angold, Erklani, Costello, & Rutter, 1996). Similarly, one study that asked adolescents to give reports in two interviews regarding the duration of their depressed mood found that about 31% of participants in one interview reported a duration of more than 1 year and in another interview reported a duration of less than 1 year (Lewinsohn & Essau, 2002). To help young people make more reliable reports about the timing of depressive symptoms, Orvaschel (2004) recommended obtaining information about symptom onset from parents and grounding time to events, such as asking about the child's feelings today, yesterday, since school started, since his or her birthday, since summer vacation, and so on. Of course, MHPs should also assess for key depressive symptoms in developmentally appropriate ways. For example, clinicians can ask young children whether they feel hungry and how their clothes fit and ask their parents about weight gain or loss (Orvaschel, 2004). With adolescents who are often concerned about reporting stigmatizing behavior such as suicidal thoughts or actions, clinicians should emphasize confidentiality and include self-report measures or computer-administered interviews (e.g., the computerized version of the DICA, the voice version of the DISC) to which they may be more forthcoming than in face-to-face interviews (Rourke & Reich, 2004; Wasserman et al., 2005).

Developed for youth 6 to 17 years of age, the K–SADS has been called the "most useful of the clinical interview schedules available" for depressive disorders (Kutcher & Marton, 1996, p. 102). This was supported by a comparative study of the diagnostic validity of the interview schedules (G. A. Carlson, Kashani, DeFatima, Vaidya, & Daniel, 1987). Its reliability and validity ratings are superior to those of DISC, DICA (Compas, 1997), and the less studied CAPA, and it also requires less training and cost to the clinician than the other interviews. The K–SADS was found to be used more frequently than the DISC, DICA, and CAPA in a review of published studies involving adolescent depression diagnosis (Brooks & Kutcher, 2001). It was revised to accommodate DSM–IV criteria and generates reliable and valid child psychiatric diagnoses, including MDD and bipolar disorder (J. Kaufman et al., 1997; Shanee, Apter, & Weizman, 1997), with solid evidence of interrater reliability and convergent validity (Klein et al., 2005). The K–SADS has also been shown valid for use with abused youth (e.g., Egeland, 1997). The K–SADS can be used to assess current and past psychopathology as well as symptom severity levels (frequency, intensity and duration). Thus, as for anxiety disorders, it appears to be the best semistructured interview for courtroom modification assessment purposes. See Table 9.3 for more information about its psychometric properties.

After mood disorders in children and adolescents began to be recognized in the 1980s, most of the available depression rating scales were developed, and these continue to be studied and widely used today, along with newer measures (K. Myers & Winters, 2002). Scales can be administered by the clinician or filled out by the child or adolescent (self-report), parent, and teacher. The purpose of symptom rating scales is to assist in screening for internalizing problems or for determining the severity of depressive symptoms. They are cheaper, faster, simpler, more direct, and require less expertise to administer than interviews (Brooks & Kutcher, 2001; W. M. Reynolds, 2006). These are not clinically valid diagnostic instruments, however, and therefore should not be used to diagnose depressive disorders in youth (Kutcher & Marton, 1996). Instead, they can be used in a complementary fashion with diagnostic interviews, as previously described. Given the limitations of existing depression scales for youth, including insufficient reliability, poor construct validity, lack of discriminant validity data, and low sensitivity to change, it is recommended that more than one scale be used to evaluate internalizing constructs, including depression, until more robust or ideal measures are developed (Brooks & Kutcher, 2001; K. Myers & Winters, 2002).

For more comprehensive reviews of the various measures of depression, readers are referred to the following resources:

- Angold and Fisher's (1999) discussion of the structured and semistructured interviewer-based interviews with children: ADIS: C, CAPA, CAS, DICA, Missouri Assessment of Genetics Interview for Children (MAGIC), and K–SADS;
- Brooks and Kutcher's (2001) review of 12 measures for adolescent depression: K–SADS, DISC, DICA–R and DICA–IV, CAPA, Hamilton Depression Rating Scales (HDRS), Montgomery–Asberg Depression Rating Scales (MADRS), Children's Depression Rating Scale—Revised (CDRS–R), Beck Depression Inventory (BDI), Children's Depression Inventory (CDI), Mood and Feelings Questionnaire (MFQ and SMFQ), Reynolds Adolescent Depression Scale (RADS), Center for Epidemiologic Studies Depression Scales (CES–D and CES–DC);
- K. Myers and Winters's (2002) thorough discussion of widely used measures in the published literature, including the following related to mood disorders: BDI, HDRS, RADS, Reynolds Child Depression Scale (RCDS), CES–D and CES–DC, CDI, Children's Depression Scale (CDS), Depression Self Rating

TABLE 9.3
Depression Assessment Instruments for Use in Courtroom Modification Assessments With Children and Adolescents

Depression Measures	Age range	Reliability data	Validity data	Severity level/ cutoff scores	Features/summary	Weaknesses
The Schedule for Affective Disorders and Schizophrenia for School-Age Children: Present and Lifetime Version (K–SADS–PL) Original citation: J. Kaufman et al., 1997 Other K–SADS versions include the K–SADS–P (Present episode), K–SADS–E (Epidemiological version), K–SADS–L (Lifetime version), and K–SADS–IVR Available at http://www.wpic.pitt. edu/ksads/default.htm Restrictions on use are as follows: "This instrument is copyrighted. Usage is freely permitted without further permission for uses which meet one or more of the following: Clinical usage in a not-for-profit institution, Usage in an IRB [internal review board] approved research protocol. All other uses require written permission of the principal author, Dr. Kaufman, including but not limited to the following: Redistribution of the instrument in printed, electronic or other forms, Commercial use of the instrument."	6/7–18 years	Internal consistency • Earlier version: K–SADS–P—one study's alphas ranged from .68 to .84 for depression summary scales; another had alphas of .76 to .89 (Brooks & Kutcher, 2001) Interrater and test-retest reliability - Interrater reliability in utilization of skip-out options across 20 diagnostic areas surveyed averaged 99.7% (93%–100%) - ITest–retest: kappas MDD = .90 (present) and = 1.00 (lifetime); MDD and dysthymia kappas = .90 (present) and = 1.00 (lifetime); DDNOS kappas = .86 (lifetime); bipolar I or NOS kappas = 1.00 (present) and = 1.00 (lifetime) • Sample: 52 subjects aged 6–17 years, about 30 with MDD; interval of 1–3 days, different interviewer (Brooks & Kutcher, 2001)	Concurrent validity • Sample of 55 psychiatric outpatients and 11 normal control youth who screened positive for current depression also scored significantly higher on the CDI, the BDI, and the CBCL Internalizing scale (J. Kaufman & Schweder, 2004). • Sample: youth whose screening interview indicated the need for depressive disorder supplement ($n = 37$) scored significantly higher than others ($n = 29$) on the BDI and CDI (Brooks & Kutcher, 2001) Predictive validity • K–SADS–P and –E: Children with current/past depressive disorder (using K–SADS) at 9 years showed more depressive symptoms (using DISC) at 11 and 13 years than those at 9 years who did not show depressive disorder (Brooks & Kutcher, 2001)	The severity/ intensity and timing/duration of symptoms are scored with probes used during screening interview process with child and parent on a 0–3 scale: 0 = *no information;* 1 = *not present;* 2 = *subthreshold;* 3 = *threshold* If treated with medication, severity is noted according to the most intense severity before taking or when not taking medication. Summary diagnoses for each disorder are placed on a 1–4 scale: 1 = *no disorder,* 4 = *definite disorder*	• Semistructured interview used by trained clinicians to assess current and lifetime *DSM–III–R* and *DSM–IV* differential diagnoses, including MDD, dysthymia, depressive disorder NOS, atypical depression, adjustment disorder with depressed mood, mania, bipolar disorder NOS. • Used extensively in research and clinical situations. • Administered first to preadolescents then to parent; with adolescents, the order is reversed. • Three-component structure: - Begins with 10–15 minute unstructured introductory interview, followed by an 82-item screening interview in which core symptoms of each diagnostic area are rated on a 4-point scale and skip-out criteria are used, followed by the use of five diagnostic supplements based on need, including	• Administration time • Requires extensive training (several weeks with no training; 2 hours for a skilled clinician/ researcher), clinical experience, and *DSM–IV* familiarity. • Does not include *ICD–10* diagnoses. • Not intended to measure or monitor change. • Currently no computerized versions available. • Limited reliability and validity data "suggest adequacy" (Brooks & Kutcher, 2001).

Instrument	Age	Reliability	Validity	Scoring / Norms	Description / Comments
The Schedule for Affective Disorders and Schizophrenia for School-Age Children: Present and Lifetime Version (K–SADS–PL) (Continued)		- IKappa for MDD was .54; for the depression summary, scales ranged from .67 to .81 - ICC of individual symptoms "acceptable" for 12 of 14 items ranged from .51 to .88. ICCs between informants on 11 of 12 items ranged from .5 to .85 • Sample: 20 subjects aged 7–17 years, 10 with MDD (Brooks & Kutcher, 2001): Test-retest kappas = .90 (present) and = 1.00 (lifetime) found by pairs of raters performed 2–38 days apart • Sample using Spanish language version: MDD diagnosis, kappa = .76 (Ulloa et al., 2006)			affective disorders. • Clinician uses common answer sheet for child and caretaker interviews and produces a summary rating, using clinical judgment, producing diagnoses for each disorder on 1–4 scale. • Duration: Complete process can take 1.5–3 hours; 35–45 minutes per interviewee with control subjects, 1.25 hours with clinical patients. • Translated into at least 16 languages, many with without published psychometrics.
Children's Depression Inventory (CDI) Original citation: Kovacs (1992) Multi-Health Systems, Inc.,, P.O. Box 950, North Tonawanda, NY 14120-0950; https://www.mhs.com/index.htm; Tel: (800) 456-3003 Fax: (888) 540-4484; e-mail: customerservice@mhs.com Contact information: Maria Kovacs University of Pittsburgh School of Medicine, Western Psychiatric Institute & Clinic, 3811 O'Hara St., Pittsburgh, PA 15213; Tel: (412) 624-2043; Fax: (412) 624-0060	7–17 years	Internal consistency • Original sample of 1,266 students (592 boys, aged 7–15 years; 674 girls aged 7–16 years) and 134 clinically diagnosed children. 23% of sample were African American, American Indian, or Hispanic; alpha for total score = .85; five factors ranged from .59 to .68 (Nezu, Ronan, Meadows, & McClure, 2000) • Most studies with clinical and nonclinical samples show alphas > .80 (Brooks & Kutcher, 2001; Comer & Kendall, 2005)	Concurrent validity (Brooks & Kutcher, 2001) • RADS: 2,460 adolescents, $r = .73$ • DSRS: 82 6–13-year-olds, $r = .81$ • CDRS–R $r = .89$ for females ($n = 29$), .41 for males ($n = 16$) Discriminative validity • Mixed evidence; some studies demonstrate the CDI can discriminate those with depressive disorders from other disorders or from nondepressed youth, but	Severity of each item is scored on a 3-point scale: 0 = *absence of the symptom*, 2 = *definite symptom* Cutoff scores: • Kovacs (1992) proposed a cutoff score of 12 of 13 for clinical populations and 19 of 20 for nonclinical populations; however, these	• One of the best known and most frequently used self-report measures of depression for children. • Twenty-seven-item child self-report questionnaire screening severity of depressive symptoms over the past 2 weeks; items tapping disturbed mood, anhedonia, negative self-evaluation, ineffectiveness, interpersonal problems. • Yields five empirically derived factor scores and an overall score by • Downward extension of BDI; 27 items (the first 18 correspond to the BDI); Items posses cognitive bias. • Five factor structure not consistently supported, including with ethnically diverse samples (e.g., Craighead,

(continues)

TABLE 9.3

Depression Assessment Instruments for Use in Courtroom Modification Assessments With Children and Adolescents *(Continued)*

Depression Measures	Age range	Reliability data	Validity data	Severity level/ cutoff scores	Features/summary	Weaknesses
Children's Depression Inventory (CDI) *(Continued)*		Test–retest reliability • Original sample: range from .74 to .83 for 2- to 3-week intervals • Most studies report rs close to .70, with wide range: .38 (69 healthy fifth and sixth graders, 1-week interval) to .88 (108 healthy 7–12-year-olds, 4- to 6-week intervals) (Brooks & Kutcher, 2001)	other studies have not (Comer & Kendall, 2005; Silverman & Rabian, 1999) • Young children tend to get lower scores than adolescents • CDI's proposed cutoff scores have poor sensitivity; it will miss 86% of depressed children (Matthey & Petrovski, 2002) Sensitivity to change (Brooks & Kutcher, 2001) • Demonstrated, but caution is needed because of score dropping on second administration, even with without treatment	have been criticized or not upheld in subsequent studies • Cutoff scores differ by clinical and community settings; they should not be used for diagnosis, (Matthey & Petrovski, 2002; Timbremont, Braet, & Dreessen, 2004)	summing the ratings (0–54); scores are converted to *t* scores based on age range (7–12 or 13–17); five factors are negative mood, ineffectiveness, negative self-esteem, interpersonal problems, anhedonia. • First-grade reading level • Duration: 10–20 minutes • Alternative forms: a 10-item short form; paper and pencil or computerized formats. • Translated to other languages, including Arabic, Bulgarian, Croatian, Portuguese, Spanish, French (Canadian), Italian, Japanese, Norwegian, Russian, Ukrainian, Afrikaans, Dutch, German, Hebrew, French (European), Hungarian, Lithuanian, Swedish, Spanish (European), Polish, Turkish, and South African English.	Smucker, Craighead, & Ilardi, 1998; Steele et al., 2006) • Cutoff scores criticized. • Poor and mixed evidence for discriminative ability. • Recommended for use as a continuous measure rather than a categorical measure of depression in clinical samples (Comer & Kendall, 2005).
Children's Depression Rating Scale—Revised (CDRS–R)	6–12 years; also widely used with	Internal consistency • Clinical sample from a depression clinic (*n* = 78,	Convergent validity • Correlations with Global Ratings of Depression = .87,	Symptom areas rated on a 7-point scale (2 indicates	• Brief clinician rating scale of the presence and severity of depressive	• Modeled after the adult *Hamilton*

Instrument	Reliability	Validity	Description	Comments
Children's Depression Rating Scale—Revised (CDRS–R) *(Continued)* Original citation: Poznanski & Mokros (1996) Available from Western Psychological Services 12031 Wilshire Blvd. Los Angeles, CA 90025-1251 Tel: (800) 648-8857 Fax: (310) 478-7838 http://www.wpspublish.com/	60 met *DSM–III* criteria for depressive disorder, 15 others had another diagnosis); item correlations ranged from .28 to .78 • Nonreferred sample (*n* = 223), alpha = .85; item correlations ranged from .36 to .71 (Nezu et al., 2000) • 314 MDD patients 7–17 years, alpha = .70 (Guo et al., 2006) Interrater reliability • Four child psychiatrists, reliability was *r* = .92 (Nezu et al., 2000) • Interinformant reliability: "poor"; cross-informant item correlations ranged from –.01 to .42 in 110 children aged 6–12 years (community sample) and parents, with total score *r* = .38; similar data with clinical sample *n* = 34 (Brooks & Kutcher, 2001) Test–retest reliability • Clinical sample (*n* = 52), 2 weeks apart, blind to first rating, *r* = .8 (Nezu et al., 2000) • Sample (*n* = 53): clinic referred 6–12-year-olds, 2-week interval, *r* = .86 (Brooks & Kutcher, 2001)	correlation with modified Hamilton Rating Scale for Depression (*n* = 36) = .48 (Nezu et al., 2006) • Sample (*n* = 48): 12–18-year-olds, distinguished between acutely and chronically depressed (Brooks & Kutcher, 2001) • HDRS: *n* = 16 male, 29 female 12–18-year-olds with depression, *r* = .92 (overall), .84 (male), .94 (female) • CDI: *n* = 16 male, 29 female depressed 12–18-year-olds, *r* = .41 (male), .89 (female) • RADS: *n* = 16 male, 29 female depressed 12–18-year-olds, *r* = .48 (male), .86 (female) • Sample of *n* = 142 clinical adolescents and their parents CDRS–R with MFQ-R. Average AUC = .87 (Daviss et al., 2006) Discriminant validity • Sample (Nezu et al., 2006): children diagnosed with depression (*M* = 53.68, *SD* = 15.7) scored higher than either the nonclinical group (*M* = 27.8, *SD* = 8.9) or the other disorder group (*M* = 34.12, *SD* = 8.4) Sensitivity to change (Brooks & Kutcher, 2001): "proven in children; limited data in adolescents"	symptoms in children. • Semistructured interview with the child (or an adult who knows the child well) consisting of 14 items evaluated by the trained interviewer in response to the child's verbal responses and caretaker or teacher input (rated on 7-point scale) and 3 items based on clinician-observed nonverbal behavior. • Items include impaired schoolwork, difficulty having fun, social withdrawal, appetite disturbance, sleep disturbance, excessive fatigue, physical complaints, irritability, excessive guilt, low self-esteem, depressed feelings, morbid ideation, suicidal ideation, excessive weeping, depressed facial affect, listless speech, hypoactivity. • Duration: 15–30 minutes	*Rating Scale for Depression.* • More clarity needed regarding combining data from different informants. • Reliability: "good in children; limited data in adolescents" (Brooks & Kutcher, 2001). • Sensitivity to change questioned in adolescents (Brooks & Kutcher, 2001) but is frequently used in medication treatment trials and studies.

adolescents (K. Myers & Winters, 2002)

problems may exist, and 3–7 are of increasing clinical significance); three are rated on a 5-point scale Clinician calculates a summary score (17–113) and a *t* score
• *t* scores 55–64 indicate further evaluation needed
• *t* scores ≥ 65 indicate there is likely to be a significant disorder
• Original samples found mean *t* score of 71 for the clinical sample and 53 for the nonclinical sample (Nezu et al., 2000)

(continues)

TABLE 9.3
Depression Assessment Instruments for Use in Courtroom Modification Assessments With Children and Adolescents (Continued)

Depression Measures	Age range	Reliability data	Validity data	Severity level/cutoff scores	Features/summary	Weaknesses
Mood and Feelings Questionnaire (MFQ; Costello & Angold, 1988); Short Mood and Feelings Questionnaire (SMFQ; Angold, Costello et al., 1995) Child (MFQ–C; SMFQ–C) and Parent (MFQ–P; SMFQ–P) versions available Available at http://devepi.mc.duke.edu/MFQ.html Contact information: Anita Chalmers; Tel: (919) 687-4686, extension 230; e-mail: achalmers@psych.duhs.duke.edu Usage Information from Web site: "COPYRIGHT PERMISSION: Should you wish to administer the MFQ to your clients or for your research study, please describe your proposed use and write to the above address to receive a letter of copyright approval from the first author, Adrian Angold, MRCPsych, at no charge. Citation in published work would be appreciated."	7–18 years	Internal consistency • Brooks and Kutcher, 2001 (citing Wood et al., 1995): Sample: MFQ (n = 104) 10–19-year-old outpatients and parents, alphas = .94 (children) and = .92 (parents); (citing Angold et al., 1995) SMFQ, 6-17-year-old outpatients/parents, alphas = .85 (children) and = .87 (parents); • Sample (n = 470) clinical and control children and adolescents, MFQ–C alpha = .95, MFQ–P alpha = .96 (Daviss et al., 2006) • Sample: n = 2,465 12.5–15.7-year-old Norwegian school youth, MFQ alpha = .91 (Sund, Larsson, & Wichstrom, 2001) Test–retest reliability • Sample (n = 15): 10–19-year-olds with MDD, 18 days, ICC = .78, with 7.6% drop in means; 30 psychiatric inpatients, 1-week interval, ICC = .75 (Brooks & Kutcher, 2001, citing Costello et al., 1991) • Sample of 83 youth with ADHD, 1 month, MFQ–C	Concurrent validity • Sample (Brooks & Kutcher, 2001, citing Angold et al., 1995): MFQ–C: CDI, r = .67 (full) and .62 (short); DISC-C, r = .58 (full) and .65 (short); MFQ–P: CDI, r = .24 (full) and .31 (short); DISC–P r = .40 (full) and .43 (short) Criterion validity • Brooks & Kutcher, 2001, citing Wood et al, 1995, K-SADS MDD diagnoses; MFQ–C AUC = .82, MFQ–P AUC = .69; cut point = 27 yielded 78% sensitivity and specificity • SMFQ (Brooks & Kutcher, 2001, citing Thapar & McGuffin, 1998): with CAPA DSM–III–R diagnoses (parent), AUC was .72 for SMFQ–C and .90 for SMFQ–P • Sample (n = 470): clinical and control children and adolescents (Daviss et al., 2006), "moderate to high criterion validity for discriminating MDE or any mood disorders in this sample" (p. 932), for overall sample, AUC = .85, cut	Rate items as 0 = not true; 1 = sometimes true; 2 = not true Optimal cut points vary across and within samples in studies (e.g., MFQ–C of 29 or 27 and MFQ–P of 27 or 21); clinicians should use them with caution (Daviss et al., 2006)	• Child self-report screening tool designed to assess DSM criteria for MDD • Full MFQ has 30–35 items (score range 0–64); Short SMFQ has 13 items (score range 0–26). • MFQ used extensively in epidemiological and clinical research. • MFQ and SMFQ used with diverse international populations. • Simple format and wording; can be read to younger children. • Parallel parent versions of MFQ and SMFQ available. • Unidimensional factor structure; choice of statistical methods to study measure may influence model results (Sharp, Goodyer, & Croudace, 2006). • Duration: 5–10 minutes	• SMFQ is biased toward affective and cognitive symptoms; does not assess appetite, sleep, weight, and suicidal ideation (Brooks & Kutcher, 2001). • Limited discriminative validity against other self-report measures. • More evidence is needed to support averaging of MFQ–C and MFQ–P scores.

Measure	Age	Reliability/Validity	Scoring	Comments
Mood and Feelings Questionnaire (MFQ; Costello & Angold, 1988); Short Mood and Feelings Questionnaire (SMFQ; Angold, Costello et al., 1995) *(Continued)*		ICC = .80, MFQ–P ICC = .80 (Davis et al., 2006) • Sample (n = 2,465) of 12.5-15.7-year-old Norwegian school youth: 3 week, r = .84; 3 month, r = .80 (Sund et al., 2001) Parent–child concordance: • "weak" (citing Angold et al., 1995); sample (n = 48) of 6–17-year-old psychiatric outpatients (n = 125) 6–11-year-old control subjects, and their parents: r = .25 for MFQ, r = .30 for SMFQ (Brooks & Kutcher, 2001) • Sample (n = 470); clinical and control sample children and adolescents, MFQ–C with MFQ–P, r = .61 (Davis et al., 2006)	point = 29 for MFQ–C (sen 68%, spe 88%), AUC = .86, cut point = 27 for MFQ–P (sen 61%, spe 85%) (except 27, cut point, did not significantly discriminate MDD for youth with anxiety disorders); cut point = 32 for MFQ–Average (sen 58%, spe 94%) Sensitivity to change • "mixed results" (Brooks & Kutcher, 2001, p. 363)	
The Reynolds Adolescent Depression Scale—Second Edition (RADS–2). Contact and principal developer: William M. Reynolds, PhD, Professor and Chair, Department of Psychology, Humboldt State University; Tel: (707) 826-3162 e-mail: wr9@humboldt.edu Available from Psychological Assessment Resources, Inc., 16204 North Florida Ave., Lutz, FL 33549; (800) 331-8378; http://www3.parinc.com/	11–20 years	Internal consistency (Reynolds, 2004) • Sample n = 9,052 adolescents: alpha = 0.93 for the total scale, subscales ranged from .8 to .87 • Clinical sample (n = 101 adolescents): alpha = .94 for total scale, subscales ranged from .81 to .87 Test–retest reliability • Sample (n = 1,765 adolescents in school setting): r = .85 total scale, with subscales from .77 to .84, 2 weeks Convergent validity (Reynolds, 2004) • Sample (n = 485 adolescents): RADS–2 and panic disorder scale, r = 0.56; OCD, r = .49; generalized anxiety disorder, r = .63; social phobia, r = .55; separation anxiety, r = .37; PTSD, r = .7; similar findings in a sample (n = 167) of adolescent psychiatric inpatients and outpatients • Previous version showed convergence with anxiety, self-concept, loneliness, suicidal ideation, and hopelessness constructs	Items rated on 4-point scale to indicate symptom frequency: *almost never, hardly ever, sometimes, most of the time* The measure provides standard scores (t scores) and percentile ranks) - Empirically derived clinical cutoff score (not for diagnosis	• Brief 30-item adolescent self-report measure assessing the frequency and clinical severity of depressive symptoms. • Items not changed from RADS (previous version). • Symptoms congruent with *DSM–IV* and *ICD–10*. • Four factorially derived subscales derived from school-based sample of 9,052 adolescents from eight states and one Canadian province; 30% were non-Caucasian; equal number of male • Does not cover all depressive symptoms; does not provide a formal *DSM* diagnosis. • As with other a self-report measures, youth may not respond openly and may deny, underreport, or overendorse symptoms. • Discriminant

(continues)

TABLE 9.3

Depression Assessment Instruments for Use in Courtroom Modification Assessments With Children and Adolescents *(Continued)*

Depression Measures	Age range	Reliability data	Validity data	Severity level/cutoff scores	Features/summary	Weaknesses
The Reynolds Adolescent Depression Scale—Second Edition (RADS–2). *(Continued)*		• Clinical sample (*n* = 70 adolescents with psychiatric disorders): 2 week interval *r* = .89 for the total scale, subscales .81–.87	Criterion-related validity (Reynolds, 2004) • Hamilton Depression Rating Scale (HAMD): Sample (*n* = 485 12–19-year-olds), *r* = .82. Subscales and HAMD ranged from *r* = .54 to .79 • Adolescent Psychopathology Scale (APS) • Sample (*n* = 485 adolescents): *r* = .76 with MD Scale, *r* = .74 with the DD Scale. RADS–2 Subscale correlations with MD scale ranged .424 to .70 and with DD scale .49 to .69 • BDI: Sample (*n* = 70) of adolescents with clinical diagnoses: *r* = .8; subscale *r* = .66 for dysphoric mood; *r* = .66 for anhedonia/negative affect; *r* = .77 for negative self-evaluation; *r* = .64 for somatic complaints. Discriminant validity (Reynolds, 2004) • Previous version found low relationships with unrelated constructs including social desirability, academic and cognitive ability, self-report of antisocial behavior	of depression) used to identify adolescents most likely to manifest clinical levels of depressive symptoms • Cutoff score derived from sample (*n* = 107) of adolescents with MDD and an age- and gender-matched group of school-based adolescents. • Cutoff *t* score is 61 (equal to raw score of 76) (corresponds with previous RADS cutoff score of 77) to differentiate between MDD and school sample (sen 92%, spe 84%, hit rate 88%) • RADS cutoff score of 77 misclassifies one third of depressed adolescents as not depressed (Brooks & Kutcher, 2001)	and female subjects, aged 11–13 years, 14–16 years, 17–20 years • Dysphoric Mood: eight items, evaluates disturbance of mood, sadness, crying behavior, loneliness, irritability, worry, self-pity. • Anhedonia/Negative Affect: seven items, represents a behavioral component in depression. • Negative Self-Evaluation: eight items including negative feelings about oneself; primarily cognitive. • Somatic Complaints: seven items that evaluate somatic and vegetative complaints. • Total depression score: the sum of all items, a global assessment. • Duration: 5–10 minutes • Group or individual administration • Second-grade reading level; Flesch–Kincaid Grade 1.1 reading level; 96% Flesch Reading Ease Index; with instructions, values	validity "not well studied" (K. Myers & Winters, 2002, p. 641); "not the best self-report instrument for detecting changes in depressive symptoms over time" (Brooks & Kutcher, 2001, p. 364). • No computer scoring available.

	Grades (ages)	Psychometric properties	Description / scoring	Comments
The Reynolds Adolescent Depression Scale—Second Edition (RADS–2). *(Continued)*				rise to a 1.8-grade level and 92% ease of reading; may be read to adolescents with learning difficulties or disabilities. • Parent version available • Previous version available in languages other than English, and studies found it consistent with the U.S. measure; "RADS is applicable to diverse populations" (K. Myers & Winters, 2002, p. 641).
Reynolds Child Depression Scale (RCDS) Original citation: W. M. Reynolds (1989) Contact: William M. Reynolds, PhD, Professor and Chair, Department of Psychology, Humboldt State University; Tel: (707) 826-3162; e-mail: wr9@humboldt.edu Available from Psychological Assessment Resources, Inc., 16204 North Florida Ave., Lutz, FL 33549; (800) 331-8378; http://www.3.parinc.com/	Grades 3–6 (8–12 years)	Internal consistency • Normative sample ($n = 1,620$ children); alpha = .90 Test–retest reliability (Nezu et al., 2000): • Sample 2-week interval (24 fifth graders): $r = .82$. • Sample ($n = 220$ children grades 3–6): 4-week interval: $r = .85$. Convergent validity • Manual cites $r = .73$ with the CDI and $r = -.63$ with a measure of self-esteem Divergent validity • Manual notes that there are six critical items designed to discriminate between clinically and nonclinically depressed children Sensitivity to change • Shown sensitive to effects of CBT in research study (Nezu et al., 2000, citing Stark, Reynolds, & Kaslow, 1987)	Twenty-nine items on a 4-point scale: *almost never, sometimes, a lot of the time, all of the time* One item with five faces with different emotions (happy to sad) Children asked to indicate frequency, over the past 2 weeks, that they have felt each way Range of scores is from 30–121; higher scores indicate more depressive symptoms Cutoff score = 74 indicates the	• Brief self-report measure of depressive symptoms (30 items) constructed based on *DSM–III*. • Can be administered to individuals, small groups, or classrooms. • Second-grade reading level • Duration: 10–20 minutes • Parent version available • Greater weight given to anhedonia and dysphoric mood (Nezu et al., 2000). • Studied most with schoolchildren; utility in clinical samples is less clear and instrument may not be sensitive to treatment effects (K. Myers & Winters, 2002). • RCSD scores do not correlate well with caregiver and teacher

(continues)

TABLE 9.3
Depression Assessment Instruments for Use in Courtroom Modification Assessments With Children and Adolescents   *(Continued)*

Depression Measures	Age range	Reliability data	Validity data	Severity level/cutoff scores	Features/summary	Weaknesses
Reynolds Child Depression Scale (RCDS) *(Continued)*				school-based child needs further evaluation (spe 97%, sen 73%, hit rate 94%)		depression ratings (K. Myers & Winters, 2002). • Cutoff scores are not established for other populations.

Note. ADHD = attention-deficit/hyperactivity disorder; AUC = area under the curve; BDI = Beck Depression Inventory; CBCL = Child Behavior Checklist; CDI = Children's Depression Inventory; DD = dysthymic disorder; DISC = Diagnostic Interview Schedule for Children; DDNOS = dysthymic disorder, not otherwise specified; DSRS = Depression Self-Rating Scale; DSM–III = *Diagnostic and Statistical Manual of Mental Disorders, Third Edition; DSM–III–R = Diagnostic and Statistical Manual of Mental Disorders, Third Edition, Revised; DSM–IV = Diagnostic and Statistical Manual of Mental Disorders, Fourth Edition;* ICC = interclass correlation coefficient; ICD–10 = *International Classification of Diseases, Tenth Edition;* MDD = major depressive disorder; MDE = major depressive episode; NOS = not otherwise specified; sen = sensitivity; spe = specificity.

Scale (DSRS), CDRS–R, and Mania Rating Scale (MRS);

- Nezu et al.'s (2000) *Practitioner's Guide to Empirically Based Measures of Depression*, which contains 36 measures of depression, depressive symptomatology, and depressive mood in adults and older adolescents, 15 depression measures for special populations (7 of which pertain to children and adolescents): CDI, CDRS–R, K–SADS–PL, Multiscore Depression Inventory for Children (MDI–C), RADS, RCDS, Youth Depression Adjective Checklist (Y–DACL), and 42 measures of depression-related constructs;
- Silverman and Rabian's (1999) chapter on anxiety and mood includes descriptions of the following self-rating scales for depression (CDI, Children's Depression Scale [CDS], CES–DS, DSRS, MFQ, RCDS), as well as constructs related to depression (Hopelessness Scale for Children [HSC]; Children's Attributional Style Questionnaire; Automatic Thoughts Questionnaire); and
- Winters, Myers, and Proud's (2002) thorough review of scales assessing suicidality, cognitive style, and self-esteem.

For courtroom modification assessment purposes, there are five severity or symptom screening measures recommended for use. See Table 9.3 for more details about these measures and their psychometric properties.

Consistent with recommendations made by other reviewers, different scales should be used when assessing children from nonclinical and clinical (i.e., in community or residential treatment) populations. For nonclinical children and adolescents, the Reynolds Adolescent or Child Depression Scales (RADS–2; W. M. Reynolds, 2004; RCDS, W. M. Reynolds, 1989) can be used because they "offer a clear construct, overall good psychometric properties, and experience with thousands of youths" (K. Myers & Winters, 2002, p. 646) from different ethnic and socioeconomic backgrounds. The RCDS, RADS, and RADS–2 have been used with children and adolescents exposed to violence, abuse, or other stressful life events (Delahanty, Nugent, Christopher, & Walsh, 2005; Perks & Jameson, 1999; W. M. Reynolds, 2004). Children aged 8 to 13 and adolescents aged 11 to 20 years are asked to rate the frequency of *DSM* depression-related items over the past 2 weeks on a 4-point scale (1 = *almost never*, 2 = *hardly ever*, 3 = *sometimes*, 4 = *most/all of the time*). Although the RADS–2 was revised to follow *DSM–IV* criteria, the RCDS is based on *DSM–III* criteria. The RADS–2 also now contains four subscales that tap into various aspects of depression: dysphoric mood, anhedonia and negative affect, negative self-evaluation, and somatic complaints (W. M. Reynolds, 2004). Both provide empirically derived cutoff scores. In the RCDS, the last item asks the child to place an X over one of five sad to happy faces that represent his or her mood. The RCDS takes approximately

10 to 20 minutes to complete; the RADS–2 takes about 5 to 10 minutes and is written at the 2nd-grade level (W. M. Reynolds, 2004). Computer scoring is in development.

For clinical samples, the CDRS–R combined with the CDI or MFQ are recommended as depression screeners (K. Myers & Winters, 2002). The Children's Depression Rating Scale—Revised (CDRS; Poznanski, Cook, & Carroll, 1979; CDRS–R, Poznanski & Mokros, 1996) is the most widely used clinician rating scale for measuring the presence and severity of depression in youth and is considered the gold standard in drug trials. Adapted from the adult Hamilton Rating Scale for Depression, the CDRS was developed for use with children aged 6 to 12 but is also used widely with teenagers (K. Myers & Winters, 2002). Of relevance to courtroom modification assessments, the CRDS–R was used in a study of 6- to 12-year-old urban school children of White, Hispanic, and African American backgrounds who reported violent events occurring to themselves, a relative, or a friend (Freeman, Mokros, & Poznanski, 1993). Taking about 15 to 30 minutes to administer, the CDRS–R asks the clinician to present 14 items to the child (and independently to a parent or other adult informant) and complete three items based on the clinician's observations of the child's nonverbal behavior (i.e., facial affect, tempo of language, and level of activity). Rated on a 7-point scale (2 indicates problems may exist; 3–7 signal increasing clinical significance), the 14 symptom areas differ from DSM depression criteria, are biased toward physiological symptoms (Brooks & Kutcher, 2003), and include the following: Impaired Schoolwork, Difficulty Having Fun, Social Withdrawal, Appetite Disturbance, Sleep Disturbance, Excessive Fatigue, Physical Complaints, Irritability, Excessive Guilt, Low Self-Esteem, Depressed Feelings, Morbid Ideation, Suicidal Ideation, and Excessive Weeping. Its factor structure is undergoing empirical study, and its efficiency and ability to integrate information from multiple sources, including observations of the child's behaviors during the interview, are strengths for its clinical use (Guo, Nilsson, Heiligenstein, Wilson, & Emslie, 2006; Nezu et al., 2000).

The (CDI (Kovacs, 1980) is the "most frequently used, and best studied, scale for juvenile depression, its correlates . . . and associated factors . . . [which] has been used with many nationalities and translated into several languages" (K. Myers & Winters, 2002, p. 643). The CDI has been used in a controlled study with sexually abused children and adolescents (McLeer et al., 1998) and in African American youth exposed to violence (Fitzpatrick, 1993). Originally developed as a downward extension of the Beck Depression Inventory, the CDI consists of 27 items, with three response options of varying severity. It was designed for a wide range of ages, 7 to 17 years, with a first-grade reading level (Pearson Education, 2007). It has been found to be biased toward cognitive symptoms (Brooks & Kutcher, 2001). Despite its strengths (reliability, internal consistency, sensitivity to change), other psychometric properties have been criticized (e.g., Barreto &

McManus, 1997), especially related to its construct and discriminant validity with minority youth (Compas, 1997; Craighead, Smucker, Craighead, & Ilardi, 1998; Laurent et al., 1999; K. Myers & Winters, 2002; Steele et al., 2006). More work is needed to establish optimum cutoff scores, among the many available (Brooks & Kutcher, 2001; Matthey & Petrovski, 2002; Timbremont, Braet, & Dreessen, 2004). As a result, the CDI should not be used as a sole screening instrument with children (Kresanov, Tuominen, Piha, & Almqvist, 1998; K. Myers & Winters, 2002).

Some clinicians may want to use the Beck Depression Inventory (BDI; Beck, Ward, Mendelson, Mock, & Erbaugh, 1961; BDI–II, Beck, Steer, & Brown, 1996) with older adolescents because it is considered the "gold standard of adult self-report depression instruments" (Brooks & Kutcher, 2001, p. 358). The BDI–II is a 21-item self-report measure in which respondents rate *DSM–IV*-related depressive symptoms in terms of severity level. Although some find it appropriate for clinical use with certain adolescents (Kutcher & Marton, 1996; W. M. Reynolds, 2006), including abused youth (e.g., Kress & Vandenberg, 1998), concerns about its sensitivity and specificity in adolescents as well as a paucity of ethnically diverse norms (Brooks & Kutcher, 2001; Dozois & Covin, 2004) do not support its use in courtroom modification assessments at this time. However, the more recently developed Beck Depression Inventory for Youth (BDI–Y; Beck, Beck, & Jolly, 2001) is being investigated with diverse populations and shows promise (e.g., Stapleton, Sander, & Stark, 2007).

The 33- and 34-item MFQ (Costello & Angold, 1988) and its 13-item short version (SMFQ; Angold, Costello, et al., 1995; Messer et al., 1995) are also newer self-report instruments that have shown promise for use with 7- to 18-year-olds. Developed for epidemiological screening purposes, the MFQ items cover *DSM–III–R* symptoms and other items, including loneliness and feeling ugly or unloved, experienced in the past 2 weeks. The SMFQ reveals "a substantial bias toward affective and cognitive symptoms and does not assess changes in weight or appetite, disturbance of sleep patterns, or suicidal ideation" (Brooks & Kutcher, 2001, p. 362) but does include the somatic symptoms of tiredness and restlessness. Items are rated on a 3-point scale ranging from 0 to 2 (0 = *not true*, 1 = *sometimes true*, and 2 = *true*) and take 5 to 10 minutes to complete. The MFQ has shown good test–retest reliability, internal consistency, criterion and convergent validity, with adequate discriminant validity; data also support the internal consistency, criterion, and construct validity of the SMHQ (Brooks & Kutcher, 2001; Daviss et al., 2006; Klein et al., 2005; Sharp, Goodyer & Croudace, 2006). Parent versions of both forms are available, and studies reveal that when used together with the child version, the measure does a better job in discriminating mood disorders than either version used alone (Daviss et al., 2006). Considered one of the best screeners for depression by the National Institute for Health and Clinical Excellence (2005), an independent organization located in

England, the MFQ and SMFQ have been used with diverse groups of young people, including U.S. juvenile justice samples (Kuo, Vander Stoep, & Stewart, 2005), Mongolian youth exposed to domestic violence and physical punishment (Kohrt, Kohrt, Waldman, Saltzman, & Carrion, 2004), Palestinian children experiencing war-related trauma (Thabet, Abed, & Vostanis, 2004), and Ukrainian street children (Kerfoot, Koshyl, Roganov, Mikhailichenko, Gorbova, & Pottage, 2007).

CONCLUSION

Fears, worries, anxiety, sadness, apathy, and somatic problems are part of the human condition, and children and adolescents can experience the psychological and psychiatric internalizing disorders of anxiety and depression that can be disabling and chronic. Stressful events, such as courtroom testimony, can lead to depression and anxiety in some children and adolescents, including those who have allegedly been abused. However, assessment of these clinical conditions is a challenging process. "Thinking about risk and resilience in a contextually and dimensionally sensitive manner does not lend itself to quick diagnosis or for parents and a culture looking for simple answers to complex issues" (Carrey & Ungar, 2007, p. 507).

When conducting a courtroom modification assessment at this point in time, one should therefore address any current anxiety and depression symptom frequency, intensity, duration, and course using currently available reliable and valid instruments, which can provide some evidence of future symptoms and behaviors. As we recommended with PTSD instruments (see chap. 7, this volume), multiple measures and supplemental questions are needed given the limitations of current interviews and screening instruments (e.g., psychometric, developmental, cultural), as well as the comorbidity of anxiety and depression in children and adolescents. Given that "different reporters may be sensitive to different types of information" (Sternberg et al., 2006, p. 286), these measures should involve responses from multiple sources, including the child.

To review, although they are time-consuming, we recommended that structured and semistructured interviews (i.e., ADIS–IV: C/P; K–SADS–PL) be used as they provide for more reliable *DSM–IV* diagnosis of these disorders with a wide age range of children (as young as 6–8 years and as old as 16–18 years) and address symptom frequency, severity, and duration. If MHPs choose to start with shorter screening measures before implementing longer interviews, we advise that a combination of screening measures and supplemental contextually sensitive questions be used for a range of disorders including both anxiety (e.g, MASC) and depression (e.g, RADS–2 with nonclinical populations). Continued research with all measures reviewed herein is needed to assess developmentally and ethnoculturally diverse populations of youth more effectively. Such research may also involve the development of new measures and approaches to more fully understand and address factors such as underreporting, somatic symptoms, and other expressions of emotional distress in children and adolescents, as well as factors that affect and promote coping and resilience.

10

COMMUNICATION ABILITIES, DISORDERS, AND COURTROOM MODIFICATION EVALUATIONS

Mental health professionals (MHPs) who perform courtroom modification evaluations must possess a working knowledge of children's communication abilities, problem areas, and disabilities because communication abilities and disorders may affect two legal issues in the United States. First, as discussed at the start of chapter 2, a child is deemed competent to testify only if he or she is able to communicate at the time of trial. Second, as discussed in chapter 3, the MHP testimony may be used to help the court determine, as required in some jurisdictions, whether a courtroom modification can be granted because of the child's unavailability or because the child's testimony in the presence of the defendant would result in that child suffering trauma/emotional distress such that he or she could not reasonably communicate in the courtroom.

An assessment of the child witness's current communication abilities allows MHPs to competently interview the child, select linguistically and culturally appropriate measures, screen for language or related communication difficulties, evaluate the work of collateral sources (e.g., taped or transcribed interviews conducted by other professionals), and provide an opinion to the court about the child's need for a modification(s). It can also inform recommendations made to the court or other legal professionals regarding the need for appropriate questioning styles. For example, in Britain,

Home Office guidance documents advise legal professionals to pay "careful attention to the communication requirements of the witness," including the need to

- slow down their speech rate;
- allow extra time for the witness to take in what has just been said;
- provide time for the witness to prepare a response;
- be patient if the witness replies slowly, especially if an intermediary is being used;
- avoid immediately posing the next question; and
- avoid interrupting. (Cooke & Davies, 2001, p. 86)

If communication problems are detected during the MHP's screening process, a referral to a speech–language pathologist and/or other specialist (e.g., audiologist, neuropsychologist, forensic linguist) for a thorough evaluation is critical. Because communication is "an extremely complex process, where linguistic, social and cognitive skills combine simultaneously" (Cross, 1999, p. 249), an in-depth knowledge of each field is often beyond the competency of MHPs. Comprehensive language assessments typically include "tests of hearing, social development and play, nonverbal communication, attention and nonverbal cognition, and family and cultural patterns of language and communication" (Kelley, Jones, & Fein, 2004, p. 192). If communication problems are not detected, Cross (1999) warned that "adult–child interactions may be based on inappropriate expectations and interpretations of the child's behaviour" (p. 254), and such children may be perceived as more "difficult" to deal with (p. 250). Also, research on a sample of allegedly maltreated Swedish children with developmental, communication, and other "mental disorders" who testified in cases found "that the courts often made decisions largely in ignorance of the capabilities, behavior, and limitations of vulnerable witnesses (Cederborg & Lamb, 2006, p. 539).

Consideration of language issues, which may include the use of screening measures, should therefore be part of the MHP's initial work in the case. To assist the MHP in this task, this chapter begins with a review of definitional and cultural issues related to language abilities. It then discusses some problems related to language that may present in some child witnesses and common ways to screen for them. It is beyond the scope of this chapter to provide a comprehensive discussion of the vast fields of speech, language, and communication, as well as their links to the considerable literature on related issues of memory, accuracy, and suggestibility in the context of child witness testimony and investigative interviews (see, e.g., Aldridge & Wood, 1998; Ceci & Bruck, 1993b, 1995, 1998; Hewitt, 1999; Pipe, Lamb, Orbach, & Esplin, 2004; Poole & Lamb, 1998; Quas et al., 2000; Warren & Marsil, 2002; Westcott, Davies, & Bull, 2002). MHPs should consult with speech and language professionals, as appropriate, as a part of competent multidisciplinary practice (e.g., American Speech–Language–Hearing Association [ASHA]; http://www.asha.org, the professional, scientific, and credentialing association for audiologists, speech–language pathologists, and speech, language, and hearing scientists; National Black Association for Speech–Language and Hearing, http://nbaslh.org).

CHILDREN'S LANGUAGE ABILITIES

Language, in its various forms, is "one of the central components of being human . . . an essential constituent of human cognition, culture, and day-to-day lives" (Kelley et al., 2004, p. 191). Although we most often think of language as involving verbal expression, it also includes nonverbal expression, such as through body language, sign language, or computer-assisted means, as well as the ability to process and understand what others express. For this reason, child clinicians are often trained to be aware of their clients' expressive (what they can say or demonstrate) and receptive (what they can understand) language abilities, and the *Diagnostic and Statistical Manual of Mental Disorders, Fourth Edition* (DSM–IV; American Psychiatric Association [APA], 1994) Communication Disorders usually first diagnosed in young people (discussed subsequently). Generally, children understand more than they can express. When working with very young or impaired children, clinicians should therefore also be knowledgeable about prelinguistic forms of communication, including babbling, joint attention (i.e., the use of procedures, such as showing a toy, to coordinate attention between interactive social partners with respect to objects or events"; Mundy et al., 1986, p. 657), pointing, play, and other behaviors used to communicate (e.g., acting out; Hewitt, 1999; Kelley et al., 2004). However, working with deaf or hearing impaired children requires consultation with experts on deaf communication to address fully the needs of these children (Tiapula, 2005), as is true when working with children with other developmental disabilities (Anderson & Heath, 2006a, 2006b). Such children may be at increased risk for abuse, and their unique needs may not be taken into account in the legal system (Cederborg & Lamb, 2006). Although there is normal variation to the process of expressive language development, it typically begins about age 1 with one- to two-word expressions, increases to two- or three-word sentences by age 2, and proceeds to full sentences that are understandable to most adults by age 3 (Saywitz, 2002). Preschoolers still continue to express themselves with nonverbal cues, which "carry a significant portion of meaning" (Steward et al., 1993, p. 27).

Clinicians may be less aware of particular linguistic concepts related to receptive and expressive language abilities. Understanding the concepts is important because adults differ from children in "intelligibility, vocabulary, grammar, conversational style, and in their ability to detect and cope with misunderstanding" (Saywitz, 2002, p. 4). The four major components of language reflect these areas of difference and develop in tandem with each other as children learn to communicate (Feinstein & Phillips, 2006; Kelley et al., 2004; Steward et al., 1993):

1. phonology (the sounds of language and rules for combining them; phonemes are the basic sound components of language) and prosody (the understanding and use of the intonation patterns of a language),
2. morphology (study of word formation; morphemes are the smallest meaningful linguistic units) and syntax (rules for combining words or their equivalents and the relationships among the elements of a sentence),
3. semantics (how vocabulary and meaning develops), and
4. pragmatics and discourse–conversational competence (the social functions and uses of language).

"Adult-like communicative competence" in these domains does not fully develop until the child reaches 10 to 12 years of age (Saywitz, 2002, p. 4).

In other words, to understand where a child is in his or her language development and to know how to communicate most effectively with the child, MHPs need to consider issues related to the form (phonology, morphology, syntax), content (semantics), and use of language (pragmatics, discourse; Cross, 1999). Although, as already noted, a full discussion is beyond the scope of this chapter, the following sections contain information of most relevance to MHPs.

Form

The first area of form concerns the production and perception of language sounds. By age 6 months, infants are typically able to distinguish and categorize all the possible phonemes ("the smallest units of a language that can change the meaning of a word, for example, substituting the h in *hat* with c creates *cat*, a significant change in meaning"; Kelley et al., 2004, p. 194). Kelley et al. further noted that by 12 months, they specialize only in the sounds of their native language, then proceed to produce them in about the same order. Because the ability to produce sounds takes longer than the ability to understand them, with many sounds not being mastered until age 4, pronunciation is not consistent (Poole & Lamb, 1998). Given the developmental course of phonemes pronunciation, it is normal for young children to have difficulty with making certain consonant sounds (i.e., fricatives; e.g., *f* and *v*; liquids, e.g., *l* and *r*; and their blends; Kelley et al., 2004). Sounds can be deleted, added, substituted, or reversed (Poole & Lamb, 1998). For dialectical variations used by some African American and Latino and Latina children, see Bernthal and Bankson (1993); for assessing phonological differences and disorders in bilingual children, see Goldstein and Fabiano (2007). Saywitz (2002) illustrated how normal phoneme production errors can affect interviews with young children:

> When asked how a suspect had moved an object across the room without leaving fingerprints, a four-year-old who had been found by the police at the crime site stated, "*Tom pull swing.*" The boy meant to convey that the perpetrator had pulled the object with a *string.* In the speech of the preschooler, "w" is often substituted for "r," especially in a consonant blend. (p. 4)

The other area of form is morphology and syntax. Children also acquire these language components in predictable manners, first learning word order and then other rules, such as past-tense endings (Kelley et al., 2004). For this reason, young children often leave off endings they have not mastered, such as –ed from past-tense verbs (Saywitz, 2002). Children best understand sentence and question word order when it follows the pattern they first learn of subject–verb–object (e.g., John hit the doll) and therefore have the most difficulty with passive voice order (e.g., the doll was hit) because mastery of this skill does not emerge until about 10 to 13 years (Poole & Lamb, 1998). From age 5 to 10 years (primary school years), children come to master past and future tenses and understand complex sentence constructions, including embedded sentences (multiple verbs or clauses are included, e.g., "After you finished playing, did the man who was eating talk to you?"); long, complex, or multiple questions; negations (e.g., "Didn't I tell you to pick up your clothes?"); and tag questions (e.g., "he hit you, didn't he?"; and pointing words (pronouns, e.g., *he, she,* and *him, her*). Given the difficulties that even some adults have with these more sophisticated aspects of syntax, it is best that interviewers avoid or compensate for them, such as using several short sentences instead of long ones and use specific names of people instead of pronouns (Poole & Lamb; Saywitz, 2002; Steward et al., 1993). Otherwise the child will place more effort on understanding the interviewer and have fewer resources with which to respond (Dockrell, 2004). Just as with phonology, differences occur across cultures with regard to syntax and semantics (McCauley, 2001).

Content

Children progress from simple vocabulary understanding to what is known as metalinguistic awareness, "understanding the nature of words and the meanings contained within them" (Kelley et al., 2004, p. 204). Children quickly learn words, with estimates of approximately 5 to 8 new words a day between the ages of 1 and 6, such that by "age 6, the average child has a working vocabulary of between 8,000 and 14,000 words" (Poole & Lamb, 1998, p. 161). However, very young children often use words without understanding what they mean (A. G. Walker & Warren, 1995). Some words are considered problematic for children, including "touch," "remember," "more–less," "some–all"; the articles "the" and "a"; words such as "this–that," "here–there," "come–go," "bring–take"; kinship terms (their usage also varies by cultural groups); and legal terms. Furthermore, some words are only understood in familiar contexts, such as words related to time, because temporal concepts are not developed until ages 8 to 10 (Poole & Lamb, 1998). Because context involves culture and can affect the way that questions about time are answered, cultural differences should be considered in addition to age; for example, "it is common for Native American children to mark life events by seasons, ceremonies, and daily activities [rather than] dates or days of the week" (Blahauvietz, 2005, p. 1). Although preschoolers can express themselves in well-formed sentences and can tell others about "who, what where, and often how . . . they cannot give good responses to when or how many" (Hewitt, 1999, p. 35).

Use

The ability to communicate socially involves appropriate interaction skills and the ability to understand rules of conversation (Cross, 1999), called *pragmatics*. These rules are culturally constructed, so interpretations about "appropriateness" can only be made by MHPs familiar with the cultural norms of the child being interviewed in his or her context. There are four main aspects of pragmatics: (a) quantity (the right amount of information given to your conversation partner; not too much or too little), (b) quality (an expectation that you will tell the truth), (c) relevance (staying on topic), and (d) manner (taking turns, not interrupting, being understandable, considering social and cognitive status of the partner; Kelley et al., 2004). Children as young as 1 year have been shown to have a well-developed sense of taking turns in conversation (Warren & McCloskey, 1997). Because young children often repeat phases said to them to mark turn taking or keep the conversation going when they do not understand the other person, adults can misunderstand and treat the repetition as an affirmation (Poole & Lamb, 1998). An example from Saywitz (1988) illustrates this point:

> Attorney: Is she your daddy's momma?
>
> Jenny: Huh? (doesn't understand the question)
>
> Attorney: Is she your daddy's momma? (leading question requiring only a nod)
>
> Jenny: Daddy's momma (repeated the end of the sentence). (pp. 38–39)

Although turn taking can be observed in 1-year-olds, relevance or staying on topic is an aspect of child development that takes longer for children to develop (Warren & McCloskey, 1997). A related concept to topic focus is discourse, or the way children put words and sentences together to form paragraphs and narratives (stories; Kelley et al., 2004). Different cultural groups structure conversations and stories differently (Hester, 1996; McCabe, 1996; Poole & Lamb, 1998). For example, whereas "Academic English" expects narratives to be "topic centered" with "dialogue organized hierarchically" under the topic with a beginning, middle, and end, some African American children follow a "topic associating" style that is organized by "implicitly associated personal anecdotes" with topic shifts "signaled by shifts in intonation and tempo, shifts that many . . . are not trained to detect" (Poole & Lamb, pp. 177–178). Cultural differences also exist in how children respond to questions verbally (e.g., the use of *yes* to be polite in Japanese culture) and nonverbally (e.g., the use of averted gaze as a sign of respect; Blahauvietz, 2005; Fontes, 2005; Poole & Lamb, 1998).

When confronted with problematic aspects of form (linguistically complex questions) or content (unfamiliar or sophisticated vocabulary) that they do not understand, even school-age children do not often ask for clarification or otherwise display their misunderstanding (Saywitz, 2002). Asking for clarification develops gradually during early and middle childhood (Pool & Lamb, 1998). Also, the forensic context is one that can produce pragmatic misunderstanding in children and adults given a different set of conversation rules (Lamb & Brown, 2006; Saywitz, 2002). Several authors have provided helpful guidelines (e.g., Hewitt, 1999; Poole & Lamb, 1998; Saywitz, Goodman, & Lyon, 2002) to assist MHPs in talking with children in a developmentally appropriate fashion to elicit more reliable reports (see Table 10.1). Other resources described in chapter 5 of this volume regarding effective interview practices can and should also be consulted.

COMMUNICATION PROBLEMS AND DISORDERS

Problems in communication include a wide variety of impairments in hearing, speech, and language, including "articulation problems, voice disorders, fluency problems (such as stuttering), aphasia (difficulty in using words, usually as a result of a brain injury), and delays in speech and/or language" (Council for Exceptional Children, 1990, ¶1). Children with speech or language delays may have difficulty following directions, answering questions, and speaking in a way that others can easily comprehend. Cross (1999) estimated that 5% of school-age children in the general population have speech and language problems. Other estimates show that "[u]p to 15% of children have a language disorder (American Academy of Child and Adolescent Psychiatry, 1998; APA, 2000; Castrogiovanni, 2002; U.S. Department of

TABLE 10.1
Guidelines for Talking With Children

Language component	Guidelines for talking with children
Phonology	Speak to the child using proper pronunciation. Do not use baby talk. Do not guess what a child might have said. If a comment is uninterpretable, ask the child to repeat the comment. Remember that the child may pronounce words differently than an adult would. If there might be another interpretation of what the child said (e.g., *body* or *potty*), clarify the meaning of the target word by asking a follow-up question (e.g., "I'm not sure I understand where he peed. Tell me more about where he peed.").
Vocabulary	A word might not mean the same thing to the child and the interviewer. Instead, the child's usage may be more restrictive (bathing suits, shoes, or pajamas may not be *clothes* to the child; only hands may be capable of *touching*); more inclusive (*in* might mean *in* or *between*); or idiosyncratic (i.e., having no counterpart in typical adult speech). Avoid introducing new words, such as the names of specific persons or body parts, until the child first uses those words. The ability to answer questions about the time of an event is very limited before 8 to 10 years of age. Try to narrow down the time of an event by asking about activities or events that children understand, such as whether it was a school day or what the child was doing that day. Even the words *before* and *after* might produce inconsistent answers from children under the age of 7 (e.g., "Did it happen before Christmas?"). When the child mentions a specific person, ask follow-up questions to make sure that the identification is unambiguous. Beware of *shifters*, words whose meaning depends on the speaker's context, location, or relationship (e.g., come/go, here/there, a/the, kinship terms). Avoid complicated legal terms or other adult jargon.
Syntax	Use sentences with subject–verb–object word orders. Avoid the passive voice. Avoid embedding clauses. Place the primary question *before* qualifications. For example, say "What did you do when he hit you?" rather than "When he hit you, what did you do?" Ask about only one concept per question. Avoid *negatives*, as in "Did you *not* see who it was?" Do not use tag questions, such as "This is a daddy doll, *isn't it*?" Be redundant. Words such as *she, he, that,* or *it* may be ambiguous. When possible, use the referent rather than a pointing word that refers back to a referent. Children learn to answer *what, who,* and *where* questions earlier than *when, how,* and *why* questions. Avoid nominalization. That is, do not convert verbs to nouns (e.g., "the poking").

(continues)

TABLE 10.1
Guidelines for Talking With Children   *(Continued)*

Language component	Guidelines for talking with children
Pragmatics	Different cultural groups have different norms for conversing with authority figures or strangers. Avoid correcting a child's nonverbal behavior unless it is interfering with your ability to hear the child or otherwise impending the interview.
	Language diversity includes diversity in the way conversations are structured. Be tolerant of talk that seems off topic and avoid interrupting children while they may be speaking.
	Children may believe that it is polite to agree with a stranger. It is especially important to avoid leading or yes–no format questions with children who might always be expected to comply even when adults are wrong.

Note. From *Investigative Interviews of Children: A Guide for Helping Professionals* (pp. 179–180), by D. A. Poole and M. E. Lamb, 1998, Washington, DC: American Psychological Association. Copyright 1998 by the American Psychological Association.

Education, 1995)" (Feinstein & Phillips, 2006, p. 204). Prevalence rates vary according to age, the specific type and severity of communication impairments studied, and the methods and measures used to study them (DeThorne et al., 2006; McKinnon, McLeod, & Reilly, 2007).

Causes of delays or disorders of speech and language are complex and include factors such as genetics, environment, hearing loss, as well as other conditions such as learning disabilities, cerebral palsy, mental retardation, cleft lip, or cleft palate (Council for Exceptional Children, 1990; DeThorne et al., 2006), traumatic brain injury, and autism (Kelley et al., 2004). Environmental risk factors include "adverse family conditions, low socio-economic status, psychosocial stress, parental mental illness, perinatal complications and premature birth . . . [and c]hildren in an abusive situation" (Cross, 1999, p. 251). Delays in speech and language have been related to maltreatment (Coster & Cicchetti, 1993; Coster, Gersten, Beeghly, & Cicchetti, 1989; Fox, Long, & Anglois, 1988; Wolfe & McEachran, 1997), perhaps because of its related impairments in cognitive development (Perez & Widom, 1994; Wiehe, 1996). Emotional and behavioral problems therefore often co-occur with communication problems (Cross, 1999), and all are relevant to the courtroom modification evaluation.

In addition to considering the normal development differences and delays in children's language as compared with adults' language (reviewed in the previous section), as well as other conditions that may affect a child's communication competency, MHPs should also be aware of certain *DSM–IV* disorders of speech and language that have particular relevance for the courtroom modification assessment. Organized by linguistic categories, disorders related to form include phonological disorder and stuttering; disorders related to content and use include expressive language disorder and mixed receptive–expressive language disorder. These disorders are discussed next, along with common screening tools.

Selective mutism, a unique "Other Disorder of Childhood" (not a communication disorder but a disorder involving a selective refusal to speak), is explained at the end of this section.

Diagnostic and Statistical Manual of Mental Disorders: Disorders of Form

Phonological disorder and stuttering are disorders related to the sounds of words. Difficulties with sound and word production could impair the ability of the child witness to make him- or herself heard and understood in the courtroom. The text revision of the *DSM–IV* (*DSM–IV–TR*) describes the essential feature of phonological disorder as follows:

> a failure to use developmentally expected speech sounds that are appropriate for the individual's age and dialect (Criterion A). This may involve errors in sounds production, use, representation, or organization such as, but not limited to, substitutions of one sound for another (use of /t/ for target /k/ sound) or omissions of sounds (e.g., final consonants). (APA, 2000, p. 65)

The severity of this disorder "ranges from little to no effect on speech intelligibility to completely unintelligible speech" by family members and those outside the family (APA, 2000, p. 64). Phonological disorder is more prevalent in boys than girls (APA, 2000). Spontaneous remission by age 6 occurs in three fourths of children with mild to moderate cases of phonological disorder (APA, 2000). Evaluation by speech and language specialists for articulation problems includes the use of standardized assessment tests, as well as evaluation of spontaneous and elicited samples of the child's speech, in ways that take into account the child's culture and language (or languages as in the case of bilingual or multilingual children; Kelley et al., 2004).

Stuttering is a communication problem and disorder that affects the normal fluency of a person's speech. It is characterized by disruptions in how a person produces sounds, known as *disfluencies*. Although many people occasionally make brief disfluencies, such as when one repeats words or uses interjections such as "um" or "OK," disfluencies can get in the way of communication when someone produces them too frequently, does not resolve them quickly (perhaps as a way to avoid another word that the person typically "gets stuck on"), or is negatively affected by emotions such as anxiety or frustration (ASHA, 1997–2007c).

The *DSM–IV–TR* (APA, 2000) diagnostic criteria for stuttering are as follows:

A. Disturbance in the normal fluency and time patterning of speech (inappropriate for the individual's age), characterized by frequent occurrences of one or more of the following:

(1) sound and syllable repetitions
(2) sound prolongations
(3) interjections
(4) broken words (e.g., pause within a word)
(5) audible or silent blocking (filled or unfilled pauses in speech)
(6) circumlocutions (word substitutions to avoid problematic words)
(7) words produced with an excess of physical tension
(8) monosyllabic whole-word repetitions (e.g., "I-I-I-I see him")

B. The disturbance in fluency interferes with academic or occupational achievement with social communication.

C. If a speech–motor or sensory deficit is present, the speech difficulties are in excess of those usually associated with these problems. (p. 68)

Stuttering or stammering may also be "accompanied by motor movements (e.g., eye blinks, tics, tremors of the lips or face, jerking of the head, breathing movements, or fist clenching)" (p. 67).

Beginning in childhood, typically between the ages of 2 and 7 years and before age 10 in 98% of cases, stuttering is more common in boys than girls (3:1 ratio; APA, 2000). Onset is most often gradual, with the child unaware of it; disfluencies become more common over time, following a "waxing and waning course" (APA, 2000, p. 68). As the child's awareness grows, he or she may try to find ways to avoid the disfluencies and experience anxiety, frustration, and low self-esteem, which also may negatively affect social functioning (APA, 2000). How others react to stuttering will also affect the impact of stuttering on the child's functioning, because children who stutter can be teased, excluded from activities, bullied at school, or negatively stereotyped, which can lead to anxiety and other problems (ASHA, 1997–2007c; Blood, Blood, Tellis, & Gabel, 2003; Howell, 2007; Turnbull, 2006). Although youth who stutter may be stereotyped as more anxious or nervous than their peers who do not stutter, research has not always found that children and adolescents who stutter have clinically significant anxiety as compared with youth who do not stutter (Blood, Blood, Maloney, Meyer, & Qualls, 2007).

Although stuttering can persist over the life span, recovery estimates range from 20% to 80% (APA, 2000), with most preschoolers (approximately 75%) who begin to stutter eventually stopping (ASHA, 1997–2007b; McKinnon et al., 2007) and about 50% of children aged 7 to 12 stopping (Howell, 2007). About one in five children who stutter have a chronic perseverative form of stuttering (Feinstein & Phillips, 2006). To predict whether a child is likely to continue to stutter, referral to a speech and language pathologist is recommended as the professional who can best select appropriate methods (typically involving tests, observations, and interviews) to estimate the child's risk for continuing to stutter (ASHA, 1997–2007a). Although there is a lack of agreement in the speech–language pathologist community about which specific risk factors are most important to consider in evaluations, factors noted by many stuttering disorder specialists include the following:

> a positive family history of stuttering, stuttering that has continued for 6 months or longer, the presence of concomitant speech or language disorders, and the existence of strong fears or concerns about stuttering on the part of the child or the family. (ASHA, 1997–2007a, ¶ 3)

Similar assessment procedures are used by speech and langauge specialists for older children and adults (ASHA, 1997–2006a). Regardless of age, "stress or anxiety has been shown to exacerbate Stuttering" (APA, 2000, p. 67), and these are relevant contextual factors to consider in the courtroom modification assessment.

Diagnostic and Statistical Manual of Mental Disorders: Disorders of Content and Use

Expressive language disorder and mixed receptive–expressive language disorder reflect significant impairments in a person's ability to express oneself and/or understand the verbal speech or sign language of others, as considered in the person's developmental, cultural, and linguistic contexts. Symptoms of expressive language problems include "having a markedly limited vocabulary, making errors in tense, or having difficulty recalling words or producing sentences with developmentally appropriate length" (APA, 2000, p. 61). Receptive language symptoms include "difficulty understanding words, sentences, or specific types of words, such as spatial terms" (APA, 2000, p. 64), which are often hard to assess because the child may act in inconsistent ways. Children with receptive language difficulties "may 'switch off' in response to language they do not understand" (Cross, 1999, p. 254). More specifically, the *DSM–IV–TR* notes that

> [t]he child may intermittently appear not to hear or to be confused or not paying attention when spoken to. The child may follow commands incorrectly, or not at all, and give tangential or inappropriate responses to questions. The child may be exceptionally quiet or, conversely, very talkative. (APA, 2000, p. 63)

These disorders can be acquired as a result of a neurological insult or medical condition, such as head trauma, or are termed *developmental* when there is not a known cause. As with phonological disorder and stuttering, these developmental conditions are more common in boys than girls.

As noted earlier, screening for receptive and expressive language problems assists the MHP in knowing when to refer a child for more extensive testing by speech and language pathologists, audiologists, neurologists, or other specialists, which can be required for diagnosis of these disorders. The *DSM–IV–TR* (APA, 2000) criteria for expressive and mixed receptive and expressive language disorders specifically refer to the need to use standardized, individually administered measures of nonverbal intellectual capacity and of expressive and receptive language abilities when making a diagnosis, with the substitution of a nonstandardized functional assessment when standardized measures are not available or appropriate (e.g., culturally, linguistically). Although some information about receptive and expressive language abilities can be captured by standardized intelligence tests, which may be a part of the child's educational file, they can be biased (e.g., verbally, culturally). Commonly used screening instruments with acceptable psychometric properties that should also be reviewed for cultural and linguistic bias (Kelley et al., 2004) include (Volkmar & Marans, 1999) the following:

- The Peabody Picture Vocabulary Test—III (PPVT–III; Dunn & Dunn, 1997), a measure of receptive vocabulary for children 2.5 years of age and older. It was found to be more appropriate than its predecessor version with an urban, at-risk sample of African American preschoolers (Washington & Craig, 1999). Test items are representative of racial and gender diversity. The Test de Vocabulario en Imagenes Peabody is also available for Spanish-speaking children and adolescents.
- The Expressive Vocabulary Test (Williams, 1997) was designed to be the expressive vocabulary and word retrieval counterpoint to the PPVT–III.
- The Expressive and Receptive One-Word Picture Vocabulary Tests (Brownell, 2000) are used with children aged 2 to 18 years. The Expressive One-Word Picture Vocabulary Test: Spanish—Bilingual Edition assesses the expressive vocabulary of individuals who are bilingual in Spanish and English.
- The Reynell Developmental Language Scales—U.S. Edition (Reynell & Grueber, 1990) is a test of verbal comprehension and expressive language best used with children 1 to 5 years of age.
- The Clinical Evaluation of Language Fundamentals—Fourth Edition (CELF; Semel, Wiig, & Secord, 2003) is used to identify receptive and expressive language abilities in children 6 to 21 years of age, with subtests assessing language content, form, and pragmatics, as well as short-term auditory memory. A Spanish CELF is available. The CELF—Preschool version (CELF–P–II; Wiig, Secord, & Semel, 2006) is available for use with children 3 to 6 years of age.
- The MacArthur Communication Development Inventory

(Fenson et al., 1993) is a parent self-report checklist and form that assesses vocabulary comprehension, vocabulary production and gestures, and sentence complexity with children 8 to 30 months of age or when a child has "minimal functional language" from mid to high socioeconomic status households (Schreibman, Stahmer, & Akshoomoff, 2006, p. 509). A Spanish version is also available (Jackson-Maldonado et al., 2003).

Selective Mutism

Selective mutism (SM) is a disorder of childhood that is characterized by "the persistent failure to speak in specific social situations (e.g., school, with playmates) where speaking is expected, despite speaking in other situations" (APA, 2000, p. 125). The majority of children with SM speak in their homes with family members but avoid social interactions in which they will be required to speak outside of the home, such as at school, in eating establishments, and in other public places (Crundwell, 2006; Vecchio & Kearney, 2007), which could include courtrooms. Children with severe cases may also "refuse to speak on the telephone, answer the door at home, or speak at home to people they do not know" (Vecchio & Kearney, 2007, p. 38). Instead of talking in such situations, children with SM may use "gestures, nodding, pulling, pushing, or monosyllabic utterances" to communicate (Krysanski, 2003, p. 30). For this reason, SM is typically first noticed as a clinical problem when the child enters school, even though onset typically occurs before a child is 5 years old (APA, 2000). It is considered a disorder when other *DSM–IV–TR* criteria are also met:

- B. The disturbance interferes with educational or occupational achievement or with social communication.
- C. The duration of the disturbance is at least 1 month (not limited to the first month of school).
- D. The failure to speak is not due to a lack of knowledge of, or comfort with, the spoken language required in the social situation.
- E. The disturbance is not better accounted for by a Communication Disorder (e.g., Stuttering) and does not occur exlusively during the course of a Pervasive Developmental Disorder, Schizophrenia, or other Psychotic Disorder. (APA, p. 125)

It has also been recommended that bilingual children who meet criteria be diagnosed with SM only if their condition is present in both native and nonnative languages and persists for at least 6 months (Toppelberg, Tabors, Coggins, Lum, & Burger, 2005).

SM is an "apparently rare" disorder "found in fewer than 1% of individuals seen in mental health settings" (APA, 2000, p. 126), although some school-based sources feel it is underreported (Cleator & Hand, 2001; Garcia et al., 2006). SM occurs cross-culturally and affects children from diverse social and economic backgrounds (McInnes, Fung, Manassis, Fiksenbaum, & Tannock, 2004; Vecchio & Kearney, 2007). Yet migration and bilingualism have been found to be risk factors for SM (Steinhausen, Wachter, Laimbock, & Metzke, 2006), with prevalence rates at least 3 times higher for immigrant and other English-language minority children (Toppelberg et al., 2005). Some researchers report SM as slightly more common in girls than boys (e.g., Krysanski, 2003; McInnes et al., 2004) perhaps because of studies involving clinical samples (Cohan, Chavira, & Stein, 2006) in which girls report experiencing more anxiety than boys (Sharp, Sherman, & Gross, 2007), whereas others find it equally as common (e.g., Yeganeh, Beidel, & Turner, 2006). With remission rates ranging from 39% to 100%, SM can be a chronic condition, which can negatively affect a child's social and academic development (McInnes et al., 2004; Steinhausen et al., 2006; but see Crundwell, 2006).

SM was first identified in 1877 as *aphasia voluntaria* by the German physician Kussmaul, who emphasized the voluntary nature of the person's decision not to speak (Krysanski, 2003). In 1934, Mortiz Tanner, the Swiss pioneer of child psychiatry, replaced that term with *elective mutism*, which is still used today by the 10th revision of the *International Classification of Diseases* (Krysanski, 2003; Steinhausen et al., 2006; World Health Organization, 2005). The term *elective* reflected the etiological explanation of the time for the disorder; it was considered to be "a form of defiance or passive oppositional behavior in response to either an overprotective or controlling parental style" (McInnes et al., 2004, p. 304). The *DSM–IV* replaced elective mutism with *selective* mutism to emphasize the select situations or social contexts in which the child with this disorder does not speak, a position consistent with newer anxiety-based etiological explanations for the disorder (Dow, Sonies, Scheib, Moss, & Leonard, 1995; Garcia et al., 2006; Krysanski, 2003), notably social anxiety (Sharp et al., 2007; Vecchio & Kearney, 2007). Furthermore, "in clinical settings, children with Selective Mutism are almost always given an additional diagnosis of an Anxiety Disorder (especially Social Phobia)" (APA, 2000, p. 126; see also American Academy of Child & Adolescent Psychiatry, 2007; Garcia et al., 2006; Yeganeh et al., 2006). Other possible etiological explanations for SM include oppositional behavior, which lacks rigorous empirical support (Sharp et al., 2007), or organic or medical causes, such as hearing or neurological problems (Krysanski, 2003). Still, there is considerable debate about the cause(s) of selective mutism and how it should be classified, conceptualized, and treated (Cleator & Hand, 2001; Krysanski, 2003; Sharp et al., 2007), although evidence exists to support behavioral and cognitive–behavioral treatment approaches (Cohan, Chavira, & Stein, 2006).

Children with SM present as a heterogeneous group. Although various studies reveal different associated features of SM, some children show internalizing problems, such as being excessively shy, afraid of social embarassment, anxious (e.g., blushing, avoiding eye contact, being noticeably fidgety or rigid), socially isolated, clingy, compulsive, or sensitive (Crundwell, 2006; Krysanski, 2003). Similarly, a history of sensitive or behaviorally inhibited temperment during infancy and genetic factors are often reported (Garcia et al., 2006; Joseph, 1999; Krysanski, 2003; Steinhausen et al., 2006; Toppelberg et al., 2005). On the externalizing side, oppositional behaviors, such as temper tantrums, being stubborn, controlling, negative, strong willed and aggressive, as well as parental behaviors that reinforce the refusal to speak have also been reported in this population (Crundwell, 2006; Dow et al., 1995; Yeganeh et al., 2006).

Sometimes language deficits are associated with SM. The presence of speech and language disorders, including phonological disorder and receptive and expressive language delay, in this population is variable; rates range from 11% to 50% (Cleator & Hand, 2001; Yeganeh et al., 2006). Other comorbid disorders include the anxiety disorders, pervasive developmental disorders, depression, elimination problems, and obsessive–compulsive features (Krysanski, 2003); major life events and traumas have also been cited as risk factors for the development of SM (Krysanski, 2003; Steinhausen et al., 2006), but empirical evidence does not fully support this association (Garcia et al., 2006; Sharp et al., 2007).

Assessment of this "rare and perplexing disorder" (McInnes et al., 2004, p. 304) is challenging and requires collaboration with an interdisciplinary team, as was true for the communication disorders discussed earlier. Dow et al. (1995) recommended psychiatric, neurological, developmental, and speech–language assessments. Bilingual speech–language pathologists and cotherapists or translators should be included on the team in cases involving immigrant or language minority children (Toppelberg et al., 2005). After rapport is established with the child, which can be challenging with children with SM (Vecchio & Kearney, 2007), nonverbal cognitive and receptive language abilities can be assessed (Cleator & Hand, 2001; Dow et al., 1995; McInnes et al., 2004). The assessment of expressive langauge abilities can be even more challenging, involving parental report, taped samples of the child's speech, standardized structured interviews and checklists, as well as narrative assessments (Cleator & Hand, 2001; Crundwell, 2006; Krysanski, 2003; McInnes et al., 2001).

CONCLUSION

Communication is a central requirement for being able to testify. Impairments in the ability to give competent testimony may be addressed by a courtroom modification that will enable the child to communicate verbally or with demonstrative aids, such as communication boards or electronic equipment (Cooke & Davies, 2001). Thus, this chapter has reviewed children's language abilities and communication problems and disorders to prepare MHPs to conduct courtroom modification evaluations. During the evaluation, if the MHP's screening efforts reveal a potential communication problem associated with trauma/emotional distress, referrals to members of a multidisciplinary team will be warranted to provide a more thorough assessment of the child's condition and needs. Then, following guidelines discussed in chapter 5 of this volume, the MHP can use this information in his or her evaluation to determine the child's past and present communication abilities and/or disorders and whether any past or current communication problem or disorder may be triggered or exacerbated by distress due to confrontation with the defendant.

It is unknown to what extent children with communication difficulties or disorders testify in court. Children with learning and intellectual disabilities, especially when they are alleged victims of abuse or sole witnesses against the defendant, rarely give testimony because of concerns about their credibility and suggestibility (Cooke & Davies, 2001; Henry & Gudjonsson, 2007). Yet it is widely recognized that children with disabilities are at higher risk for maltreatment. Modifications may help provide such children with a way to share their voices about alleged abuse with the court.

11

CONCLUSION AND FUTURE DIRECTIONS

The U.S. Supreme Court in *Maryland v. Craig* (1990b) required that, at a minimum, trial courts determine three things before imposing a courtroom modification that raises Confrontation Clause concerns: (a) that the procedure is necessary to protect the welfare of the particular child witness; (b) that the child witness would be traumatized by the presence of the defendant, not by the courtroom generally; and (c) that the trauma/emotional distress suffered by a child witness in the presence of the defendant is more than *de minimis* (i.e., more than mere nervousness, excitement, or reluctance to testify). Because MHPs are often involved in providing expert testimony on these three issues, this book has provided a structured approach to conducting courtroom modification evaluations and to providing related expert testimony.

The first step in this approach involves the MHP becoming familiar with the various courtroom modifications for child witnesses and the legal standards required for their use in their jurisdiction. Chapters 2 and 3 examined the possible alternative courtroom procedures available for child witnesses, which may or may not implicate the defendant's Confrontation Clause rights, and the legal issues surrounding their use. Courtroom modifications presenting confrontational concerns, which we reviewed in chapter 3, included the following:

- use of remote testimony (closed-circuit television [CCTV]);
- use of videotaped testimony or depositions;

- use of videotaped investigative interview and other hearsay statements;
- courtroom design changes, namely, the use of devices (e.g., screens) to shield child witnesses from seeing the defendant, and the use of physical courtroom changes (e.g., altered seating arrangements); and
- instructions to child witnesses on how to avoid eye contact while in the physical presence of the defendant.

We then recommended that MHPs review the empirical support for these modifications and provided a review and critique of this science in chapter 4. One important goal of that chapter was to determine whether science supports the use of these modifications as protective, probative, and nonprejudicial. Remote testimony (CCTV, videotaped testimony or depositions), or videotaped investigative interviews and statements that are offered as hearsay testimony in lieu of the child's testimony met our standards for use in child witness modification hearings. A similar approach can be used with modifications that do not raise Confrontation Clause concerns (see chap. 2).

With knowledge of the relevant law and science relating to courtroom modifications, MHPs are then ready to use our analytic framework for conducting a courtroom modification evaluation. Our proposed approach (see chap. 5) starts with MHPs taking a critical look at themselves to ensure that they possess the necessary qualifications and take on an appropriate role as a child evaluator and expert witness in courtroom modification cases. We then highlighted guiding principles for conducting a courtroom modification evaluation, which covered freedom from bias including using culturally sensitive evaluations, using objective and defensible methods, using multiple sources of information and multiple methods, and selecting reliable and valid assessment instruments. Finally, we described how to apply assessment methods to address the three *Craig* requirements. Our proposed methodology involves the ethical and clinically sound use of multiple sources of relevant and reliable information to evaluate the child's clinical condition, functional abilities, and relationship to the defendant in the case.

Chapters 7, 8, 9, and 10 augmented our analytic approach by providing a detailed review of clinical conditions related to child trauma and communication difficulties that may be indicative of the need for a courtroom modification, including posttraumatic stress disorder (PTSD), dissociation, fear, anxiety, depression, and communication disorders. These chapters scrutinized the validity and reliability of the potential instruments and methods for evaluating the presence, severity (i.e., is it and will it likely be more than *de minimis*?), and likely future course of each of the child witness's clinical and functional problem areas.

The MHP's evaluation and conclusions will, of necessity, vary on the basis of the requirements of the legal standard in one's jurisdiction and the unique needs and clinical presentation of a child in his or her context. Because testifying can be a positive, neutral, or negative experience for children who have allegedly been abused (Sandler, 2006; Small & Melton, 1994; Wade, 2002), it is important to obtain their input about what, if anything, they think is needed to help them cope with testifying (Plotnikoff & Woolfson, 2004; Wade, 2002). Ultimately, however, it is the court that must decide whether a procedure is necessary to protect this child witness (the first *Craig* factor). Because each case will require a particularized *necessity* determination for the proposed modification(s) for a specific child, the MHP's expert testimony, and other relevant information (e.g., lay testimony, testimony of the child witness, prior court decisions) will be helpful, if not essential, for the judge's determination.

SUGGESTIONS REGARDING MODIFICATIONS

When a courtroom modification is needed, what type ought to be promoted? Modifications should assist the child in coping with his or her trauma symptoms, even though the problem area may still exist if the modification is granted. In addition, the modification should assist the child by taking away additional stressful factors that may precipitate a display of that problem area or disorder or increase symptoms. This latter condition is important to consider because children with psychological problems may not only be more vulnerable to stress (Saywitz, 1997) but may also experience exacerbated psychological difficulties with face-to-face confrontation with the defendant (Briere, 1992).

Unfortunately, no research has been conducted comparing various modifications on their effectiveness in reducing the child's emotional distress or trauma. Although we do not know what is the most effective modification for reducing a child's emotional distress/trauma, empirical evidence (as reviewed in chap. 4) generally tells us that, among the modifications that implicate the Confrontation Clause, videotaped investigative interviews or statements offered as hearsay testimony in lieu of the child's testimony would best minimize emotional distress in youth. However, as discussed in chapter 3, this practice may not continue to be an option because of the influence of *Crawford* (2004) and its progeny. Other modifications, such as CCTV and videotaped testimony, may become more common (Lyon, 2004; S. McMahon, 2006). Of these, in general, CCTV would also be helpful, with videotaped testimony and depositions less helpful. These procedures should also best facilitate the child's ability to communicate with the court while not prejudicing the courtroom proceedings against the defendant.

The following discussion provides some guidance about how these general recommendations might be applied to cases in which a child witness is found to have significant problems with symptoms of PTSD, depression, or anxiety. These recommendations are offered for cases generally and have not been empirically tested. MHPs are required to assess each child on a case-by-case basis and should consider the child's wishes, opinions, and perspectives regarding his or her own needs when making suggestions to the court regarding any modifications for that child. In their decision making, MHPs should also evaluate the potential helpfulness of other modifications that we reviewed in chapter 2 that do not implicate the Confrontation Clause.

The symptoms of depression, anxiety, and PTSD of most relevance to courtroom modification evaluations include irritability, hyperarousal, social withdrawal or avoidance, fear, difficulty concentrating, reexperiencing, and problems in communicating with others (especially for anxious children in the context of a feared event). If these symptoms were found likely to occur during future courtroom testimony, appropriate environmental interventions for these children should attempt to address them.

Specifically, symptoms of irritability and hyperarousal may be improved by cognitive–behavioral and interpersonal psychotherapy approaches, such as learning relaxation and problem-solving skills or by the therapeutic alliance generally (J. A. Cohen, Mannarino, & Deblinger, 2006; Kutcher & Marton, 1996). In addition, children may be put at ease by the presence of familiar people in familiar settings, which also has the benefit of improving children's information processing and communication abilities (Saywitz & Camparo, 1998). Thus, the presence of supportive people while the child is interviewed or testifying may help reduce the presentation of irritable mood and improve the child's ability to testify.

The presence of large numbers of or certain people may produce withdrawal or avoidance symptoms in some children. Withdrawal, fear, and avoidance symptoms may be addressed by reducing large numbers of people and/or the presence of particular symptom-provoking people in the testimony room. Fear of the defendant may cause some children not to reveal what they know about that person (Goodman, Levine, Melton, & Ogden, 1991). Similarly, the symptoms of difficulty concentrating, reexperiencing, one's mind going blank, numbing, and problems communicating with others may be helped by reducing distractions and triggers of these problems. Appropriate environmental interventions for child witnesses with severe PTSD should reduce the frequency of traumatic reminders and unnecessary reexposure to abuse-related stimuli, including graphic depictions of the alleged abuse (van der Kolk, McFarlane, & Weisaeth, 1996). In addition to minimizing a child's distress, reducing distractions, removing spectators, and providing support people can optimize the child's information processing abilities and maximize reliability in the courtroom (Saywitz, 1997; Saywitz & Camparo, 1998; Whitcomb, Goodman, Runyan, & Hoak, 1994).

Alternatively, or at the same time, children and adolescents can be taught cognitive–behavioral techniques to help themselves reduce their fears, anxieties, and stress, such as progressive relaxation or stress inoculation training (J. A. Cohen et al., 2006; Sas, 1991). Preparing children for court and empowering them to cope with testimonial stressors can also help them to recover from adverse consequences and help their testimony to be as complete as possible (Copen, 2000; Saywitz, 1997; Small & Melton, 1994).

Regarding courtroom modifications that implicate the Confrontation Clause, the best option to protect vulnerable alleged child witnesses from trauma associated with confrontation, clinically significant anxiety, PTSD, and/or depression is to admit a videotaped investigative interview as hearsay testimony in lieu of the child's testimony. By not testifying or providing a deposition, the child will encounter fewer numbers of people with whom he or she will have to relate his or her experiences, because most investigative interviews are conducted by only one person. Moreover, the setting of investigative videotapes is neutral and likely to be more comfortable and child-friendly (and thus more familiar) than a courtroom or the videotaped testimony setting, especially if they are made at a children's advocacy center (Walsh, Jones, & Cross, 2003). Such an environment coupled with the abilities of trained child forensic interviewers (as opposed to attorneys who are not routinely trained to speak with children) might help to ameliorate the child's tension, jumpiness, flinching, fight-or-flight reaction, and other PTSD-arousal or anxiety-related responses. In addition, signs of numbing or detachment could be monitored both during the interview (by the interviewer and observers) and after it (by professionals who review the videotape). Results of this analysis could be used by MHPs to justify a conclusion about the need to reduce the number of times a child would have to experience a feared event or trigger of depressive, anxious, or posttraumatic symptomology, such as describing the alleged abusive incidents in detail or being exposed to other reminders of the alleged abuse (e.g., the defendant). If this option is not legally available, videotaped investigative interviews could be admitted along with CCTV testimony, as is done in other countries (e.g., England; see Cordon, Goodman, & Anderson, 2003; Hamlyn et al., 2004).

CCTV is generally the second most appropriate modification for child witnesses with depression, anxiety, and PTSD. Even though this procedure requires the child to relate his or her allegations another time (in addition to the forensic or investigative interviews and other forms of questioning), the child is removed from the traditional courtroom. The safe and separate environment provided in CCTV arrangements has been shown to be less stressful and to facilitate communication with the court, including the defense. Support persons or items (e.g., teddy bear) should be of particular interest, because they are also helpful in this environment and have been noted as particularly helpful for child witnesses (J. E. B. Myers, 1996a). Finally, the live nature of CCTV testimony allows for immediate modifications to legal procedures or questions in an attempt to respond to the child's needs (e.g., bathroom break) or any fluctuations in the child's responses and behaviors (e.g., "spacing out").

The least helpful alternative procedures that implicate the Confrontation Clause are likely to be videotaped investigative interviews admitted as hearsay statements in conjunction with the child's in-court or videotaped testimony. These procedures are not likely to be recommended by MHP evaluators for certain vulnerable child witnesses because they involve the child testifying in the presence of a large number of people, including the defendant. In fact, the "defendant's physical proximity may be closer to the victim [during videotaped testimony] than in normal courtroom settings and be more intimidating" (American Prosecutors Research Institute [APRI], 2004, p. 450). Directly exposing some children to reminders of the alleged abuse and potentially hostile adult(s) might trigger or worsen anxious or PTSD symptomology (more than *de minimis* distress) in some cases. Experiencing severe depressive and/or anxious symptoms has been shown to impede some children's ability to communicate with the court (Goodman et al., 1991; Saywitz, 1997; Saywitz & Camparo, 1998). Children have also expressed confrontation fears related to entering and exiting the witness stand and the courtroom. Such fears might represent a learned response to, or traumatic reminder of, the alleged abuse or alleged abuser. Thus, when a child has learned over time that he or she could not control or avoid the alleged abuse or abuser, he or she might experience fear and anxiety when being required to enter or exit a courtroom or videotaped testimony room where the defendant is present.

FUTURE DIRECTIONS

Given knowledge of the courtroom modification process and its relationship to possible modifications, we conclude the book by discussing key issues for further and future consideration. These include assuring fair treatment for both witnesses and defendants in modification hearings, increasing the effectiveness of modifications, enacting legal reforms, and conducting needed research to improve the value of MHPs' testimony in these hearings.

Assuring Fair Treatment

Many MHPs find themselves called to testify as expert witnesses or are attracted by the lucrative nature of the position, yet they are unprepared for the role or its responsibilities (Welder, 2000). To serve the court, MHPs need to come equipped with appropriate qualifications and knowledge so that they can assist "the trial judge by careful psychological observation, factual reporting and reasoned inferences: Nothing more is needed, and nothing less is acceptable" (Saunders, 1993, p. 57). Working to uphold an objective stance in their science and practice can help avoid the common criticism that their opinions can be bought (Ogloff, 2002). In courtroom modification cases, MHPs should keep foremost in mind the court's goal of balancing the rights of the defendant with the needs of the child witness. Being objective means questioning and rejecting assumptions such as the following: All children in abuse cases have been abused, all children need modifications, and children's needs always trump defendants' rights. A key to a fair evaluation is honest, ongoing self-examination, including consultation with trusted colleagues regarding the extent and boundaries of their knowledge and competencies as well as identification of potential sources of bias (see recommendations in chap. 5, this volume). In addition, the MHP's written or oral evaluation should be appropriately stated to the court, grounding opinions in the evidence and acknowledging the limitations of one's knowledge (Gross & Mnookin, 2003).

Increasing the Effectiveness of Modifications

Research evidence has shown that "the legal process itself can add to children's trauma motivated changes in the legal system and greater consideration of the unique needs of child victims" and witnesses (Ghetti, Alexander, & Goodman, 2002, p. 241), with the result that national and international legal reforms have changed the way that child witnesses are treated in the courts. Through familiar legal channels (e.g., the American Bar Association [ABA] has a Center on Children and the Law), attorneys and judges can receive training and access materials on child development, accompanied by practical legal implications of this knowledge such as ways to effectively communicate with child witnesses (e.g., A. G. Walker, 2000). This is vital because studies consistently show that a child's perceived credibility as a witness is directly influenced by the attorney's ability to interact and communicate effectively with the child (see Bharti & Heath, 1997; Cashmore & Bussey, 1996; Saywitz & Goodman, 1996). In other words, a child's performance as a witness depends on whether the prosecutor asks age and developmentally appropriate questions (¶3).

With such knowledge, judges can take an active role in managing cases to ensure that "the proceedings, generally, and any questions put to the child, in particular, enable the child to participate in the proceedings at a level that is consistent with that child's level of development" (Esam, 2002, p. 311).

Additionally, as we reviewed in chapters 2 and 3, children can be prepared in advance for courtroom testimony with special programs that help reduce anxiety (e.g., Copen, 2000; "Kids in Court," Finnegan, 2000;

"Court Prep Group," Sisterman Keeney, Amacher, & Kastanakis, 1992). They also can give their testimony remotely (using videotape or CCTV) or in the courtroom with supportive items, people, settings, and/or schedules. Forensic evaluations of child witnesses can help the court determine which of the available modifications, if any, would be most effective for a particular child witness.

"Impeding this progress, however, is a lack of awareness of the reforms, a lack of training on how to implement them, and a lack of funding to conduct preparation programs and to retrofit courtrooms with new technology" (Welder, 2000, p. 169). It is hoped that this book will contribute to increased awareness of courtroom modifications by the parties who can influence the use of such procedures—namely, MHPs, attorneys, victim advocates, judges, and child protection professionals. Adoption of legal reforms in the United States, as discussed subsequently, as well as internationally (Beresford, 2005; Bottoms & Goodman, 1996), may also assist in informing greater numbers of professionals about the needs of child witnesses and the legality of available modifications.

Consultation and training can assist courts in implementing alternative procedures for child witnesses. Many organizations provide opportunities for training MHPs, attorneys, and judges in working with child witnesses, including, but not limited to, the APRI (2007), American Professional Society on the Abuse of Children (2007), National Council of Juvenile and Family Court Judges (2007), and the federal Office for Victims of Crime (2007).

Although some procedures can be expensive to purchase and implement (e.g., CCTV), others are not (e.g., allowing a child to have a doll during testimony). Existing grants, such as the federal Children's Justice Act (Administration for Children & Families, 2007), have funded modification projects (including training and equipment), children's advocacy centers, and multidisciplinary trainings for courts (judges, guardians *ad litem*, court-appointed special advocates), child protection agencies, and law enforcement agencies). The National Child Traumatic Stress Network (2007), funded through the Center for Mental Health Services (2007), part of the U.S. Department of Health and Human Services' Substance Abuse Mental Health Services Administration (2007), appears to be an untapped source of support for addressing the needs of traumatized youth in the criminal justice system (other funding resources can be found at http://www.childwelfare.gov/systemwide/funding/).

Given the monetary and logistical resources involved in implementing new procedures, additional research that examines which measures are more helpful for children and least prejudicial to the defense are warranted (Ghetti et al., 2002). To accomplish this goal, it is essential that legal professionals open their practices and courtrooms to research and program evaluations, as such "real world" research is necessary to complement lab- or university-based studies.

Enacting Proposals for Legal Reforms

Since the mid-1980s, there have been proposals for reform in the law pertaining to courtroom modifications for child witnesses. Their purpose was to raise awareness regarding the unique needs of children who have increasingly become involved in court cases and to suggest procedures for improving the treatment of child witnesses without offending defendants' rights (e.g., ABA Criminal Justice Section, 1985; Task Force on Child Witnesses of the American Bar Association Criminal Justice Section, 2002; U.S. Department of Justice, Office of Justice Programs, Office for Victims of Crimes, 1999; National Conference of Commissioners on Uniform State Laws [NCCUSL], 2002). The result has been that the states have enacted a wide variety of procedures and modifications. In addition, J. E. B. Myers (1996a), noting that "few efforts have been made to distill the patchwork of reforms into a comprehensive Child Witness Code" (p. 171), offered a model Child Witness Code to fill the void.

As can be seen from the review of modifications in chapters 2 and 3, the need for legal reform still exists. Although it is beyond the scope of this book to consider all proposed modifications and model rules, including that proposed by J. E. B. Myers (1996a), we discuss the most recent proposals (NCCUSL, 1999, 2002). The NCCUSL (2007), a nonpartisan organization formed more than 100 years ago to promote uniformity across state laws, issued two pieces of model legislation regarding child witnesses: a special child hearsay exception and a child witness act. Given the influence of NCCUSL in state legislatures, its work deserves mention.

NCCUSL updated its proposed Uniform Rules of Evidence (URE) on the special child hearsay exception, which had not been addressed since 1986. Proposed Rule 807(a)(2) of the URE (NCCUSL, 1999) provides that a child must either testify at the proceeding or the court must allow a statement of a child to be introduced through an alternative method recognized under applicable state law. The exception applies only to "a child under [7] years of age describing an alleged act of neglect, physical or sexual abuse, or sexual contact performed against, with, or on the child by another individual." Because this model law was drafted before *Crawford v. Washington* (2004), its constitutionality is in doubt; it adopts the old reliability and trustworthiness analysis of *Ohio v. Roberts* (1980) and *Idaho v. Wright* (1990), instead of the testimonial analysis of *Crawford* (see chap. 3, this volume). Of course, if the U.S. Supreme Court would distinguish *Crawford*, making an exception to allow special hearsay statutes for alleged child abuse victims to be admitted on the basis of a judicial determination of reliability rather than a testimonial analysis, as one legal commentator has proposed (Thompson, 2005), then such a model law could still work.

In 2002, NCCUSL drafted its Child Witness Act, which provides the "applicable state procedure" referred to in the URE. This legal reform gives courts

> a clear and legally sound means of protecting child witnesses from the emotional trauma associated with giving testimony, while at the same time protecting the 6th Amendment rights of defendants and respondents. . . . [and] clear standards for the use of these methods, without displacing an enacting state's existing mechanisms and means of addressing this issue [in criminal and non-criminal proceedings]. (NCCUSL, 2001, ¶ 7)

The ABA approved the act in February 2003, and it has subsequently been adopted in a few states (e.g., Idaho Code § 9-1801 [2007]).

The Act refers to "alternative methods" for child testimony. Broadly defined, it incorporates existing authorized practices, such as CCTV, videotaped testimony, videotaped interviews, and courtroom design changes, as well as "other similar methods either currently employed or through technology yet to be developed or recognized in the future." The Act does not specify the type of criminal case or the child's status of being an alleged victim of the crime. It also does not change a state's age restrictions. When it defines a child witness (i.e., "children under [13] who are competent to testify and . . . called to testify in the proceeding"), however, it supports an age restriction on the use of modifications. Although lower than the age of eligibility of some states, 13 years old and younger contrasts with the even lower age threshold of 6 or 7 years old and younger than Justice Antonin Scalia appeared to be in favor of in *Danner v. Kentucky* (1998; see chap. 3, this volume).

For criminal cases, the Act uses the standard higher than in the *Craig* test (i.e., "serious emotional trauma"; "substantially impair the child's ability to communicate") as is used in the majority of states (see chap. 3). It also uses a higher standard of persuasion (i.e., clear and convincing evidence) than is used in a few states (see chap. 3). Specifically, Section 5 provides that in criminal proceedings, the judge may allow an alternative procedure in two situations:

1. The child may testify otherwise than in an open forum in the presence and full view of the finder of fact if the presiding officer finds by clear and convincing evidence that the child would suffer serious emotional trauma that would substantially impair the child's ability to communicate with the finder of fact if required to testify in the open forum.
2. The child may testify other than face-to-face with the defendant if the presiding officer finds by clear and convincing evidence that the child would suffer serious emotional trauma that

would substantially impair the child's ability to communicate with the finder of fact if required to be confronted face-to-face by the defendant.

If either of these standards is met, the Act directs the judge to consider a number of additional factors (e.g., other alternatives for reducing emotional trauma to the child, nature and degree of emotional trauma the child may suffer if an alternative method is not used), as is done in some state case law (see chap. 3), before making the finding.

The Child Witness Act has been criticized because it was written broadly to cover child witnesses in all cases and was not limited to those in child abuse cases (Grearson, 2004). For example, it has been noted that the model act does not specifically address the important public policy approved by *Craig* (i.e., to recognize "the state interest in protecting child witnesses from the trauma of testifying in a child abuse case" [p. 855]). However, this criticism appears to miss the fact that a broader rule allows for this public policy to be maintained, as well as opening the door for the ability to protect other people who may be vulnerable in the courtroom, as is done in other countries (e.g., England and Wales). The public policy rationale for imposing a modification in *Craig* could be included under the language in another of its sections, Section 7. It directs the judge "to employ an alternative method that is no more restrictive of the rights of the parties than is necessary under the circumstances to serve the purposes of the order," which would include the URE child hearsay exception for statements of children regarding alleged abuse.

Thus, although helpful uniform codes have been proposed, the need remains for updating such codes to comport with more recent legal decisions, such as *Crawford* (2004). In addition, uniform codes should attempt to implement a coherent and consistent standard based on the results of existing social science research (see chap. 4, this volume), as well as that which will be conducted in the future. For example, younger children are not the only ones who could benefit from courtroom modifications (Quas, Goodman, & Ghetti, 2005), although the law favors modifications for young children over adolescents.

Conducting Needed Research

Many research questions and issues vital to the goals of securing justice and fair treatment for all involved in child witness cases remain unanswered. With regard to courtroom modification evaluations, there are at least two areas of inquiry:

1. First, an examination of how courtroom modification evaluations are actually being conducted in the field, whether they

follow recommended practices, and the effectiveness of such practices must be undertaken.

2. Researchers must develop improved (valid and reliable) subjective and objective ways to measure stress and emotional distress in youth of all ages in the forensic context (Clifford, 2002), especially the context of testifying in front of the defendant. As part of this effort, the development of clinically useful and empirically based risk assessment protocols for more than *de minimis* emotional distress in child witnesses, as is being done in the area of violence risk assessment (for a review, see, e.g., Borum, 1996; Elbogen, 2002; Melton et al., 1997; Monahan et al., 2001), is warranted.

As to the effectiveness and effects of courtroom modifications, future research could redress issues and gaps in knowledge that we discussed in chapter 4 and test the validity of our recommendations for use of the modifications in specific cases (see Suggestions Regarding Modifications, this chapter). For example, one approach to determining the effectiveness of modifications is to develop more systematic data collection about the use of alternative courtroom procedures. In England and Wales, Esam (2002) suggested the development of a research or management program to obtain and track the following information:

- How many child witness cases are prosecuted each year?
- What are the ages of the child witnesses?
- How many cases result in convictions, and how does this relate to the conviction rate for prosecutions generally?
- How many cases fail to get to court because the child witness does not feel able to give evidence (or because a parent/carer considers that it would not be in the child's interests to give evidence)?
- How many cases do not go to court because the police decide not to proceed, and what are the reasons for these decisions?
- How many cases do not go to court because the Crown Prosecution Service decides not to proceed, and what are the reasons for these decisions?
- How many cases involve retrials?
- How many cases accept reduced pleas?
- How many cases fail because of technical problems with the video equipment?
- How many cases fail because of inadequate/poor-quality video evidence?
- What is the success rate of local service level agreements?
- How long are these cases taking to come to trial? (p. 312)

However, relying solely on answering these questions is insufficient. For example, they do not address whether modifications in the courtroom affect jurors' perceptions of the child's credibility (e.g., Ghetti et al., 2002).

To address fully the efficacy question, studies are needed that not only broaden the study of the effectiveness and effects of courtroom modifications but that also contrast the different modifications and compare psychological outcomes and the impact the modifications have on the fairness of the trial (e.g., CCTV vs. screens vs. traditional in-court testimony vs. not testifying). Some evidence is available for gauging short-term effects, but it is unclear whether they have long-term effects on children's feelings, as well as their perceptions of the legal system (Ghetti et al., 2002). For this reason, longitudinal research is needed to assess the negative and positive effects of various forms of children's involvement with the U.S. legal system (Edelstein et al., 2002), including courtroom testimony in criminal, family, civil, and juvenile cases, as well as with legal systems in other countries. Research in this area published in the early 1990s found that some children experienced fear and anxiety when testifying in front of the accused (e.g., Goodman, Levine, & Melton, 1992; Runyan et al., 1988; Sas, Austin, Wolfe, & Hurley, 1991), and that such testimony can have long-term emotional effects (Ghetti et al., 2002; Quas et al., 2005). Because changes to procedures in the past 15 years may affect children's experiences, they also should be examined.

As part of this effort, professionals need to consider and include children's voices (Wade, 2002). To that end, research should focus on children's perceptions of the legal process and their reactions to it, including testifying in court with and without various modifications. Some qualitative studies in the United Kingdom have been conducted with children regarding their experiences as witnesses with courtroom modifications (Hamlyn, Phelps, Turtle, & Sattar, 2004; Murray, 1995; Plotnikoff & Woolfson, 2004; Wade, 2002), and such work is needed in the United States. Moreover, consulting with children and adolescents about what would most help them testify is also recommended (Sandler, 2006; Wade, 2002).

Individual child characteristics (taking into account racial, ethnic, cultural, and socioeconomic differences) should also be considered in the research informing courtroom modifications. For example, one question to explore is the relationship between children and adolescents' knowledge of the legal system, their fears or stress about testifying, and their performance on the stand (Crawford & Bull, 2006b; Saywitz, Goodman, & Lyon, 2002). Although one study found that children with more legal knowledge were less stressed about taking the stand in a mock trial than those with less knowledge (Goodman et al., 1998), more work is needed in this area with older and more diverse samples of children and adolescents, as well as in the context of actual cases.

In addition, research needs to identify children who cope well with the stresses of criminal justice system involvement, including in-court testimony and the factors that help to protect them from emotional distress. Work in the early 1990s identified maternal support as one such buffering factor (Everson & Boat, 1989; Goodman, Pyle-Taub, et al., 1992; Sas, Hurley, Hatch, Malla, & Dick, 1993); more work is needed to tease out factors that contribute to such maternal and interpersonal support. For example, studies could examine the efficacy of programs designed to prepare children for court, which could affect more children than those who actually end up testifying. Little systematic evaluation of these programs has been conducted, but it is needed to identify ways that might reduce stress, improve performance, and not unduly influence children's testimony (Saywitz et al., 2002).

Finally, research is needed to inform future use of modifications for child witnesses and to overcome any hurdles to implementing those modifications found to be effective. For example, studies should test the assumptions of legal professionals that the child testifying live in the courtroom provides the maximum effect, as well as the assumptions behind the pros and cons of the various modifications (see APRI, 2004, for a listing of pros and cons of CCTV, videotaped testimony or depositions, and videotaping interviews).

CONCLUSION

It is our hope that this book will promote the knowledge and skills needed by MHPs to provide services that will effectively respond to the needs of allegedly abused children, their attorneys, and the courts. With this knowledge, MHPs may contribute to finding new ways to provide for children and their families in the community. It takes a community to ensure that children and their families understand and have access to services to which that they may be entitled, and we hope that this book will be a part of that effort for children who may serve as witnesses in abuse cases.

We also hope that our review and analysis will stimulate further discourse on improving public policies in this area. Policymakers can do much to generate more comprehensive laws, if not more uniformity in the law. Although policy revision is needed, our work can "effectively influence social programs, policy, or law only to the extent that it comes to the attention of professionals 'in the trenches': social workers, attorneys, judges, legislators, the public, and others (Grisso & Melton, 1987)" (Bottoms et al., 2002, p. 101). For this reason, we also urge psychological scientists and mental health professionals to make legal and policy professionals (e.g., attorneys, judges, legislators) aware of past, current, and new social science research that will improve the factual underpinnings for policy revision in this important area.

REFERENCES

Aber, J. L., & Allen, J. P. (1987). Effects of maltreatment on young children's socioemotional development: An attachment theory perspective. *Developmental Psychology, 23,* 406–414.

Achenbach, T. M. (1993a). *Empirically based taxonomy: How to use syndromes and profile types derived from the CBCL/4–18, TRF, and YSR.* Burlington: Department of Psychiatry, University of Vermont.

Achenbach, T. M. (1993b). Implications of multiaxial empirically based assessment for behavior therapy with children. *Behavior Therapy, 24,* 91–116.

Achenbach, T. M. (2005). Advancing assessment of children and adolescents: Commentary on evidence-based assessment of child and adolescent disorders. *Journal of Clinical Child and Adolescent Psychology, 34,* 541–547.

Ackerman, P. T., Newton, J. E. O., McPherson, W. B., Jones, J. G., & Dykman, R. A. (1998). Prevalence of post traumatic stress disorder and other psychiatric diagnoses in three groups of abused children (sexual, physical, and both). *Child Abuse & Neglect, 22,* 759–774.

Adam, B. S., Everett, B. L., & O'Neal, E. (1992). PTSD in physically and sexually abused psychiatrically hospitalized children. *Child Psychiatry and Human Development, 23,* 3–8.

Adams, R. E., & Burkowski, W. M. (2007). Relationships with mothers and peers moderate the association between childhood sexual abuse and anxiety disorders. *Child Abuse & Neglect, 31,* 645–656.

Administration for Children & Families. (2007). *Children's justice act.* Retrieved August 24, 2007, from http://www.acf.hhs.gov/programs/cb/programs_fund/state_tribal/justice_act.htm

Ala. Code § 15-25-2 (2007).

Ala. Code § 15-25-3 (2007).

Ala. Code § 15-25-31 (2007).

Alaska Stat. § 12.40.110 (2007).

Alaska Stat. § 12.45.046 (2007).

Aldridge, M., & Wood, J. (1998). *Interviewing children: A guide for child care and forensic practitioners.* Chichester, NY: Wiley.

Alexander, E. K., & Lord, J. H. (1994, July). *Impact statements: A victim's right to speak, a nation's responsibility to listen,* OVC report (NCJ 154395). Retrieved August 22, 2007, from http://www.ojp.usdoj.gov/ovc/publications/infores/impact/welcome.html

Allen, S. N. (1994). Psychological assessment of post-traumatic stress disorder: Psychometrics, current trends, and future directions. *Psychiatric Clinics of North America, 17,* 327–349.

Al-Mateen, C. S. (2002). Effects of witnessing violence on children and adolescents. In D. H. Schetky & E. P. Benedek (Eds.), *Principles and practice of child and adolescent forensic psychiatry* (pp. 213–224). Washington, DC: American Psychiatric Publishing.

Amaya-Jackson, L., & March, J. S. (1995). Posttraumatic stress disorder. In J. S. March (Ed.), *Anxiety disorders in children and adolescents* (pp. 276–300). New York: Guilford Press.

American Academy of Child & Adolescent Psychiatry. (1997a). Practice parameters for the assessment and treatment of children and adolescents with anxiety disorders. *Journal of the American Academy of Child & Adolescent Psychiatry, 36*(Suppl. 10). Retrieved August 22, 2007, from http://www.aacap.org/galleries/PracticeParameters/forensic.pdf

American Academy of Child & Adolescent Psychiatry. (1997b). Practice parameters for the forensic evaluation of children and adolescents who may have been physically or sexually abused. *Journal of the American Academy of Child & Adolescent Psychiatry, 36*(Suppl. 10), 37s–56s.

American Academy of Child & Adolescent Psychiatry. (1998). Practice parameters for the assessment and treatment of children and adolescents with depressive disorders. Washington, DC: Author. Retrieved August 24, 2007, from http://www.aacap.org/galleries/PracticeParameters/Depress.pdf

American Academy of Child & Adolescent Psychiatry. (2007). Practice parameters for the assessment and treatment of children and adolescents with anxiety disorders. *Journal of the American Academy of Child & Adolescent Psychiatry, 46,* 267–283.

American Academy of Psychiatry and the Law. (2005). *Ethical guidelines for the practice of forensic psychiatry.* Bloomfield, CT: Author. Retrieved July 17, 2007, from https://www.aapl.org/pdf/ETHICSGDLNS.pdf

American Bar Association. (1996). *Standards of practice for lawyers representing children in abuse and neglect cases.* Retrieved July 17, 2007, from http://www.abanet.org/child/repstandwhole.pdf

American Bar Association Criminal Justice Section. (1985). *Guidelines for the fair treatment of child witnesses in cases where child abuse is alleged.* Retrieved August 23, 2007, from http://www.abanet.org/child/witnesses-abuse-cases.doc

American Counseling Association. (2005). *ACA code of ethics.* Alexandria, VA: Author. Retrieved July 17, 2007, from http://www.counseling.org/Resources/CodeOfEthics/TP/Home/CT2.aspx

American Professional Society on the Abuse of Children. (1990). *Practice guidelines: Psychosocial evaluation of suspected sexual abuse in young children.* Chicago: Author.

American Professional Society on the Abuse of Children. (1995). *Guidelines for the use of anatomical dolls.* Chicago: Author.

American Professional Society on the Abuse of Children. (1997). *Psychosocial evaluation of suspected psychological maltreatment in children and adolescents.* Chicago: Author.

American Professional Society on the Abuse of Children. (1998). *Practice guidelines: Psychosocial evaluation of suspected sexual abuse in children* (2nd ed.). Chicago: Author.

American Professional Society on the Abuse of Children. (2002). *Investigative interviewing in cases of alleged child abuse.* Chicago: Author.

American Professional Society on the Abuse of Children. (2007). [Home page]. Retrieved July 4, 2007, from http://www.apsac.org

American Prosecutors Research Institute. (2007). Retrieved July 4, 2007, from http://www.ndaa.org/apri/index.html

American Prosecutors Research Institute National Center for Prosecution of Child Abuse. (2004). *Investigation and prosecution of child abuse* (3rd ed.). Thousand Oaks, CA: Sage.

American Psychiatric Association. (1980). *Diagnostic and statistical manual of mental disorders* (3rd ed.). Washington, DC: Author.

American Psychiatric Association. (1987). *Diagnostic and statistical manual of mental disorders* (3rd ed., rev.). Washington, DC: Author.

American Psychiatric Association. (1994). *Diagnostic and statistical manual of mental disorders* (4th ed.). Washington, DC: Author.

American Psychiatric Association. (2000). *Diagnostic and statistical manual of mental disorders* (4th ed., text revision). Washington, DC: Author.

American Psychological Association. (1994). Guidelines for child custody evaluations in divorce proceedings. *American Psychologist, 49,* 677–680.

American Psychological Association. (1995). *Twenty-four questions (and answers) about professional practice in the area of child abuse.* Washington, DC: Author.

American Psychological Association. (2002a). Ethical principles of psychologists and code of conduct. *American Psychologist, 57,* 1060–1073.

American Psychological Association. (2002b). *Guidelines on multicultural education, training, research, practice, and organizational change for psychologists.* Retrieved January 19, 2008, from http://www.apa.org/pi/multiculturalguidelines.pdf

American Psychological Association Ad Hoc Committee on Legal and Ethical Issues in the Treatment of Interpersonal Violence. (2008). *Potential problems for psychologists working with the area of interpersonal violence.* Retrieved January 24, 2008, from http://www.apa.org/pi/potential.html

American Psychological Association Committee on Professional Practice and Standards. (1998). *Guidelines for psychological evaluations in child protection matters.* Washington, DC: American Psychological Association. Retrieved August 23, 2007, from http://www.apa.org/practice/childprotection.html

American Psychological Association Council of Representatives. (1991). *The use of anatomically detailed dolls in forensic evaluations.* Retrieved August 23, 2007, from http://www.apa.org/pi/cyfres.html#anatodolls

American Speech–Language–Hearing Association. (1997–2007a). *Assessment and diagnosis.* Retrieved January 19, 2008, from http://www.asha.org/public/speech/disorders/stutter/AssessDiag.htm

American Speech–Language–Hearing Association. (1997–2007b). *Onset and developmental course.* Retrieved January 19, 2008, from http://www.asha.org/public/speech/disorders/stutter/onstdevcrs.htm

American Speech–Language–Hearing Association. (1997–2007c). *Stuttering.* Retrieved January 19, 2008, from http://www.asha.org/public/speech/disorders/stuttering.htm

Anastasi, A., & Urbina, S. (1997). *Psychological testing*. Upper Saddle River, NJ: Prentice Hall.

Anderson, J., & Heath, R. T. (2006a). Forensic interviews of children who have developmental disabilities: Part 1 of 2. *Update, 19,* 1–2. Retrieved August 23, 2007, from http://www.ndaa.org/publications/newsletters/update_vol_19_number_1_2006.pdf

Anderson, J., & Heath, R. T. (2006b). Forensic interviews of children who have developmental disabilities: Part 2 of 2. *Update, 19,* 1–2. Retrieved August 23, 2007, from http://www.ndaa.org/publications/newsletters/update_vol_19_number_2_2006.pdf

Anderson, J. C. (1994). Epidemiological issues. In T. H. Ollendick, N. J. King, & W. Yule (Eds.), *International handbook of phobic and anxiety disorders in children and adolescents* (pp. 43–66). New York: Plenum Press.

Angold, A., Costello, E. J., & Erkanli, A. (1999). Comorbidity. *Journal of Child Psychology and Psychiatry and Allied Disciplines, 40,* 57–87.

Angold, A., Costello, E. J., Messer, S. C., Pickles, A., Winder, F., & Silver, D. (1995). The development of a short questionnaire for use in epidemiological studies of depression in children and adolescents. *International Journal of Methods in Psychiatric Research, 5,* 237–249.

Angold, A., Erkanli, A., Costello, E. J., & Rutter, M. (1996). Precision, reliability and accuracy in the dating of symptom onsets in child and adolescent psychopathology. *Journal of Child Psychology and Psychiatry, 37,* 57–664.

Angold, A., & Fisher, P. W. (1999). Interviewer-based interviews. In D. Shaffer, C. P. Lucas, & J. E. Richters (Eds.), *Diagnostic assessment in child and adolescent psychopathology* (pp. 34–64). New York: Guilford Press.

Angold, A., Prendergast, M., Co, A., Harrington, R., Simonoff, E., & Rutter, M. (1995). The Child and Adolescent Psychiatric Assessment (CAPA). *Psychological Medicine, 25,* 739–753.

Annotation. *Closed-circuit television witness examination,* 61 American Law Reports 4th 1155 (2007).

Applegate, R. (2006). Taking child witnesses out of the Crown Court: A live link initiative. *International Review of Victimology, 13,* 179–200.

Ariz. Rev. Stat. § 13-4252 (2007).

Ark. Code Ann. § 16-43-1001 (2007).

Armagh, D. (1998). A safety net for our children: Protecting our children. *Juvenile Justice, 5,* 9–15.

Armstrong, J., Putnam, F. W., Carlson, E., Libero, D. Z., & Smith, S. (1997). Development and validation of a measure of adolescent dissociation: The Adolescent Dissociative Experiences Scale. *Journal of Nervous and Mental Disease, 185,* 491–497.

Arnold, B. R., & Matus, Y. E. (2000). Test translation and cultural equivalence methodologies for use with diverse populations. In I. Cuellar & F. A. Paniagua (Eds.), *Handbook of multicultural mental health: Assessment and treatment of diverse populations* (pp. 121–136). San Diego, CA: Academic Press.

Askowitz, L. R., & Graham, M. H. (1994). The reliability of expert psychological testimony in child sexual abuse prosecutions. *Cardozo Law Review, 15,* 2027–2101.

Atlas, J. A., & Hiott, J. (1994). Dissociative experiences in a group of adolescents with history of abuse. *Perceptual and Motor Skills, 78,* 121–122.

Atlas, J. A., Wolfson, M. A., & Lipschitz, D. S. (1995). Dissociation and somatization in adolescent inpatients with and without history of abuse. *Psychological Reports, 76,* 1101–1102.

Austin, A. A., & Chorpita, B. F. (2004a). Temperament, anxiety, and depression: Comparisons across five ethnic groups of children. *Journal of Clinical Child and Adolescent Psychology, 33,* 216–226.

Austin, A. A., & Chorpita, B. F. (2004b). Temperament, anxiety, and depression: Construct, convergent, and discriminative validity of the Social Phobia Anxiety Inventory for Children (SPAI–C). *Psychological Assessment, 3,* 235–240.

Avilas, D., Javier, R. A., Drucker, P., Mora, L., Salhany, J., Konstan-Pines, J., & Kupferman, F. (2006). Assessing the effect of community violence in minority children. *Journal of Social Distress and the Homeless, 15,* 294–316.

Baker-Ward, L., & Ornstein, P. A. (2002). Cognitive underpinnings. In H. Westcott, G. Davies, & R. Bull (Eds.), *Children's testimony in context: A handbook of psychological research and forensic practice* (pp. 21–37). New York: Wiley.

Bala, N. (1999). Child witnesses in the Canadian criminal courts: Recognizing their capacities and needs. *Psychology, Public Policy, and Law, 5,* 323–354.

Baldwin, J. S., & Dadds, M. R. (2007). Reliability and validity of parent and child versions of the Multidimensional Anxiety Scale for Children in Community Samples. *Journal of the American Academy of Child & Adolescent Psychiatry, 46,* 252–260.

Barkley, R. A. (1997). Attention-deficit/hyperactivity disorder. In E. J. Mash & L. G. Terdal (Eds.), *Assessment of childhood disorders* (3rd ed., pp. 71–129). New York: Guilford Press.

Barlow, D. H. (2002). *Anxiety and its disorders: The nature and treatment of anxiety and panic* (2nd ed.). New York: Guilford Press.

Barlow, D. H., Allen, L. B., & Choate, M. L. (2004). Towards a unified treatment for emotional disorders. *Behavior Therapy, 35,* 205–230.

Barreto, S., & McManus, M. (1997). Casting the net for "depression" among ethnic minority children from high-risk urban communities. *Clinical Psychology Review, 17,* 823–845.

Barrios, B., & Hartmann, D. P. (1988). Recent developments in single-subject methodology: Methods for analyzing generalization, maintenance, and multicomponent treatments. In M. Hersen, R. M. Eisler, & P. M. Miller (Eds.), *Progress in behavior modification* (Vol. 22, pp. 11–47). New York: Academic Press.

Barrios, B. A., & Hartmann, D. P. (1997). Fears and anxieties. In E. J. Mash & L. G. Terdal (Eds.), *Assessment of childhood disorders* (3rd ed., pp. 230–327). New York: Guilford Press.

Beck, A. T., Steer, R. A., & Brown, G. K. (1996). *Beck Depression Inventory manual* (2nd ed.). San Antonio, TX: Psychological Corporation.

Beck, A. T., Ward, C. H., Mendelson, M., Mock, J. E., & Erbaugh, J. K. (1961). An inventory for measuring depression. *Archives of General Psychology, 4,* 561–571.

Beck, J. S., Beck, A. T., & Jolly, J. B. (2001). *Beck Youth Inventories.* San Antonio, TX: Psychological Corporation.

Becker, J. V., Alpert, J. L., BigFoot, D. S., Bonner, B. L., Geddie, L. F., Henggeler, S., et al. (1995). Empirical research on child abuse treatment: Report by the child abuse and neglect treatment working group. *Journal of Clinical Child Psychology, 24*(Suppl.), 23–46.

Beidel, D. C., Turner, S. M., Hamlin, K., & Morris, T. L. (2000). The Social Phobia and Anxiety Inventory for Children (SPAI–C): External and discriminative validity. *Behavior Therapy, 31,* 75–87.

Beidel, D. C., Turner, S. M., & Morris T. L. (1995). A new inventory to assess childhood social anxiety and phobia: The Social Phobia and Anxiety Inventory for Children. *Psychological Assessment, 7,* 73–79.

Beidel, D. C., Turner, S. M., & Morris, T. L. (1998). *Social Phobia and Anxiety Inventory for Children (SPAI–C) user's manual.* New York: Multi-Health Systems.

Beloof, D. E. (1999). The third model of criminal process: The victim participation model. *Utah Law Review,* 289–328.

Bennett, K. J. (2003). Legal and social issues surrounding closed-circuit television testimony of child victims and witnesses. *Journal of Aggression, Maltreatment & Trauma, 8,* 233–271.

Beresford, S. (2005). Child witnesses and the international criminal justice system: Does the International Criminal Court protect the most vulnerable? *Journal of International Criminal Justice, 3,* 721–748.

Berliner, L. (1998). The use of expert testimony in child sexual abuse cases. In S. J. Ceci & H. Hembrooke (Eds.), *Expert witnesses in child abuse cases: What can and should be said in court* (pp. 11–28). Washington, DC: American Pyschological Association.

Berliner, L., & Conte, J. R. (1993). Sexual abuse evaluations: Conceptual and empirical obstacles. *Child Abuse & Neglect, 17,* 111–125.

Berliner, L., & Conte, J. R. (1995). The effects of disclosure and intervention on sexually abused children. *Child Abuse & Neglect, 19,* 371–384.

Berliner, L., & Lieb, R. (2001). *Child sexual abuse investigations: Testing documentation methods* (Document No. 01-01-4102). Olympia: Washington State Institute for Public Policy.

Berman, S. L., Silverman, W. K., & Kurtines, W. M. (2002). The effects of community violence on children and adolescents: Intervention and social policy. In B. L. Bottoms, M. B. Kovera, & B. D. McAuliff (Eds.), *Children, social science, and the law* (pp. 301–321). New York: Cambridge University Press.

Bernstein, E. M., & Putnam, F. W. (1986). Development, reliability, and validity of a dissociation scale. *Journal of Nervous and Mental Disease, 174,* 727–735.

Bernstein, G. A., Borchardt, C. M., & Perwien, A. R. (1996). Anxiety disorders in children and adolescents: A review of the past 10 years. *Journal of the American Academy of Child & Adolescent Psychiatry, 35,* 1110–1119.

Bernstein, I. H., Ellason, J. W., Ross, C. A., & Vanderlinden, J. (2001). On the dimensionalities of the Dissociative Experiences Scale (DES) and the Dissociation Questionnaire (DIS–Q). *Journal of Trauma & Dissociation, 2*, 103–123.

Bernthal, J. E., & Bankson, J. W. (1993). *Articulation and phonological disorders* (3rd ed.). Engelwood Cliffs, NJ: Prentice Hall.

Bharti, K., & Heath, W. P. (1997). Perceptions of a child as witness: Effects of leading questions and the type of relationship between child and defendant. *Psychological Reports, 80*, 979–986.

Bhatia, S. K., & Bhatia, S. C. (2007). Childhood and adolescent depression. *American Family Physician, 75*, 73–80.

Bidjerano, T. (2006). Factor structure of a Bulgarian translation of the Revised Children's Manifest Anxiety Scale. *Psychological Reports, 99*, 943–952.

Birmaher, B., & Brent, D. (1998). Practice parameters for the assessment and treatment of children and adolescents with depressive disorders. *Journal of the American Academy of Child & Adolescent Psychiatry, 37*(Suppl. 10), 63S–83S.

Birmaher, B., Brent, D. A., Chiappetta, L., Bridge, J., Monga, S., & Baugher, M. (1999). Psychometric properties of the Screen for Child Anxiety Related Emotional Disorders (SCARED): A replication study. *Journal of the American Academy of Child & Adolescent Psychiatry, 38*, 1230–1236.

Birmaher, B., Khetarpal, S., Brent, D., Cully, M., Balach, L., Kaufman, J., & Neer, S. M. (1997). The screen for child anxiety related emotional disorders (SCARED): Scale construction and psychometric characteristics. *Journal of the American Academy of Child & Adolescent Psychiatry, 36*, 545–553.

Birmaher, B., Ryan, N. D., & Williamson, D. E. (1996). Depression in children and adolescents: Clinical features and pathogenesis. In K. I. Shulman, M. Tohen, & S. P. Kutcher (Eds.), *Mood disorders across the life span* (pp. 51–81). New York: Wiley.

Blahauvietz, S. (2005). Key factors in forensic interviews with Native American children. *Update, 18*, 1–2. Retrieved August 23, 2007, from http://www.ndaa-apri.org/publications/newsletters/update_index.html

Blank, A. S. (1991). Psychological treatment of war veterans: A challenge for mental health professionals. *Medical Hypnoanalysis, 6*, 91–96.

Blank, A. S. (1993). The longitudinal course of posttraumatic stress disorder. In J. R. T. Davidson & E. B. Foa (Eds.), *Posttraumatic stress disorder: DSM–IV and beyond* (pp. 3–22). Washington, DC: American Psychiatric Press.

Blood, G. W., Blood, I. M., Maloney, K., Meyer, C., & Qualls, C. D. (2007). Anxiety levels in adolescents who stutter. *Journal of Communication Disorders, 40*, 452–469.

Blood, G. W., Blood, I. M., Tellis, G. M., & Gabel, R. M. (2003). A preliminary study of self-esteem, stigma, and disclosure in adolescents who stutter. *Journal of Fluency Disorders, 28*, 143–159.

Blumenthal, J. A. (2001). Reading the text of the confrontation clause: "To be" or not "to be"? *University of Pennsylvania Journal of Constitutional Law, 3*, 722–749.

Boatright v. State, 192 Ga. App. 112, 385 S.E.2d 298 (Ga. Ct. App. 1989).

Boeschen, L. E., Sales, B. D., & Koss, M. P. (1998). Rape trauma experts in the courtroom. *Psychology, Public Policy, and Law, 4*, 414–432.

Borum, R. (1996). Improving the clinical practice of violence risk assessment. *American Psychologist, 51*, 945–956.

Bottoms, B. L., & Goodman, E. S. (Eds.). (1996). *International perspectives on child abuse and children's testimony: Psychological research and law.* Thousand Oaks, CA: Sage.

Bottoms, B. L., Repucci, N. D., Tweed, J. A., & Nysse-Carris, K. L. (2002). Children, psychology, and law: Reflections on past and future contributions to science and policy. In J. R. P. Ogloff (Ed.), *Taking psychology and law into the twenty-first century* (pp. 62–119). New York: Kluwer Academic/Plenum Press.

Bowlby, J. (1988). *A secure base: Parent–child attachment and healthy human development.* New York: Basic Books.

Brannon, L. C. (1994). The trauma of testifying in court for child victims of sexual assault v. the accused's right to confrontation. *Law and Psychology Review, 18,* 439–460.

Brennan, M., & Brennan, R. E. (1988). *Strange language: Child victims under cross examination* (3rd ed.) Wagga Wagga, Australia: Riverina Murray Institute of Higher Education.

Brett, E. A. (1993). Classification of PTSD in *DSM–IV:* Anxiety disorder, dissociative disorder, or stress disorder. In J. R. Davidson & Foa, E. B. (Eds.), *PTSD: DSM–IV and beyond* (pp. 191–206). Washington, DC: American Psychiatric Publishing.

Briere, J. (n. d.). *Trauma Symptom Checklist for Children (TSCC).* Retrieved June 13, 2007, from http://www.johnbriere.com/tscc.htm

Briere, J. N. (1992). Child abuse trauma: Theory and treatment of the lasting effects. Newbury Park, CA: Sage.

Briere, J. (1996a). *Trauma Symptom Checklist for Children: Professional manual.* Odessa, FL: Psychological Assessment Resources.

Briere, J. (1996b). Psychometric review of the Trauma Symptom Checklist for Children. In B. H. Stamm (Ed.), *Measurement of stress, trauma, and adaptation* (pp. 43–68). Lutherville, MD: Sidran Foundation and Press.

Briere, J. (2004). *Psychological assessment of adult posttraumatic states: Phenomenology, diagnosis, and measurement* (2nd ed.). Washington, DC: American Psychological Association.

Briere, J., Cotman, A., Harris, K., & Smiljanich, K. (1992, August). *The Trauma Symptom Inventory: Preliminary data on reliability and validity.* Paper presented at the annual meeting of the American Psychological Association, Washington, DC.

Briere, J., Elliott, D. M., Harris, K., & Cotman, D. (1995). Trauma Symptom Inventory: Psychometrics and association with childhood and adult victimization in clinical samples. *Journal of Interpersonal Violence, 10,* 387–401.

Briere, J., Johnson, K., Bissada, A., Damon, L., Crouch, J., Gil, E., et al. (2001). The Trauma Symptom Checklist for Young Children (TSCYC): Reliability and association with abuse exposure in a multi-site study. *Child Abuse & Neglect: The International Journal, 25*, 1001–1014.

Briere, J., & Runtz, M. (1988). Multivariate correlates of childhood psychological and physical maltreatment among university women. *Child Abuse & Neglect, 12*, 331–341.

Briere, J., & Runtz, M. (1990a). Augmenting Hopkins SCL scales to measure dissociative symptoms: Data from two nonclinical samples. *Journal of Research in Personality, 55*, 376–379.

Briere, J., & Runtz, M. (1990b). Differential adult symptomology associated with three types of child abuse histories. *Child Abuse & Neglect, 14*, 357–364.

Brooks, S. J., & Kutcher, S. (2001). Diagnosis and measurement of adolescent depression: A review of commonly utilized instruments. *Journal of Child and Adolescent Psychopharmacology, 11*, 341–376.

Brooks, S. J., & Kutcher, S. (2003). Diagnosis and measurement of anxiety disorder in adolescents: A review of commonly used instruments. *Journal of Child and Adolescent Psychopharmacology, 13*, 351–400.

Brosky, B. A., & Lally, S. J. (2004). Prevalence of trauma, PTSD, and dissociation in court-referred adolescents. *Journal of Interpersonal Violence, 19*, 801–814.

Brown, D. (2001). The new 702: How it affects the use of experts. *APRI Update, 14*(3). Retrieved August 24, 2007, from http://www.ndaa-apri.org/publications/newsletter/update_index.html

Brown, D., & Pipe, M. (2003). Individual differences in children's event memory reports and the narrative elaboration technique. *Journal of Applied Psychology, 88*, 195–206.

Brown, E. J., & Goodman, R. F. (2005). Childhood traumatic grief: An exploration of the construct in children bereaved on September 11. *Journal of Clinical Child and Adolescent Psychology, 34*, 248–259.

Brown, J., Cohen, P., Johnson, J. G., & Smailes, M. (1999). Childhood abuse and neglect: Specificity of effects on adolescent and young adult depression and suicidality. *Journal of the American Academy of Child & Adolescent Psychiatry, 38*, 1490–1496.

Brownell, R. (2000). *Expressive and Receptive One-Word Picture Vocabulary Tests.* San Antonio, TX: Psychological Corporation.

Bruck, M. (1998). The trials and tribulations of a novice expert witness. In S. J. Ceci & H. Hembrooke (Eds.), *Expert witnesses in child abuse cases: What can and should be said in court* (pp. 85–104). Washington, DC: American Psychological Association.

Bruck, M., & Ceci, S. J. (1995). Amicus brief for the case of State of New Jersey v. Michaels presented by Committee of Concerned Social Scientists. *Psychology, Public Policy, and Law, 1*, 272–322.

Bruck, M., & Ceci, S. J. (2004). Forensic developmental psychology: Unveiling four common misconceptions. *Current Directions in Psychological Science, 13*, 229–232.

Bruck, M., Ceci, S. J., & Francoeur, E. (1999). The accuracy of mothers' memories of conversations with their preschool children. *Journal of Experimental Psychology: Applied, 5,* 89–106.

Bruck, M., Ceci, S. J., & Principe, G. F. (2006). The child and the law. In K. A. Renninger, I. E. Sigel, W. Damon, & R. M. Lerner (Eds.), *Handbook of child psychology: Vol. 4, Child psychology in practice* (6th ed., pp. 776–816). Hoboken, NJ: Wiley.

Brunner, R., Parzer, P., Schuld, V., & Resch, F. (2000). Dissociative symptomatology and traumatogenic factors in adolescent psychiatric patients. *Journal of Nervous & Mental Disease, 188,* 71–77.

Bryant, R. A. (2003). Early predictors of posttraumatic stress disorder. *Biological Psychiatry, 53,* 789–795.

Bryant, R. A., Salmon, K., Sinclair, E., & Davidson, P. (2007). Heart rate as a predictor of posttraumatic stress disorder in children. *General Hospital Psychiatry, 29,* 66–68.

Buck, J. A. (2006). Hearsay testimony in child sexual abuse cases. In S. M. Sturt (Ed.), *New developments in child abuse research* (pp. 73–93). New York: Nova Science.

Bulkley, J. A., Feller, J. N., Stern, P., & Roe, R. (1996). Child abuse and neglect: Laws and legal proceedings. In J. Briere, L. Berliner, J. A. Bulkley, C. Jenny, & T. Reid (Eds.), *The APSAC handbook on child maltreatment* (pp. 271–296). Thousand Oaks, CA: Sage.

Bursztajn, H. J., & Brodsky, A. (1998). Ethical and effective testimony after *Daubert.* In L. E. Lifson & R. I. Simon (Eds.), *The mental health practitioner and the law: A comprehensive handbook* (pp. 262–280). Cambridge, MA: Harvard University Press.

Burton, M., Evans, R., & Sanders, A. (2006). Are special measures for vulnerable and intimidated witnesses working? Evidence from the criminal and justice agencies. *Home Office Online Report.* Retrieved August 3, 2007, from http://www.homeoffice.gov.uk/rds/pdfs06/rdsolr0106.pdf

Cal. Evid. Code § 240 (2007).

Cal. Evid. Code § 1228 (2007).

Cal. Penal Code § 868.8(a) (2007).

Cal. Penal Code § 868.8(b) (2007).

Cal. Penal Code § 868.8(d) (2007).

Cal. Penal Code § 859.1 (2007).

Cal. Penal Code § 999s (2007).

Cal. Penal Code § 1346 (2007).

California v. Green, 399 U.S. 149 (1970).

Campbell, T. W. (1997). Indicators of child sexual abuse and their unreliability. *American Journal of Forensic Psychology, 15,* 5–18.

Canino, G. (2004). Are somatic symptoms and related distress more prevalent in Hispanic/Latino youth? Some methodological considerations. *Journal of Clinical Child and Adolescent Psychology, 33,* 272–275.

Canino, G., & Bravo, M. (1999). The translation and adaptation of diagnostic instruments for cross-cultural use. In D. Shaffer, C. P. Lucas, & J. E. Richters (Eds.), *Diagnostic assessment in child and adolescent psychopathology* (pp. 285–298). New York: Guilford Press.

Cardeña, E., & Weiner, L. A. (2004). Evaluation of dissociation throughout the lifespan. *Psychotherapy: Theory, Research, Practice, Training, 41,* 496–508.

Carlson, E. B. (1997). *Trauma assessments: A clinician's guide.* New York: Guilford Press.

Carlson, E. B., & Dutton, M. A. (2003). Assessing experiences and responses of crime victims. *Journal of Traumatic Stress, 16,* 133–148.

Carlson, E. B., Furby, L., Armstrong, J., & Shales, J. (1997). A conceptual framework for long-term psychological effects of traumatic childhood abuse. *Child Maltreatment, 2,* 272–295.

Carlson, G. A., Kashani, J. H., DeFatima, T. M., Vaidya, A., & Daniel, A. E. (1987). Comparison of two structured interviews on a psychiatrically hospitalized population of children. *Journal of the American Academy of Child & Adolescent Psychiatry, 26,* 645–648.

Carmines, E. G. (1979). *Reliability and validity assessment.* Thousand Oaks, CA: Sage.

Carrey, N., & Ungar, M. (2007). Resilience theory and the *Diagnostic and Statistical Manual:* Incompatible bed fellows? *Child & Adolescent Psychiatric Clinics of North America, 16,* 497–513.

Carrion, V. G., & Steiner, H. (2000). Trauma and dissociation in delinquent adolescents. *Journal of the American Academy of Child & Adolescent Psychiatry, 39,* 353–359.

Carter, C. A., Bottoms, B. L., & Levine, M. (1996). Linguistic and socioemotional influences on the accuracy of children's reports. *Law and Human Behavior, 20,* 335–358.

Carter, L. S., Wiethhorn, L. A., & Behrman, R. E. (1999). Domestic violence and children: Analysis and recommendations. *Future of Children, 9,* 4–20.

Cashmore, J. (2002). Innovative procedures for child witnesses. In H. L. Westcott, G. M. Davies, & R. H. C. Bull (Eds.), *Children's testimony: A handbook of psychological research and forensic practice* (pp. 203–217). West Sussex, England: Wiley.

Cashmore, J., & Bussey, K. (1996). Judicial perceptions of child witness competence. *Law & Human Behavior, 20,* 313–334.

Cashmore, J., & De Haas, N. (1992). *The use of closed-circuit television for child witnesses in the ACT.* Sydney: The Australian Law Reform Commission.

Cashmore, J., & Trimboli, L. (2006). *An evaluation of the NSW child sexual assault specialist jurisdiction pilot.* Sydney: NSW Bureau of Crime Statistics and Research. Retrieved August 3, 2007, from http://www.lawlink.nsw.gov.au/lawlink/bocsar/ll_bocsar.nsf/vwFiles/r57.pdf/$file/r57.pdf

Casper, R. C., Belanoff, J., & Offer, D. (1996). Gender differences, but not racial group differences, in self-reported psychiatric symptoms in adolescents. *Journal of the American Academy of Child & Adolescent Psychiatry, 35,* 500–508.

Castillo, R. J. (1994). Spirit possession in South Asia: Dissociation or hysteria? Part 2: Case histories. *Culture, Medicine, and Psychiatry, 18,* 141–162.

Ceci, S. J., & Bruck, M. (1993a). Children's recollections: Translating research into policy. *SRCD Social Policy Reports, 7*(3).

Ceci, S. J., & Bruck, M. (1993b). Suggestibility of the child witness: A historical review and synthesis. *Psychological Bulletin, 113,* 403–439.

Ceci, S. J., & Bruck, M. (1995). *Jeopardy in the courtroom: A scientific analysis of children's testimony.* Washington, DC: American Psychological Association.

Ceci, S. J., & Bruck, M. (1998). Children's testimony: Applied and basic issues. In W. Damon (Ed.), *Handbook of child psychology: Vol. 4. Child psychology in practice* (5th ed., pp. 713–774). New York: Wiley.

Ceci, S. J., & Hembrooke, H. (1998). *Expert witnesses in child abuse cases: What can and should be said in court.* Washington, DC: American Psychological Association.

Cederborg, A., & Lamb, M. E. (2006). How does the legal system respond when children with learning difficulties are victimized? *Child Abuse & Neglect, 30,* 537–547.

Center for Mental Health Services. (2007). *Child and adolescent mental health.* Retrieved July 4, 2007, from http://mentalhealth.samhsa.gov/child/childhealth.asp

Cezero-Jimenez, M., & Frias, D. (1994). Emotional and cognitive adjustment in abused children. *Child Abuse & Neglect, 18,* 923–932.

Chaffin, M., Silovsky, J. F., & Vaughn, C. (2005). Temporal concordance of anxiety disorders and child sexual abuse: Implications for direct versus artifactual effects of sexual abuse. *Journal of Clinical Child and Adolescent Psychology, 34,* 210–222.

Chaffin, M., Wherry, J. N., & Dykman, R. (1997). School age children's coping with sexual abuse: Abuse stresses and symptoms associated with four coping strategies. *Child Abuse & Neglect, 21,* 227–240.

Chambers, W. J., Puig-Antich, J., Hirsch, M., Paez, P., Ambrosini, P. J., Tabrizi, M. A., et al. (1985). The assessment of affective disorders in children and adolescents by semi-structured interview: Test–retest reliability of the schedule for affective disorders and schizophrenia for school age children, present episode version. *Archives of General Psychiatry, 42,* 696–702.

Chandy, J. M., Blum, R. W., & Resnick, M. D. (1996). Female adolescents with a history of sexual abuse: Risk outcome and protective factors. *Journal of Interpersonal Violence, 11,* 503–518.

Chase, C. A. (2003). The five faces of the confrontation clause. *Houston Law Review, 40,* 1003–1079.

Cherryman, J., King, N., & Bull, R. (1999). Child witness investigative interviews: An analysis of the use of children's video recorded evidence in North Yorkshire. *International Journal of Police Science and Management, 2,* 50–56.

Child Victims' and Child Witnesses' Rights Act, 18 U.S.C. § 3509 (2007).

Child Welfare Information Gateway (n.d.). *Funding information for programs*. Retrieved June 22, 2007, from http://www.childwelfare.gov/systemwide/funding/

Child Welfare Information Gateway. (2003, July). *Reporting penalties*. Retrieved June 22, 2007, from http://www.childwelfare.gov/systemwide/laws_policies/statutes/report.pdf

Choi, H. (2002). Understanding adolescent depression in ethnocultural context. *ANS Advances in Nursing Science, 25*, 75–85.

Chorpita, B. F., Daleiden, E. L., Moffitt, C., Yim, L., & Umemoto, L. A. (2000). Assessment of tripartite factors of emotion in children and adolescents: I. Structural validity and normative data of an affect and arousal scale. *Journal of Psychopathology and Behavioral Assessment, 22*, 141–160.

Chorpita, B. F., Moffitt, C. E., & Gray, J. A. (2005). Psychometric properties of the Revised Child Anxiety and Depression Scale in a clinical sample. *Behaviour Research and Therapy, 43*, 309–322.

Chorpita, B. F., Tracey, S. A., Brown, T. A., Collica, T. J., & Barlow, D. H. (1997). Assessment of worry in children and adolescents: An adaptation of the Penn State Worry Questionnaire. *Behaviour Research and Therapy, 35*, 569–581.

Chorpita, B. F., Yim, L., Moffitt, C., Umemoto, L. A., & Francis, S. E. (2000). Assessment of symptoms of DSM-IV anxiety and depression in children: A revised child anxiety and depression scale. *Behaviour Research and Therapy, 38*, 835–855.

Chu, J. A., & Dill, D. L. (1990). Dissociative symptoms in relation to childhood physical and sexual abuse. *American Journal of Psychiatry, 147*, 887–892.

Clark, L. A., & Watson, D. (1991). Tripartite model of anxiety and depression: Psychometric evidence and taxonomic implications. *Journal of Abnormal Psychology, 100*, 316–336.

Clark, S. J. (2003). An accuser-obligation approach to the confrontation clause. *Nebraska Law Review, 81*, 1258–1280.

Cleator, H., & Hand, L. (2001). Selective mutism: How a successful speech and language assessment really is possible. *International Journal of Language & Communication Disorders, 36*, 126–131.

Clifford, B. R. (2002). Methodological issues in the study of children's testimony. In H. L. Westcott, G. M. Davies, & R. H. C. Bull (Eds.), *Children's testimony: A handbook of psychological research and forensic practice* (pp. 331–344). West Sussex, England: Wiley.

Cohan, S. L., Chavira, D. A., & Stein, M. B. (2006). *Journal of Child Psychology and Psychiatry, 47*, 1085–1097.

Cohen, J. A., Deblinger, E., Mannarino, A. P., & de Arellano, M. A. (2001). The importance of culture in treating abused and neglected children: An empirical review. *Child Maltreatment, 6*, 148–157.

Cohen, J. A., & Mannarino, A. P. (2000). Predictors of treatment outcome in sexually abused children. *Child Abuse & Neglect, 24*, 983–994.

Cohen, J. A., Mannarino, A. P., & Deblinger, E. (2006). *Treating trauma and traumatic grief in children and adolescents*. New York: Guilford Press.

Cohen, J. A., Mannarino, A. P., Padlo, S., Greenberg, T., & Seslow, C. (2005). Childhood traumatic grief—development, epidemiology, assessment, and treatment. In K. A. Kendall-Tackett & S. M. Giacomoni (Eds.), *Child victimization: Maltreatment, bullying and dating violence, prevention and intervention* (pp. 7-1–7-15). Kingston, NJ: Civic Research Institute.

Cohen, P., & Kasen, S. (1999). The context of assessment: Culture, race, and socioeconomic status as influences on the assessment of children. In D. Shaffer, C. P. Lucas, & J. E. Richters (Eds.), *Diagnostic assessment in child and adolescent psychopathology* (pp. 299–318). New York: Guilford Press.

Colo. Rev. Stat. § 13-25-129 (2006).

Colo. Rev. Stat. § 18-3-413 (2006).

Colo. Rev. Stat. § 18-6-401.3 (2006).

Colorado ex rel. R.A.S., 111 P.3d 487 (Colo. App. Ct. 2004).

Comer, J. S., & Kendall, P. C. (2005). High-end specificity of the Children's Depressive Inventory in a sample of anxiety-disordered youth. *Depression and Anxiety, 22*(1), 11–19.

Committee on Ethical Guidelines for Forensic Psychologists. (1991). Specialty guidelines for forensic psychologists. *Law and Human Behavior, 15*(6), 655–665.

Commonweath v. Allshouse, 924 A.2d 1215, 2007 Pa. Super. 109 (Pa. Super. 2007).

Commonwealth v. Bergstrom, 402 Mass. 534, 524 N.E.2d 366 (Mass. 1988).

Commonwealth v. Brusgulis, 398 Mass. 325, 496 N.E.2d 652 (Mass. 1986).

Commonwealth v. Conefrey, 410 Mass. 1, 570 N.E.2d 1384 (Mass. 1991). *aff'd* Commonwealth v. Conefrey, 37 Mass. App. Ct. 290, 640 N.E.2d 116 (1994), *rev'd* [on other grounds than citation] Commonwealth v. Conefrey, 420 Mass. 508, 650 N.E.2d 1268 (Mass. 1995).

Commonwealth v. DeOliveira, 447 Mass. 56 (2006).

Commonwealth v. Spear, 43 Mass. App. Ct. 583, 686 N.E.2d 1037 (Mass. App. Ct. 1997).

Commonwealth v. Trowbridge, 419 Mass. 750, 647 N.E.2d 413 (Mass. 1995).

Commonwealth v. Willis, 716 S.W.2d 224 (Ky. 1986).

Compas, B. E. (1997). Depression in children and adolescents. In E. J. Mash & L. G. Terdal (Eds.), *Assessment of childhood disorders* (3rd ed., pp. 197–229). New York: Guilford Press.

Conn. Gen. Stat. § 54-86g (2003).

Conte, J., Briere, J., & Sexton, D. (1989, August). *Moderators of the long-term effects of sexual abuse.* Paper presented at the annual meeting of the American Psychological Association, New Orleans.

Conte, J. R. (1992). Has this child been sexually abused? Dilemmas for the mental health professional who seeks the answer. *Criminal Justice and Behavior, 19,* 54–73.

Cook, A., Blaustein, M., Spinazzola, J., & van der Kolk, B. (Eds.). (2003). *Complex trauma in children and adolescents*. White Paper from the National Child Traumatic Stress Network Complex Trauma Task Force. Retrieved July 5, 2007, from http://www.nctsnet.org/nctsn_assets/pdfs/edu_materials/Complex Trauma_All.pdf

Cooke, P., & Davies, G. (2001). Achieving best evidence from witnesses with learning disabilities: New guidance. *British Journal of Learning Disabilities, 29,* 84–87.

Coons, P. M. (1996). Clinical phenomenology of 25 children and adolescents with dissociative disorders. *Child & Adolescent Psychiatric Clinics of North America, 5,* 361–374.

Copen, L. M. (2000). *Preparing children for court: A practitioner's guide*. Thousand Oaks, CA: Sage.

Cordon, I. M., Goodman, G. S., & Anderson, S. J. (2003). Children in court. In P. J. van Koppen & S. D. Penrod (Eds.), *Adversarial versus inquisitive justice: Psychological perspective on criminal justice systems* (pp. 167–189). New York: Kluwer Academic/Plenum Press.

Costello, E. J., & Angold, A. (1988). Scales to assess child and adolescent depression: Checklists, screens, and nets. *Journal of the American Academy of Child & Adolescent Psychiatry, 27,* 726–737.

Costello, E. J., Angold, A., March, J., & Fairbank, J. (1998). Life events and posttraumatic stress: The development of a new measure for children and adolescents. *Psychological Medicine, 28,* 1275–1288.

Costello, E. J., Costello, A. J., Edelbrock, C., Burns, B. J., Dulcan, M. K., Brent, D., et al. (1988). Psychiatric disorders in pediatric primary care: Prevalence and risk factors. *Archives of General Psychiatry, 45,* 1107–1116.

Costello, E. J., Erkanli, A., Fairbank, J. A., & Angold, A. (2002). The prevalence of potentially traumatic events in childhood and adolescence. *Journal of Traumatic Stress, 15,* 91–112.

Coster, W. J., & Cicchetti, D. (1993). Research in the communicative development of maltreated children: Clinical implications. *Topics in Language Disorders, 13,* 25–38.

Coster, W. J., Gersten, M. S., Beeghly, M., & Cicchetti, D. (1989). Communicative functioning in maltreated toddlers. *Developmental Psychology, 25,* 777–793.

Council for Exceptional Children. (1990). *Children with communication disorders*. Retrieved August 23, 2007, from http://www.thememoryhole.org/edu/eric/ed321504.html (ERIC Digest E470, revised 419)

Coy v. Iowa, 487 U.S. 1012 (1988).

Craig v. State, 76 Md.App. 250, 544 A.2d 784 (Md. Ct. Spec. App. 1988).

Craig v. State, 316 Md. 551, 560 A.2d 1120 (Md. 1989).

Craig v. State, 322 Md. 418, 588 A.2d 328 (Md. 1991).

Craighead, W. E., Smucker, M. R., Craighead, L. W., & Ilardi, S. S. (1998). Factor analysis of the Children's Depression Inventory in a community sample. *Psychological Assessment, 10,* 156–165.

Crawford, E., & Bull, R. (2006a). Child witness support and preparation: Are parents/caregivers ignored? *Child Abuse Review, 15,* 243–256.

Crawford, E., & Bull, R. (2006b). Teenagers' difficulties with key words regarding the criminal court process. *Psychology, Crime & Law, 12,* 653–667.

Crawford v. Washington, 541 U.S. 36 (2004).

Cromer, L., Stevens, C., DePrince, A. P., & Pears, K. (2006). The relationship between executive attention and dissociation in children. *Journal of Trauma & Dissociation, 7,* 135–143.

Cross, M. (1999). Lost for words. *Child & Family Social Work, 4,* 249–257.

Cross, T. P., Finkelhor, D., & Ormrod, R. (2005). Police involvement in child protective services investigations: Literature review and secondary data analysis. *Child Maltreatment, 10,* 224–244.

Crowe, M., Ward, N., Dunnachie, B., & Roberts, M. (2006). Characteristics of adolescent depression. *International Journal of Mental Health Nursing, 15,* 10–15.

Crundwell, R. M. A. (2006). Identifying and teaching children with selective mutism. *Teaching Exceptional Children, 38,* 48–54.

Daigneault, I., Tourigny, M., & Hébert, M. (2006). Self-attributions of blame in sexually abused adolescents: A mediational model. *Journal of Traumatic Stress, 19,* 153–157.

Daleiden, E., Chorpita, B. F., & Lu, W. (2000). Assessment of tripartite factors of emotion in children and adolescents: II. Concurrent validity of the affect and arousal scales for children. *Journal of Psychopathology and Behavioral Assessment, 22,* 161–182.

Dalenberg, C. J., & Palesh, O. G. (2004). Relationship between child abuse history, trauma, and dissociation in Russian college students. *Child Abuse & Neglect, 28,* 461–474.

Dalgleish, T., Meiser-Stedman, R., & Smith, P. (2005). Cognitive aspects of posttraumatic stress reactions and their treatment in children and adolescents: An empirical review and some recommendations. *Behavioural and Cognitive Psychotherapy, 33,* 459–486.

Dana, R. H. (2001). Clinical diagnosis of multicultural populations in the United States. In L. A. Suzuki, J. G. Ponterotto, & P. J. Meller (Eds.), *Handbook of multicultural assessment: Clinical, psychological, and educational applications* (2nd ed., pp. 101–131) [Electronic resource]. San Francisco: Jossey-Bass.

Dana, R. H. (2005). *Multicultural assessment: Principles, applications and examples.* Mahwah, NJ: Erlbaum.

Danielson, C. K., de Arellano, M. A., & Kilpatrick, D. G. (2005). Child maltreatment in depressed adolescents: Differences in symptomatology based on history of abuse. *Child Maltreatment, 10,* 37–48.

Danner v. Kentucky, 525 U.S. 1010 (1998).

Davies, G. (1999). The impact of television on the presentation and reception of children's testimony. *International Journal of Law and Psychiatry, 22,* 241–256.

Davies, G., & Noon, E. (1991). *An evaluation of the live link for child witnesses.* London: A report commissioned and published by the Home Office.

Davies, G., & Noon, E. (1993). Video links: Their impact on child witness trials. *Issues in Criminological & Legal Psychology, 20, 22–26.*

Davies, G., & Westcott, H. L. (1995). The child witness in the courtroom: Empowerment or protection? In M. S. Zaragoza, J. R. Graham, G. C. N. Hall, R. Hirschman, & Y. S. Ben-Porath (Eds.), *Memory and testimony in the child witness* (pp. 199–213). Thousand Oaks, CA: Sage.

Davies, G., Wilson, C., Mitchell, R., & Milsom, J. (1995). *Videotaping children's evidence: An evaluation.* London: Home Office.

Davis, G., Hoyano, L., Keenan, C., Maitland, L., & Morgan, R. (1999). *An assessment of the admissibility and sufficiency of evidence in child abuse prosecutions. A Report for the Home Office by the Department of Law, University of Bristol.* London: Home Office, Information and Publications Group, Research Development and Statistics Directorate.

Davis, S. L., & Bottoms, B. L. (2002). The effects of social support on the accuracy of children's reports: Implications for the forensic interview. In M. L. Eisen, J. A. Quas, & G. S. Goodman (Eds.), *Memory and suggestibility in the forensic interview* (pp. 437–457). Mahwah, NJ: Erlbaum.

Davis v. Washington, 547 U.S. 813, 126 S. Ct. 2266, 165 L. Ed. 2d 224 (2006).

Daviss, W. B., Birmaher, B., Melhem, N. A., Axelson, D. A., Michaels, S. M., & Brent, D. A. (2006). Criterion validity of the Mood and Feelings Questionnaire for depressive episodes in clinic and non-clinic subjects. *Journal of Child Psychology and Psychiatry, 47,* 927–934.

Dawes, R. M., Faust, D., & Meehl, P. E. (1989). Clinical versus actuarial judgment. *Science, 243,* 1668–1674.

De Los Reyes, A., & Kazdin, A. E. (2005). Informant discrepancies in the assessment of childhood psychopathology: A critical review, theoretical framework, and recommendations for further study. *Psychological Bulletin, 131,* 483–509.

DeBellis, M. D. (1997). Posttraumatic stress disorder and acute stress disorder. In R. T. Ammerman & M. Herson (Eds.), *Handbook of prevention and treatment with children and adolescents: Intervention in the real world context* (pp. 455–494). New York: Guilford Press.

DeBellis, M. D., Keshavan, M. S., Clark, D. B., Casey, B. J., Giedd, J. N., Boring, A. M., et al. (1999). Developmental traumatology: II. Brain development. *Biological Psychiatry, 45,* 1271–1284.

DeBellis, M. D., Keshavan, M. S., Shifflett, H., Beers, S. R., Hall, J., & Moritz, G. (2002). Brain structures in pediatric maltreatment-related posttraumatic stress disorder: A sociodemographically matched study. *Biological Psychiatry, 52,* 1066–1078.

Del. Code Ann. tit. 11, § 3513 (2007).

Delahanty, D. L., Nugent, N. R., Christopher, N. C., & Walsh, M. (2005). Initial urinary epinephrine and cortisol levels predict acute PTSD symptoms in child trauma victims. *Psychoneuroendocrinology, 30,* 121–128.

Dell, P. F. (2001). Why the diagnostic criteria for dissociative identity disorder should be changed. *Journal of Trauma & Dissociation, 2,* 7–37.

Dell, P. F. (2006). The multidimensional inventory of dissociation (MID): A comprehensive measure of pathological dissociation. *Journal of Trauma & Dissociation, 7,* 77–106.

Derogatis, L. (1993). *Brief Symptom Inventory: Administration, scoring and procedures manual.* Minneapolis, MN: National Computer Systems.

Deters, P. B., Novins, D. K., Fickenscher, A., & Beals, J. (2006). Trauma and posttraumatic Stress Disorder symptomatology: Patterns among American Indian adolescents in substance abuse treatment. *American Journal of Orthopsychiatry, 7,* 335–345.

DeThorne, L. S., Hart, S. A., Petrill, S. A., Deater-Deckard, K., Thompson, L. A., Schatschneider, C., & Davison, M. D. (2006). Children's history of speech-language difficulties: Genetic influences and associations with reading-related measures. *Journal of Speech, Language, and Hearing Research, 49,* 1280–1293.

Dezwirek-Sas, L. (1992). Empowering child witnesses for sexual abuse prosecution. In H. Dent & R. Flin (Eds.), *Children as witnesses* (pp. 181–200). Chichester, England: Wiley.

Diamanduros, T. D. (2004). Traumatic stress symptomatology in sexually abused boys. *Dissertation Abstracts International, 65* (03), 1542. (UMI No. 3124944)

Dickstein, L. J. (2002). Domestic abuse as a risk factor for children and youth. In D. H. Schetky & E. P. Benedek (Eds.), *Principles and practice of child and adolescent forensic psychiatry* (pp. 205–212). Washington, DC: American Psychiatric Publishing.

Dion, K. K. (2006). On the development of identity: Perspectives from immigrant families. In R. Mahalingam (Ed.), *Cultural psychology of immigrants* (pp. 299–314). Mahwah, NJ: Erlbaum.

Diseth, T. H. (2006). Dissociation following traumatic medical treatment procedures in childhood: A longitudinal follow-up. *Development and Psychopathology, 18,* 233–251.

Dockrell, J. E. (2004). How can studies of memory and language enhance the authenticity, validity and reliability of interviews? *British Journal of Learning Disabilities, 32,* 161–165.

Doerfler, L. A., Connor, D. F., Volungis, A. M., & Toscano, P. F. (2007). Panic disorder in clinically referred children and adolescents. *Child Psychiatry and Human Development, 38,* 57–71.

Dow, S. P., Sonies, B. C., Scheib, D., Moss, S. E., & Leonard, H. L. (1995). Practical guidelines for the assessment and treatment of selective mutism. *Journal of the American Academy of Child & Adolescent Psychiatry, 34,* 836–845.

Downs, D. A. (Ed.). (1996). *More than victims: Battered women, the syndrome society, and the law.* Chicago: University of Chicago Press.

Dozois, D. J. A., & Covin, R. (2004). The Beck Depression Inventory-II (BDI-II), Beck Hopelessness Scale (BHS), and Beck Scale for Suicide Ideation (BSS). In M. Hersen (Series Ed.), M. J. Hilsenroth, & D. L. Segal (Vol. Eds.), *Comprehensive handbook of psychological assessment: Vol. 2. Personality Assessment* (pp. 50–69). New York: Wiley.

Draijer, N., & Langeland, W. (1999). Childhood trauma and perceived parental dysfunction in the etiology of dissociative symptoms in psychiatric inpatients. *American Journal of Psychiatry, 156*, 379–385.

Drake, E. B., Bush, S. F., & van Gorp, W. G. (2001). Evaluation and assessment of PTSD in children and adolescents. In E. Spencer (Ed.), *PTSD in children and adolescents* (pp. 1–31). Washington, DC: American Psychiatric Publishing.

Dubner, A. E., & Motta, R. W. (1999). Sexually and physically abused foster care children and posttraumatic stress disorder. *Journal of Consulting & Clinical Psychology, 67*, 367–373.

Dunn, L. M., & Dunn, L. (1997). *Peabody Picture Vocabulary Test* (3rd ed.). Circle Pines, MN: American Guidance Service.

Dykman, R. A., McPherson, B., Ackerman, P. T., Newton, J. E. O., Mooney, D. M., Wherry, J., et al. (1997). Internalizing and externalizing characteristics of sexually and/or physically abused children. *Integrative Physiological & Behavioral Science, 32*, 62–83.

Dyregrov, A., & Yule, W. (2006). A review of PTSD in children. *Child and Adolescent Mental Health, 11*, 176–184.

Dziech, B. W., & Schudson, C. B. (1991). *On trial: America's courts and their treatment of sexually abused children* (2nd ed.). Boston: Beacon Press.

Eaton, T. E., Ball, P. J., & O'Callaghan, M. G. (2001). Child-witness and defendant credibility: Child evidence presentation mode and judicial instructions. *Journal of Applied Social Psychology, 31*, 1849–1858.

Edelbrock, C., Costello, A. J., Dulcan, M. K., Conover, N. C., & Kala, R. (1986). Parent–child agreement on child psychiatric symptoms assessed via structured interview. *Journal of Child Psychology and Psychiatry, 27*, 181–190.

Edelson, J. L. (1999). The overlap between child maltreatment and woman battering. *Violence Against Woman, 5*, 134–154.

Edelstein, R. S., Goodman, G. S., Ghetti, S., Alexander, K. W., Quas, J. A., Redlich, A. D., et al. (2002). Child witnesses' experiences post-court: Effects of legal involvement. In H. L. Westcott, G. M. Davies, & R. H. C. Bull (Eds.), *Children's testimony: A handbook of psychological research and forensic practice* (pp. 261–277). West Sussex, England: Wiley.

Edwards, L. P., & Sagatun, I. J. (1995). Who speaks for the child? Symposium: Domestic violence, child abuse, and the law. *University of Chicago Law School Roundtable, 2*, 67–94.

Egeland, B. (1989, October). *A longitudinal study of high risk families: Issues and findings.* Paper presented at the Research Forum on Issues in the Longitudinal Study of Child Maltreatment, Toronto, Ontario, Canada.

Egeland, B. (1997). Mediators of the effects of child maltreatment on developmental adaptation in adolescence. In D. Cicchetti & S. L. Toth (Eds.), *Developmental perspectives on trauma: Theory, research, and intervention* (pp. 403–434). Rochester, NY: University of Rochester Press.

Egger, H. L., & Angold, A. (2004). The Preschool Age Psychiatric Assessment (PAPA): A structured parent interview for diagnosing psychiatric disorders in preschool children. In R. DelCarmen-Wiggins & A. Carter (Eds.), *Handbook of infant, toddler, and preschool mental health assessment* (pp. 223–243). New York: Oxford University Press.

Egger, H. L., Ascher, B., & Angold, A. (1999). *The Preschool Age Psychiatric Assessment (PAPA).* Durham, NC: Duke University Medical Center.

Egger, H. L., Erkanli, A., & Keeler, G. (2006). The test–retest reliability of the Preschool Age Psychiatric Assessment. *Journal of the American Academy of Child & Adolescent Psychiatry, 45,* 538–549.

18 U.S.C.S. § 3509(b)(1) (2007).

18 U.S.C.S. § 3509(b)(1)(B)(ii) (2007).

18 U.S.C.S. § 3509(b)(2) (2007).

18 U.S.C.S. § 3509(b)(2)(B)(i)(II) (2007).

Elbogen, E. B. (2002). The process of violence risk assessment: A review of descriptive research. *Aggression and Violent Behavior, 7,* 591–604.

Elders, M. J., & Albert, A. E. (1998). Adolescent pregnancy and sexual abuse. *JAMA, 280,* 648–649.

Epkins, C. C. (2002). A comparison of two self-report measures of children's social anxiety in clinic and community samples. *Journal of Clinical Child and Adolescent Psychology, 31,* 69–79.

Esam, B. (2002). Young witnesses: Still no justice. In H. L. Westcott, G. M. Davies, & R. H. C. Bull (Eds.), *Children's testimony: A handbook of psychological research and forensic practice* (pp. 309–323). West Sussex, England: Wiley.

Essau, C. A. (2007). Course and outcome of major depressive disorder in non-referred adolescents. *Journal of Affective Disorders, 99,* 191–201.

Eth, S., & Pynoos, R. S. (1985). *Post-traumatic stress disorder in children.* Washington, DC: American Psychiatric Publishing.

Evers-Szostak, M., & Sanders, S. (1992). The Children's Perceptual Alteration Scale (CPAS): A measure of children's dissociation. *Dissociation, 5,* 91–97.

Everson, M. D., & Boat, B. W. (1989). False allegations of sexual abuse by children and adolescents. *Journal of the American Academy of Child & Adolescent Psychiatry, 28,* 230–240.

Everson, M. D., & Boat, B. W. (1994). Putting the anatomical doll controversy in perspective: An examination of the major uses and criticisms of the dolls in child sexual abuse evaluations. *Child Abuse & Neglect, 18,* 113–129.

Faller, K. C. (2003). *Understanding and assessing child sexual maltreatment* (2nd ed.). Thousand Oaks, CA: Sage.

Famularo, R., Fenton, T., Kinscherff, R., & Augustyn, M. (1996). Psychiatric co-morbidity in childhood posttraumatic stress disorder. *Child Abuse & Neglect, 20,* 953–961.

Famularo, R., Fenton, T., Kinscherff, R., Ayoub, C., & Barnum, R. (1994). Maternal and child posttraumatic stress disorder in cases of child maltreatment. *Child Abuse & Neglect, 18,* 27–36.

Fantuzzo, J. W., & Mohr, W. K. (1999). Prevalence and effects of child exposure to domestic violence. *The Future of Children, 9,* 21–32.

Farley, M., & Keaney, J. C. (1997). Physical symptoms, somatization, and dissociation in women survivors of childhood sexual assault. *Women & Health, 25,* 33–45.

Farrington, A., Waller, G., Smerden, J., & Faupel, A. W. (2001). The Adolescent Dissociative Experience Scale: Psychometric properties and differences in scores across age groups. *Journal of Nervous and Mental Disorders, 189,* 722–727.

Fed. R. Evid. 611(a).

Fed. R. Evid. 611(c).

Fed. R. Evid. 801(c).

Fed. R. Evid. 803.

Fed. R. Evid. 804.

Fed. R. Evid. 807.

Fed. R. Evid. 1101.

Feeny, N. C., Foa, E. B., Treadwell, K. R. H., & March, J. (2004). Posttraumatic stress disorder in youth: A critical review of the cognitive and behavioral treatment outcome literature. *Professional Psychology: Research and Practice, 35,* 466–476.

Feigenson, N., & Dunn, M. A. (2003). New visual technologies in court: Directions for research. *Law and Human Behavior, 27,* 109–126.

Feindler, E. L., Rathus, J. H., & Silver, L. B. (2003). *Assessment of family violence: A handbook for researchers and practitioners.* Washington, DC: American Psychological Association.

Feinstein, C., & Phillips, J. M. (2006). Developmental disorders of communication, motor skills, and learning. In M. K. Dulcan & J. M. Wiener (Eds.), *Essentials of child and adolescent psychiatry* (pp. 203–229). Washington, DC: American Psychiatric Publishing.

Fenson, L., Dale, P. S., Reznick, J. S., Thai, D. J., Bates, E., Hartung, J. P., et al. (1993). *The MacArthur Communicative Development Inventories: User's guide and technical manual.* San Diego, CA: Singular.

Ferdinand, R. F. (2007). Predicting anxiety diagnoses with the Youth Self-Report, *Depression and Anxiety, 24,* 32–40.

Ferdinand, R. F. (2007). Validity of the CBCL/YSR *DSM–IV* scales Anxiety Problems and Affective Problems. *Journal of Anxiety Disorders, 22,* 126–134.

Ferdinand, R. F., Dieleman, G., Ormel, J., & Verhulst, F. C. (2007). Homotypic versus heterotypic continuity of anxiety symptoms in young adolescents: Evidence for distinctions between *DSM–IV* subtypes. *Journal of Abnormal Child Psychology, 35,* 325–333.

Ferdinand, R. F., van Lang, N. D. J., Ormel, J., & Verhulst, F. C. (2006). No distinctions between different types of anxiety symptoms in pre-adolescents from the general population. *Anxiety Disorders, 20,* 207–221.

Fergusson, D. M., Horwood, L. J., & Lynskey, M. T. (1996). Childhood sexual abuse and psychiatric disorder in young adulthood: II. Psychiatric outcomes of childhood sexual abuse. *Journal of the American Academy of Child & Adolescent Psychiatry, 35,* 1365–1374.

Filbert, B. G. (1997). Disorder and syndrome evidence. In R. G. Lande & D. T. Armitage (Eds.), *Principles and practice of military forensic psychiatry* (pp. 187–198). Springfield, IL: Charles C Thomas.

Finkelhor, D. (1992). Preface. In J. N. Briere (Ed.), *Child abuse trauma: Theory and treatment of the lasting effects*. Newbury Park, CA: Sage.

Finkelhor, D., & Browne, A. (1985). The traumatic impact of child sexual abuse: A conceptualization. *American Journal of Orthopsychiatry, 55,* 530–541.

Finkelhor, D., Hotaling, G., Lewis, I. A., & Smith, C. (1989). Sexual abuse in a national study of adult men and women: Prevalence, characteristics, and risk factors. *Child Abuse & Neglect, 14,* 19–28.

Finkelhor, D., & Kendall-Tackett, K. (1997). A developmental perspective on the childhood impact of crime, abuse, and violent victimization. In D. Cicchetti & S. Toth (Eds.), *Rochester symposium on developmental psychopathology and developmental perspectives on trauma* (pp. 1–32). Rochester, NY: University of Rochester Press.

Finkelhor, D., Ormrod, R. K., & Turner, H. A. (2007). Poly-victimization: A neglected component in child victimization. *Child Abuse & Neglect, 31,* 7–26.

Finkelhor, D., & Putnam, C. (2004). Protecting the privacy of child crime victims. *Update, 17*(2). Retrieved August 23, 2007, from http://www.unh.edu/ccrc/pdf/CV98-APRI.pdf

Finnegan, M. J. (2000). Creating and administering a kids court program. *APRI Update, 13*(5). Retrieved August 23, 2007, from http://www.ndaa-apri.org/publications/newsletters/update_volume_13_number_5_2000.html

Finzi, R., Har-Even, D., Shnit, D., & Weizman, A. (2002). Psychosocial characterization of physically abused children from low socioeconomic households in comparison to neglected and nonmaltreated children. *Journal of Child and Family Studies, 11,* 441–453.

Fisher, C. B. (1995). The American Psychological Association's ethics code and the validation of sexual abuse in day-care settings. *Psychology, Public Policy, and Law, 1,* 461–468.

Fisher, C. B., & Whiting, K. A. (1998). How valid are child sexual abuse validations? In S. J. Ceci & H. Hembrooke (Eds.), *Expert witnesses in child abuse cases: What can and should be said in court* (pp. 159–184). Washington, DC: American Psychological Association.

Fisher, R. P., Brennan, K. H., & McCauley, M. R. (2002). The cognitive interview methods to enhance eyewitness recall. In M. L. Eisen, J. A. Quas, & G. S. Goodman (Eds.), *Memory and suggestibility in the forensic interview* (pp. 265–286). Mahwah, NJ: Erlbaum.

Fitzpatrick, K. M. (1993). Exposure to violence and presence of depression among low-income African-American youth. *Journal of Consulting and Clinical Psychology, 61,* 528–531.

Fivush, R. (2002). The development of autobiographical memory. In H. L. Westcott, G. M. Davies, & R. H. C. Bull (Eds.), *Children's testimony: A handbook of psychological research and forensic practice* (pp. 55–68). West Sussex, England: Wiley.

Fla. Stat. ch. 90.612 (2007).

Fla. Stat. ch. 92.54 (2007).

Fla. Stat. ch. 918.16 (2007).

Fletcher, K. E. (1996). Childhood posttraumatic stress disorder. In E. J. Mash & R. A. Barkley (Eds.), *Child psychopathology* (pp. 242–276). New York: Guilford Press.

Fletcher, K. E. (2005). *Scales for Assessing Posttraumatic Responses of Children.* Retrieved June 5, 2007, from http://users.umassmed.edu/Kenneth.Fletcher/scales.html

Flin, R. (1990). Child witnesses in criminal courts. *Children & Society, 4,* 264–283.

Flin, R. H. (1993). Hearing and testing children's evidence: The British experience. In G. Goodman & B. Bottoms (Eds.), *Child victims, child witnesses* (pp. 279–300). New York: Guilford Press.

Flin, R. H., Bull, R., Boon, J., & Knox, A. (1992). *Child witnesses in Scottish criminal prosecutions.* Report to the Scottish Home and Health Department. Glasgow: Glasgow College of Technology.

Flin, R. H., Stevenson, Y., & Davies, G. M. (1989) Children's knowledge of legal proceedings. *British Journal of Psychology, 80,* 285–297.

Flisher, A. J., Kramer, R. A., Hoven, C. W., & Greenwald, S. (1997). Psychosocial characteristics of physically abused children and adolescents. *Journal of the American Academy of Child & Adolescent Psychiatry, 36,* 123–131.

Foa, E. B., Riggs, D. S., Dancu, C. V., & Rothbaum, B. O. (1993). Reliability and validity of a brief instrument for assessing post-traumatic stress disorder. *Journal of Traumatic Stress, 6,* 459–473.

Foa, E. B., Treadwell, K., Johnson, K., & Feeny, N. (2001). Child PTSD Symptom Scale (CPSS): Validation of a measure for children with PTSD. *Journal of Clinical Child Psychology, 30,* 376–384.

Fonseca, A. C., & Perrin, S. (2001). Clinical phenomenology, classification and assessment of anxiety disorders in children and adolescents. In W. K. Silverman & P. D. A. Treffers (Eds.), *Anxiety disorders in children and adolescents: Research, assessment and intervention* (pp. 126–158). Cambridge, England: Cambridge University Press.

Fontes, L. A. (2005). *Child abuse and culture: Working with diverse families.* New York: Guilford Press.

42 Pa. Cons. Stat. § 5983 (2006).

42 Pa. Cons. Stat. § 5984.1 (2006).

Fox, L., Long, S. H., & Anglois, A. (1988). Patterns of language comprehension deficit in abused and neglected children. *Journal of Speech and Hearing Disorders, 53,* 239–244.

Foy, D. W., Madvig, B. T., Pynoos, R. S., & Camilleri, A. J. (1996). Etiologic factors in the development of posttraumatic stress disorder in children and adolescents. *Journal of School Psychology, 34,* 133–145.

Frederick, C., Pynoos, R., & Nader, K. (1992). *Childhood PTS Reaction Index (CPTS–RI)*. (Available from K. Nader, P.O. Box 2251, Laguna Hills, CA 92654)

Freeman, L. N., Mokros, H., & Poznanski, E. (1993). Violent events reported by normal urban school-aged children: Characteristics and depression correlates. *Journal of the American Academy of Child & Adolescent Psychiatry, 32,* 419–423.

Friedman, M. J., Foa, E. B., & Charney, D. S. (Eds.). (2003). Editorial: Toward evidence-based early interventions for acutely traumatized adults and children. *Biological Psychiatry, 53,* 765–768.

Friedman, R. D. (2002). Children as victims and witnesses in the criminal trial process: The conundrum of children, confrontation, and hearsay. *Law and Contemporary Problems, 65,* 243–255.

Friedman, R. L. (2002). The Confrontation Clause in search of a paradigm: Has public policy trumped the Constitution? *Pace Law Review, 22,* 455–508.

Friedrich, W. N. (1995). Evaluation and treatment: The clinical use of the Child Sexual Behavior Inventory: Commonly asked questions. *American Professional Society on the Abuse of Children (APSAC) Advisor, 8,* 1, 17–20.

Friedrich, W. N. (2002). *Psychological assessment of sexually abused children and their families.* Thousand Oaks, CA: Sage.

Friedrich, W. N., Gerber, P. N., Koplin, B., Davis, M., Giese, J., Mykelbust, C., et al. (2001). Multimodal assessment of dissociation in adolescents: Inpatients and juvenile sex offenders. *Sexual Abuse: A Journal of Research and Treatment, 13,* 167–177.

Friedrich, W. N., Jaworski, T. M., Huxsahl, J. E., & Bengtson, B. S. (1997). Dissociative and sexual behaviors in children and adolescents with sexual abuse and psychiatric histories. *Journal of Interpersonal Violence, 12,* 155–171.

Ga. Code Ann. § 16–5–70 (2007).

Gabarino, J., Dubrow, N., Kostelny, K., & Pardo, C. (1998). *Children in danger: Coping with the consequences of community violence.* San Francisco: Jossey-Bass.

Garber, J., & Horowitz, J. L. (2002). Depression in children. In I. H. Gotlib & C. L. Hammen (Eds.), *Handbook of depression* (pp. 510–540). New York: Guilford Press.

Garcia, A. M., Freeman, J. B., Ale, C. M., Black, B., & Leonard, H. L. (2006). Specific phobia, panic disorder, social phobia, and selective mutism. In M. K. Dulcan & J. M. Wiener (Eds.), *Essentials of child and adolescent psychiatry* (pp. 455–477). Washington, DC: American Psychiatric Publishing.

Garcia-Lopez, L. J., Olivares, J., Hidalgo, M. D., Beidel, D. C., & Turner, S. M. (2001). Psychometric properties if the Social Phobia and Anxiety Inventory, the Social Anxiety Scale for Adolescents, the Fear of Negative Evaluation Scale, and the Social Avoidance and Distress Scale in an Adolescent Spanish-Speaking Sample. *Journal of Psychopathology and Behavioral Assessment, 23,* 51–59.

Gee, C. B. (2004). Assessment of anxiety and depression in Asian American youth. *Journal of Clinical Child and Adolescent Psychology, 33,* 269–271.

Ghetti, S., Alexander, K. W., & Goodman, G. S. (2002). Legal involvement in child sexual abuse cases: Consequences and interventions. *International Journal of Law and Psychiatry, 25*, 235–251.

Gier By & Through Gier v. Educational Serv. Unit No. 16, 845 F. Supp. 1342 (D. Neb. 1994), *aff'd*, 66 F.3d 940 (8th Cir. 1995).

Ginsburg, G. S., Riddle, M. A., & Davies, M. (2006). Somatic symptoms in children and adolescents with anxiety disorders. *Journal of the American Academy of Child & Adolescent Psychiatry, 45*, 1179–1187.

Globe Newspaper Co. v. Super. Ct., 457 U.S. 596 (1982).

Goenjian, A., Pynoos, R. S., Steinberg, A. M., Najarian, L. M., Asarnow, J. R., Karayan, I., et al. (1995). Psychiatric comorbidity in children after the 1988 earthquake in Armenia. *Journal of the American Academy of Child & Adolescent Psychiatry, 34*, 1174–1184.

Golding, J. M., Bradshaw, G. S., Dunlap, E. E., & Hodell, E. C. (2007). The impact of mock jury gender composition on deliberations and conviction rates in a child sexual assault trial. *Child Maltreatment, 12*, 182–190.

Golding, J. M., Sanchez, R. P., & Sego, S. A. (1997). The believability of hearsay testimony in a child sexual assault trial. *Law and Human Behavior, 21*, 299–326.

Goldstein, B. A., & Fabiano, L. (2007, February 13). Assessment and intervention for bilingual children with phonological disorders. *The ASHA Leader, 6–7*, 26–27, 31.

Gomes-Schwartz, B., Horowitz, J. M., & Cardarelli, A. P. (1990). *Child sexual abuse: The initial effects.* Newbury Park, CA: Sage.

Goodman, G. S., Batterman-Faunce, J. M., Schaaf, J. M., & Kenney, R. (2002). Nearly 4 years after an event: Children's eye witness memory and adult's perceptions of children's accuracy. *Child Abuse & Neglect, 26*, 849–884.

Goodman, G. S., Bottoms, B. L., Schwartz-Kenney, B., & Rudy, L. (1991). Children's memory for a stressful event: Improving children's reports. *Journal of Narrative and Life History, 1*, 69–99.

Goodman, G. S., Levine, M., & Melton, G. B. (1992). The best evidence produces the best law. *Law & Human Behavior, 16*, 244–251.

Goodman, G. S., Levine, M., Melton, G. B., & Ogden, D. W. (1991). Child witnesses and the confrontation clause: The American Psychological Association brief in *Maryland v. Craig. Law and Human Behavior, 15*, 13–29.

Goodman, G. S., & Melinder, A. (2007). Child witness research and forensic interviews of young children: A review. *Legal and Criminological Psychology, 12*, 1–19.

Goodman, G. S., Myers, J. E. B., Qin, J., Quas, J. A., Castelli, P., Redlich, A. D., et al. (2006). Hearsay versus children's testimony: Effects of truthful and deceptive statements on jurors' decisions. *Law and Human Behavior, 30*, 363–401.

Goodman, G. S., Myers, J. E. B., Qin, J., Quas, J., Shuder, M., Rogers, L., et al. (1996, March). *Effects of hearsay testimony on juror's decisions in cases involving child witnesses.* In B. L. Bottoms & M. Epstein (Chairs), *Juror decision making in child sexual abuse cases.* Symposium conducted at the biennial convention of the American Psychology and Law Society, Hilton Head, SC.

Goodman, G. S., Pyle-Taub, E., Jones, D. P. H., England, P., Port, L. K., Rudy, L., et al. (1992). Testifying in criminal court: Emotional effects on child sexual assault victims. *Monographs of the Society for Development in Child Research, 57,* (Serial No. 229, No. 5).

Goodman, G. S., Quas, J. A., Bulkley, J., & Shapiro, C. (1999). Innovations for child witnesses: A national survey. *Psychology, Public Policy, and Law, 5,* 255–281.

Goodman, G. S., Tobey, A. E., Batterman-Faunce, J. M., Orcutt, H., Thomas, S., & Shapiro, C. (1998). Face-to-face confrontation: Effects of closed-circuit technology on children's eyewitness testimony and jurors' decisions. *Law and Human Behavior, 22,* 165–203.

Graziano, A. M., DeGiovanni, I. S., & Garcia, K. (1979). Behavioral treatment of children's fears: A review. *Psychology Bulletin, 86,* 804–830.

Grearson, K. M. (2004). Proposed Uniform Child Witness Testimony Act: An impermissible abridgement of criminal defendants' rights. *Boston College Law Review, 45,* 467–498.

Greaves-Lord, K., Ferdinand, R. F., Sondeijker, F. E. P. L., Dietrich, A., Oldehinkel, A. J., Rosmalen, J. G. M., et al. (2007). Testing the tripartite model in young adolescents: Is hyperarousal specific for anxiety and not depression? *Journal of Affective Disorders, 102,* 55–63.

Greco, L. A., & Morris, T. L. (2004). Assessment. In T. L. Morris & J. S. March (Eds.), *Anxiety disorders in children and adolescents* (2nd ed., pp. 98–121). New York: Guilford Press.

Green, A. H. (1993). Child abuse, neglect and depression. In H. S. Koplewicz & E. Klass (Eds.), *Depression in children and adolescents* (pp. 55–62). Philadelphia: Harwood Academic.

Greenberg, L. R., & Gould, J. W. (2001). The treating expert: A hybrid role with firm boundaries. *Professional Psychology: Research and Practice, 32,* 469–478.

Greenberg, S. A., & Shuman, D. W. (1997). Irreconcilable conflict between therapeutic and forensic roles. *Professional Psychology: Research & Practice, 28,* 50–57.

Greenhill, L. L., Pine, D., March, J., Birmaher, B., & Riddle, M. (1998). Assessment issues in treatment research of pediatric anxiety disorders: What is working, what is not working, what is missing, and what needs improvement. *Psychopharmacology Bulletin, 34,* 155–164.

Grisso, T. (1988). *Competency to stand trial evaluations: A manual for practice.* Sarasota, FL: Professional Resource Exchange.

Grisso, T. (1998). *Forensic evaluation of juveniles.* Sarasota, FL: Professional Resource Press.

Grisso, T. (2003). *Evaluating competencies: Forensic assessments and instruments* (2nd ed.). New York: Kluwer Academic/Plenum Press.

Grisso, T., & Melton, G. B. (1987). Getting child development research to legal practitioners: Which way to the trenches? In G. B. Melton (Ed.), *Reforming the law: Impact of child development research* (pp. 146–178). New York: Guilford Press.

Grisso, T., & Underwood, L. A. (2004). *Screening and assessing mental health and substance use disorders among youth in the juvenile justice system. A resource guide for practitioners* (Report NCJ 204956). Rockville, MD: Office of Juvenile Justice and Delinquency Prevention.

Gross, S. R., & Mnookin, J. L. (2003). Expert information and expert evidence: A preliminary taxonomy. *Seton Hall Law Review, 34,* 141–189.

Grove, W. M., & Meehl, P. E. (1997). Comparative efficiency of formal (mechanical, algorithmic) and informal (subjective, impressionistic) prediction procedures: The clinical/statistical controversy. *Psychology, Public Policy, and the Law, 2,* 293–323.

Guo, Y., Nilsson, M. E., Heiligenstein, J., Wilson, M. G., & Emslie, G. (2006). An exploratory factor analysis of the Children's Depression Rating Scale—Revised. *Journal of Child and Adolescent Psychopharmacology, 16,* 482–491.

Hafemeister, T. J. (1996). Protecting child witnesses: Judicial efforts to minimize trauma and reduce evidentiary barriers. *Violence and Victims, 11,* 71–92.

Hall, S. R. (1995). *A multidisciplinary manual for the use of televised alternative procedures (videotaped interviews and videotaped and closed-circuit testimony) with victims and non-victim child witnesses.* Phoenix, AZ: Governor's Division for Children.

Halleck, S. L., Hoge, S. K., Miller, R. D., Sadoff, R. L., & Halleck, N. H. (1992). The use of psychiatric diagnosis in the legal process: Task force report of the American Psychiatric Association. *Bulletin of the American Academy of Psychiatry & Law, 20,* 481–499.

Hamlyn, B., Phelps, A., Turtle, J., & Sattar, G. (2004). *Are special measures working? Evidence from surveys of vulnerable and intimidated witnesses.* Retrieved January 20, 2008, from http://www.homeoffice.gov.uk/rds/pdfs04/hors283.pdf

Hammon v. Indiana, 546 U.S. 1088 (2006), *rev'd by* Davis v. Washington, 126 S. Ct. 2266, 165 L. Ed. 2d 224 (2006), *remanded to* Hammon v. State, 853 N.E.2d 477 (Ind. 2006).

Hankin, B. L., Abramson, L. Y., Moffitt, T. E., Silva, P. A., McGee, R., & Angell, K. E. (1998). Development of depression from preadolescence to young adulthood: Emerging gender differences in a 10-year longitudinal study. *Journal of Abnormal Psychology, 107,* 96–110.

Hankin, B. L., Mermelstein, R., & Roesch, L. (2007). Sex differences in adolescent depression: Stress exposure and reactivity models. *Child Development, 78,* 279–295.

Hanson, R. F., Saunders, B. E., Kilpatrick, D. G., Resnick, H., Crouch, J. A., & Duncan, R. (2001). Impact of childhood rape and aggravated assault on adult mental health. *American Journal of Orthopsychiatry, 71,* 108–119.

Haralambie, A. M. (1995). The role of the child's attorney in protecting the child throughout the litigation process. *North Dakota Law Review, 71,* 939–986.

Harmon, A. (2005). Child testimony via two-way closed circuit television: A new perspective on *Maryland v. Craig* in *United States v. Turning Bear* and *United States v. Bordeaux. North Carolina Journal of Law & Technology, 7,* 157–179.

Haugaard, J. J. (2004). Recognizing and treating uncommon behavioral and emotional disorders in children and adolescents who have been severely maltreated: Dissociative disorders. *Child Maltreatment, 9,* 146–153.

Haugaard, J. J. (2005). Commentary: Implications of longitudinal research with child witnesses for developmental theory, public policy, and intervention strategies. *Monographs of the Society for Research in Child Development, 70,* 129–139.

Haugaard, J., & Reppucci, N. D. (1988). *The sexual abuse of children.* San Francisco: Jossey-Bass.

Haw. R. Evid. 804(b)(6) (2007).

Hawkins, S. S., & Radcliffe, J. (2006). Current measures of PSTD for children and adolescents. *Journal of Pediatric Psychology, 31,* 420–430.

Hayes, S. H. (1997). Reactive attachment disorder: Recommendations for school counselors. *School Counselor, 44,* 353–361.

Hayward, C., Gotlib, I. H., Schraedley, P. K., & Litt, I. F. (1999). Ethnic differences in the association between pubertal status and symptoms of depression in adolescent girls. *Journal of Adolescent Health, 25,* 143–149.

Heilbrun, K. (2001). *Principles of forensic mental health assessment.* New York: Kluwer Academic/Plenum Press.

Heiman, M. L. (1992). Putting the puzzle together: Validating allegations of child sexual abuse. *Journal of Child Psychology & Psychiatry, 33,* 311–329.

Henderson, E. (2002). Persuading and controlling: The theory of cross-examination in relation to children. In H. L. Westcott, G. M. Davies, & R. H. C. Bull (Eds.), *Children's testimony: A handbook of psychological research and forensic practice* (pp. 279–293). West Sussex, England: Wiley.

Henry, J. (1997). System intervention trauma to child sexual abuse victims following disclosure. *Journal of Interpersonal Violence, 12,* 499–512.

Henry, J. (1999). Videotaping child disclosure interviews: Exploratory study of children's experiences and perceptions. *Journal of Child Sexual Abuse, 8,* 35–49.

Henry, L. A., & Gudjonsson, G. H. (2007). Individual and developmental differences in eyewitness recall and suggestibility in children with intellectual disabilities. *Applied Cognitive Psychology, 21,* 361–381.

Herjanic, B., & Campbell, W. (1977). Differentiating psychiatrically disturbed children on the basis of a structured interview. *Journal of Abnormal Child Psychology, 5,* 127–134.

Herman, J. (2003). The mental health of crime victims: Impact of legal intervention. *Journal of Traumatic Stress, 16,* 159–166.

Herman, J., & Hirschman, L. (1981). *Father–daughter incest.* Cambridge, MA: Harvard University Press.

Hershkowitz, I., Fisher, S., Lamb, M. E., & Horowitz, D. (2007). Improving credibility assessment in child sexual abuse allegations: The role of the NICHD investigative interview protocol. *Child Abuse & Neglect, 31,* 99–110.

Hester, E. J. (1996). Narratives of young African American children. In A. G. Kamhi, K. E. Pollock, & J. L. Harris (Eds.), *Communication development and disorders in African American children: Research, assessment, and intervention* (pp. 227–245). Baltimore: Brookes Publishing.

Hewitt, S. K. (1999). *Assessing allegations of sexual abuse in preschool children: Understanding small voices.* Thousand Oaks, CA: Sage.

Higa, C. K., Fernandez, S. N., Nakamura, B. J., Chorpita, B. F., & Daleiden, E. L. (2006). Parental assessment of childhood social phobia: Psychometric properties of the Social Phobia and Anxiety Inventory for Children–Parent Report. *Journal of Clinical Child and Adolescent Psychology, 35,* 590–597.

Hill, P. E., & Hill, S. M. (1987). Videotaping children's testimony: An empirical view. *Michigan Law Review, 85,* 809–833.

Hiltz, B., & Bauer, G. (2003). Drawings in forensic interviews of children. *Update, 16*(3). Retrieved August 24, 2007, from http://www.ndaa-apri.org/publications/newsletters/update_volume_16_number_3_2003.html

Hjemdal, O., Friborg, O., Stiles, T. C., Martinussen, M., & Rosenvinge, J. H. (2006). A new scale for adolescent resilience: Grasping the central protective resources behind healthy development. *Measurement and Evaluation in Counseling and Development, 39,* 84–96.

Hobson, C. L. (1990). Appointed counsel to protect the child victim's rights. *Pacific Law Journal, 21,* 691–730

Hochheiser v. Superior Court, 161 Cal. App. 3d 777, 208 Cal Rptr 273 (1984).

Hofflich, S. A., Hughes, A. A., & Kendall, P. C. (2006). Somatic complaints and childhood anxiety disorders. *International Journal of Clinical and Health Psychology, 6,* 229–242.

Holmes, L. S., & Finnegan, M. J. (2002). The use of anatomical diagrams in child sexual abuse forensic interviews. *Update, 15*(5). Retrieved August 25, 2007, from http://www.ndaa.org/publications/newsletters/update_volume_15_number_5_2002.html

Hornstein, N. L. (1996). Dissociative disorders in children and adolescents. In L. K. Michelson & W. J. Ray (Eds.), *Handbook of dissociation: Theoretical, empirical, and clinical perspectives* (pp. 139–162). New York: Plenum Press.

Hoverstein v. Iowa, 998 F.2d 614 (8th Cir. 1993).

Howell, P. (2007). Signs of developmental stuttering up to age eight and at 12 plus. *Clinical Psychology Review, 27,* 287–306.

Hsu, L., & Alden, L. (2007). Social anxiety in Chinese- and European-heritage students: The effect of assessment format and judgments of impairment. *Behavior Therapy, 38,* 120–131.

Hudson, D. L. (2004, April 30). New clout for confrontation clause: Citing U.S. Supreme Court, Maryland court overturns child sex-abuse conviction. *ABA Journal eReport.* Retrieved February 8, 2008, from http://www.abajournal.com/contact

Hyman, I., Berna, J., Snook, P., DuCette, J., & Kohr, M. (2002). *Manual for the My Worst Experience Scales.* Los Angeles, CA: Western Psychological Services.

Ickovics, J. R., Meade, C. S., Kershaw, T. S., Milan, S., Lewis, J. B., & Ethier, K. A. (2006). Urban teens: Trauma, posttraumatic growth, and emotional distress among female adolescents [Special issue]. *Journal of Consulting and Clinical Psychology, 74,* 841–850.

Idaho Code § 9–1801 (2007).

Idaho v. Wright, 497 U.S. 805 (1990).

Imhoff, M. C., & Baker-Ward, L. (1999). Preschoolers' suggestibility: Effects of developmentally appropriate language and interviewer supportiveness. *Applied Developmental Psychology, 20,* 407–429.

In re Amber B., 191 Cal. App. 3d 682, 236 Cal. Rptr. 623 (Cal. Ct. App. 1987).

In re Rolandis G., 352 Ill. App. 3d 776, 817 N.E.2d 183 (Ill. App. Ct. 2004).

In re Stradford, 119 N.C. App. 654, 460 S.E.2d 173 (N.C. Ct. App. 1995).

Ind. Code Ann. § 35-37-4-6 (2007).

Ind. Code Ann. § 35-37-4-8 (2007).

International Society for the Study of Dissociation. (2004). Guidelines for the evaluation and treatment of dissociative symptoms in children and adolescents. *Journal of Trauma & Dissociation, 5,* 119–150. Retrieved August 26, 2007, from http://www.isst-d.org/education/ChildGuidelines-ISSTD-2003.pdf

International Society for the Study of Dissociation. (2005). Guidelines for treating dissociative identity disorder in adults. *Journal of Trauma & Dissociation, 6,* 69–149.

Iowa Code § 915.37 (2006).

Iowa Code § 915.38 (2006).

Ivarsson, T. (2006). Normative data for the Multidimensional Anxiety Scale for Children (MASC) in Swedish adolescents. *Nordic Journal of Psychiatry, 60,* 107–113.

Jackson v. State, 290 Ark. 375, 720 S.W.2d 282 (Ark. 1986).

Jackson-Maldonado, D., Thal, D. J., Fenson, L., Marchman, V.A., Newton, T., & Conboy, B. (2003). *MacArthur Inventarios del Desarrollo de Habilidades Comunicativas: User's guide and technical manual.* Baltimore: Brookes Publishing.

Jaycox, L. H., Stein, B. D., Kataoka, S. H., Wong, M., Fink, A., Escudero, P., et al. (2002). Violence exposure, posttraumatic stress disorder, and depressive symptoms among recent immigrant school children. *Journal of the American Academy of Child & Adolescent Psychiatry, 41,* 1104–1110.

Jehu, D. (1988). *Beyond sexual abuse: Therapy with women who were childhood victims.* Chichester, England: Wiley.

Jensen, B. J., & Haynes, S. N. (1986). Self-report questionnaires and inventories. In A. R. Ciminero, K. S. Calhoun, & H. E. Adam (Eds.), *Handbook of behavioral assessment* (2nd ed., pp. 150–175). New York: Wiley.

Johnson, R. M., Kotch, J. B., Catellier, D. J., Winsor, J. R., Dufort, V., Hunter, W., et al. (2002). Adverse behavioral and emotional outcomes from child abuse and witnessed violence. *Child Maltreatment, 7,* 179–186.

Jones, D., & McGraw, E. M. (1987). Reliable and fictitious accounts of sexual abuse to children. *Journal of Interpersonal Violence, 2,* 27–45.

Jones, J. M. (2007). Exposure to chronic community violence: Resilience in African American children. *Journal of Black Psychology, 33,* 125–149.

Jones, L., & Finkelhor, D. (2001). *The decline of sexual abuse cases.* Retrieved August 26, 2007, from http://www.ncjrs.org/pdffiles1/ojjdp/184741.pdf

Jones, L. M., Cross, T. P., Walsh, W. A., & Simone, M. (2005). Criminal investigations of child abuse: The research behind "best practices." *Trauma, Violence, & Abuse, 6,* 254–268.

Joseph, P. (1999). Selective mutism—The child who doesn't speak at school. *Pediatrics, 104,* 308–309.

Kan. Stat. Ann. § 22-3433 (2006).

Kan. Stat. Ann. § 22-3434 (2006).

Kan. Stat. Ann. § 60-460(dd) (2006).

Kaplan, S. J., Pelcovitz, D., & Labruna, V. (1999). Child and adolescent abuse and neglect research: A review of the past 10 years. Part I: Physical and emotional abuse and neglect. *Journal of the American Academy of Child & Adolescent Psychiatry, 38,* 1214–1222.

Kaplan, S. J., Pelcovitz, D., Salzinger, S., & Mandel, F. (1997). Adolescent physical abuse and suicide attempts. *Journal of the American Academy of Child & Adolescent Psychiatry, 36,* 799–808.

Kaplow, J. B., Dodge, K. A., Amaya-Jackson, L., & Saxe, G. N. (2005). Pathways to PTSD: Part II. Sexually abused children. *American Journal of Psychiatry, 162,* 1305–1310.

Kaplow, J. B., Saxe, G. N., Putnam, F. W., Pynoos, R. S., & Lieberman, A. F. (2006). The long-term consequences of early childhood trauma: A case study and discussion. *Psychiatry, 69,* 362–375.

Kaplow, J. B., & Widom, C. S. (2007). Age of onset of child maltreatment predicts long-term mental health outcomes. *Journal of Abnormal Psychology, 116,* 176–187.

Kaslow, N. J., Morris, M. K., & Rehm, L. P. (1998). Childhood depression. In R. J. Morris & T. R. Kratochwill, *The practice of child therapy* (3rd ed., pp. 48–90). Boston: Allyn & Bacon.

Kassam-Adams, N., & Winston, F. K. (2004). Predicting child PTSD: The relationship between acute stress disorder and PTSD in injured children. *Journal of the American Academy of Child & Adolescent Psychiatry, 43,* 403–411.

Kaufman, J., Birmaher, B., Brent, D., Rao, U., Flynn, C., Moreci, P., et al. (1997). Schedule for Affective Disorders and Schizophrenia for School-Age Children—Present and Lifetime version: Initial reliability and validity data. *Journal of the American Academy of Child & Adolescent Psychiatry, 36,* 980–989.

Kaufman, J., & Charney, D. (2001). Effects of early stress on brain structure and function: Implications for understanding the relationship between child maltreatment and depression. *Development and Psychopathology, 13,* 451–471.

Kaufman, J., & Schweder, A. E. (2004). The Schedule for Affective Disorders and Schizophrenia for School-Age Children: Present and Lifetime Version (K–

SADS–PL). In M. J. Hilsenroth & D. L. Segal (Eds.), *Comprehensive handbook of psychological assessment: Vol. 2. Personality assessment* (pp. 247–255). New York: Wiley.

Kaufman, R. M., & Perry, B. D. (2000, January). Understanding juvenile and family court: Special focus on competency, capacity and hearsay. *Child Trauma Academy, Interdisciplinary Education Series, 3*(2). Retrieved August 23, 2007, from http://www.childtrauma.org/ctamaterials/Juv_Fam_Ct.asp

Kaushall, P. (1999). Child confessions: Assessing the validity of child confessions and interrogations. *Forensic Examiner, 8*(3–4), 29–30.

Kaysen, D., Resick, P. A., & Wise, D. (2003). Living in danger: The impact of chronic traumatization and the traumatic context on posttraumatic stress disorder. *Trauma, Violence, & Abuse, 4,* 247–264.

Kazdin, A. E. (2005). Evidence-based assessment for children and adolescents: Issues in measurement development and clinical application. *Journal of Clinical Child and Adolescent Psychology, 34,* 548–558.

Kazdin, A. E., & Marciano, P. L. (1998). Childhood and adolescent depression. In E. J. Mash & R. A. Barkley (Eds.), *Treatment of childhood disorders* (2nd ed., pp. 211–248). New York: Guilford Press.

Kehn, A., Grey, J. M., & Nunez, N. L. (2007). Hearsay testimony: Protecting the needs of children at the expense of the defendant's right to a fair trial. *Journal of Forensic Psychology Practice, 7,* 59–66.

Kelley, E., Jones, G., & Fein D. (2004). Language assessment in children. In G. Goldstein & S. R. Beers (Eds.), *Comprehensive handbook of psychological assessment: Vol. 1. Intellectual and neuropsychological assessment* (pp. 191–215). Hoboken, NJ: Wiley.

Kelley, B., Thornberry, T. P., & Smith, C. A. (1997, August). In the wake of child maltreatment. *OJJDP Juvenile Justice Bulletin.* Rockville, MD: Office of Juvenile Justice and Delinquency Prevention, U.S. Department of Justice.

Kempe, C. H., Silverman, F. N., Steele, B. F., Drogemueller, W., & Silver, H. K. (1962). The battered child syndrome. *Journal of the American Medical Association, 181,* 17–24.

Kenardy, J., Smith, A., Spence, S. H., Lilley, P., Newcombe, P., Dob, R., et al. (2007). Dissociation in children's trauma narratives: An exploratory investigation. *Journal of Anxiety Disorders, 21,* 456–466.

Kendall, P. C., Cantwell, D. P., & Kazdin, A. E. (1989). Depression in children and adolescents: Assessment issues and recommendations. *Cognitive Therapy and Research, 13,* 109–146.

Kendall, P. C., Kortlander, E., Chansky, T. E., & Brady, E. U. (1992). Comorbidity of anxiety and depression in youth: Treatment implications. *Journal of Consulting and Clinical Psychology, 60,* 869–880.

Kendall-Tackett, K. (2002). The health effects of childhood abuse: Four pathways by which abuse can influence health. *Child Abuse & Neglect, 26,* 715–729.

Kendall-Tackett, K. A., Williams, L. M., & Finkelhor, D. (1993). Impact of sexual abuse on children: A review and synthesis of recent empirical studies. *Psychological Bulletin, 113,* 164–180.

Kentucky v. Stincer, 482 U.S. 730 (1987).

Keren, M., & Tyano, S. (2006). Depression in infancy. *Child & Adolescent Psychiatric Clinics of North America, 15,* 883–897.

Kerfoot, M., Koshyl, V., Roganov, O., Mikhailichenko, K., Gorbova, I., & Pottage, D. (2007). The health and well-being of neglected, abused and exploited children: The Kyiv Street Children Project. *Child Abuse & Neglect, 31,* 27–37.

Kerig, P. K., & Fedorowicz, A. E. (1999). Assessing maltreatment of children of battered women: Methodological and ethical concerns. *Child Maltreatment, 4,* 103–115.

Kermani, E. J. (1993). Child sexual abuse revisited by the U.S. Supreme Court. *Journal of the American Academy of Child & Adolescent Psychiatry, 32,* 971–974.

Kilpatrick, D. G., Ruggiero, K. J., Acierno, R., Saunders, B. E., Resnick, H. S., & Best, C. L. (2003). Violence and risk of PTSD, major depression, substance abuse/dependence, and comorbidity: Results from the national survey of adolescents. *Journal of Consulting and Clinical Psychology, 71,* 692–700.

Kinard, E. M. (1998). Depressive symptoms in maltreated children from mother, teacher, and child perspective. *Violence & Victims, 13,* 131–147.

Kiser, L. J., Heston, J., Millsap, P. A., & Pruitt, D. B. (1991). Physical and sexual abuse in childhood: Relationship with post-traumatic stress disorder. *Journal of the American Academy of Child & Adolescent Psychiatry, 30,* 776–783.

Kisiel, C. L., & Lyons, J. S. (2001). Dissociation as a mediator of psychopathology among sexually abused children and adolescents. *American Journal of Psychiatry, 158,* 1034–1039.

Klein, D., & Riso, L. P. (1993). Psychiatric disorders: Problems of boundaries and comorbidity. In C. G. Costello (Ed.), *Basic issues in psychopathology* (pp. 19–66). New York: Guilford Press.

Klein, D. N., Dougherty, L. R., & Olino, T. M. (2005). Toward guidelines for evidence-based assessment of depression in children and adolescents. *Journal of Clinical Child and Adolescent Psychology, 34,* 412–432.

Ko, S. (2005). Promoting culturally competent trauma-informed practices. *NCTSN Culture & Trauma Briefs, 1.* Retrieved August 23, 2007, from http://www.nctsnet.org/nctsn_assets/pdfs/culture_and_trauma_brief.pdf#search='nctsn%20promoting%20culturally%20competent%20traumainformed%20practices

Koenen, K., Moffitt, T. E., Poulton, R., Martin, J., & Caspi, A. (2007). Early childhood factors associated with the development of post-traumatic stress disorder: Results from a longitudinal birth cohort. *Psychological Medicine, 37,* 181–192.

Kohlmann, R. H. (1996). The presumption of innocence: Patching the tattered cloak after *Maryland v. Craig. St. Mary's Law Journal, 27,* 389–395.

Köhnken, G. (2002). A German perspective on children's testimony. In H. L. Westcott, G. M. Davies, & R. H. C. Bull (Eds.), *Children's testimony: A handbook of psychological research and forensic practice* (pp. 233–244). West Sussex, England: Wiley.

Kohrt, H. E., Kohrt, B. A., Waldman, I., Saltzman, K., & Carrion, V. G. (2004). An ecological–transactional model of significant risk factors for child psychopathology in Outer Mongolia. *Child Psychiatry and Human Development, 35,* 163–181.

Kolko, D. J., Moser, T. M., & Weldy, S. R. (1988). Behavioral/emotional indicators of sexual abuse in child psychiatric inpatients: A controlled comparison with physical abuse. *Child Abuse & Neglect, 12,* 529–541.

Kolko, D. J., & Swenson, C. C. (2002). *Assessing and treating physically abused children and their families: A cognitive-behavioral approach.* Thousand Oaks, CA: Sage.

Konner, M. (2007). Trauma, adaptation, and resilience: A cross-cultural and evolutionary perspective. In L. J. Kirmayer, R. Lemelson, & M. Barad (Eds.), *Understanding trauma: Integrating biological, clinical, and cultural perspectives* (pp. 300–338). New York: Cambridge University Press.

Koocher, G. P., Goodman, G. S., White, C. S., Friedrich, W. N., Sivan, A.B., & Reynolds, C. R. (1995). Psychological science and the use of anatomically detailed dolls in child sexual-abuse assessments [Electronic version]. *Psychological Bulletin, 118,* 199–222.

Koopman, C., Carrion, V., Butler, L. D., Sudhakar, S., Palmer, L., & Steiner, H. (2004). Relationships of dissociation and childhood abuse and neglect with heart rate in delinquent adolescents. *Journal of Traumatic Stress, 17,* 47–54.

Koss, M. P., Bailey, J. A., & Yuan, N. P. (2003). Depression and PTSD in survivors of male violence: Research and training initiatives to facilitate recovery. *Psychology of Women Quarterly, 27,* 130–142.

Kovacs, M. (1980). Rating scales to assess depression in school-aged children. *Acta Paediatrica, 46,* 305–315.

Kovacs, M. (1992). *Children's Depression Inventory manual.* North Tonawanda, NY: Multi-Health Systems.

Kovacs, M., Gatsonis, C., Paulauskas, S. L., & Richards, C. (1989). Depressive disorders in childhood. IV. A longitudinal study of comorbidity with and risk for anxiety disorders. *Archives of General Psychiatry, 46,* 776–782.

Kovera, M. B., & Borgida, E. (1996). Children on the witness stand: The use of expert testimony and other procedural innovations in U.S. child sexual abuse trials. In B. L. Bottoms & G. S. Goodman (Eds.), *International perspectives on child abuse and children's testimony: Psychological research and law* (pp. 201–220). Thousand Oaks, CA: Sage.

Kovera, M. B., Gresham, A. W., Borgida, E., Gray, E., & Regan, P. C. (1997). Does expert testimony inform or influence juror decision-making? A social cognitive analysis. *Journal of Applied Social Psychology, 82,* 178–191.

Kratochwill, T. R. (1996). Posttraumatic stress disorder in children and adolescents: Commentary and recommendations. *Journal of School Psychology, 34,* 185–188.

Kresanov, K., Tuominen, J., Piha, J., & Almqvist, F. (1998). Validity of child psychiatric screening methods. *European Child & Adolescent Psychiatry, 7,* 85–95.

Kress, F., & Vandenberg, B. (1998). Depression and attribution in abused children and their nonoffending caregivers. *Psychological Reports, 83,* 1285–1286.

Krysanski, V. L. (2003). A brief review of the selective mutism literature. *The Journal of Psychology, 137,* 29–40.

Kuo, E. S., Vander Stoep, A., & Stewart, D. G. (2005). Using the Short Mood and Feelings Questionnaire to detect depression in detained adolescents. *Assessment, 12*, 374–383.

Kutcher, S. P., & Marton, P. (1996). Treatment of adolescent depression. In K. I. Shulman, M. Tohen, & S. P. Kutcher (Eds.), *Mood disorders across the life span* (pp. 101–126). New York: Wiley.

Ky. Rev. Stat. § 421.350 (2006), as amended by Ky. Acts 19 (2007).

Ky. Rev. Stat. § 26A.140 (2006).

La. Rev. Stat. § 15:283 (2007).

La. Rev. Stat. § 15:440.5 (2007).

Lamb, M. E. (1994). The investigation of child sexual abuse: An interdisciplinary consensus statement. *Expert Evidence, 2*, 151–156.

Lamb, M. E., & Brown, D. A. (2006). Conversational apprentices: Helping children become competent informants about their own experiences. *British Journal of Developmental Psychology, 24*, 215–234.

Lambert, S. F., Cooley, M. R., Campbell, K. D. M., Benoit, M. Z., & Stansbury, R. (2004). Assessing anxiety sensitivity in inner-city African American children: Psychometric properties of the Childhood Anxiety Sensitivity Index. *Journal of Clinical Child and Adolescent Psychology, 33*, 248–259.

Lamken, J. A. (n.d.). *Petition for a writ of certiorari* [Vogelsberg v. Wisconsin]. Retrieved July 10, 2007, from http://www-personal.umich.edu/~rdfrdman/Vogelsbergpetition1.pdf

Landolt, M. A., Vollrath, M., Ribi, K., Gnehm, H. E., & Sennhauser, F. H. (2003). Incidence and associations of parental and child posttraumatic stress symptoms in pediatric patients. *Journal of Child Psychology and Psychiatry, 44*, 1199–1207.

Lang, P. J. (1968). Fear reduction and fear behavior: Problems in treating a construct. In J. M. Shlien (Ed.), *Research in psychotherapy* (Vol. 3, pp. 90–102). Washington, DC: American Psychological Association.

Langley, A. K., Bergman, L. R., & Piacentini, J. C. (2002). Assessment of childhood anxiety. *International Review of Psychiatry, 14*, 102–113.

Lanktree, C. B., Briere, J., & Zaidi, L. Y. (1991). Incidence and impacts of sexual abuse in a child outpatient sample: The role of direct inquiry. *Child Abuse & Neglect, 15*, 447–453.

Lanning, K. V. (2002). Criminal investigation of sexual victimization of children. In J. E. B. Myers, L. Berliner, J. Briere, C. T. Hendrix, C. Jenny, & T. A. Reid (Eds.), *The APSAC handbook on child maltreatment* (2nd ed., pp. 329–347). Thousand Oaks, CA: Sage.

Laor, N., Wolmer, L., Kora, M., Yucel, D., Spirman, S., & Yazgan, Y. (2002). Posttraumatic, dissociative and grief symptoms in Turkish children exposed to the 1999 earthquakes. *Journal of Nervous and Mental Disease, 190*, 824–832.

LaPlante v. Crosby, 736 So. 2d 1190, *cert. denied* 546 U.S. 961 (2005).

Laurent, J., Cantanzaro, S. J., & Joiner, T. E. (2004). Development and preliminary validation of the physiological hyperarousal scale for children. *Psychological Assessment, 16*, 373–380.

Laurent, J., Catanzaro, S. J., Joiner, T. E., Rudolph, K. D., Potter, K. I., Lambert, S., et al. (1999). A measure of positive and negative affect for children: Scale development and preliminary validation. *Psychological Assessment, 11*, 326–338.

Lawlor, R. J. (1998). The expert witness in child sexual abuse cases: A clinician's view. In S. J. Ceci & H. Hembrooke (Eds.), *Expert witnesses in child abuse cases: What can and should be said in court* (pp. 105–122). Washington, DC: American Psychological Association.

Lewinsohn, P. M., & Essau, C. A. (2002). Depression in adolescents. In I. H. Gotlib & C. L. Hammen (Eds.), *Handbook of depression* (pp. 541–559). New York: Guilford Press.

Lewis, D. O. (1996). Diagnostic evaluation of the child and adolescent with dissociative identity disorder/multiple personality disorder. *Child & Adolescent Psychiatric Clinics of North America, 5*, 303–331.

Lewis, D. O., & Yeager, C. A. (1994). Abuse, dissociative phenomena and childhood multiple personality disorder. *Child & Adolescent Psychiatric Clinics of North America, 3*, 729–743.

Li, H., & Morris, R. J. (2007). Assessing fears and related anxieties in children and adolescents with learning disabilities or mild mental retardation. *Research in Developmental Disabilities, 28*, 445–447.

Lind, E. A., & Tyler, T. R. (1988). *The social psychology of procedural justice.* New York: Plenum Press.

Lindberg, M. A., Chapman, M. T., Samsock, D., Thomas, S. W., & Lindberg, A. W. (2003). Comparisons of three different investigative interview techniques with young children. *Journal of Genetic Psychology, 164*, 5–28.

Lindsay, D. S. (2002). Children's source monitoring. In H. L. Westcott, G. M. Davies, & R. H. C. Bull (Eds.), *Children's testimony: A handbook of psychological research and forensic practice* (pp. 83–98). West Sussex, England: Wiley.

Lindsay, R. C. L., Ross, D. F., Lea, J. A., & Carr, C. (1995). What's fair when a child testifies? *Journal of Applied Social Psychology, 25*, 870–888.

Liner, D. (1989). Dissociation and hypnotizability in abused children. *Dissertation Abstracts International, 6359.* (UMI No. 8919575)

Linning, L. M., & Kearney, C. A. (2004). Post-traumatic stress disorder in maltreated youth: A study of diagnostic comorbidity and child factors. *Journal of Interpersonal Violence, 19*, 1087–1101.

Lipovsky, J. A. (1994). The impact of court on children: Research findings and practical recommendations. *Journal of Interpersonal Violence, 9*, 238–257.

Lipovsky, J., & Stern, P. (1997). Preparing children for court: An interdisciplinary view. *Child Maltreatment, 2*, 150–163.

Lipschitz, D. S., Winegar, R. K., Hartnick, E., Foote, B., & Southwick, S. M. (1999). Posttraumatic stress disorder in hospitalized adolescents: Psychiatric comorbidity and clinical correlates. *Journal of the American Academy of Child & Adolescent Psychiatry, 38*, 385–392.

Lomholt v. Iowa, 327 F.3d 748 (8th Cir. 2003).

Lonigan, C. J., Phillips, B. M., & Richey, J. A. (2003). Posttraumatic stress disorder in children: Diagnosis, assessment, and associated features. *Child & Adolescent Psychiatric Clinics of North America, 12,* 171–194.

Lubit, R., Hartwell, N., van Gorp, W. G., & Eth, S. (2002). Forensic evaluation of trauma syndromes. *Child & Adolescent Psychiatric Clinics of North America, 11,* 823–857.

Luby, J. L., Belden, A. C., & Spitznagel, E. (2006). Risk factors for preschool depression: The mediating role of early stressful life events. *Journal of Child Psychology and Psychiatry, 47,* 1292–1298.

Luby, J. L., Mrakotsky, C., & Heffelfinger, A. (2003). Modification of *DSM–IV* criteria for depressed preschool children. *American Journal of Psychiatry, 160,* 1169–1172.

Luby, J. L., Mrakotsky, C. M., Heffelfinger, A., Brown, K., & Spitznagel, E. (2004). Characteristics of depressed preschoolers with and without anhedonia: Evidence for a melancholic depressive sub-type in young children. *American Journal of Psychiatry, 161,* 1998–2004.

Lucas, C. P., Fisher, P., & Luby, J. (1998). *Young-Child DISC–IV research draft: Diagnostic Interview Schedule for Children.* New York: Division of Child Psychiatry, Joy and William Ruane Center to Identify and Treat Mood Disorders, Columbia University.

Lusk, R., & Waterman, J. (1986). Effects of sexual abuse on children. In K. MacFarlane & J. Waterman (Eds.), *Sexual abuse of young children* (pp. 15–29). New York: Guilford Press.

Lyneham, H. J., Abbott, M. J., & Rapee, R. M. (2007). Interrater reliability of the Anxiety Disorders Interview Schedule for *DSM–IV*: Child and parent version. *Journal of the American Academy of Child & Adolescent Psychiatry, 46,* 731–736.

Lyon, T. D. (2004, Spring). The Supreme Court and reluctant witnesses: Crawford v. Washington. *Section on Child Maltreatment Newsletter, Division 37, American Psychological Association, 9,* 1–2.

Lyons, J. A. (1988). Posttraumatic stress disorder in children and adolescents: A review of the literature. In S. Chess & C. Thomas (Eds.), *Annual progress in child psychiatry and development* (pp. 451–467). New York: Brunner/Mazel.

Macfie, J., Cicchetti, D., & Toth, S. L. (2001). The development of dissociation in maltreated preschool-aged children. *Development & Psychopathology, 13,* 233–254.

Malenbaum, R., & Russell, A. T. (1987). Multiple personality disorder in an eleven-year-old boy and his mother. *Journal of the American Academy of Child & Adolescent Psychiatry, 26,* 436–439.

Malinosky-Rummell, R. R., & Hoier, T. S. (1991). Validating measures of dissociation in sexually abused and nonabused children. *Behavioral Assessment, 13,* 341–357.

Manson, S. M. (1995). Culture and major depression: Current challenges in the diagnosis of mood disorders. *Psychiatric Clinics of North America, 18,* 487–501.

Manson, S. M. (1996). The wounded spirit: A cultural formulation of posttraumatic stress disorder. *Culture, Medicine and Psychiatry, 20,* 489–498.

March, J. S. (1995). Cognitive–behavioral psychotherapy for children and adolescents with OCD: A review and recommendations for treatment. *Journal of the American Academy of Child & Adolescent Psychiatry, 34,* 7–18.

March, J. S. (1998). Assessment of pediatric post-traumatic stress disorder. In P. Saigh & J. Bremner (Eds.), *Posttraumatic stress disorder: A comprehensive approach to assessment and treatment* (pp. 199–218). Needham Heights, MA: Allyn & Bacon.

March, J. S. (2003). Acute stress disorder in youth: A multivariate prediction model. *Biological Psychiatry, 53,* 809–816.

March, J. S., Mulle, K., Stallings, P., Erhardt, D., & Conners, C. K. (1995). Assessment. In J. S. March (Ed.), *Anxiety disorders in children and adolescents* (pp. 125–147). New York: Guilford Press.

March, J. S., Parker, J. D. A., Sullivan, K., Stallings, P., & Conners, K. (1997). The Multidimensional Anxiety Scale for Children (MASC): Factor, structure, reliability, and validity. *Journal of the American Academy of Child & Adolescent Psychiatry, 36,* 554–565.

March, J. S., Sullivan, K., & James, P. (1999). Test–retest reliability of the Multidimensional Anxiety Scale for Children. *Journal of Anxiety Disorders, 13,* 349–358.

Margolin, G., & Gordis, E. (2000). The effects of family and community violence on children. *Annual Review of Psychology, 51,* 445–479.

Marks, I. (1987). The development of normal fear: A review. *Journal of Child Psychology and Psychiatry, 28,* 667–697.

Marks, R. G. (1995). Should we believe the people who believe the children: The need for a new sexual abuse tender years hearsay exception statute. *Harvard Journal on Legislation, 32,* 207–254.

Marsil, D. F., Montoya, J., Ross, D., & Graham, L. (2002). Children as victims and witnesses in the criminal trial process: Child witness policy: Law interfacing with social science. *Law and Contemporary Problems, 65,* 209–242.

Mart, E. (2006). *Getting started in forensic psychology practice: How to create a forensic specialty in your mental health practice.* Hoboken, NJ: Wiley.

Martinez-Taboas, A. (1995). *A sociocultural analysis of Merskey's approach.* Northvale, NJ: Jason Aronson.

Martinez-Taboas, A., Canino, G., Wang, M. Q., Garcia, P., & Bravo, M. (2006). Prevalence and victimization correlates of pathological dissociation in a community sample of youths. *Journal of Traumatic Stress, 19,* 439–448.

Martinez-Taboas, A., Shrout, P. E., Canino, G., Chavez, L. M., Ramirez, R., Bravo, M., et al. (2004). The psychometric properties of a shortened version of the Spanish Adolescent Dissociative Experiences Scale. *Journal of Trauma & Dissociation, 5,* 33–54.

Marx v. State, 987 S.W.2d 577 (Tex. Crim. App. 1999), *cert. denied,* Marx v. Texas, 528 U.S. 1034 (1999).

Maryland v. Craig, 76 Md. App. 250, 544 A.2d 784 (Md. Ct. Spec. App. 1988); *rev'd* 316 Md. 551, 560 A.2d 1120 (1989), *cert. granted,* 493 U.S. 1041 (1990a), *vacated* 497 U.S. 836 (1990b).

Mash, E. J., & Hunsley, J. (2005). Evidence-based assessment of child and adolescent disorders: Issues and challenges. *Journal of Clinical Child and Adolescent Psychology, 34,* 362–379.

Mash, E. J., & Terdal, L. G. (1997a). Assessment of child and family disturbance: A behavioral-systems approach. In E. J. Mash & L. G. Terdal (Eds.), *Assessment of childhood disorders* (3rd ed., pp. 3–70). New York: Guilford Press.

Mash, E. J., & Terdal, L. G. (1997b). *Assessment of childhood disorders* (3rd ed.). New York: Guilford Press.

Mass. Gen. Laws Ann. ch. 233, § 81 (2007).

Mass. Gen. Laws Ann. ch. 278, § 16 D (2007).

Masten, A., & Coatsworth, J. (1998). The development of competence in favorable and unfavorable environments: Lessons from research of successful children. *American Psychologist, 53,* 205–220.

Matthey, S., & Petrovski, P. (2002). The Children's Depression Inventory: Error in cutoff scores for screening purposes. *Psychological Assessment, 14,* 146–149.

Mayer, A. (1990). *Child sexual abuse and the courts: A manual for therapists.* Montreal, Quebec, Canada: Learning Publications.

McAuliff, B. D., & Kovera, M. B. (2000, March). *Accommodating children in court: How do jurors view alternative testimonial procedures?* Paper presented at the American Psychology–Law Society conference, New Orleans, LA.

McAuliff, B. D., & Kovera, M. B. (2002). The status of evidentiary and procedural innovations in child abuse proceedings. In B. L. Bottoms, M. B. Kovera, & B. D. McAuliff (Eds.), *Children, social science, and the law* (pp. 412–445). New York: Cambridge University Press.

McCabe, A. (1996). Evaluating narrative discourse skills. In K. N. Cole, P. S. Dale, & D. J. Thal (Eds.), *Assessment of communication and language* (Vol. 6, pp. 121–141). Baltimore: Brookes Publishing.

McCauley, R. J. (2001). *Assessment of language disorders in children.* Mahwah, NJ: Erlbaum.

McCauley, M., Schwartz-Kenny, B. M., Epstein, M. A., & Tucker, E. J. (2000). United States. In B. M. Schwartz-Kenny, M. McCauley, & M. A. Epstein (Eds.), *Child abuse: A global view* (pp. 241–255). Westport, CT: Greenwood Press.

McDermott, B. M., & Palmer, L. J. (2002). Postdisaster emotional distress, depression and event-related variables: Findings across child and adolescent developmental stages. *Australian and New Zealand Journal of Psychiatry, 36,* 754–761.

McGough, L. S. (1994). *Child witnesses: Fragile voices in the American legal system.* New Haven, CT: Yale University Press.

McGough, L. S. (1999). Hearing and believing hearsay. *Psychology, Public Policy, and Law, 5,* 485–498.

McGough, L. S. (2002). Children as victims and witnesses in the criminal trial process: Good enough for government work: The constitutional duty to preserve forensic interviews of child victims. *Law and Contemporary Problems, 65,* 175–205.

McInnes, A., Fung, D., Manassis, K., Fiksenbaum, L., & Tannock, R. (2004). Narrative skills in children with selective mutism: An exploratory study. *American Journal of Speech–Language Pathology, 13*, 304–315.

McKinnon, D. H., McLeod, S., & Reilly, S. (2007). The prevalence of stuttering, voice, and speech-sound disorders in primary school students in Australia. *Language, Speech, and Hearing Services in Schools, 38*, 5–15.

McLeer, S., Callaghan, M., Henry, D., & Wallen, J. (1994). Psychiatric disorders in sexually abused children. *Journal of the American Academy of Child & Adolescent Psychiatry, 33*, 313–319.

McLeer, S. V., Dixon, J. F., Henry, D., Ruggiero, K., Escovitz, K., Niedda, T., et al. (1998). Psychopathology in non-clinically referred sexually abused children. *Journal of the American Academy of Child & Adolescent Psychiatry, 37*, 1326–1333.

McLeod, B.D., Wood, J. J., & Weisz, J. R. (2007). Examining the association between parenting and childhood anxiety: A meta-analysis. *Clinical Psychology Review, 27*, 155–172.

McMahon, R. J., & Estes, A. M. (1997). Conduct problems. In E. J. Mash & L. G. Terdal (Eds.), *Assessment of childhood disorders* (3rd ed., pp. 130–198). New York: Guilford Press.

McMahon, S. (2006). The turbulent aftermath of *Crawford v. Washington*: Where do child abuse victims' statements stand? *Hastings Constitutional Law Quarterly, 33*, 361–395.

McNally, R. J. (1996). Assessment of posttraumatic stress disorder in children and adolescents. *Journal of School Psychology, 34*, 147–161.

Meehl, P. E. (1954). *Clinical vs. statistical prediction*. Minneapolis: University of Minnesota Press.

Meinig, M. B. (1991). Profile of Roland Summit [Interview]. *Violence Update, 1*, 6–7.

Meisenheimer, K. (1993, April). Point/counterpoint: Videotaping of child interviews. *Violence Update, 3*, 10.

Meiser-Stedman, R. (2002). Towards a cognitive–behavioral model of PTSD in children and adolescents. *Clinical Child and Family Psychology Review, 5*, 217–232.

Meiser-Stedman, R., Dalgleish, T., Smith, P., Yule, W., & Glucksman, E. (2007). Diagnostic, demographic, memory quality, and cognitive variables associated with acute stress disorder in children and adolescents. *Journal of Abnormal Psychology, 116*, 65–79.

Meiser-Stedman, R., Smith, P., Glucksman, E., Yule, W., & Dalgleish, T. (2007). Parent and child agreement for acute stress disorder, post-traumatic stress disorder and other psychopathology in a prospective study of children and adolescents exposed to single-event trauma. *Journal of Abnormal Child Psychology, 35*, 191–201.

Melinder, A. (2002). Children's memory of a mildly stressful event—What help is helpful? In M. S. Korsnes, A. Raftopoulos, & A. Demetriou (Eds.), *Studies of the* mind: Proceedings of the first Norwegian Cypriot Meeting on Cognitive Psychology and Neuropsychology (pp. 25–31). Nicosia: Cyprus University Press.

Melton, G. B. (1994). Expert opinions: "Not for cosmic understanding." In B. D. Sales & G. R. VandenBos (Eds.), *Psychology in litigation and legislation* (pp. 55–99). Washington, DC: American Psychological Association.

Melton, G. B., & Limber, S. (1989). Psychologists' involvement in cases of child maltreatment: Limits of role and expertise. *American Psychologist, 44,* 1225–1233.

Melton, G. B., & Limber, S. (1991). Caution in child maltreatment cases. *American Psychologist, 46,* 81–84.

Melton, G. B., Petrila, J., Poythress, N. G., & Slobogin, C. (1997). *Psychological evaluations for the courts: A handbook for mental health professionals and lawyers.* New York: Guilford Press.

Memorandum of good practice. (1992). Department of Home and Health. London: Her Majesty's Stationery Office.

Mennen, F. E. (1995). The relationship of race/ethnicity to symptoms in childhood sexual abuse. *Child Abuse & Neglect, 19,* 114–125.

Mennen, F. E. (2004). PTSD symptoms in abused Latino children. *Child and Adolescent Social Work Journal, 21,* 477–493.

Merikangas, K. R. (1990). Comorbidity for anxiety and depression: Review of family and genetic studies. In J. D. Maser & C. R. Cloninger (Eds.), *Comorbidity of mood and anxiety disorders* (pp. 331–348). Washington, DC: American Psychiatric Press.

Messer, S. C., Angold, A., Costello, E. J., Loeber, R., Van Kammen, W., & Stouthamer-Loeber, M. (1995). Development of a short questionnaire for use in epidemiological studies of depression in children and adolescents: Factor composition and structure across development. *International Journal of Methods in Psychiatric Research, 5,* 251–262.

Meyer, R. G. (1993). *The clinician's handbook: Integrated diagnostics, assessment and intervention in adult and adolescent psychopathology.* Boston: Allyn & Bacon.

Mich. Comp. Laws § 600.2163a (2007).

Milan, S., Ickovics, J. R., Kershaw, T., Lewis, J., Meade, C., & Ethier, K. (2004). Prevalence, course, and predictors of emotional distress in pregnant and parenting adolescents. *Journal of Consulting and Clinical Psychology, 72,* 328–340.

Miller, T. W., & Veltkamp, L. J. (1995). Assessment of sexual abuse and trauma: Clinical measures. *Child Psychiatry and Human Development, 26,* 3–10.

Mills, J. (2004). Structuralization, trauma, and attachment. *Psychoanalytic Psychology, 21,* 154–160.

Minn. Stat. § 595.02 (2006).

Mo. Rev. Stat. § 491.075 (2007).

Mo. Rev. Stat. § 492.304 (2007).

Moffitt, T. E., Caspi, A., Harrington, H., Milne, B. J., Melchior, M., Goldberg, D., et al. (2007). Generalized anxiety disorder and depression: Childhood risk factors in a birth cohort followed to age 32. *Psychological Medicine, 37,* 441–452.

Mohlen, H., Parzer, P., Resch, F., & Brunner, R. (2005). Psychological support for war-traumatized child and adolescent refugees: Evaluation of a short-term treatment program. *Australian and New Zealand Journal of Psychiatry, 39*, 81–87.

Monahan, J., Steadman, H., Silver, E., Appelbaum, P., Robbins, P., Mulvey, E., et al. (2001). *Rethinking risk assessment: The MacArthur Study of Mental Disorder and Violence.* New York: Oxford University Press.

Monahon, C. (1997). *Children and trauma: A guide for parents and professionals.* San Francisco: Jossey-Bass.

Montoya, J. (1992). On truth and shielding in child abuse trials. *Hastings Law Journal, 43*, 1259–1319.

Montoya, J. (1999). Child hearsay statutes: At once over-inclusive and under-inclusive. *Psychology, Public Policy, and Law, 5*, 304–322.

Morris, R. J., & Kratochwill, T. R. (1998). Childhood fears and phobias. In R. J. Morris & T. R. Kratochwill, *The practice of child therapy* (3rd ed., pp. 91–131). Boston: Allyn & Bacon.

Mosteller, R. P. (2005). *Crawford v. Washington*: Encouraging and ensuring the confrontation of witnesses. *University of Richmond Law Review, 39*, 511–626.

Moston, S., & Engelberg, T. (1992). The effects of social support on children's eyewitness testimony. *Applied Cognitive Psychology, 6*, 61–75.

Mundy, P., Sigman, M., Ungerer, J., & Sherman, T. (1986). Defining the social deficits of autism: The contribution of nonverbal communication measures. *Journal of Child Psychology and Psychiatry and Allied Disciplines, 27*, 657–669.

Muris, P., Merckelbach, H., Gadet, B., Moulaert, V., & Tierney, S. (1999). Sensitivity for treatment effects of the screen for child anxiety related emotional disorders. *Journal of Psychopathology and Behavioral Assessment, 21*, 323–335.

Muris, P., Merckelbach, H., & Peeters, E. (2003). The links between the Adolescent Dissociative Experiences Scale (A-DES), fantasy proneness, and anxiety symptoms. *Journal of Nervous and Mental Disease, 191*, 18–24.

Muris, P., Merckelbach, H., Van Brakel, A., & Mayer, B. (1999). The revised version of the screen for child anxiety related emotional disorders (SCARED–R): Further evidence for its reliability and validity. *Anxiety, Stress, & Coping: An International Journal, 12*, 411–425.

Murray, K. (1995). *Live television link: An evaluation of its use by child witnesses in Scottish criminal trials.* Edinburgh, Scotland: The Scottish Office Central Research Unit.

Myers, J. E. B. (1992a). *Evidence in child abuse and neglect cases.* New York: Wiley Law.

Myers, J. E. B. (1992b). *Legal issues in child abuse and neglect.* Newbury Park, CA: Sage.

Myers, J. E. B. (1992c). Steps toward forensically relevant research. In G. S. Goodman, E. P. Taub, D. P. H. Jones, P. England, L. K. Port, L. Rudy, & L. Prado, Testifying in criminal court. *Monographs of the Society for Research in Child Development, 57*(5, Serial No. 229), 143–152.

Myers, J. E. B. (1993). Investigative interviews of children: Should they be video-taped? *Notre Dame Journal of Law, Ethics, & Public Policy, 7*, 371–386.

Myers, J. E. B. (1996a). A decade of international reform to accommodate child witnesses: Steps toward a child witness code. *Pacific Law Journal, 28*, 169–241.

Myers, J. E. B. (1996b). Expert testimony. In J. Briere, L. Berliner, J. A. Bulkley, C. Jenny, & T. Reid (Eds.), *The APSAC handbook on child maltreatment* (pp. 319–340). Thousand Oaks, CA: Sage.

Myers, J. E. B. (1997). *Evidence in child abuse and neglect cases* (3rd ed.). Frederick, MD: Aspen Law & Business.

Myers, J. E. B. (1998). *Legal issues in child abuse and neglect practice* (2nd ed.). Thousand Oaks, CA: Sage.

Myers, J. E. B. (2000). *Evidence in child abuse and neglect cases* (3rd ed., 2000 Cumulative Supplement). Frederick, MD: Aspen Law and Business.

Myers, J. E. B., Cordon, I., Ghetti, S., & Goodman, G. S. (2002). Hearsay exceptions: Adjusting the ratio of intuition to psychological science. *Law and Contemporary Problems, 65*, 3–46.

Myers, J. E. B., Redlich, A. D., Goodman, G. S., Prizmich, L. P., & Imwinkelried, E. (1999). Jurors' perceptions of hearsay in child sexual abuse cases. *Psychology, Public Policy, and Law, 5*, 388–419.

Myers, J. E. B., Saywitz, K. J., & Goodman, G. S. (1996). Psychological research on children as witnesses: Practical implications for forensic interviews and courtroom testimony. *Pacific Law Journal, 28*, 3–92.

Myers, J. E. B., & Stern, P. (2002). Expert testimony: Current research and practice implications. In J. E. B. Myers, L. Berliner, J. Briere, C. T. Hendrix, C. Jenny, & T. A. Reid. (Eds.), *The APSAC handbook on child maltreatment* (2nd ed., pp. 379–401). Thousand Oaks, CA: Sage.

Myers, K., & Winters, N. C. (2002). Ten-year review of rating scales: II. Scales for internalizing disorders. *Journal of the American Academy of Child & Adolescent Psychiatry, 41*, 634–659.

Nader, K. O. (1997). Assessing traumatic experiences in children. In J. P. Wilson & T. M. Keane (Eds.), *Assessing psychological trauma and PTSD* (pp. 291–348). New York: Guilford Press.

Nader, K. O., Kriegler, J., Blake, D., Pynoos, R., Newman, E., & Weather, F. (2002). *The Clinician-Administered PTSD Scale, Child and Adolescent Version (CAPS–CA)*. White River Junction, VT: National Center for PTSD.

Nader, K. O., Kriegler, J. A., Blake, D. D., & Pynoos, R. S. (1994). *Clinician Administered PTSD Scale, Child and Adolescent Version (CAPS–C)*. White River Junction, VT: National Center for PTSD.

Nader, K. O., Newman, E., Weathers, F. W., Kaloupek, D. G., Kriegler, J. A., Blake, D. D., et al. (1998). *Clinician-Administered PTSD Scale for Children and Adolescents for DSM–IV, CAPS–CA*. White River Junction, VT: National Center for PTSD and UCLA Trauma Psychiatry Program.

Nader, K. O., Stuber, M., & Pynoos, R. (1991). Posttraumatic stress reactions in preschool children with catastrophic illness: Assessment needs. *Comprehensive Mental Health Care, 1*, 223–239.

Natali, L. M. (2007). *Commentary. Federal Rules of Criminal Procedure. Title IV. Arraignment and Preparation for Trial. Rule 15. Depositions.* Louisville, CO: National Institute for Trial Advocacy.

National Center for Prosecution of Child Abuse. (2004, June). *Legislation and case law regarding the competency of child witnesses to testify in criminal proceedings.* Retrieved August 26, 2007, from http://www.ndaa-apri.org/pdf/competency_statutory_updates.pdf

National Center for Study of Corporal Punishment and Alternatives in the Schools. (1992). *My Worst Experiences Survey.* Philadelphia: Temple University Press.

National Child Traumatic Stress Network. (2007). *Child traumatic stress introduction.* Retrieved July 4, 2007, from http://www.nctsnet.org/nccts/nav.do?pid=hom_main

National Conference of Commissioners on Uniform State Laws. (1999). *Uniform Rules of Evidence Act 1999.* Retrieved August 23, 2007, from http://www.law.upenn.edu/bll/archives/ulc/ulc.htm

National Conference of Commissioners on Uniform State Laws. (2001). *Summary: Uniform child witness testimony by alternative methods act.* Retrieved August 26, 2007, from http://www.nccusl.org/update/uniformact_summaries/uniformacts-s-ucwtbama.asp

National Conference of Commissioners on Uniform State Laws. (2002). *Uniform child witness testimony by alternative methods act.* Retrieved January 20, 2008, from http://www.law.upenn.edu/bll/archives/ulc/ucwtbama/2002final.htm

National Conference of Commissioners on Uniform State Laws. (2007). Retrieved July 4, 2007, from http://www.nccusl.org/Update/

National Council of Juvenile and Family Court Judges. (2007). [Home page]. Retrieved July 4, 2007, from http://www.ncjfcj.org/

National Institute for Health and Clinical Excellence. (2005, September). *Depression in children and young people: Identification and management in primary, community and secondary care (Clinical Guideline 28).* London: Author.

N.D. Cent. Code § 12.1-35-04 (2007).

N.D. Cent. Code § 31-04-04.1 (2007).

Neal-Barnett, A. (2004). Orphans no more: A commentary on anxiety and African-American youth. *Journal of Clinical Child and Adolescent Psychology, 33,* 276–278.

Neumann, D. A., Housekamp, B. M., Pollock, V. E., & Briere, J. (1996). The long-term sequelae of childhood sexual abuse in women: A meta-analytic review. *Child Maltreatment, 1,* 6–16.

Newspapers, Inc. v. Commonwealth, 222 Va. 574, 281 S.E.2d 915 (Va. 1981).

Nezu, A. M., Nezu, C. M., McClure, K. S., & Zwick, M. L. (2002). Assessment of depression. In I. H. Gotlib & C. L. Hammen (Eds.), *Handbook of depression* (pp. 61–85). New York: Guilford Press.

Nezu, A. M., Ronan, G. F., Meadows, E. A., & McClure, K. S. (Eds.). (2000). *Practitioner's guide to empirically based measures of depression.* Hingham, MA: Kluwer Academic.

N.H. Rev. Stat. Ann. § 517:13-a (2007).

N.H. Super. Ct. R. 93-A (2007).

Nilsson, D., & Svedin, C. G. (2006). Dissociation among Swedish adolescents and the connection to trauma: An evaluation of the Swedish version of Adolescent Dissociative Experience Scale. *Journal of Nervous and Mental Disease, 194,* 684–689.

N.J. Stat. § 2A:84A-32.4 (2007).

N.J. Stat. § 9:6-8.104 (2007).

N.M. Stat. Ann. § 30-9-17 (2007).

Norasakkunkit, V., & Kalick, S. M. (2002). Culture, ethnicity, and emotional distress measures: The role of self-construal and self-enhancement. *Journal of Cross-Cultural Psychology, 33,* 56–70.

Nored, L. S. (2005). *Crawford v. Washington:* Implications for the presentation of child-witness testimony in child-abuse cases. *Mississippi College Law Review, 25,* 97–108.

Norris, F. H., & Riad, J. K. (1997). Standardized self-report measures of civilian trauma and posttraumatic stress disorder. In J. P. Wilson & T. M. Keane (Eds.), *Assessing psychological trauma and PTSD* (pp. 7–42). New York: Guilford Press.

Nunnally, J. C., & Bernstein, I. (1994). *Psychometric theory* (3rd ed.). New York: McGraw-Hill.

N.Y. Crim. Proc. Law §§ 190.25, .30, .32 (2007).

Oates, R. K., & Tong, L. (1987). Sexual abuse of children: An area with room for professional reforms. *Medical Journal of Australia, 147,* 544–548.

O'Brien, E. J. (2000). Are courts-martial ready for prime time? Televised testimony and other developments in the law of confrontation. *Army Lawyer, 330,* 63–78.

O'Brien, L. S. (1998). *Traumatic events and mental health.* New York: Cambridge University Press.

Office for Victims of Crime. (2007). Retrieved on July 4, 2007, from http://www.ojp. usdoj.gov/ovc/

Ogawa, J. R., Sroufe, L. A., Weinfield, N. S., Carlson, E. A., & Egeland, B. (1997). Development and the fragmented self: Longitudinal study of dissociative symptomology in a nonclinical sample. *Development and Psychopathology, 9,* 855–879.

Ogloff, J. R. P. (2002). Two steps forward and one step backward: The law and psychology movement(s) in the 20th century. In J. R. P. Ogloff (Ed.), *Taking psychology and law into the twenty-first century* (pp. 1–33). New York: Kluwer Academic/Plenum Press.

O'Grady, C. (1996, January). *Child witnesses and jury trials: An evaluation of the use of closed circuit television and removable screens in Western Australia.* Report prepared for the Ministry of Justice, Western Australia, Perth.

Ohan, J. L., Myers, K., & Collett, B. R. (2002). Ten-year review of rating scales. IV: Scales assessing trauma and its effects. *Journal of the American Academy of Child & Adolescent Psychiatry, 41,* 1401–1422.

Ohio Rev. Code Ann. § 2937.11 (Anderson 1996).

Ohio v. Roberts, 448 U.S. 56 (1980).

Okla. Stat. Ann. tit. 10, § 7003–4.2 (2007).

Okla. Stat. Ann. tit. 12, § 2611.4 (2007).

Okla. Stat. Ann. tit. 22, § 765 (2007).

Olafson, E., & Kenniston, J. (2004, Winter). The child forensic interview training institute of the childhood trust, Cincinnati Children's Hospital. *APSAC Advisor, 16*, 11–19.

O'Leary, C. C., Frank, D. A., Grant-Knight, W., Beeghly, M., Augustyn, M., Rose-Jacobs, R., et al. (2006). Suicidal ideation among urban nine and ten year olds. *Developmental & Behavioral Pediatrics, 27*, 33–39.

Olivares, J., Garcia-Lopez, L. J., Hidalgo, M. D., La Greca, A. M., Turner, S. M., & Beidel, D. C. (2002). A pilot study on normative data for two social anxiety measures: The Social Phobia and Anxiety Inventory and the Social Anxiety Scale for Adolescents. *International Journal of Clinical and Health Psychology, 2*, 467–476.

Olson, R. C. (2005). *Pinal County protocols for the multidisciplinary investigation of child abuse*. Retrieved August 26, 2007, from http://parent-wise.org/protocol/pinal.pdf

Or. Rev. Stat. § 40.460 (2005).

Or. Rev. Stat. § 163.160 (2005).

Orcutt, H. K., Goodman, G. S., & Tobey, A. E. (2001). Detecting deception in children's testimony: Factfinders' abilities to reach the truth in open court and closed-circuit trials. *Law and Human Behavior, 25*, 339–372.

Ornstein, P. A., Merritt, K. A., Baker-Ward, L., Furtado, E., Gordon, B. N., & Principe, G. (1998). Children's knowledge, expectation, and long-term retention. *Applied Cognitive Psychology, 12*, 387–405.

Ortiz v. State, 188 Ga. App. 532, 374 S.E.2d 92 (Ga. 1988).

Orvaschel, H. (2004). Depressive disorders. In M. Hersen (Ed.), *Psychological assessment in clinical practice: A pragmatic guide* (pp. 269–296). New York: Brunner-Routledge.

Osofsky, J. D. (1995). The effects of exposure to violence on young children, *American Psychologist, 50*, 782–788.

Ostrowski, S. A., Christopher, N. C., & Delahanty, D. L. (2007).The impact of maternal posttraumatic stress disorder symptoms and child gender on risk for persistent posttraumatic stress disorder symptoms in child trauma victims. *Journal of Pediatric Psychology, 32*, 338–342.

Padilla, A. M. (2001). Issues in culturally appropriate assessment. In L. A. Suzuki, J. G. Ponterotto, P. J. Meller (Eds.), *Handbook of multicultural assessment: Clinical, psychological, and educational applications* (2nd ed., pp. 1–28) [Electronic resource]. San Francisco: Jossey-Bass.

Pathak, M. K., & Thompson, W. C. (1999). From child to witness to jury: Effects of suggestion on the transmission and evaluation of hearsay. *Psychology, Public Policy, and Law, 5*, 372–387.

Pearson Education, Inc. (2007). *The Children's Depression Inventory.* Retrieved August 25, 2007, from http://www.pearsonassessments.com/tests/cdi.htm

Pelcovitz, D., & Kaplan, S. (1996). Post-traumatic stress disorder in children and adolescents. *Child & Adolescent Psychiatric Clinics of North America, 5,* 449–469.

Pence, D., & Wilson, C. (1994). Team investigation of child sexual abuse: The uneasy alliance. In J. R. Conte (Series Ed.), *Interpersonal violence: The practice series, Vol. 6.* Thousand Oaks, CA: Sage.

Penfold, S. P. (1995). Mendacious moms or devious dads? Some perplexing issues in child custody/sexual abuse allegation disputes. *Canadian Journal of Psychiatry, 40,* 337–341.

People v. Cortes, 4 Misc. 3d 575, 781 N.Y.S.2d 401 (N.Y. Misc. 2004).

People v. Geno, 261 Mich. App. 624, 683 N.W.2d 687 (Mich. Ct. App. 2004).

People v. Seum Sisavath, 118 Cal. App. 4th 1396; 13 Cal. Rptr. 3d 753 (Cal. Ct. App. 2004).

People v. Sharp, 29 Cal. App. 4th 1772, 36 Cal. Rptr. 2d 117 (Cal. Ct. App. 1994), *overruled* [on other grounds], People v. Martinez, 11 Cal. 4th 434, 903 P.2d 1037, 45 Cal. Rptr. 2d 905 (1995).

People v. Vigil, 104 P.3d 258 (Colo. Ct. App. 2004), *aff'd in part, rev'd in part,* Vigil v. People, 2006 Colo. LEXIS 810 (Colo. Oct. 2, 2006), *abrogated, in part* [on a different matter], People v. Ramirez, 155 P.3d 371 (2007), *cert. denied,* Vigil v. Colorado, 127 S. Ct. 86, 166 L. Ed. 2d 72 (2006).

People v. Vigil, 127 P.3d 916 (Colo. 2006), *cert. denied,* Vigil v. People, 2006 Colo. LEXIS 810 (Colo. Oct. 2, 2006), *abrogated, in part* [on a different matter], People v. Ramirez, 155 P.3d 371 (2007), *cert. denied,* Vigil v. Colorado, 127 S. Ct. 86, 166 L. Ed. 2d 72 (2006).

Perez, C., & Widom, C. (1994). Childhood victimization and long-term intellectual and academic outcomes. *Child Abuse & Neglect, 18,* 617–633.

Perks, S. M., & Jameson, M. (1999). The effects of witnessing domestic violence on behavioural problems and depressive symptomatology: A community sample of pupils from St Lucia. *West Indian Medical Journal, 48,* 208–211.

Perrin, S., Smith, P., & Yule, W. (2000). Practitioner review: The assessment and treatment of post-traumatic stress disorder in children and adolescents. *Journal of Child Psychology and Psychiatry, 41*(3), 277–289.

Perry, B. D. (1996). Neurobiological sequelae of childhood trauma: PTSD in children. In M. M. Murburg (Ed.), *Catecholamine function in posttraumatic stress disorder: Emerging concepts* (pp. 233–255). Washington, DC: American Psychiatric Press.

Perry, N. W., McAuliff, B. D., Tam, P., Claycomb, L., Dostal, C., & Flanagan, C. (1995). When lawyers question children: Is justice served? *Law and Human Behavior, 19,* 609–629.

Pervanidou, P., & Chrousos, G. P. (2007). Post-traumatic stress disorder in children and adolescents: From Sigmund Freud's "trauma" to psychopathology and the (dys)metabolic syndrome. *Hormone and Metabolic Research, 39,* 413–419.

Peters, D. (1991). The influence of arousal and stress on the child witness. In J. Doris (Ed.), *The suggestibility of children's recollections* (pp. 60–76). Washington, DC: American Psychological Association.

Peterson, D. R. (2004). Science, scientism, and professional responsibility. *Clinical Psychology: Science and Practice, 11,* 196–210.

Peterson, G. (1991). Children coping with trauma: Diagnosis of "dissociation identity disorder." *Dissociation, 4,* 152–164.

Pezdek, K., & Hinz, T. (2002). The construction of false events in memory. In H. L. Westcott, G. M. Davies, & R. H. C. Bull (Eds.), *Children's testimony: A handbook of psychological research and forensic practice* (pp. 99–116). West Sussex, England: Wiley.

Pfefferbaum, B. (1997). Posttraumatic stress disorder in children: A review of the past 10 years. *Journal of the American Academy of Child & Adolescent Psychiatry, 36,* 1503–1511.

Phillips, A. (2004a). Weathering the storm after *Crawford v. Washington:* Part 1 of 2. *Update, 17,* 1–5.

Phillips, A. (2004b). Weathering the storm after *Crawford v. Washington:* Part 2 of 2. *Update, 17,* 1–5.

Phillips, A. (2005a, July–August). Child forensic interviews after *Crawford v. Washington:* Testimonial or not? *The Prosecutor, 39.* Retrieved August 25, 2007, from http://ndaa-apri.org/publications/ndaa/toc_july_august_2005.html

Phillips, A. (2005b). Out of harm's way: Hearings that are safe from the impact of *Crawford v. Washington:* Part 1 of 2. *Update, 18,* 1–2.

Phillips, A. (2005c). Out of harm's way: Hearings that are safe from the impact of *Crawford v. Washington:* Part 2 of 2. *Update, 18,* 1–2.

Phillips, A. (2006a). A ray of hope in the wake of *Crawford v. Washington:* An analysis of *Bobadilla v. Minnesota:* Part 1 of 2. *APRI Update, 18,* 1–2.

Phillips, A. (2006b). A ray of hope in the wake of *Crawford v. Washington:* An analysis of *Bobadilla v. Minnesota:* Part 2 of 2. *APRI Update, 18,* 1–2.

Phillips v. State, 505 So. 2d 1075, 1077 (Ala. Crim. App. 1986).

Piers, C. (1998). Contemporary trauma theory and its relation to character. *Psychoanalytic Psychology, 15,* 14–33.

Pipe, M., & Henaghan, M. (1996). Child witnesses in New Zealand. In B. L. Bottoms & G. S. Goodman (Eds.), *International perspectives on child witnesses* (pp. 145–167). Thousand Oaks, CA: Sage.

Pipe, M., Lamb, M. E., Orbach, Y., & Esplin, P. W. (2004). Recent research on children's testimony about experienced and witnessed events. *Developmental Review, 24,* 440–468.

Pittman v. State, 178 Ga. App. 693, 344 S.E.2d 511 (Ga. Ct. App. 1986).

Pizzi, W. T., & Perron, W. (1996). Crime victims in German courtrooms: A comparative perspective on American problems. *Stanford Journal of International Law, 31,* 37–64.

Plotnikoff, J., & Woolfson, R. (1995). *Evaluation of the child witness pack. The support and preparation of child witnesses.* London: Home Office.

Plotnikoff, J., & Woolfson, R. (2004). *Executive summary. In their own words: The experiences of 50 young witnesses in criminal proceedings.* London: National Society for the Prevention of Cruelty to Children. Retrieved August 3, 2007, from http://www.nspcc.org.uk/Inform/Publications/Downloads/InTheirOwnWords pdf gf25460.pdf

Poole, D. A., & Lamb, M. E. (1998). *Investigative interviews of children: A guide for helping professionals.* Washington, DC: American Psychological Association.

Powell, M., & Thomson, D. (2002). Children's memories for repeated events. In H. L. Westcott, G. M. Davies, & R. H. C. Bull (Eds.), *Children's testimony: A handbook of psychological research and forensic practice* (pp. 69–82). West Sussex, England: Wiley.

Poznanski, E. O., Cook, S. C., & Carroll, B. J. (1979). A depression rating scale for children. *Pediatrics, 64,* 442–450.

Poznanski, E. O., & Mokros, H. B. (1996). *Children's Depression Rating Scale—Revised (CDRS–R).* Los Angeles: Western Psychological Services.

Praver, F. (2002). *The Angie/Andy parent rating scales.* Locust Valley, NY: Author.

Praver, F., DiGiuseppe, R., Pelcovitz, D., Mandel, F. S., & Gaines, R. (2000). A preliminary study of a cartoon measure for children's reactions to chronic trauma. *Child Maltreatment, 5,* 273–285.

Press-Enterprise Co. v. Superior Court, 464 U.S. 501 (1985).

Prohl, J., Resch, F., Parzer, P., & Brunner, R. (2001). Relationship between dissociative symptomatology and declarative and procedural memory in adolescent psychiatric patients. *Journal of Nervous Mental Disease, 189,* 602–607.

Puliafico, A. C., Comer, J. S., & Kendall, P. C. (2007). Social phobia in youth: The diagnostic utility of feared social situations. *Psychological Assessment, 19,* 152–158.

Putnam, F. W. (1990). *Child Dissociation Checklist (CDCL).* Unpublished manuscript.

Putnam, F. W. (1993). Dissociative disorders in children: Behavioral profiles and problems. *Child Abuse & Neglect, 17,* 39–45.

Putnam, F. W. (1997). *Dissociation in children and adolescents: A developmental perspective.* New York: Guilford Press.

Putnam, F. W. (2006, Winter). The impact of trauma on child development. *Juvenile and Family Court Journal, 57,* 1–11.

Putnam, F. W., Helmers, K., Horowitz, L. A., & Trickett, P. K. (1995). Hypnotizability and dissociativity in sexually abused girls. *Child Abuse & Neglect, 19,* 645–655.

Putnam, F. W., Helmers, K., & Trickett, P. K. (1993). Development, reliability, and validity of a child dissociation scale. *Child Abuse & Neglect, 17,* 731–741.

Putnam, F. W., Hornstein, N., & Peterson, G. (1996). Clinical phenomenology of child and adolescent dissociative disorders: Gender and age effects. *Child & Adolescent Psychiatric Clinics of North America, 5,* 303–442.

Putnam, F. W., & Peterson, G. (1994). Further validation of the Child Dissociative Checklist. *Dissociation, 7*, 204–211.

Pynoos, R. S. (1994). Traumatic stress and developmental psychopathology in children and adolescents. In R. S. Pynoos (Eds.), *Posttraumatic stress disorder: A clinical review*. Baltimore: Sidran Foundation and Press.

Pynoos, R. S., Goenjian, A. K., & Steinberg, A. M. (1998). A public mental health approach to the postdisaster treatment of children and adolescents. *Child & Adolescent Psychiatric Clinics of North America, 7*, 195–210.

Pynoos, R. S., Steinberg, A. M., & Goenjian, A. (1996). Traumatic stress in childhood and adolescence: Recent developments and current controversies In B. A. van der Kolk, A. C. McFarlane, & L. Weisaeth (Eds.), *Traumatic stress: The effects of overwhelming experience on mind, body, and society* (pp. 331–358). New York: Guilford Press.

Pynoos, R. S., Steinberg, A. M., & Wraith, R. (1995). A developmental model of childhood traumatic stress. In D. Cicchetti & D. Cohen (Eds.), *Developmental psychopathology: Vol. 2. Risk, disorder, and adaptation* (pp. 72–95). New York: Wiley.

Qouta, S., Punamäki, R-L., & Sarraj, E. E. (2003). Prevalence and determinants of PTSD among Palestinian children exposed to military violence. *European Child & Adolescent Psychiatry, 12*, 265–272.

Quas, J. A., DeCecco, V., Bulkley, J., & Goodman, G. S. (1996). District attorneys' views of innovative practices for child witnesses. *American Psychology–Law Society Newsletter, 16*, 5–8.

Quas, J. A., Goodman, G. S., & Ghetti, S. (2005). Childhood sexual assault victims: Long-term outcomes after testifying in criminal court. *Monographs of the Society for Research in Child Development, 70*, 1–145.

Quas, J. A., Goodman, G. S., Ghetti, S., & Redlich, A. D. (2000). Questioning the child witness: What can we conclude from the research thus far? *Trauma, Violence & Abuse, 1*, 223–249.

Quinn, K. (1995). Guidelines for the psychiatric evaluation of posttraumatic stress disorder in children and adolescents. In R. Simon (Ed.), *Posttraumatic stress disorder in litigation* (pp. 85–98). Washington, DC: American Psychiatric Press.

Rabalais, A. E., Ruggiero, K. J., & Scotti, J. R. (2002). Multicultural issues in the response of children to disasters. In A. M. La Greca, W. K. Silverman, E. M. Vernberg, & M. C. Roberts (Eds.), *Helping children cope with disasters and terrorism* (pp. 73–99). Washington, DC: American Psychological Association

Rabkin, J. G., & Klein, D. F. (1987). The clinical measurement of depressive disorders. In A. J. Marsella, R. M. A. Hirschfeld, & M. N. Katz (Eds.), *The measurement of depression* (pp. 30–83). New York: Guilford Press.

Raeder, M. S. (2003). Hot topics in confrontation clause cases and creating a more workable confrontation clause framework without starting over. *Quinnipiac Law Review, 21*, 1013–1046.

Raeder, M. S. (2005a, Summer). Domestic violence, child abuse, and trustworthiness exceptions after Crawford. *Criminal Justice Magazine, 20*(2). Retrieved August 25, 2007, from http://www.abanet.org/crimjust/cjmag/20–2/raeder.html

Raeder, M. S. (2005b). Remember the ladies and the children too: *Crawford's* impact on domestic violence and child abuse cases. *Brooklyn Law Review, 71,* 311–389.

Rao, P. A., Beidel, B. C., Turner, S. M., Ammerman, R. T., Crosby, L. E., & Sallee, F. R. (2007). Social anxiety disorder in children and adolescents: Descriptive psychopathology. *Behavior Research and Therapy, 45,* 1181–1191.

Reagor, P. A., Kasten, J. D., & Morelli, N. (1992). A checklist for screening dissociative disorders in children and adolescents. *Dissociation, 5,* 1–19.

Realmuto, G. M., Masten, A., Carole, L. F., Hubbard, J., Groteluschen, A., & Chun, B. (1992). Adolescent survivors of massive childhood trauma in Cambodia: Life events and current symptoms. *Journal of Traumatic Stress, 5,* 589–599.

Redlich, A. D., Myers, J. E. B., Goodman, G. S., & Qin, J. (2002). A comparison of two forms of hearsay in child sexual abuse cases. *Child Maltreatment, 7,* 312–328.

Reich, W. (2000). Diagnostic Interview for Children and Adolescents (DICA). *Journal of the American Academy of Child & Adolescent Psychiatry, 29,* 59–66.

Reich, W., Shayka, J. J., & Taibleson, C. (1991). *Diagnostic Interview for Children and Adolescents (DICA).* St. Louis, MO: Washington University.

Renick, P. A. (2001). *Stress and trauma.* Philadelphia: Taylor & Francis.

Research Units on Pediatric Psychopharmacology Anxiety Study Group. (2002). The Pediatric Anxiety Rating Scale (PARS): Development and psychometric properties. *Journal of the American Academy of Child & Adolescent Psychiatry, 41,* 1061–1069.

Reutter v. State, 866 P.2d 1298 (Alaska Ct. App. 1994), *cert. denied,* Reutter v. Crandel, 522 U.S. 851, 118 S. Ct. 142 (1997).

Reynell, J., & Grueber, C. P. (1990). *Reynell Developmental Language Scales—U.S. edition.* Los Angeles: Western Psychological Services.

Reynolds, C. R., & Richmond, B. O. (1979). Factor structure and construct validity of "What I think and feel": The Revised Children's Manifest Anxiety Scale. *Journal of Personality Assessment, 43,* 281–283.

Reynolds, C. R., & Richmond, B. O. (1985). *Revised Children's Manifest Anxiety Scale: Manual.* Los Angeles: Western Psychological Services.

Reynolds, W. M. (1989). *The Reynolds Child Depression Scale: Professional manual.* Odessa, FL: Psychological Assessment Services.

Reynolds, W. M. (2004). The Reynolds Adolescent Depression Scale—Second edition (RADS–2). In M. Hersen (Series Ed.), M. J. Hilsenroth, & D. L. Segal (Vol. Eds.), *Comprehensive handbook of psychological assessment: Vol. 2. Personality Assessment* (pp. 224–236). New York: Wiley.

Reynolds, W. M. (2006). Depression. In M. Hersen (Ed.), *Clinician's handbook of child behavioral assessment* (pp. 291–311). Burlington, MA: Elsevier.

Rhue, J. W., Lynn, S. J., & Sandberg, D. (1995). Dissociation, fantasy and imagination in childhood: A comparison of physically abused, sexually abused, and non-abused children. *Contemporary Hypnosis, 12,* 131–136.

R.I. Gen. Laws § 11-37-13.1 (2007).

R.I. Gen. Laws § 11-37-13.2 (2007).

Rice, F., Harold, G. T., Shelton, K. H., & Thapar, A. (2006). Family conflict inter-acts with genetic liability in predicting childhood and adolescent depression. *Journal of the American Academy of Child & Adolescent Psychiatry, 45,* 841–848.

Rimsza, M. E., Berg, R. A., & Locke, C. (1988). Sexual abuse: Somatic and emo-tional reactions. *Child Abuse & Neglect, 12,* 201–208.

Roberts, W., & Strayer, J. (1987). Parents' responses to the emotional distress of their children: Relations with children's competence. *Developmental Psychology, 23,* 415–422.

Roesler, T. A., & McKenzie, N. (1994). Effects of childhood trauma on psycho-logical functioning in adults sexually abused as children. *Journal of Nervous and Mental Disease, 182,* 145–150.

Romey v. Vanyur, 9 F. Supp. 2d 565 (D.N.C. 1998).

Rosen, P. J., Milich, R., & Harris, M. J. (2007). Victims of their own cognitions: Implicit social cognitions, emotional distress, and peer victimization. *Journal of Applied Developmental Psychology, 28,* 211–226.

Rosenberg, J. (2001). Forensic aspects of PTSD in children and adolescents. In S. Eth (Ed.), *PTSD in children and adolescents* (pp. 33–36). Washington, DC: American Psychiatric Publishing.

Ross, C. A., Heber, S., Norton, G. R., Anderson, D., Anderson, G., & Barchet, P. (1989). The Dissociative Disorders Interview Schedule: A structured interview. *Dissociation, 11,* 169–189.

Ross, D. F., Hopkins, S., Hanson E., Lindsay, R. C. L., Hazen, K., & Eslinger, T. (1994). The impact of protective shields and videotape testimony on convic-tion rates in a simulated trial of child sexual abuse. *Law & Human Behavior, 18,* 553–566.

Ross, D. F., Lindsay, R. C. L., & Marsil, D. F. (1999). The impact of hearsay testi-mony on conviction rates in trials of child sexual abuse: Toward balancing the rights of defendants and child witnesses. *Psychology, Public Policy, and Law, 5,* 439–455.

Ross, D. F., Warren, A. R., & McGough, L. S. (1999). Forward: Hearsay testimony in trials involving child witnesses. *Psychology, Public Policy, and Law, 5,* 251–254.

Rourke, K. M., & Reich, W. (2004). The Diagnostic Interview for Children and Adolescents (DICA). In M. J. Hilsenroth & D. L. Segal (Vol. Eds.), *Com-prehensive handbook of psychological assessment: Vol. 2. Personality assessment* (pp. 271–280). New York: Wiley.

Roza, S. J., Hofstra, M. B., van der Ende, J., & Verhulst, F. C. (2003). Stable predic-tion of mood and anxiety disorders based on behavioral and emotional prob-lems in childhood: A 14-year follow-up during childhood, adolescence, and young adulthood. *American Journal of Psychiatry, 160,* 2116–2121.

Runyan, D. K., Everson, M. D., Edelsohn, G. A., Hunter, W. M., & Coulter, M. L. (1988). Impact of legal intervention on sexually abused children. *Pediatrics, 113,* 647–653.

Rutter, M. (2007). Commentary: Resilience, competence, and coping. *Child Abuse & Neglect, 31,* 205–209.

Ryan, G., Lane, S., Davis, J., & Issac, C. (1987). Juvenile sex offenders: Development and correction. *Child Abuse & Neglect, 11,* 385–395.

Rynn, M. A., Barber, J. P., Khalid-Khan, S., Siqueland, L., Dembiski, M., McCarthy, K. S., et al. (2006). The psychometric properties of the MASC in a pediatric psychiatric sample. *Journal of Anxiety Disorders, 20,* 139–157.

Sabin, J. A., Zatzick, D. F., Jurkovich, G., & Rivara, F. P. (2006). Primary care utilization and detection of emotional distress after adolescent traumatic injury: Identifying an unmet need. *Pediatrics, 117,* 130–138.

Saigh, P. A. (1987, November). *The validity of DSM–III posttraumatic stress disorder classification as applied to adolescents.* Paper presented at the meeting of the Association for the Advancement of Behavior Therapy, Boston, MA.

Saigh, P. A. (1989). The validity of the *DSM–III* posttraumatic stress disorder classification as applied to children. *Journal of Abnormal Psychology, 98,* 189–192.

Saigh, P. A. (1991). The development of posttraumatic stress disorder following four different types of traumatization. *Behaviour Research and Therapy, 29,* 213–216.

Saigh, P. A. (1998). The effects of flooding on the memories of posttraumatic stress disorder patients. In J. D. Bremner & C. Marmer (Eds.), *Trauma, memory, and dissociation* (pp. 285–320). Washington, DC: American Psychiatric Publishing.

Saigh, P. A. (2003a). *The Children's Posttraumatic Stress Disorder Inventory.* San Antonio, TX: Psychological Corporation.

Saigh, P. A. (2003b). *The Children's Posttraumatic Stress Disorder Inventory test manual.* San Antonio, TX: Psychological Corporation.

Saigh P. A., Sack, W., Yasik, A., & Koplewicz, H. (1999). Child–adolescent posttraumatic stress disorder: Prevalence, comorbidity, and risk factors. In P. A. Saigh & J. D. Bremner (Eds.), *Posttraumatic stress disorder: A comprehensive textbook* (pp. 18–43). Needham Heights, MA: Allyn & Bacon.

Saigh, P. A., & Yasik, A. E. (2002). Diagnosing child–adolescent posttraumatic stress disorder. In S. E. Brock, P. J. Lazarus, & S. R. Jimerson (Eds.), *Best practices in school crisis prevention and intervention* (pp. 619–638). Bethesda, MD: National Association of School Psychologists.

Saigh, P. A., Yasik, A. E., & Oberfield, R. A. (2000). The Children's PTSD Inventory: Development and reliability. *Journal of Traumatic Stress, 13,* 369–380.

Saigh, P. A., Yasik, A. E., Oberfield, R., & Halamandaris, P. V. (2007). Self-reported anger among traumatized children and adolescents. *Journal of Psychopathology Behavior Assessment, 29,* 29–37.

Saigh, P. A., Yasik, A. E., Oberfield, R. A., Halamandaris, P. V., & McHugh, M. (2002). An analysis of the internalizing and externalizing behaviors of traumatized urban youth with and without PTSD. *Journal of Abnormal Psychology, 111,* 462–470.

Saigh, P. A., Yasik, A. E., Sack, W., & Koplewicz, H. (1999). Child–adolescent posttraumatic stress disorder: Prevalence, comorbidity, and risk factors. In P. A.

Saigh & J. D. Bremner (Eds.), *Posttraumatic stress disorder: A comprehensive text* (pp. 19–43). Needham Heights, MA: Allyn & Bacon.

Sales, B. D., Miller, M. O., & Hall, S. R. (2005). *Laws affecting clinical practice*. Washington, DC: American Psychological Association.

Sales, B. D., & Shuman, D. W. (2005). *Experts in court: Reconciling law, science, and professional knowledge*. Washington, DC: American Psychological Association.

Saltzman, K. M., Weems, C. F., & Carrion, V. G. (2006). IQ and posttraumatic stress symptoms in children exposed to interpersonal violence. *Child Psychiatry and Human Development, 36*(3), 261–272.

Salzer, M., & Bickman, L. (1999). The short- and long-term psychological impact of disasters: Implications for mental health interventions and policy. In R. Gist & B. Lubin (Eds.), *Response to disaster: Psychological, community, and ecological approaches* (pp. 63–82). Philadelphia: Bruner/Mazel.

Sanders, B., & Giolas, M. H. (1991). Dissociation and childhood trauma in psychologically disturbed adolescents. *American Journal of Psychiatry, 148*, 50–54.

Sandler, J. C. (2006). Alternative methods of child testimony: A review of law and research. In C. R. Barol & A. M. Bartol (Eds.), *Current perspectives in forensic psychology and criminal justice* (pp. 203–212). Thousand Oaks, CA: Sage.

Sar, V., Tutkun, H., Alyanak, B., Bakim, B., & Baral, I. (2000). Frequency of dissociative disorders among psychiatric outpatients in Turkey. *Comprehensive Psychiatry, 41*, 216–222.

Sar, V., Yargic, I., & Tutkun, H. (1996). Structured interview data on 35 cases of dissociative identity disorder in Turkey. *American Journal of Psychiatry, 153*, 1329–1333.

Sas, L. D. (1991). *Reducing the system-induced trauma for child sexual abuse victims through court preparation, assessment, and follow-up* (Final Report, Project No. 4555–1–125, National Welfare Grants Division, Health and Welfare Canada). London, Canada: London Family Court Clinic.

Sas, L., Austin, G., Wolfe, D., & Hurley, P. (1991). *Reducing the system induced trauma for child sexual abuse victims through court preparation, assessment, and follow-up*. London, Canada: London Family Court Clinic.

Sas, L. D., Hurley, P., Hatch, A., Malla, S., & Dick, T. (1993). *Three years after the verdict: A longitudinal study of the social and psychological adjustment of child witnesses referred to the child witness project*. Ottawa, Canada: Health and Welfare Canada.

Sattler, J. M. (1998). *Clinical and forensic interviewing of children and families: Guidelines for the mental health, education, pediatric, and child maltreatment fields*. San Diego, CA: Jerome Sattler Publishers.

Saunders, T. R. (1993). Some ethical and legal features of child custody disputes: A case illustration and applications. *Psychotherapy, 30*, 49–58.

Saxe, G., Chawla, N., Stoddard, F., Kassam-Adams, N., Courtney, D., Cunningham, K., et al. (2003). Child Stress Disorders Checklist: A measure of ASD and PTSD in children. *Journal of the American Academy of Child & Adolescent Psychiatry, 42*, 972–978.

Saylor, C. F., Swenson, C. C., Reynolds, S. S., & Taylor, M. (1999). The Pediatric Emotional Distress Scale: A brief screening measure for young children exposed to traumatic events. *Journal of Clinical Child Psychology, 28,* 70–81.

Saywitz, K. J. (1988). The credibility of child witnesses. *Family Advocate, 10,* 38–41.

Saywitz, K. J. (1989). Children's conceptions of the legal system: "Court is a place to play basketball." In S. J. Ceci, D. F. Ross, & M. P. Toglia (Eds.), *Perspectives on children's testimony* (pp. 131–157). New York: Springer-Verlag.

Saywitz, K. J. (1995). Improving children's testimony: The question, the answer, and the environment. In M. S. Zaragoza, J. R. Graham, C. C. N. Hall, R. Hirschman, & Y. Ben-Porath (Eds.), *Memory and testimony in the child witness* (pp. 113–140). Thousand Oaks, CA: Sage.

Saywitz, K. J. (1997, June). Identifying children in need of special court procedures. *The child witness handout.* Paper presented at the A Search for Truth: Use of Closed-Circuit and Videotaped Testimony of Children conference, Alexandria, VA.

Saywitz, K. J. (2002). Developmental underpinnings of children's testimony. In H. L. Westcott, G. M. Davies, & R. H. C. Bull (Eds.), *Children's testimony: A handbook of psychological research and forensic practice* (pp. 3–35). New York: Wiley.

Saywitz, K. J., & Camparo, L. (1998). Interviewing child witnesses: A developmental perspective. *Child Abuse & Neglect, 22,* 825–843.

Saywitz, K. J., & Goodman, G. S. (1996). Interviewing children in and out of court. In J. Briere, L. Berlinger, J. Bulkley, C. Jenny, & T. Reid (Eds.), *The APSAC handbook on child maltreatment* (2nd ed., pp. 297–305). Thousand Oaks, CA: Sage.

Saywitz, K. J., Goodman, G. S., & Lyon, T. D. (2002). Interviewing children in and out of court: Current research and practice implications. In J. E. B. Myers, L. Berliner, J. Briere, C. T. Hendrix, C. Jenny, & T. A. Reid. (Eds.), *The APSAC handbook on child maltreatment* (2nd ed., pp. 349–377). Thousand Oaks, CA: Sage.

Saywitz, K. J., Jaenicke, C., & Camparo, L. (1990). Children's knowledge of legal terminology. *Law and Human Behavior, 14,* 523–535.

Saywitz, K. J., Mannarino, A. P., Berliner, L., & Cohen, J. A. (2000). Treatment of sexually abused children and adolescents. *American Psychologist, 55,* 1040–1049.

Saywitz, K. J., & Nathanson, R. (1993). Children's testimony and their perceptions of stress in and out of the courtroom. *Child Abuse & Neglect, 17,* 613–622.

Saywitz, K. J., & Snyder, L. (1993). Improving children's testimony with preparation. In G. Goodman & B. Bottoms (Eds.), *Child victims, child witnesses: Understanding and improving children's testimony* (pp. 117–146). New York: Guilford Press.

Saywitz, K. J., & Snyder, L. (1996). Narrative elaboration: Test of a new procedure for interviewing children. *Journal of Consulting and Clinical Psychology, 64,* 1347–1357.

Sbraga, T. P., & O'Donohue, W. (2003). Post hoc reasoning in possible cases of child sexual abuse: Symptoms of inconclusive origins. *Clinical Psychology: Science and Practice, 10,* 320–334.

S.C. Code Ann. § 16-3-1550(E) (Law. Co-op. 2006).

Schaaf, J. M., Alexander, K. W., Goodman, G. S., Ghetti, S., Edelstein, R. S., & Castelli, P. (2002). In B. L. Bottoms, M. B. Kovera, & B. D. McAuliff (Eds.), *Children, social science, and the law* (pp. 342–377). New York: Cambridge University Press.

Scheeringa, M. S., Peebles, C. D., Cook, C. A., & Zeanah, C. H. (2001). Toward establishing procedural, criterion, and discriminant validity for PTSD in early childhood. *Journal of the American Academy of Child & Adolescent Psychiatry, 40,* 52–60.

Scheeringa, M. S., Wright, M. J., Hunt, J. P., & Zeanah, C. H. (2006). Factors affecting the diagnosis and prediction of PTSD symptomatology in children and adolescents. *American Journal of Psychiatry, 163,* 644–651.

Scheeringa, M. S., Zeanah, C. H., Drell, M., & Larrieu, J. (1995). Two approaches to the diagnosis of post-traumatic stress disorder in infancy and early childhood. *Journal of the American Academy of Child & Adolescent Psychiatry, 34,* 191–200.

Scheeringa, M. S., Zeanah, C. H., Myers, L., & Putnam, F. W. (2003). New findings on alternative criteria for PTSD in preschool children. *Journal of the American Academy of Child & Adolescent Psychiatry, 42*(5), 561–570.

Scheflin, A. W. (1998). Narrative truth, historical truth, and forensic truth. In L. E. Lifson & R. I. Simon (Eds.), *The mental health practitioner and the law: A comprehensive handbook* (pp. 299–328). Cambridge, MA: Harvard University Press.

Schetky, D. H. (2003). PTSD in children and adolescents: An overview with guidelines for forensic assessment. In R. I. Simon (Ed.), *Posttraumatic stress disorder in litigation: Guidelines for forensic assessment* (2nd ed., pp. 91–118). Washington, DC: American Psychiatric Publishing.

Schetky, D. H., & Guyer, M. J. (2002). Psychic trauma and civil litigation. In D. H. Schetky & E. P. Benedek (Eds.), *Principles and practice of child and adolescent forensic psychiatry* (pp. 355–364). Washington, DC: American Psychiatric Publishing.

Schniering, C. A., Hudson, J. L., & Rapee, R. M. (2000). Issues in the diagnosis and assessment of anxiety disorders in children and adolescents. *Clinical Psychology Review, 20,* 453–478.

Schniering, C. A., & Lyneham, H. J. (2007). The Children's Automatic Thoughts Scale in a clinical sample: Psychometric properties and clinical utility. *Behaviour Research and Therapy, 45,* 1931–1940.

Schreibman, L., Stahmer, A. C., & Akshoomoff, N. (2006). Pervasive development disorders. In M. Hersen (Ed.), *Clinician's handbook of child behavioral assessment* (pp. 503–525). San Diego, CA: Elsevier.

Schroeder, C. S., & Gordon, B. N. (2002). *Assessment and treatment of childhood problems: A clinician's guide* (2nd ed.). New York: Guilford Press.

Schwab-Stone, M., Fallon, T., Brigs, M., & Crowther, B. (1994). Reliability of diagnostic reporting for children ages 6–11: A test–retest study of the Diagnostic Interview Schedule for Children—Revised. *American Journal of Psychiatry, 151,* 1048–1054.

Schwartz, J. A., Gladstone, T. R. G., & Kaslow, N. J. (1998). Depressive disorders. In T. H. Ollendick & M. Hersen (Eds.), *Handbook of child psychopathology* (3rd ed., pp. 269–289). New York: Plenum Publishers.

S.D. Codified Laws § 26-8A-30 (Michie 2007).

Seeley, S. M., Perosa, S. L., & Perosa, L. M. (2004). A validation study of the Adolescent Dissociative Experiences Scale. *Child Abuse & Neglect, 28,* 755–769.

Seligman, L. D., & Ollendick, T. H. (1998). Comorbidity of anxiety and depression in children and adolescents: An integrative review. *Clinical Child and Family Psychology Review, 1,* 125–144.

Semel, E., Wiig, E. H., & Secord, W. A. (2003). *The Clinical Evaluation of Language Fundamentals—4.* San Antonio, TX: Harcourt Assessment. Retrieved August 26, 2007, from http://harcourtassessment.com/HAIWEB/Cultures/en-us/Productdetail.htm?Pid=015-8037-200

725 Ill. Comp. Stat. 5/106B-5 (West 2007).

Sgroi, S. M. (1982). *Handbook of clinical intervention in child sexual abuse.* Lexington, MA: Lexington Books.

Shaffer, D. (1989, October). *The Diagnostic Interview Schedule for Children (DISC–2): Its development and administration.* Paper presented at the annual meeting of the American Academy of Child & Adolescent Psychiatry, New York.

Shaffer, D., Fisher, P., Lucas, C., Dulcan, M., & Schwab-Stone, M. (2000). The Diagnostic Interview Schedule for Children, Version VI (DISC–IV): Description, differences from previous versions, and reliability of some common diagnoses. *Journal of the American Academy of Child & Adolescent Psychiatry, 39,* 28–38.

Shaffer, D., Fisher, P., Piacentini, J., Schwab-Stone, M., & Wicks, J. (1992). *The Diagnostic Interview Schedule for Children* (DISC). Unpublished manuscript. (Available from the authors: Columbia NIMH DISC Training Center, Division of Child and Adolescent Psychiatry, Unit 78, New York State Psychiatric Institute, 722 West 168th Street, New York, NY 10032)

Shanee, N., Apter, A., & Weizman, A. (1997). Psychometric properties of the K–SADS–PL in an Israeli adolescent clinical population. *Israel Journal of Psychiatry & Related Sciences, 34,* 179–186.

Shapiro, D. L. (1991). *Forensic psychological assessment: An integrative approach.* Boston: Allyn & Bacon.

Sharp, C., Goodyer, I. M., & Croudace, T. J. (2006). The Short Mood and Feelings Questionnaire (SMFQ): A unidimensional item response theory and categorical data factor analysis of self-report ratings from a community sample of 7- through 11-year-old children. *Journal of Abnormal Child Psychology, 34,* 365–377.

Sharp, W. G., Sherman, C., & Gross, A. M. (2007). *Journal of Anxiety Disorders, 21,* 568–579.

Shipman, K. L., Rossman, B. B. R., & West, J. C. (1999). Co-occurrence of spousal violence and child abuse: Conceptual implications. *Child Maltreatment, 4,* 93–102.

Shuman, D. W. (2003). Persistent reexperiences in psychiatry and law: Current and future trends for the role of PTSD in litigation. In R. I. Simon (Ed.), *Posttraumatic stress disorder in litigation: Guidelines for forensic assessment* (2nd ed., pp. 1–18). Washington, DC: American Psychiatric Publishing.

Shuman, D. W., Greenberg, S., Heilbrun, K., & Foote, W. E. (1998). An immodest proposal: Should treating mental health professionals be barred from testifying about their patients? *Behavioral Sciences & the Law, 16,* 509–523.

Shuman, D. W., & Sales, B. D. (2001). Daubert's wager. *Journal of Forensic Psychology Practice, 1,* 69–77.

Sidran Institute. (n.d.). *Dissociative Features Profile.* Retrieved from http://www.sidran.org/store/index.cfm?fuseaction=product.display&Product_ID=64

Sigal, J. A., Gibbs, M. S., Rubin, C., Bartlett, B., Orosy-Fildes, C., Ceravolo, A., et al. (1993). Courtroom reforms and juror's perceptions in child sexual abuse trials. *Family Violence & Sexual Assault Bulletin, 9,* 19.

Silberg, J. L. (1998). Afterword. In J. L. Silberg (Ed.), *The dissociative child* (2nd ed., pp. 333–349). Lutherville, MD: Sidran Foundation and Press.

Silberg, J. L. (2000). Fifteen years of dissociation in maltreated children: Where do we go from here? *Child Maltreatment, 5,* 119–136.

Silverman, W. K., & Albano, A. M. (1996). *Anxiety Disorders Interview Schedule for DSM–IV: Child and parent version.* San Antonio, TX: Psychological Corporation/Graywind.

Silverman, W. K., & Eisen, A. R. (1992). Age differences in the reliability of parent and child reports of child anxious symptomology using a structured interview. *Journal of the American Academy of Child & Adolescent Psychiatry, 31,* 117–124.

Silverman, W. K., Fleisig, W., Rabian, B., & Peterson, R. A. (1991). Child anxiety sensitivity index. *Journal of Child Psychology, 20,* 162–168.

Silverman, W. K., & La Greca, A. M. (2002). Children experiencing disasters: Definitions, reactions, and predictor of outcomes. In A. M. La Greca, W. K. Silverman, E. M. Vernberg, & M. C. Roberts (Eds.), *Helping children cope with disasters and terrorism* (pp. 11–30). Washington, DC: American Psychological Association.

Silverman, W. K., & Lopez, B. (2004). Anxiety disorders. In M. Hersen (Ed.), *Psychological assessment in clinical practice: A pragmatic guide* (pp. 269–296). New York: Brunner-Routledge.

Silverman, W. K., & Nelles, W. B. (1988). The Anxiety Disorders Interview Schedule for Children. *Journal of the American Academy of Child & Adolescent Psychiatry, 27,* 772–778.

Silverman, W. K., & Ollendick, T. H. (2005). Evidence-based assessment of anxiety and its disorders in children and adolescents. *Journal of Clinical Child and Adolescent Psychology, 34,* 380–411.

Silverman, W. K., & Rabian, B. (1995). Test–retest reliability of the DSM–III–R childhood anxiety disorders symptoms using the Anxiety Disorders Interview Schedule for Children. *Journal of Anxiety Disorders, 9,* 139–150.

Silverman, W. K., & Rabian, B. (1999). Rating scales for anxiety and mood disorders. In D. Shaffer, C. P. Lucas, & J. E. Richters (Eds.), *Diagnostic assessment in child and adolescent psychopathology* (pp. 127–166). New York: Guilford Press.

Silverman, W. K., Saavedra, L. M., & Pina, A. A. (2001). Test–retest reliability of anxiety symptoms and diagnoses using the Anxiety Disorders Interview Schedule for DSM–IV: Child and Parent Version (ADIS for DSM–IV: C/P). *Journal of the American Academy of Child & Adolescent Psychiatry, 40,* 937–944.

Silverman, W. K., & Serafini, L. T. (1998). Assessment of child behavior problems: Internalizing disorders. In A. S. Bellack & M. Herson (Eds.), *Behavioral assessment: A practical handbook* (4th ed., pp. 342–360). Boston: Allyn & Bacon.

Simon, R. I. (2003). *Posttraumatic stress disorder in litigation: Guidelines for forensic assessment.* Washington, DC: American Psychiatric Publishing.

Sisterman Keeney, K., Amacher, E., & Kastanakis, J. A. (1992). The Court Prep Group: A vital part of the court process. In H. Dent & R. Flin (Eds.), *Children as witnesses* (pp. 201–209). Chichester, England: Wiley.

Slovic, P., Monahan, J., & MacGregor, D. G. (2000). Violence risk assessment and risk communication: The effects of using actual cases, providing instruction, and employing probability versus frequency formats. *Law & Human Behavior, 24,* 271–296.

Small, M. A., & Melton, G. B. (1994). Evaluation of child witnesses for confrontation by criminal defendants. *Professional Psychology: Research and Practice, 25,* 228–233.

Smith, B., Elstein, S., Trost, T., & Bulkley, J. (1993). *The prosecution of child sexual and physical abuse cases.* Washington, DC: American Bar Association.

Smith, S. R., & Carlson, E. B. (1996). Reliability and validity of the Adolescent Dissociative Experiences Scale. *Dissociation, 9,* 125–129.

Somer, E., & Braunstein, A. (1999). Are children exposed to interparental violence being psychologically maltreated? *Aggression & Violent Behavior, 4*(4), 449–456.

Somervell v. Florida, 883 So. 2d 836 (Fla. 5th D.C.A. 2004).

Sorenson, T., & Snow, B. (1991). How children tell: The process of disclosure in child sexual abuse. *Child Welfare, 70,* 3–15.

Sparta, S. N. (2003). Assessment of childhood trauma. In A. M. Goldstein (Ed.), *Handbook of psychology: Forensic psychology* (Vol. 11, pp. 209–231). New York: Wiley.

Spence, S. H. (1994, November). *The structure and assessment of anxiety in children.* Paper presented at the meeting of the Association for the Advancement of Behavior Therapy, San Diego, CA.

Spence, S. H. (1998). A measure of anxiety symptoms among children. *Behaviour Research and Therapy, 36,* 545–566.

Spence, S. H., Barrett, P. M., & Turner, C. M. (2003). Psychometric properties of the Spence Children's Anxiety Scale with young adolescents. *Journal of Anxiety Disorders, 17,* 605–625.

Spencer, J. R., & Flin, R. H. (1990). *The evidence of children: The law and the psychology*. London: Blackstone Press.

Spilsbury, J. C., Drotar, D., Burant, C., Flannery, D., Creeden, R., & Friedman, S. (2005). Psychometric properties of the Pediatric Emotional Distress Scale in a diverse sample of children exposed to interpersonal violence. *Journal of Clinical Child and Adolescent Psychology, 34*, 758–764.

Stalets, M. M., & Luby, J. L. (2006). Preschool depression. *Child & Adolescent Psychiatric Clinics of North America, 15*, 899–917.

Stallings, P., & March, J. S. (1995). Assessment. In J. S. March (Ed.), *Anxiety disorders in children and adolescents* (pp. 125–147). New York: Guilford Press.

Stapleton, L. M., Sander, J. B., & Stark, K. D. (2007). Psychometric properties of the Beck Depression Inventory for Youth in a sample of girls. *Psychological Assessment, 19*, 230–235.

State v. Apilando, 79 Haw. 128, 900 P.2d 135 (Haw. 1995).

State v. Bobadilla, 709 N.W.2d 243 (Minn. 2006).

State v. Bronson, 258 Conn. 42, 779 A.2d 95 (Conn. 2001).

State v. Cameron, 168 Vt. 421, 721 A.2d 493 (Vt. 1998).

State v. Deuter, 839 S.W.2d 391 (Tenn. 1992).

State v. Ford, 626 So. 2d 1338 (Fla. 1993).

State v. Hunsaker, 39 Wash. App. 489, 693 P.2d 724 (Wash. Ct. App. 1984).

State v. Hussy, 521 A.2d 278 (Me. 1987).

State v. Mack, 337 Ore. 586, 101 P.3d 349 (Or. 2004).

State v. Mannion, 19 Utah 505, 57 P. 542 (Utah, 1899).

State v. Michaels, 264 N.J. Super. 579, 625 A.2d 489 (App. Div. 1993), *aff'd*, 642 A.2d 1372 (1994).

State v. Nutter, 258 N.J. Super. 41, 609 A.2d 65 (App. Div. 1992).

State v. Pitt, 209 Ore. App. 270, 147 P.3d 940 (Ore. App. 2006), *opinion adhered to on rehearing, with opinion*, 212 Or. App. 523, 159 P.3d 329 (Ore. App. 2007).

State v. Snowden, 385 Md. 64, 867 A.2d 314 (Md. 2005).

State v. T. E., 342 N.J. Super. 14, 775 A.2d 686 (App. Div. 2001).

State v. Vaught, 268 Neb. 316, 682 N.W.2d 284 (Neb. 2004).

State v. Vogelsberg, WI App. 228 (Wis. Ct. App. 2006), *rev. denied* State v. Vogelsberg, 731 N.W.2d 636 (Wis. Sup. Ct. 2007).

Steele, R. G., Little, T. D., Hardi, S. S., Forehand, R., Brody, G. H., & Hunter, H. L. (2006). A confirmatory comparison of the factor structure of the Children's Depression Inventory between European American and African American youth. *Journal of Child and Family Studies, 15*, 779–794.

Steele, R. G., Phipps, S., & Srivastava, D. K. (1999). Low-end specificity of childhood measures of emotional distress: Consistent effects for anxiety and depressive symptoms in a nonclinical population. *Journal of Personality Assessment, 73*, 276–289.

Steinberg, A. M., Brymer, M., Decker, K., & Pynoos, R. S. (2004). The UCLA PTSD Reaction Index. *Current Psychiatry Reports*, 6, 96–100.

Steinberg, M. (1994). *Structured Clinical Interview for DSM–IV Dissociative Disorders (SCID–D)*. Washington, DC: American Psychiatric Publishing.

Steinberg, M. (1996). The psychological assessment of dissociation. In L. K. Michelson & W. J. Ray (Eds.), *Handbook of dissociation: Theoretical, empirical, and clinical perspectives* (pp. 251–268). New York: Plenum Press.

Steinberg, M. (2000). Advances in the clinical assessment of dissociation: The SCID–D–R. *Bulletin of the Menninger Clinic*, 64, 146–163.

Steinberg, M. (2001). Updating diagnostic criteria for dissociative disorders: Learning from scientific advances. *Journal of Trauma & Dissociation*, 291, 59–63.

Steinberg, M., Rounsaville, B., & Cicchetti, D. (1990). The Structured Clinical Interview for *DSM–III–R* Dissociative Disorders: Preliminary report on a new diagnostic instrument. *American Journal of Psychiatry*, 147, 76–82.

Steinberg, M., & Steinberg, A. (1995). Using the SCID–D to assess dissociative identity disorder in adolescents: Three case studies. *Bulletin of the Menninger Clinic*, 59, 221–231.

Steinhausen, H., Wachter, M., Laimbock, K., & Metzke, W. (2006). A long-term outcome study of selective mutism in childhood. *Journal of Child Psychology and Psychiatry*, 47, 751–756.

Sternberg, K. J., Lamb, M. E., Esplin, P. W., Orbach, Y., & Hershkowitz, I. (2002). Using a structured interview protocol to improve the quality of investigative interviews. In M. L. Eisen, J. A. Quas, & G. S. Goodman (Eds.), *Memory and suggestibility in the forensic interview* (pp. 409–436). Mahwah, NJ: Erlbaum.

Sternberg, K. J., Lamb, M. E., Guterman, E., & Abbott, C. B. (2006). Effects of early and later family violence on children's behavior problems and depression: A longitudinal, multi-informant perspective. *Child Abuse & Neglect*, 30, 283–306

Stevenson, J. (1999). The treatment of the long-term sequelae of child abuse. *Journal of Child Psychology and Psychiatry*, 40, 89–111.

Steward, M. S., Bussey, K., Goodman, G. S., & Saywitz, K. J. (1993). Implications of developmental research for interviewing children. *Child Abuse & Neglect*, 17, 25–37.

Steward, M. S., & Steward, D. S. (1996). Interviewing young children about body touch and handling. *Monographs of the Society for Research in Child Development*, 61(4–5), 1–214.

Storch, E. A., Maisa-Warner, C., Dent, H. C., Roberti, J. W., & Fisher, P. H. (2003). Psychometric evaluation of the Social Anxiety Scale for Adolescents and the Social Phobia and Anxiety Inventory for Children: Construct validity and normative data. *Journal of Anxiety Disorders*, 18, 665–679.

Storr, C. L., Ialongo, N. S., Anthony, J. C., & Breslau, N. (2007). Childhood antecedents of exposure to traumatic events and posttraumatic stress disorder. *American Journal of Psychiatry*, 164, 199–125.

Strand, V. C., Sarmiento, T. L., & Pasquale, L. E. (2005). Assessment and screening tools for trauma in children and adolescents: A review. *Trauma, Violence, & Abuse, 6*, 55–78.

Stuber, M. L., & Shemesh, E. (2003). Posttraumatic stress responses in children with life-threatening illnesses. *Child & Adolescent Psychiatric Clinics of North America, 12*, 195–209.

Substance Abuse Mental Health Services Administration. (2007). [Home page]. Retrieved July 4, 2007, from http://www.samhsa.gov/

Summit, R. (1983). The child sexual abuse accommodation syndrome. *Child Abuse & Neglect, 7*, 177–192.

Sund, A. M., Larsson, B., & Wichstrøm, L. (2001). Depressive symptoms among young Norwegian adolescents as measured by the Mood and Feelings Questionnaire (MFQ). *European Child & Adolescent Psychiatry, 10*, 222–229.

Suryani, L. K., & Jensen, G. D. (1992). Psychiatrist, traditional healer, and culture integrated in clinical practice in Bali. *Medical Anthropology, 13*, 301–314.

Svedin, C. G., Nilsson, D., & Lindell, C. (2004). Traumatic experiences and dissociative symptoms among Swedish adolescents: A pilot study using Dis–Q–Sweden. *Nordic Journal of Psychiatry, 58*, 349–355.

Swanston, H. Y., Tebbutt, J. S., O'Toole, B. I., & Oates, R. K. (1997). Sexually abused children 5 years after presentation: A case-control study. *Pediatrics, 100*, 600–608.

Swim, J. K., Borgida, E., & McCoy, K. (1993). Videotaped versus in-court witness testimony: Does protecting the child witness jeopardize due process? *Journal of Applied Social Psychology, 23*(8), 603–631.

Taïeb, O., Moro, M. R., Baubet, T., Revah-Lévy, A., & Flament, M. F. (2003). Posttraumatic stress symptoms after childhood cancer. *European Child & Adolescent Psychiatry, 12*(6), 255–264.

Takushi, R., & Uomoto, J. M. (2001). The clinical interview from a multicultural perspective. In L. A. Suzuki, J. G. Ponterotto, P. J. Meller (Eds.), *Handbook of multicultural assessment: Clinical, psychological, and educational applications* (2nd ed., pp. 47–66) [Electronic resource]. San Francisco: Jossey-Bass.

Talwar, V., Lee, K., Bala, N., & Lindsay, R. C. L. (2006). Adults' judgments of children's coached reports. *Law and Human Behavior, 30*, 561–570.

Task Force on Child Witnesses of the American Bar Association Criminal Justice Section. (2002). *The child witness in criminal cases*. Washington, DC: American Bar Association.

Tebo, M. G. (2003, April). The most vulnerable clients: Attorneys must deal with special issues when kids come into contact with the courts. *ABA Journal, 89*, 46–53, 63.

Tenn. Code Ann. § 24-7-117 (2007).

Tenn. Code Ann. § 24-7-120 (2007).

Terr, L. (1990). *Too scared to cry: Psychic trauma in childhood*. New York: Harper & Row.

Terr, L. C. (1991). Childhood traumas: An outline and overview. *American Journal of Psychiatry, 148,* 10–20.

Terr, L. (1994). *Unchained memories: True stories of traumatic memories, lost and found.* New York: Basic Books.

Thabet, A. A., Abed, Y., & Vostanis, P. (2004). Comorbidity of PTSD and depression among refugee children during war conflict. *Journal of Child Psychology and Psychiatry, 45,* 533–542.

Theodore, A. D., & Runyan, D. K. (2006). A survey of pediatricians' attitudes and experiences with court in cases of child maltreatment. *Child Abuse & Neglect, 30,* 1353–1363.

Thompson, E. (2005). Child sex abuse victims: How will their stories be heard after *Crawford v. Washington? Campbell Law Review, 27,* 279–300.

Tiapula, S. (2005). Learning to read the signs: Prosecution strategies for child abuse cases with deaf victims and witnesses. *Update, 18,* 1–2. Retrieved August 25, 2007, from http://www.ndaa-apri.org/publications/newsletters/update_index.html

Timbremont, B., Braet, C., & Dreessen, L. (2004). Assessing depression in youth: Relation between the Children's Depression Inventory and a structured interview. *Journal of Clinical Child and Adolescent Psychology, 33,* 149–157.

Tobey, A. E., Goodman, G. S., Batterman-Faune, J. M., Orcutt, H. K., & Sachsenmaier, T. (1995). Balancing the rights of children and defendants: Effects of closed-circuit television on children's accuracy and jurors' perceptions. In M. S. Zaragoza, J. R. Graham, G. C. N. Hall, R. Hirschman, & Y. S. Ben-Porath (Eds.), *Memory and testimony in the child witness* (pp. 214–239). Thousand Oaks, CA: Sage.

Tolin, D. F., & Foa, E. B. (2006). Sex differences in trauma and posttraumatic stress disorder: A quantitative review of 25 years of research. *Psychological Bulletin, 132,* 959–992.

Tong, L., Oates, R. K., & McDowell, M. (1987). Personality development following sexual abuse. *Child Abuse & Neglect, 11,* 371–383.

Toppelberg, C. O., Tabors, P., Coggins, A., Lum, K., & Burger, C. (2005). Differential diagnosis of selective mutism in bilingual children. *Journal of the American Academy of Child & Adolescent Psychiatry, 44,* 592–595.

Trickett, P. K., Noll, J. G., Reiffman, A., & Putnam, F. (2001). Variants of intrafamilial sexual abuse experience: Implications for short and long-term development. *Development and Psychopathology, 13,* 1001–1019.

Trochim, W. M. K. (2006). *Theory of reliability.* Retrieved August 26, 2007, from http://www.socialresearchmethods.net/kb/reliablt.htm

Trowbridge, B. C. (2003). Psychologists' roles in evaluating child witnesses. *American Journal of Forensic Psychology, 21,* 1–41.

Tsai, J. L., & Chentsova-Dutton, Y. (2002). Understanding depression across cultures. In I. H. Gotlib & C. L. Hammen (Eds), *Handbook of depression* (pp. 467–491). New York: Guilford Press.

Tubb, V. A., Wood, J. M., & Hosch, H. M. (1999). Effects of suggestive interviewing and indirect evidence on child credibility in a sexual abuse case. *Journal of Applied Social Psychology, 29*, 1111–1127.

Turnbull, J. (2006). Promoting greater understanding in peers of children who stammer. *Emotional and Behavioural Difficulties, 11*, 237–247.

Turner, S. M., Beidel, D. C., Dancu, C. V., & Stanley, M. A. (1989). An empirically derived inventory to measure social fears and anxiety: The Social Phobia and Anxiety Inventory. *Psychological Assessment, 1*, 35–40.

Tutkun, H., Sar, V., Yargic, I. I., Ozpulat, T., Yanik, M., & Kiziltan, E. (1998). Frequency of dissociative disorders among psychiatric inpatients in a Turkish university clinic. *American Journal of Psychiatry, 155*, 800–805.

Tyler, K. A. (2002). Social and emotional outcomes of childhood sexual abuse: A review of recent research. *Aggression and Violent Behavior, 7*(6), 567–589.

Uehlein, N. A. (1988). Witnesses: Child competency statutes, 60 A.L.R.4th 369.

Ulloa, R. E., Ortiz, S., Higuera, F., Nogales, I., Fresan, A., Apiquian, R., et al. (2006). The Schedule for Affective Disorders and Schizophrenia for School-Age Children: Present and Lifetime Version (K–SADS–PL). *Actas Españolas de Psiquiatría, 34*, 36–40.

Umesue, M., Matsuo, T., Iwata, N., & Tashiro, N. (1996). Dissociative disorders in Japan: A pilot study with the Dissociative Experiences Scale and a semistructured interview. *Dissociation: Progress in the Dissociative Disorders, 9*, 182–189.

Uniform Child Witness Testimony by Alternative Methods Act, Idaho Code § 9–1801–1808 (2007).

United States v. Bordeaux, 400 F.3d 548 (8th Cir. 2005).

United States v. Etimani, 328 F.3d 493 (9th Cir. 2003).

United States v. Romey, 32 M.J. 180 (C.M.A. 1991).

United States v. Thomas, 453 F.3d 838 (7th Cir. 2006).

United States v. Thompson, 31 M.J. 168 (C.M.A. 1990).

United States v. Williams, 37 M.J. 289 (C.M.A. 1993).

U.S.C.S. Fed. R. Crim. P. 15(a)(1) (2006).

U.S. Department of Health and Human Services. (n.d.). *Appendix C: Highlights of findings from child maltreatment 2001*. Retrieved August 24, 2007, from http://www.acf.hhs.gov/programs/cb/pubs/cwo01/appendix/appendc.htm

U.S. Department of Health and Human Services. (2007). *Child maltreatment 2005*. Retrieved June 1, 2007, from http://www.acf.hhs.gov/programs/cb/pubs/cm05/index.htm

U.S. Department of Justice, Office of the Attorney General. (2005, May). *Attorney general guidelines for victim and witness assistance*. Retrieved August 26, 2007, from http://www.usdoj.gov/olp/final.pdf

U.S. Department of Justice, Office of Justice Programs, Office for Victims of Crimes. (1999, June). *Breaking the cycle of violence: Recommendations to improve the criminal justice response to child victims and witnesses*. OVC monograph (No.

NCJ 176983). Retrieved August 26, 2007, from http://www.ojp.usdoj.gov/ovc/publications/factshts/monograph.htm

U.S. Department of Justice, Office of Justice Programs, Office for Victims of Crimes. (2002, January). *The crime victim's right to be present*. OVC *Bulletin* (No. NCJ 189187). Retrieved August 26, 2007, from http://www.ojp.usdoj.gov/ovc/publications/bulletins/legalseries/bulletin3/welcome.html

U.S. Department of Justice, Office of Justice Programs, Office for Victims of Crimes. (2007). *Crime Victims' Rights Act (Part of the Justice for All Act)*. Retrieved August 26, 2007, from http://www.ojp.usdoj.gov/ovc/help/cvra.html

Utah R. Crim. P. Rule 15.5 (2007).

Va. Code Ann. § 63.2–1523 (2007).

Valle, L. A., & Silovsky, J. F. (2002). Attributions and adjustment following child sexual and physical abuse. *Child Maltreatment, 7*, 9–25.

van der Kolk, B. (2003). The neurobiology of childhood trauma and abuse. *Child & Adolescent Psychiatric Clinics of North America, 12*, 293–317.

van der Kolk, B. A. (2007). The developmental impact of childhood trauma. In L. J. Kirmayer, R. Lemelson, & M. Barad (Eds.), *Understanding trauma: Integrating biological, clinical, and cultural perspectives* (pp. 224–241). New York: Cambridge University Press.

van der Kolk, B. A., McFarlane, A. C., & Weisaeth, L. (1996). *Traumatic stress: The effects of overwhelming experience on mind, body, and society*. New York: Guilford Press.

van Lang, N. D. J., Ferdinand, R. F., Oldehinkel, A. J., Ormel, J., & Verhulst, F. C. (2005). Concurrent validity of the *DSM–IV* scales Affective Problems and Anxiety Problems of the Youth Self-Report. *Behaviour Research and Therapy, 43*, 1485–1494.

Vandenberg, G. H. (1998). *Court testimony in mental health: A guide for mental health professionals and attorneys*. Springfield, IL: Charles C Thomas.

Vanderlinden, J., Van Dyck, R., Vandereycken, W., & Vertommen, H. (1991). Dissociative experiences in the general population in the Netherlands and Belgium: A study with the Dissociative Questionnaire (DIS–Q). *Dissociation, 4*, 180–184.

Vanderlinden, J., Van Dyck, R.,Vandereycken, W., & Vertommen, H. (1993). Dissociation and traumatic experiences in the general population of the Netherlands. *Hospital & Community Psychiatry, 44*, 786–788.

Varela, R. E., & Biggs, B. K. (2006). Reliability and validity of the Revised Children's Manifest Anxiety Scale (RCMAS) across samples of Mexican, Mexican-American, and European American children: A preliminary investigation. *Anxiety, Stress, and Coping, 19*, 67–80.

Varela, R. E., Vernberg, E. M., Sanchez-Sosa, J. J., Riveros, A., Mitchell, M., & Mashunkashey, J. (2004). Anxiety reporting and culturally associated interpretation biases and cognitive schemas: A comparison of Mexican, Mexican American, and European American families. *Journal of Clinical Child and Adolescent Psychology, 33*(3), 237–247.

Vecchio, J., & Kearney, C. A. (2007). Assessment and treatment of a Hispanic youth with selective mutism. *Clinical Case Studies, 6*, 34–43.

Vernberg, E. M., La Greca, A. M., Silverman, W. K., & Prinstein, M. J. (1996). Prediction of posttraumatic stress symptoms in children after Hurricane Andrew. *Journal of Abnormal Psychology, 105*, 237–248.

Vieth, V. I. (2004). Keeping the balance true: Admitting child hearsay in the wake of *Crawford v. Washington*. *Update, 16*(12). Retrieved March 23, 2008, from http://www.ncdsv.org/images/KeepingBalanceWake.pdf

Vogelsberg v. Wisconsin, 127 S. Ct. 2265, 167 L. Ed. 2d 1093 (U.S., May 14, 2007).

Volkmar, F. R., & Marans, W. D. (1999). Measures for assessing pervasive developmental and communication disorders. In D. Shaffer, C. P. Lucas, & J. E. Richters (Eds.), *Diagnostic assessment in child and adolescent psychopathology* (pp. 167–205). New York: Guilford Press.

Vt. R. Evid. § 807 (2007).

Wade, A. (2002). New measures and new challenges: Children's experiences of the court process. In H. L. Westcott, G. M. Davies, & R. H. C. Bull (Eds.), *Children's testimony: A handbook of psychological research and forensic practice* (pp. 219–232). West Sussex, England: Wiley.

Wakefield, H., & Underwager, R. (1981). Sexual abuse allegations in divorce and custody disputes. *Behavioral Sciences & the Law, 9*, 451–468.

Wakefield, H., & Underwager, R. (1991; updated 2007, March 21). *Sexual abuse allegations in divorce and custody disputes*. Retrieved August 26, 2007, from http://www.ipt-forensics.com/library/saadcd.htm

Walker, A. G. (2000). *Handbook on questioning children: A linguistic perspective* (2nd ed.). Washington, DC: American Bar Association.

Walker, A. G., & Warren, A. R. (1995). The language of the child abuse interview: Asking the questions, understanding the answers. In T. Ney (Ed.), *True and false allegations of child sexual abuse: Assessment and case management* (pp. 153–162). New York: Brunner/Mazel.

Walker, N. E. (2002). Children as victims and witnesses in the criminal trial process: Forensic interviews of children: The components of scientific validity and legal admissibility. *Law and Contemporary Problems, 65*, 149–178.

Walker, N. E., & Hunt, J. S. (1998). Interviewing child victim-witnesses: How you ask is what you get. In C. P. Thompson, D. J. Herrmann, J. D. Read, & D. Bruce (Eds.), *Eyewitness memory: Theoretical and applied perspectives* (pp. 55–87). Mahwah, NJ: Erlbaum.

Waller, M. A. (2001). Resilience in ecosystemic context: Evolution of the concept. *American Journal of Orthopsychiatry, 71*, 290–297.

Waller, N. G., & Meehl, P. E. (1997). *Multivariate taxometric procedures: Distinguishing types from continua*. Newbury Park, CA: Sage.

Waller v. Georgia, 467 U.S. 39 (1984).

Walsh, W., Jones, L., & Cross, T. (2003). Children's advocacy centers: One philosophy, many models. *APSAC Advisor, 15*, 3–6.

Walters, S. (2000). Effective strategies for victim advocates in child abuse cases. *APRI Update, 13*(12). Retrieved August 25, 2007, from http://www.ndaa.org/publications/newsletters/update_volume_13_number_12_2000.html

Walters, S., Holmes, L., Bauer, G., & Vieth, V. (2003). *Finding words: Half a nation by 2010: Interviewing children and preparing for court* [Electronic version]. Alexandria, VA: American Prosecutors Research Institute. Retrieved August 25, 2007, from http://www.ndaa.org/pdf/finding_words_2003.pdf

Walton, E. (1994). The confrontation clause and the child victim of sexual abuse. *Child & Adolescent Social Work Journal, 11*, 195–207.

Warren, A. R., & Marsil, D. F. (2002). Why children's suggestibility remains a serious concern. *Law and Contemporary Problems, 65*, 127–147.

Warren, A. R., & McCloskey, L. A. (1997). Language in social contexts. In J. Berko-Gleason (Ed.), *The development of language* (4th ed., pp 210–258). New York: Allyn & Bacon.

Warren, A. R., & McGough, L. (1996). Research on children's suggestibility: Implications for the investigative interview. In G. Goodman & B. Bottoms (Eds.), *International perspectives on child witnesses* (pp. 12–44). Thousand Oaks, CA: Sage.

Warren, A. R., Nunez, N., Keeney, J. M., Buck, J. A., & Smith, B. (2002). The believability of children and their interviewers' hearsay testimony: When less is more. *Journal of Applied Social Psychology, 87*, 846–857.

Warren, A. R., & Woodall, C. E. (1999). The reliability of hearsay testimony: How well do interviewers recall their interviews with children? *Psychology, Public Policy, and Law, 5*, 355–371.

Warren-Leubecker, A., Tate, C., Hinton, I., & Ozbeck, N. (1989). What do children know about the legal system and when do they know it? First steps down a less traveled path in child witness research. In S. Ceci, M. Toglia, & D. Ross (Eds.), *Perspectives on children's testimony* (pp. 158–183). New York: Springer-Verlag.

Wash. Rev. Code § 9A.44.150 (2007).

Wash. Rev. Code § 10.46.085 (2007).

Washington, J., & Craig, H. (1999). Performances of at-risk, African American preschoolers on the Peabody Picture Vocabulary Test—III. *Language, Speech, and Hearing Services in Schools, 30*, 75–82.

Wasserman, G. A., McReynolds, L. S., Fisher, P., & Lucas, C. P. (2005). Diagnostic Interview Schedule for Children: Present State Voice Version. In T. Grisso, G. Vincent, & D. Seagrave (Eds.), *Mental health screening and assessment in juvenile justice* (pp. 234–239). New York: Guilford Press.

Watters, T., Brineman, J., & Wright, S. (2007). Between a rock and a hard place: Why hearsay testimony may be a necessary evil in child sexual abuse cases. *Journal of Forensic Psychology Practice, 7*, 47–57.

Weaver, T. L., & Clum, G. A. (1995). Psychological distress associated with interpersonal violence: A meta-analysis. *Clinical Psychology Review, 15*, 115–140.

Weems, C. F., Silverman, W. K., Rapee, R. R., & Pina, A. A. (2003). The role of control in childhood anxiety disorders. *Cognitive Therapy and Research, 27*, 557–568.

Weinstein, J. B., Berger, M. A., & McLaughlin, J. M. (1998). *Wienstein's Federal Evidence*. New York: Matthew Bender.

Welder, A. N. (2000). Sexual abuse victimization and the child witness in Canada: Legal, ethical, and professional issues for psychologists. *Canadian Psychology, 41,* 160–173.

Westcott, H. L. (2006). Child witness testimony: What do we know and where are we going? *Child and Family Law Quarterly, 18*(2), 175–190.

Westcott, H. L., Davies, G. M., & Bull, R. H. C. (Eds.). (2002). *Children's testimony: A handbook of psychological research and forensic practice*. Chichester, England: Wiley.

Westcott, H. L., Davies, G. M., & Clifford, B. R. (1991). Adult's perceptions of children's videotaped truthful and deceptive statements. *Children & Society, 5,* 123–135.

Westcott, H. L., Davies, G. M., & Spencer, J. R. (1999). Children, hearsay and the courts: A perspective from the UK. *Psychology, Public Policy, and Law, 5,* 282–303.

Westen, D., & Weinberger, J. (2004). When clinical description becomes statistical prediction. *American Psychologist, 59,* 595–613.

Wherry, J. N., Jolly, J. B., Feldman, J., Adam, B., & Manjanatha, S. (1994). The Child Dissociative Checklist: Preliminary findings of a screening instrument. *Child Abuse & Neglect, 3,* 51–66.

Whiffen, V. E., & MacIntosh, H. B. (2005). Mediators of the link between childhood sexual abuse and emotional distress: A critical review. *Trauma, Violence, & Abuse, 6,* 24–39.

Whitcomb, D. (1988). *Guardians ad litem in the criminal courts*. Washington, DC: Office of Communications and Research Utilization, National Institute of Justice, U.S. Department of Justice.

Whitcomb, D. (1991). Improving the investigation and prosecution of child sexual-abuse cases: Research findings, questions, and implications for public policy. In D. D. Knudsen & J. L. Miller (Eds.), *Abused and battered: Social and legal responses of family violence* (pp. 181–190). Hawthorne, NY: Aldine de Gruyter.

Whitcomb, D. (1992a). Legal reforms on behalf of child witnesses: Recent developments in American courts. In H. Dent & R. Flin (Eds.), *Children as witnesses* (pp. 151–166). Chichester, England: Wiley.

Whitcomb, D. (1992b). *When the victim is a child* (2nd ed.). Washington, DC: U.S. Department of Justice.

Whitcomb, D. (2003). Legal interventions for child victims. *Journal of Traumatic Stress, 16,* 149–157.

Whitcomb, D., De Vos, E., Cross, T. P., Peeler, N. A., Runyan, D. K., Humter, W. M., et al. (1994). *Child victim as witness research and development program*. Washington, DC: U.S. Department of Justice.

Whitcomb, D., Goodman, G. S., Runyan, D. K., & Hoak, S. (1994). *The emotional effects of testifying on sexually abused children*. Washington, DC: U.S. Department of Justice, Office of Justice Programs, National Institute of Justice.

White, S., & Edlestein, B. (1991). Behavioral assessment and investigatory interviewing. *Behavioral Assessment, 13*, 245–264.

White, S., Halpin, B. M., Strom, G. A., & Santilli, G. (1988). Behavioral comparisons of young sexually abused, neglected, and nonreferred children. *Journal of Clinical Child Psychiatry, 17*, 53–61.

White v. Illinois, 502 U.S. 346 (1992).

Whorton v. Bockting, 127 S. Ct. 1173, 167 L. Ed. 2d 1 (2007).

Widom, C. S. (1999). Posttraumatic stress disorder in abused and neglected children grown up. *American Journal of Psychiatry, 156*, 1223–1229.

Wiehe, V. R. (1996). *Working with child abuse and neglect: A primer.* Thousand Oaks, CA: Sage.

Wiig, E. H., Secord, W. A., & Semel, E. (2006). *The Clinical Evaluation of Language Fundamentals—Spanish edition.* San Antonio, TX: Harcourt Assessment. Retrieved August 26, 2007, from http://harcourtassessment.com/haiweb/cultures/en-us/productdetail.htm?pid=015-8038-41x

Willis, C. E., & Wrightsman, L. S. (1995). Effects of victim gaze behavior and prior relationship on rape culpability attributions. *Journal of Interpersonal Violence, 10*, 367–377.

Williams, K. T. (1997). *The Expressive Vocabulary Test.* Circle Pines, MN: American Guidance Service.

Winston, F. K., Kassam-Adams, N., Vivarelli-O'Neill, C., Ford, J., Newman, E., Baxt, C., et al. (2002). Acute stress disorder symptoms in children and their parents after pediatric traffic injury. *Pediatrics, 109*, 90–99.

Winters, N. C., Myers, K., & Proud, L. (2002). Ten-year review of rating scales: III. Scales assessing suicidality, cognitive style, and self esteem. *Journal of the American Academy of Child & Adolescent Psychiatry, 41*, 1150–1181.

Wis. Stat. § 908.08 (2006).

Wis. Stat. § 967.04 (2006).

Wis. Stat. § 971.105 (2006).

Wis. Stat. § 972.11 (2003).

Wolfe, D. A., & McEachran, A. (1997). Child physical abuse and neglect. In E. J. Mash & L. G. Terdal (Eds.), *Assessment of childhood disorders* (3rd ed., pp. 523–568). New York: Guilford Press.

Wolfe, D. A., Sas, L., & Wekerle, C. (1994). Factors associated with the development of posttraumatic stress disorder among child victims of sexual abuse. *Child Abuse & Neglect, 18*, 37–50.

World Health Organization. (2005). *International Statistical Classification of Diseases and Related Health Problems, 10th Revision—ICD-10* (2nd ed.). Geneva: Author.

Woodruff-Borden, J., & Leyfer, O. T. (2006). Anxiety and fear. In M. Hersen (Ed.), *Clinician's handbook of child behavioral assessment* (pp. 267–289). Burlington, MA: Elsevier.

Wren, F. J., Berg, E. A., Heiden, L. A., Kinnamon, C. J., Ohlson, L. A., Bridge, J. A., et al. (2007). Childhood anxiety in a diverse primary care population: Parent–child reports, ethnicity and SCARED factor structure. *Journal of the American Academy of Child & Adolescent Psychiatry, 46,* 332–340.

Wyo. Stat. § 7-11-408 (2007).

Yang, J., Hong, S. D., Joung, Y. S., & Kim, J. (2006). Validation study of tripartite model of anxiety and depression in children and adolescents: Clinical sample in Korea. *Journal of Korean Medical Science, 21,* 1098–1102.

Yao, S., Zou, T., Zhu, X., Abela, J. R. Z., Auerbach, R. P., & Tong, X. (2007). Reliability and validity of the Chinese version of the Multidimensional Anxiety Scale for Children among Chinese secondary school students. *Child Psychiatry and Human Development, 38,* 1–16.

Yasik, A. E., Saigh, P. A., Oberfield, R. A., & Halamandaris, P. V. (2007). Posttraumatic stress disorder: Memory and learning performance in children and adolescents. *Biological Psychiatry, 61,* 382–388.

Yeats, M. A. (2004, July 30). *The West Australian experience: A judicial perspective.* Paper presented at conference of the Australian Institute of Judicial Administration: Child Witnesses—Best Practices for Courts, District Court of New South Wales, Parramatta. Retrieved August 26, 2007, from http://www.aija.org.au/child/Yeats.rtf

Yeganeh, R., Beidel, D. C., & Turner, S. M. (2006). Selective mutism: More than social anxiety? *Depression and Anxiety, 23,* 117–123.

Yehuda, R., & McFarlane, A. C. (1995). Conflict between current knowledge about posttraumatic stress disorder and its original conceptual basis. *American Journal of Psychiatry, 152,* 1705–1713.

Yorbik, O., Akbiyik, D. I., Kirmizigul, P., & Söhmen, T. (2004). Post-traumatic stress disorder symptoms in children after the 1999 Marmara earthquake in Turkey. *International Journal of Mental Health, 33,* 46–58.

Youth Justice and Criminal Evidence Act, 1999, c. 23 (U.K.).

Yozwiak, J. A., Golding, J. M., & Marsil, D. F. (2004). The impact of type of out-of-court disclosure in a child sexual assault trial. *Child Maltreatment, 9,* 325–334.

Yuille, J. C., Hunter, R., Joffe, R., & Zaparniuk, J. (1993). Interviewing children in sexual abuse cases. In G. S. Goodman & B. L. Bottoms (Eds.), *Child victims, child witnesses: Understanding and improving children's testimony* (pp. 95–115). New York: Guilford Press.

Zahn-Waxler, C., Klimes-Dougan, B., & Slattery, M. J. (2000). Internalizing problems of childhood and adolescence: Prospects, pitfalls, and progress in understanding the development of anxiety and depression. *Development and Psychopathology, 12,* 443–446.

Zajac, R., Gross, J., & Hayne, H. (2003). Asked and answered: Questioning children in the courtroom. *Psychiatry, Psychology and Law, 10,* 199–209.

Zajac, R., & Hayne, H. (2003). I don't think that's what *really* happened: The effect of cross-examination on the accuracy of children's reports. *Journal of Experimental Psychology: Applied, 9,* 187–195.

Zinbarg, R. E., & Barlow, D. H. (1996). Structure of anxiety and the anxiety disorders: A hierarchical model. *Journal of Abnormal Psychology*, *105*, 181–193.

Zoroglu, S. S., Sar, V., Tuzun, U., Tutkun, H., & Savas, H. A. (2002). Reliability and validity of the Turkish version of the Adolescent Dissociative Experiences Scale. *Psychiatry and Clinical Neurosciences*, *56*, 551–556.

TABLE OF AUTHORITIES

AUTHOR INDEX

Bursztajn, H. J., 127
Burton, M., 74, 75, 83, 85, 90, 97
Bush, S. F., 140
Bussey, K., 126, 257

Callaghan, M., 148, 163
Camilleri, A. J., 144
Camparo, L., 4, 129, 254, 256
Campbell, K. D. M., 181
Campbell, T. W., 149
Campbell, W., 224
Canino, G., 112, 113, 115, 167, 188
Cantwell, D. P., 222
Cardarelli, A. P., 188
Cardeña, E., 159, 160, 166, 177, 178
Carlson, E., 162
Carlson, E. A., 160, 165
Carlson, E. B., 14, 115, 134, 135, 136,
        139, 140, 143, 153, 159, 162,
        163, 168, 188
Carlson, G. A., 225
Carmines, E. G., 114
Carr, C., 80
Carrey, N., 230
Carrion, V. G., 150, 159, 161, 163,
        165, 174, 175, 177, 178, 230
Carter, C. A., 72, 121
Carter, L. S., 148
Cashmore, J., 13, 15, 68, 69, 70, 75, 76,
        77, 81, 89, 97, 257
Casper, R. C., 223
Caspi, A., 150
Castillo, R. J., 160
Castrogiovanni, A., 239
Catanzaro, S. J., 181
Ceci, S. J., 4, 6, 27, 87, 89, 92, 107,
        108, 120, 126, 148, 234
Cederborg, A., 234, 235
Center for Mental Health Services,
        258
Chaffin, M., 180, 188, 189
Chambers, W. G., 224
Chan, J. L., 156
Chandy, J. M., 139
Chansky, T. E., 181
Chapman, M. T., 120
Charney, D., 223
Charney, D. S., 145
Chase, C. A., 51
Chavira, D. A., 247
Chentsova-Dutton, Y., 181, 223

Cherryman, J., 87
Child Welfare Information Gateway, 7, 13
Choate, M. L., 184
Choi, H., 223
Chorpita, B. F., 149, 180, 183, 201,
        201–202, 202, 208, 209, 210, 211,
        223
Christopher, N. C., 144, 149, 227
Chrousos, G. P., 136
Chu, J. A., 164
Cicchetti, D., 164, 175, 241
Clark, L. A., 183, 187
Clark, S. J., 51, 58n11
Cleator, H., 247, 248
Clifford, B. R., 262
Clum, G. A., 135
Coatsworth, J., 139
Coggins, A., 246
Cohan, S. L., 247
Cohen, J. A., 136, 139, 144, 153, 254, 255
Cohen, P., 113, 115, 180, 224
Cohen, S. L., 247
Collett, B. R., 114, 151, 159
Collica, T. J., 209
Comer, J. S., 182, 195, 213, 214
Committee on Ethical Guidelines for
        Forensic Psychologists, 102, 104,
        105
Committee on Legal and Ethical Issues in
        the Treatment of Interpersonal
        Violence, 7
Compas, B. E., 224, 225, 229
Connor, D. E., 182
Connors, K., 209
Conover, N. C., 182
Conte, J., 188
Conte, J. R., 67, 72, 126
Cook, A., 136, 137, 138, 139, 140, 144,
        158, 223
Cook, C. A., 147
Cooke, P., 249
Cooley, M. R., 181
Coons, P. M., 165
Copen, L. M., 255, 257
Cordon, I., 88
Cordon, I. M., 88, 92, 255
Costello, A. J., 182
Costello, E. J., 133, 158, 179, 181, 216,
        217, 225, 229
Coster, W. J., 241
Cotman, D., 151, 164
Coulter, M. L., 6, 29, 72

Hodell, E. C., 96
Hofflich, S. A., 187, 209
Hofstra, M. B., 181
Hoge, S. K., 117
Hoier, T. S., 165, 169, 173, 175
Holmes, L., 46
Holmes, L. S., 27
Hong, S. D., 183
Hornstein, N., 161, 162
Hornstein, N. L., 176, 178
Horowitz, D., 96
Horowitz, J. L., 181
Horowitz, J. M., 188
Horowitz, L. A., 165
Horwood, L. J., 224
Hosch, H. M., 94
Housekamp, B. M., 164
Hoven, C. W., 223
Howell, P., 243, 243
Hoyano, L., 88
Hsu, L., 180
Hudson, D. L., 42
Hudson, J. L., 182
Hughes, A. A., 187, 209
Hunsley, J., 115, 122
Hunt, J. P., 146
Hunt, J. S., 5
Hunter, R., 120
Hunter, W. M., 6, 29, 72
Hurley, P., 8, 67, 70, 263, 264
Huxsahl, J. E., 164
Hyman, I., 154–157

Ialongo, N. S., 145
Ickovics, J. E., 139
Ilardi, S. S., 214, 229
Imhoff, M. C., 121
Imwinkelried, E., 51, 88
International Society for the Study of
    Dissociation (ISSD), 161, 162,
    163, 165, 166, 167, 177
Ivarsson, T., 198
Iwata, N., 160

Jackson-Maldonado, D., 246
Jaenicke, C., 4
James, P., 199, 209
Jameson, M., 227
Jaworski, T. M., 164
Jaycox, L. H., 146

Jensen, B. J., 208
Jensen, G. D., 160
Joffe, R., 120
Johnson, J. G., 180, 224
Johnson, K., 154
Johnson, R. M., 148
Joiner, T. E., 181
Jolly, J. B., 229
Jones, D., 7
Jones, G., 234
Jones, J. G., 136, 148
Jones, J. M., 134, 140
Jones, L., 5, 29, 255
Jones, L. M., 68, 72
Joseph, P., 248
Joung, Y. S., 183
Jurkovich, G., 132

Kala, R., 182
Kalick, S. M., 132
Kaplan, S., 151
Kaplan, S. J., 149, 180, 188, 222, 224
Kaplow, J. B., 139, 143, 147, 180
Kasen, S., 113, 115
Kashani, J. H., 225
Kaslow, N. J., 180, 184
Kassam-Adams, N., 133, 145
Kastanakis, J. A., 258
Kasten, J. D., 167, 170
Kaufman, J., 158, 194, 196, 197, 212, 223,
    224, 225
Kaufman, R. M., 48
Kaushall, P., 87, 98n
Kaysen, D., 135
Kazdin, A. E., 112, 114, 115, 222
Keaney, J. C., 164
Kearney, C. A., 146, 147, 148, 246, 247,
    248
Keeler, G., 225
Keenan, C., 88
Keeney, J. M., 91
Kehn, A., 87, 96
Kelley, B., 5, 6
Kelley, E., 234, 235, 236, 237, 238, 239,
    241, 242, 245
Kempe, C. H., 138
Kenardy, J., 144, 160, 178
Kendall, P. C., 181, 182, 187, 195, 209,
    213, 214, 222
Kendall-Tackett, K. A., 140, 148, 150, 223
Kenney, R., 78

Lucas, C. P., 224, 225
Lum, 246
Lusk, R., 70
Lyneham, H. J., 182, 195
Lynn, S. J., 165
Lynskey, M. T., 224
Lyon, T. D., 4, 13, 26, 63, 79, 120, 239, 253, 263
Lyons, J. A., 148
Lyons, J. S., 164, 175

Macfie, J., 164, 165
MacGregor, D. G., 128
MacIntosh, H. B., 139, 140
Madvig, B. T., 144
Maitland, L., 88
Malenbaum, R., 165
Malinosky-Rummell, R. R., 165, 169, 173, 175
Malla, S., 8, 67, 264
Maloney, K., 243
Manassis, K., 247
Mandel, F., 180
Mandel, F. S., 154
Mannarino, A. P., 136, 139, 144, 153, 254
Manson, S. M., 223
Marans, W. D., 245
March, J., 139, 158, 191
March, J. S., 145, 147, 149, 151, 152, 186, 190, 193, 199, 209
Marciano, P. L., 222
Margolin, G., 148
Marks, I., 184
Marks, R. G., 5
Marsil, D. F., 15, 19, 70, 84, 85, 86, 87, 92, 93, 234
Mart, E., 109, 127
Martin, J., 150
Martinez-Taboas, A., 160, 161, 163, 167, 168, 177, 178
Martinussen, M., 139
Marton, P., 225, 226, 229, 254
Mash, E., 122
Mash, E. J., 112, 114, 115
Masten, A., 139
Matsuo, T., 160
Matthey, S., 214, 229
Matus, Y. E., 110
Mayer, A., 87
Mayer, B., 209

McAuliff, B. D., 13, 15, 75, 79, 91, 92, 98
McCabe, A., 239
McCauley, M., 19
McCauley, M. R., 120
McCauley, R. J., 237
McCloskey, L. A., 238, 239
McClure, K. S., 181, 213, 221
McCoy, K., 77
McDermott, B. M., 132
McDowell, M., 70
McEachran, A., 241
McFarlane, A. C., 146, 254
McGough, L., 121
McGough, L. S., 3, 48, 48n7, 87, 93, 96
McGraw, E. M., 7
McGuffin, 216
McHugh, M., 146
McInnes, A., 247, 248
McKenzie, N., 164
McKinnon, D. H., 241, 243
McLaughlin, J. M., 49
McLeer, S., 148, 163, 228
McLeod, B. D., 182
McLeod, S., 241
McMahon, S., 63, 253
McManus, M., 228–229
McNally, R. J., 112, 150
McPherson, W. B., 136, 148
McReynolds, L. S., 224
Meadows, E. A., 213, 221
Meehl, P. E., 113, 115, 161
Meisenheimer, K., 98
Meiser-Stedman, R., 139, 140, 145, 146, 147, 149
Melinder, A., 27, 108, 120
Melton, G. B., 15, 70, 72, 76, 84, 112, 117, 126, 128, 253, 254, 255, 262, 263, 264
Memorandum of Good Practice, 120
Mendelson, M., 229
Mennen, F. E., 149, 153
Merckelbach, H., 176, 209, 210
Merikangas, K. R., 181
Mermelstein, R., 182, 223
Messer, S. C., 229
Meyer, C., 243
Meyer, R. G., 136
Mikhailichendo, K., 230
Mikros, H. B., 215
Milan, S., 132
Milich, R., 139

Ollendick, T. H., 181, 183, 184, 186–187, 187, 188, 192, 193, 194, 208, 209, 210
Olson, R. C., 30
Orbach, Y., 120, 234
Orcutt, H. K., 81
Ormel, J., 181, 202
Ormrod, R., 29
Ormrod, R. K., 135
Ornstein, P. A., 4
Orvaschel, H., 182, 221, 222, 225
Osofsky, J. D., 148
Ostrowski, S. A., 144, 149
O'Toole, B., 223
Ozbeck, N., 3

Padilla, A. M., 115
Padlo, S., 136
Palesh, O. G., 159
Palmer, L. J., 132
Pardo, C., 134
Parker, J. D. A., 209
Parzer, P., 132, 165
Pasquale, L. E., 151, 175
Pathak, M. K., 93
Paulauskas, S. L., 181
Pears, K., 159
Pearson Education, Inc., 228
Peebles, C. D., 147
Peeters, E., 176
Pelcovitz, D., 149, 151, 154, 180, 188
Pence, D., 6
Penfold, S. P., 7
Perez, C., 241
Perks, S. M., 227
Perosa, L. M., 160
Perosa, S. L., 160
Perrin, S., 112, 149, 151, 179, 181, 182, 184, 186, 187, 201, 202, 203
Perron, W., 31
Perry, B. D., 48, 149
Perry, N. W., 4, 69
Pervanidou P., 136
Perwien, A. R., 190
Peters, D., 70
Peterson, D. R., 122
Peterson, G., 161, 162, 169, 176
Peterson, R. A., 209
Petrila, J., 15, 112
Petrovski, P., 214, 229
Pezdek, K., 4

Pfefferbaum, B., 151
Phelps, A., 67, 263
Phillips, A., 43, 44, 45, 46, 47
Phillips, B. M., 112, 135, 144
Phillips, J. M., 236, 241, 243
Phipps, S., 132
Piacentini, J. C., 179, 191
Piers, C., 133
Piha, J., 229
Pina, A. A., 155, 193, 195, 209
Pine, D., 191
Pipe, M., 82, 121, 234
Pizzi, W. T., 31
Plotnikoff, J., 5, 67, 69, 73, 74, 253, 263
Pollock, V. E., 164
Poole, D. A., 234, 236, 237, 238, 239, 241n
Portage, D., 230
Poulton, R., 150
Powell, M., 4
Poythress, N. G., 15, 112
Poznanski, E., 228
Poznanski, E. O., 215, 228
Praver, F., 154
Prendergast, M., 224
Principe, G. F., 4, 27, 87
Prinstein, M. J., 139
Prizmich, L. P., 51, 88
Prohl, J., 168
Proud, L., 227
Puliafico, A. C., 182, 195
Punamämaki, R.-L., 146
Putnam, C., 23, 24
Putnam, F., 164–165
Putnam, F. W., 136, 146n, 147, 160, 161, 162, 163, 165, 167, 169, 174, 175, 176
Pyle-Taub, E., 6, 8, 264
Pynoos, R., 112, 150, 153, 155
Pynoos, R. S., 134, 137, 144, 146, 147, 153, 153–154, 154, 162

Qin, J., 95
Qouta, S., 146
Qualls, C. D., 243
Quas, J. A., 6, 13, 66, 67, 70, 72, 73, 76, 80, 87, 234, 261, 263
Quinn, K., 147

Rabalais, A. E., 144
Rabian, B., 113, 115, 209, 214, 227

SUBJECT INDEX

357

physical conditions with symptoms
similar to, 183–184
and PTSD, 144–145
relevant symptoms of, 254
and selective mutism, 247, 248
and stuttering, 243
Anxiety Control Questionnaire for
Children (ACQC), 192, 209
Anxiety Disorders Interview Schedule
(ADIS), 190, 191
Anxiety Disorders Interview Schedule
for Children for *DSM–IV*: Child
and Parent Versions (ADIS–IV:
C/P), 191, 192, 193–194, 195,
230
Anxiety Rating for Children—Revised
(ARC–R), 190, 191
Aphasia, 239
APRI (American Prosecutors Research
Institute), 5, 258
Area under receiver-operating
characteristic curve (AUC),
116
Assessment, 16
of anxiety in children, 180–189
behavioral measures of, 129
of childhood trauma, 136–137
of depression in children, 180–184,
221–224
of dissociation in children, 161–167
of PTSD in children, 143–150
See also Courtroom modification
evaluation; Diagnosis;
Evaluation
Assessment of child witnesses, 14,
111–113, 119–127
and cultural group, 109–111
and literature, 15
Assessment instruments
cut points in, 124
for depression and anxiety, 181
limitations of to be discussed, 129
for PTSD, 148, 151, 153–158
reliable and valid, 113–117
Assessment measures
for anxiety, 189–211, 230
for depression, 212–220, 224–230
for dissociation, 166–178
for posttraumatic stress disorder,
150–158
Assessment protocols, development of
needed, 262

Attachment, and resilience, 139
Attention-deficit/hyperactivity disorder,
136
Attorney for child, 22–23, 30. *See also*
Counsel for child witness;
Guardian ad litem
Australia
shielding-technique studies in, 85, 86
videotaped mock trial study in, 80
Automatic Thoughts Questionnaire, 227

BASC (Behavior Assessment System for
Children), 192
BAT (Behavioral Avoidance Test), 193
Battered child syndrome, 138
BDDI-C (Bellevue Dissociative Disorders
Interview for Children, The), 172,
175, 177
BDI–II, 229
Beck Depression Inventory (BDI), 226,
229
Beck Depression Inventory for Youth
(BDI–Y), 229
Behavioral Avoidance Test (BAT), 193
Behavior Assessment System for Children
(BASC), 192
Beidel, Deborah C., 205, 206
Bellevue Dissociative Disorders Interview
for Children, The (BDDI-C),
172–173, 175, 177
Bias(es)
from CCTV use, 80, 85–86
against child witnesses, 81
confirmation (confirmatory), 108, 127
in evaluation (guarding against),
108–109, 152, 252, 257
from screens, 84–86
Bipolar disorders, 222
Birmaher, Boris, 200
Brief Symptom Index (BSI), 132
Britain (United Kingdom)
and communication requirements,
233–234
modification research in, 67
Witness Support Service in, 72
See also England; Northern Ireland;
Scotland; Wales

CACs. *See* Child advocacy centers
CADC (Child/Adolescent Dissociative
Checklist), 167, 170, 175, 177

Canada
court preparation program in, 67–68
screens used in, 82
and videotaped interview testimony, 88, 89–90
CAPA (Child and Adolescent Psychiatric Assessment), 191, 192, 224, 225, 226
CAPA–C, 192
CAPS (Clinician-Administered PTSD Scale), 154
CAPS–C/CAPS–CA (Clinician-Administered PTSD Scale for Children and Adolescents for DSM–IV), 153, 154, 155
CARS (Children's Anxiety Rating Scale), 191
CAS (Child Assessment Schedule), 192, 226
Cases involving child witnesses, precedence given to, 9, 29–30
CASI (Child Anxiety Sensitivity Index), 191, 192, 193
Catastrophes, as trauma, 133–134
CATS (Children's Automatic Thoughts Scale), 192
CBCL (Child Behavior Checklist), 132, 190, 191, 192, 208
adolescent version of (YSR), 132, 191, 192, 208
CBCL/YSR/TRF (Child Behavior Checklist/Youth Self Report/ Teacher Report Form), 191
CCTV. See Closed-circuit television
CDC (Child Dissociative Checklist), 167, 169, 175, 176
CDI (Children's Depression Inventory), 213–214, 226, 227, 228, 228–229
CDRS, 228
CDRS–R (Children's Depression Rating Scale—Revised), 214–215, 226, 227, 228
CDS (Children's Depression Scale), 226, 227
CELF (Clinical Evaluation of Language Fundamentals—Fourth Edition), 245
Preschool version of (CELF–P–II), 245
Center for Epidemiologic Studies Depression Scales (CES–D and CES–DC), 226, 227
Chalmers, Anita, 216

Child abuse cases. See Abuse cases
Child/Adolescent Dissociative Checklist (CADC), 167, 170, 175, 177
Child and Adolescent Psychiatric Assessment (CAPA), 191, 192, 224, 225, 226
Child and Adolescent Psychiatric Assessment: Life Events Section and PTSD Module, 158
Child advocacy centers (CACs)
evaluations at, 29
interviews in, 40, 255
MHPs as consultants to, 63
Child advocates, 21, 23
Child Anxiety and Depression Scale, 183
Child Anxiety Sensitivity Index (CASI), 191, 192, 193
Child Assessment Schedule (CAS), 192, 226
Child Behavior Checklist (CBCL), 132, 190, 191, 192, 208
adolescent version of (YSR), 132, 191, 192, 208
Child Behavior Checklist/Youth Self Report/Teacher Report Form (CBCL/YSR/TRF), 191
Child custody disputes, and false allegations, 7
Child Dissociative Checklist (CDC), 167, 169, 175, 176
Child hearsay exception. See Hearsay exception, child
Child interviews. See at Interview
Child Interview for Subjective Dissociation Experiences (CISDE), 173, 175, 177
Child Obsessive Compulsive Impact Scale, 192
Child PTSD Reaction Index (CPTS–RI), 153, 155, 191
Child PTSD Symptom Scale, 154, 191
Children
coping with court stresses (research needed on), 263–264
guidelines for talking with, 240–241
limited legal understanding of, 3–4
as reporters of psychopathology or abuse, 126, 182
See also Child witnesses
Children's Attributional Style Questionnaire, 227
Children's Automatic Thoughts Scale, 192

and dissociation, 160–161, 163
and emotional distress measures, 132
and language abilities, 238
and language use, 241
multicultural appropriateness,
  109–111
and multiple personality disorder,
  160–161
and PTSD, 144, 149
and validation of assessment
  instruments, 115
Culture-bound syndromes, 140, 163
CY-BOCS (Children's Yale–Brown
  Obsessive–Compulsive Scale),
  191, 192

"Daily diary," 193
DBRS (Devereux Behavior Rating
  Scale), School form, 192
DBRS (Devereux Behavior Rating
  Scale), Teacher form, 192
DDIS (Dissociative Disorders Interview
  Schedule), 175
Deaf or hearing impaired children, 235
Deaths from child abuse, 6
Demonstrative aids and devices, 9, 22,
  27–28, 30, 31
Department of Justice, Office for Victims
  of Crimes of, 259
Depersonalization disorder, 161–162,
  162n1
Depression, 180–182, 221–224, 230
  assessment measures for, 212–220,
    224–230
  comorbidity with, 181, 183
  and emotional distress, 131–132, 140
  medical evaluation before
    examination for, 184
  and PTSD, 144–145
  relevant symptoms of, 254
Depression Self Rating Scale (DSRS),
  226–227, 227
DES (Dissociative Experiences Scale),
  167, 175, 176, 177
Developmental level of child witnesses
  and appropriate questioning, 8, 21, 26,
    31, 257
  and communication, 4–5
  and dissociative symptoms, 162
Devereux Behavior Rating Scale
  (DBRS), School form, 192

Devereux Behavior Rating Scale (DBRS),
  Teacher form, 192
DFP (Dissociative Feature Profile), 167,
  171, 175, 177
Diagnosis
  of anxiety, 180–189
  of depression, 180–184, 221–224
  of dissociation, 159–166, 178
  of posttraumatic stress disorder, 143–149
  See also at Assessment
Diagnostic Interview for Children and
  Adolescents (DICA), 191, 192,
  193, 224, 226
  computerized version of, 225
Diagnostic Interview for Children and
  Adolescents—Revised (DICA–
  R), 190, 191, 226
Diagnostic Interview Schedule for
  Children (DISC), 190, 191, 192,
  193, 224, 226
  vs. K–SADS, 225
  voice version of, 225
Diagnostic Interview Schedule for
  Children—Version IV (DISC–
  IV), 191, 192, 224
  Hispanic version of, 167
*Diagnostic and Statistical Manual of Mental
  Disorders, Third Edition (DSM–
  III)*, 145, 149
*Diagnostic and Statistical Manual of Mental
  Disorders, Third Edition, Revised
  (DSM–III–R)*, 149, 163, 189
*Diagnostic and Statistical Manual of Mental
  Disorders, Fourth Edition (DSM–
  IV)*, 136–137, 149
  anxiety disorders in, 187, 189, 230
  ASD in, 145
  and CPTS–RI, 153
  and depression, 230
  and dissociative disorders, 166, 178
  and language disorders, 235
  and mood disorders, 221, 222, 223
  and PTSD, 146,146n, 147, 157
  and SCID-D–R, 177
*Diagnostic and Statistical Manual of Mental
  Disorders, Fourth Edition, Text
  Revision (DSM–IV–TR)*, 109, 140
  anxiety and depression in, 180, 181
  and assessment instrument, 115
  and courtroom modification evaluation,
    124, 125
  and dissociative disorders, 160, 161–162

Empowerment tradition, 68
England
    CCTV (Live Link) in, 74–77
    courtroom modification in, 66
    and effect of shielding techniques, 85
    screens used in, 82
    special measures in, 8
    study on court experience in, 67
    Victim Support and Witness Service in, 68
    and videotaped interview testimony, 88, 90
Environmental disasters, as trauma, 133–134
Environmental variables, 69
Ethical Guidelines for the Practice of Forensic Psychiatry (American Academy of Psychiatry and the Law), 102
"Ethical Principles of Psychologists and Code of Conduct" (APA), 102
Ethics codes, maintenance of competence required by, 104
Ethnicity
    and PTSD, 149
    See also African American children; Latino or Latina children; Culture
Europe, and hearsay, 88
Evaluation, 16
    at child advocacy centers, 29
    by multidisciplinary teams, 29
    See also at Assessment
"Excited utterance" exception to hearsay rule, 48, 52, 87
    in child abuse cases, 48n7
Expeditious disposition, 21, 29–30, 30
Experience, for courtroom modification evaluation, 103–104
Expertise, for courtroom modification evaluation, 103–104
Expert testimony and witnesses
    and jurors' evaluation, 98
    legal challenges to, 15–16
    necessity for use of, 55
    on need for courtroom modification, 13–15
Expressive and Receptive One-Word Picture Vocabulary Tests, 245
Expressive Vocabulary Test, 245
Eyberg Child Behavior Inventory (ECBI), 192–193
Eye contact
    child's avoidance of with defendant, 8, 52, 54, 84, 86

child's maintaining of with questioner, 98
    lack of as culturally determined, 223

Face validity, 114
Fairness (procedural), perceptions of, 80, 85
Fair treatment, assurance of, 256–257
False allegations in abuse cases, 7
False reporting, multiple perspectives in detecting, 112
Family of child, in witness support, 68
Fantasy-proneness, 177
Fear, 184–188
    confrontation, 256
    of defendant, 8, 35, 66, 127, 254
    in panic attack, 188n3
    patterns of, 185–187
    and PTSD, 188
    of sharing details about crime, 23
    in trauma, 136
    See also Distress; Emotional distress
Fear Survey Schedule for Children— Revised (FSSC–R), 190, 191, 192, 193, 208
Federal court system, 20n. *See also* Supreme Court, U.S.
Federal Rules of Criminal Procedure, Rule 15 of, 38–39
Federal Rules of Evidence, 21n
First Amendment, and courtroom closure, 24, 25
Forensic evaluation, courtroom modification. *See* Courtroom modification evaluation
Forensic interviews, 44–46
Forfeiture rule, 46, 57n, 63, 87
Fourteenth Amendment, 9
FSSC–R (Fear Survey Schedule for Children—Revised), 190, 191, 192, 193, 208
FSSC–R/II, 191
Fugue, dissociative, 162, 162n5
Functioning of child (current), in courtroom modification evaluation, 119, 112
Future directions for courtroom modification, 256
    assuring fair treatment, 256–257
    conducting needed research, 261–264

enacting proposals for legal reforms,
259–261
increasing effectiveness of
modifications, 257–258

GAD (generalized anxiety disorder), 180,
189, 189n4
GAL. *See* Guardian ad litem
Gender differences
in fear and anxiety, 184, 186
in mood disorders, 223
and PTSD, 149
in stuttering, 243
Generalized anxiety disorder (GAD), 180,
189, 189n4
Government officer, and definition of
"testimonial," 43–45
Great Britain. *See* Britain; England;
Northern Ireland; Scotland; Wales
Guardian ad litem (GAL), 8, 21, 22–23,
30, 258
appointment of, 8
right to, 31
See also Attorney for child; Counsel for
child witness
"Guidelines for Child Custody Evaluations
in Divorce Proceedings" (APA),
102

Hamilton Anxiety Rating Scale (HARS
or HAM-A), 190, 191, 192
Hamilton Depression Rating Scales
(HDRS), 226
Hamilton Rating Scale for Depression,
228
HARS (Hamilton Anxiety Rating Scale),
190, 191, 192
Hearsay exception, child, 9, 21, 47–52,
59–60, 87, 253
fairness of questioned, 92–93
protective effects of, 91
for videotape, 41–43
and well-being of child witnesses, 97–98
Hearsay rule, 47, 48
residual exception to, 48–49
Hearsay testimony, 86–96
Hispanic children
and somatic symptoms in fear or
anxiety, 187–188

See also Latino and Latina children
History of child, in courtroom
modification evaluation, 119–122
Hopelessness Scale for Children (HSC),
227

Identity of child, protection of, 21, 23–24
Illnesses, as trauma, 133
In-court testimony
content of, 108
legally relevant problems in, 118–128
principles guiding, 108–117
subject matter of, 117–118
See also Testimony of child
Individual differences
in effect of courtroom modification, 98
MHPs' consideration of, 254
in reaction to trauma, 139
and research on courtroom
modification, 263
in use of courtroom modifications, 73
Information, multiple sources of, 112–113,
118, 122, 190
Injuries, as trauma, 133
Innovative practices, 9
Interdisciplinary team (IDT)
and interviews, 40
See also Multidisciplinary teams
International Classification of Diseases, on
"elective mutism," 247
Interpersonal psychotherapy, 254
Interviewing children, 119–121, 123, 129
and interviewer bias, 108
numerical limitation on, 21, 29
See also Videotaped investigative
interviews
Interviews
notes taken on, 92
for PTSD assessment, 152
vs. self-report measures, 224
structured and semistructured vs.
unstructured, 193, 224
Interview Schedule for Children (ISC),
192
Intraclass correlation coefficient (ICC),
116
*Investigative Interviewing in Cases of Alleged
Child Abuse* (American Academy
of Child and Adolescent
Psychiatry), 102

Investigative interviews, videotaped. *See* Videotaped investigative interviews
ISC (Interview Schedule for Children), 192

Judicial control, 9
Jury instruction
and jurors' evaluation, 98
and perception of fairness, 85, 86

Kendall's tau-b, 116
Kovacs, Maria, 213
K–SADS (Schedule for Affective Disorders and Schizophrenia in School-Age Children), 191, 192, 193, 224, 225–226, 226
K–SADS–Columbia, 191
K–SADS–E (Epidemiological version), 190, 196, 212
K–SADS–IVR, 196, 212
K–SADS–L (Lifetime version), 196, 212
K–SAD–P (Present episode), 196, 212
K–SADS–PL (Schedule for Affective Disorders and Schizophrenia for School-Age Children: Present and Lifetime Version), 158, 191, 194, 196–197, 212–213, 224, 227, 230

Language
in assessment instrument, 115
non-age-appropriate, 70
Language abilities, children's, 4, 235–239
Language specialists, 234–235
Latino and Latina children
and language, 237
and somatic symptoms in fear or anxiety, 187–188
See also Hispanic children
Law, for courtroom modification evaluation, 104–105
Lay or fact witness, mental health professional as, 106
Leading questions, 9, 21, 26, 41
Legally relevant problems
and courtroom modification evaluation, 118–123
nature and source of, 125–128
severity of, 123–125

Legal professionals, and courtroom modifications, 13–14
Legal reforms, enacting proposals for, 259–261
Length of child testimony, 28–29, 30
Leyton Obsessional Inventory—Child Version (LOI–CV), 191, 192
"Lie" score, in RCMAS, 210
Literature
for courtroom modification evaluation, 106–107
for guidance on issues, 15
Live Link (UK CCTV), 74–77, 80
Log sheets, 193
LOI–CV (Leyton Obsessional Inventory—Child Version), 191, 192

MacArthur Communication Development Inventory, 245–246
MADRS (Montgomery–Ashberg Depression Rating Scales), 226
MAGIC (Missouri Assessment of Genetics Interview for Children), 226
Maltreatment cases. *See* Abuse cases
Mandated reporters, lawsuits seeking damages against, 6
Mania Rating Scale (MRS), 227
March, John R., 197
Maryland v. Craig. See Craig decision
MASC (Multidimensional Anxiety Scale for Children), 190, 191, 192, 193, 194, 197–199, 208, 209, 230
Maternal support, 140, 264
and whisper procedure, 54–55, 62
MDI–C (Multiscore Depression Inventory for Children), 227
Media
and courtroom closure, 24
misperceptions of criminal justice system learned from, 67
Memory, factors interfering with, 4, 7–8
Mental health professionals (MHPs), 13–14, 15, 264
and anxiety assessment, 190, 194, 208, 211
and children's communication, 56, 233–234, 241–242, 249 (*see also* Communication abilities and disabilities)

for competency evaluation, 20
and courtroom modification evaluation, 30, 101–102, 128–130, 251–253 (*see also at* Courtroom modification)
education, training and experience in, 103–104
knowledge of literature required in, 106–107
and legally relevant problems, 118–128
objectivity required in, 107–108
principles guiding content of, 108–117
professional standards on, 102–103
of relevant law, 104–105
and role of MHP in case, 105–108
steps to take in, 107
subject matter of, 117–118
in forensic assessment of child witness, 33
and individual differences, 98–99
and justification of number of times of child-witness exposure, 255
and law on courtroom modification, 20, 21
and legal standards on alternative procedures, 16
necessity for use of, 55
and necessity for use of modification, 61, 63
in PTSD assessment, 147, 150–152
and science supporting courtroom modifications, 65, 99
trauma-related dissociation assessment of, 166, 178
and videotaped evidence, 47
Methods
multiple, 112–113, 118, 122, 152
objective and defensible, 111–112
MFQ (Mood and Feelings Questionnaire), 216, 226, 227, 228, 229, 230
short version (SMFQ), 226, 229, 230
MID (Multidimensional Inventory of Dissociation), 175, 177
Minority groups
internalized oppression of, 134
and PTSD symptoms, 153
See also African American childen; Latino and Latina children; Culture

Misleading questions, and social support, 72
Missouri Assessment of Genetics Interview for Children (MAGIC), 226
Montgomery–Ashberg Depression Rating Scales (MADRS), 226
Mood disorders, 180
in *DSM–IV*, 221, 222
See also Depression
Mood and Feelings Questionnaire (MFQ), 216, 226, 227, 228, 229, 230
short version (SMFQ), 226, 229, 230
Morphology (language), 236, 237
MRS (Mania Rating Scale), 227
Multicultural appropriateness, 109–111; *See also* Culture
Multidimensional Anxiety Scale for Children (MASC), 190, 191, 192, 193, 194, 197–199, 208, 209, 230
Multidimensional Inventory of Dissociation (MID), 175
Multidisciplinary teams (MDTs)
for communication problems, 249
evaluations by, 29
and interviews, 40
MHPs as consultants to, 63
Multi-Health Systems, Inc., contact information for, 197, 203, 205, 213
Multiple personality disorder, and culture, 160–161
Multiple-role relationships, 105–106
Multiple sources of information and multiple methods, in courtroom modification evaluation, 112–113, 118, 122
for anxiety measures, 190
for depression measures, 224–227
for dissociation measures, 166–167
for PTSD measures, 150–152
Multiscore Depression Inventory for Children (MDI–C), 227
Mutism, selective, 246–248
My Worst Experience Survey, 154–155

Narrative elaboration techniques (NET), 121
NASSQ (Negative Affect Self-Statement Questionnaire), 192

and trauma, 136, 149
triggers of symptoms for, 152
PPVT–III (Peabody Picture Vocabulary
Test—III), 245
"Practice Parameters for the Forensic
Evaluation of Children and
Adolescents Who May Have Been
Physically or Sexually Abused"
(American Academy of Child and
Adolescent Psychiatry), 102
*Practitioner's Guide to Empirically Based
Measures of Depression* (Nezu et
al.), 227
Pragmatics, 236, 238–239
in talking with children, 241
Predictive validity, 114
Preschool Age Psychiatric Assessment
(PAPA), 225
Preschool Observational Rating Scale
(POSA), 193
Primary purpose test, 44
Private waiting area for child witnesses,
9. *See also* Waiting area for child
witnesses
Probability, in courtroom modification
evaluation, 127–128, 129
Procedural fairness, perceptions of, 80, 85
*Professional, Ethical and Legal Issues
Concerning Interpersonal Violence,
Maltreatment and Related Trauma*
(ad hoc Committee on Legal and
Ethical Issues in the Treatment
of Interpersonal Violence, APA),
103
Professional standards, adhering to,
102–103
Protection school approach, 66
PSWQC (Penn State Worry
Questionnaire for Children), 192,
209
Psychological Assessment Resources,
contact information for, 156, 204
Psychological Corporation, address of, 156
Psychological tests. *See* assessment
instruments
Psychometric adequacy, 114
indexes of, 116
*Psychosocial Evaluation of Suspected
Psychological Maltreatment
in Children and Adolescents*
(American Professional Society
on the Abuse of Children), 102

*Psychosocial Evaluation of Suspected
Sexual Abuse in Young Children*
(American Professional Society
on the Abuse of Children), 102
PTSD. *See* Posttraumatic stress disorder
PTSD Index for *DSM–IV*, 192
PTSDRI, 192
Public interest, in child's testimony, 32
Public policy(ies), 11, 264
Public support, for legislation permitting
innovative procedures, 13

Questioning techniques, 5; *See also*
Interviewing children
Questions
age appropriate, 257
on consulting and following questioning
guidelines, 120
developmentally appropriate, 8, 21, 26,
31, 257
leading, 9, 21, 26, 41
on MHP methods, 111
misleading (and social support), 72
open-ended, 121

Race
and PTSD, 149
See also African American children;
Latino or Latina children; Culture
RADS (Reynolds Adolescent Depression
Scale), 226, 227
RADS–2 (Reynolds Adolescent
Depression Scale—Second
Edition), 217–219, 227, 230
Rapport building, 121
Rarely used or underused practices, 9
Rating scales, 208; *See also* Assessment
measures
RBPC (Revised Behavior Problem
Checklist), 192
RCADS (Revised Child Anxiety and
Depression Scales), 192, 201–202,
208, 210
RCDS (Reynolds Child Depression Scale),
219–220, 226, 227–228
RCMAS (Revised Children's Manifest
Anxiety Scale), 190, 191, 192,
193, 203–204, 210–211
Recesses, 28–29
Relaxation training, 255

empirical research on need for
modifications, 66–73
See also at Courtroom modification
Scotland
CCTV (Live Link) study in, 75
courtroom modification in, 66
screens used in, 82
Screen for Child Anxiety Related
Emotional Disorders (SCARED),
191, 192, 200–201, 209–210
Screen for Child Anxiety Related
Emotional Disorders—Revised
(SCARED–R), 191, 199–200,
208, 210
Screens or partitions, 9, 52, 53, 82–83, 84,
85, 86
Seating position of child witness, 8, 53–54
Secondary victimization or
revictimization, 6–7, 66
Selective mutism, 246–248
Self-report by child
and PTSD, 152
CPTS–RI as, 153
sexual abuse not proven by, 126
Self-report measures, vs. interviews, 224
Selye, Hans, 138
Semantics, 236
Separation anxiety disorder (SAD), 180,
188, 188n2, 222
Sexual abuse or assault
child's believability about, 19
and dissociation, 164–165
PTSD frequency from, 147–148
See also Abuse and abuse cases
Shielding techniques, 52, 82–86, 97
Sidran Institute, contact information for,
168, 171
Silverman, Wendy K., 195
Sixth Amendment
Confrontation Clause of, 9–10 (*see also*
Confrontation Clause)
on speedy and public trial, 25, 29–30
SMFQ (Mood and Feelings Questionnaire,
short version), 226, 229, 230
SMQ (Stress Management
Questionnaire), 192
Social Anxiety Scale for Adolescents
(SAS–A), 191
Social Anxiety Scale for Children—
Revised (SASC–R), 190, 191,
192, 193
Social phobia, 189, 189n5

Social Phobia Anxiety Inventory (SPAI),
191, 206–207
Social Phobia Anxiety Inventory for
Children (SPAI–C), 191, 192,
205–206, 211
Social science on courtroom
modifications. *See* Science of
courtroom modifications
Social support
benefit of, 72
and cultural explanation, 110
See also Support persons and
relationships
SPAI (Social Phobia Anxiety Inventory),
191, 206–207
SPAI–C (Social Phobia Anxiety
Inventory for Children), 191, 192,
205–206, 211
Spearman's rho, 116
Special advocate
appointment of, 8
See also Attorney for child; Counsel for
child witness; Guardian ad litem
Special Phobia Anxiety Inventory for
Children (SPAI–C), 192
"Specialty Guidelines for Forensic
Psychologists" (Committee on
Ethical Guidelines for Forensic
Psychologists) 102
Speech–language pathologist, 234–235
on stuttering, 243–244
Spence Anxiety Scale, 192
Spence's Children's Anxiety Scale
(SCAS), 191, 203
SRAS (School Refusal Assessment Scale),
192
STAI (State–Trait Anxiety Inventory),
191
STAIC (State–Trait Anxiety Inventory
for Children), 190, 191, 192, 193,
208
STAI–C–PR–T, 192
Standard practices, 8–9
State laws and legislatures
and absence of legal standard, 62
on alternative procedures, 21
and CCTV, 34–35
and child hearsay exception, 49–51
and communication ability, 61–62
and courtroom closure, 25
and *Craig* standard, 12–13, 59
and permissibility of modification, 14

dissociation scale in, 175
Turner, Samuel M., 205, 206
Twenty-four Questions (and Answers) About Professional Practice in the Area of Child Abuse (APA), 103

UCLA PTSD Reaction Index, 153–154, 155
Uncertainty, in courtroom modification evaluation, 127–128, 129, 257
Underreporting, addressing of, 112–113
Underused practices, 9
Uniform Child Witness Testimony By Alternative Methods Act (2007, Idaho), 13
Uniform codes, 259–261
Uniform Rules of Evidence (URE), 259, 261
United Kingdom. *See* Britain; England; Northern Ireland; Scotland; Wales
United Nations Convention on the Rights of the Child, 31
    Article 12 of, 76

Validity of assessment instrument, 113–116
    for anxiety assessment instruments, 195–206
    for depression assessment instruments, 212–220
    of dissociation assessment instruments, 168–174
    in PTSD assessment, 152
VASA–R (Visual Analogue Scale for Anxiety—Revised), 190, 191
Vertical prosecution, 9, 30
Victimization, secondary, 6–7, 66
Victims' rights, 31–32
Videoconferencing, 9
Videotaped investigative interviews, 21, 39–47, 86–87, 88–92, 97–98, 253, 255

in conjunction with in-court or videotaped testimony, 41–42, 89–90, 97, 256
and conviction rate, 93
fairness of questioned, 92–93
as hearsay, 41–43, 86–87, 88, 92, 93–96
out-of-courtroom uses for 98
Videotaped testimony and depositions, 9, 21, 37–39
    empirical research on effect of, 74–82
    vs. investigative interviews, 40
Visual Analogue Scale for Anxiety—Revised (VASA–R), 190, 191
Vocabulary, in talking with children, 240

Waiting area for child witnesses
    private, 9
    secure, 52
    separate, 68
Wales
    CCTV (Live Link) in, 74–77
    and effect of shielding techniques, 85
    screens used in, 82
    study on court experiences in, 67
    Victim Support and Witness Service in, 68
    and videotaped interview testimony, 90
Western Psychological Services, contact information for, 203, 215
Whisper procedure, 54–55, 62
Witness Support Service, United Kingdom, 72

Youth Depression Adjective Checklist (Y–DACL), 227
Youth Justice and Criminal Evidence Act (YJCEA; 1999, Britain), 74, 76, 82
Youth Self Report Version of the CBCL (YSR), 132, 191, 192, 208

ABOUT THE AUTHORS

Susan R. Hall, JD, PhD, is an assistant professor of psychology at the Graduate School of Education and Psychology at Pepperdine University in Malibu, California. She earned a law degree and a doctorate in clinical psychology as well as psychology, policy, and law at the University of Arizona in Tucson. During her postdoctoral fellowship in child clinical psychology at the Yale University School of Medicine Child Study Center in New Haven, Connecticut, she was a Bush fellow at the Yale Center for Child Development and Social Policy. Dr. Hall has published and presented nationally on topics related to psychology, public policy, and law, including the clinical and forensic needs of children and youth exposed to violence and maltreatment. Her scholarship, including the book *Laws Affecting Clinical Practice* (with B. Sales & M. O. Miller; American Psychological Association [APA], 2005), aims to help clinicians better understand the law. Dr. Hall serves on the editorial board of the *Journal of Youth and Adolescence*, and she was the section program chair (2005–2006) and cochair (2004–2005) for the Society for Child and Family Policy and Practice, Section on Child Maltreatment (APA Division 37).

Bruce D. Sales, JD, PhD, is a professor of psychology, sociology, psychiatry, and law at the University of Arizona in Tucson, where he also directs the psychology, policy, and law program. His recent books include *Sex Offending* (with J. D. Stinson & J. V. Becker; American Psychological Association [APA], 2008); *Scientific Jury Selection* (with J. D. Lieberman; APA, 2007); *Criminal Profiling* (with S. J. Hicks; APA, 2006); *Experts in Court* (with D. Shuman; APA, 2005); *More Than the Law* (with P. W. English; APA, 2005); *Family Mediation* (with C. J. A. Beck; APA, 2001); and *Treating Adult and Juvenile Offenders With Special Needs* (coedited with J. B. Ashford & W. H. Reid; APA, 2001). Dr. Sales, the first editor of the journals *Law and Human Behavior* and *Psychology, Public Policy, and Law*, is a fellow of the APA and the Association for Psychological Science. He is an elected member of the American Law Institute and twice served as president of the American Psychology–Law Society and received their Award for Distinguished Contributions to Psychology and Law. He also received the Award for Distinguished Professional Contributions to Public Service from APA and an honorary doctor of science degree from the City University of New York for being the "founding father of forensic psychology as an academic discipline."